Friends in life and death

Two distinguished historians join forces to exploit the exceptional riches offered by the records of British and Irish Quakerdom for the student of social, demographic, and familial change during the period 1650–1900. The authors have analyzed the experiences of more than 8,000 Quaker families, involving over 30,000 individuals, to produce an unparalleled study of patterns of child-bearing, marriage, and death among a major religious grouping. Professors Vann and Eversley show how Quaker religious values delayed marriage, and the evidence suggests that in the seventeenth century English Quakers practiced family limitation, although their Irish counterparts, by contrast, became one of the most fertile of all demographic groupings. Severe urban mortality was the fate of many urban Quakers prior to 1750, but sanitary improvements seem to have reduced this, and from 1825 onwards the Quakers were in the vanguard of the move toward the small, modern family. The authors draw numerous comparisons with other demographic sectors, and *Friends in life and death* will make a substantial contribution to our understanding of the social and economic history of one of the most prominent cultural groups in early modern Britain.

Cambridge Studies in Population, Economy and Society in Past Time

---

Series Editors

PETER LASLETT, ROGER SCHOFIELD, AND E. A. WRIGLEY

ESRC Cambridge Group for the History of Population and Social Structure

and DANIEL SCOTT SMITH

University of Illinois at Chicago

Recent work in social, economic and demographic history has revealed much that was previously obscure about societal stability and change in the past. It has also suggested that crossing the conventional boundaries between these branches of history can be very rewarding.

This series will exemplify the value of interdisciplinary work of this kind, and will include books on topics such as family, kinship and neighourhood; welfare provision and social control; work and leisure; migration; urban growth; and legal structures and procedures, as well as more familiar matters. It will demonstrate that, for example, anthropology and economics have become as close intellectual neighbours to history as have political philosophy or biography.

For a full list of titles in the series, please see end of book

Friends in life and death

The British and Irish Quakers in the demographic transition, 1650–1900

RICHARD T. VANN

and

DAVID EVERSLEY

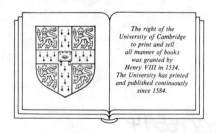

The right of the
University of Cambridge
to print and sell
all manner of books
was granted by
Henry VIII in 1534.
The University has printed
and published continuously
since 1584.

CAMBRIDGE UNIVERSITY PRESS

Cambridge
New York   Port Chester
Melbourne   Sydney

Published by the Press Syndicate of the University of Cambridge
The Pitt Building, Trumpington Street, Cambridge CB2 1RP
40 West 20th Street, New York, NY 10011–4211, USA
10 Stamford Road, Oakleigh, Victoria 3166, Australia

First published 1992

Printed in Great Britain at the University Press, Cambridge

British Library cataloguing in publication data
Vann, Richard T.
Friends in life and death: the British and Irish Quakers in the demographic
transition, 1650–1900 – (Cambridge studies in population, economy and
society in past time, v. 17).
1. Quakers. Demographic aspects, history
I. Title II. Eversley, David 1921–
304.62

Library of Congress cataloguing in publication data
Vann, Richard T.
Friends in life and death: the British and Irish Quakers in the demographic
transition, 1650–1900 / Richard T. Vann and David Eversley.
p.   cm. – (Cambridge studies in population, economy and society
in past time : 17)
Includes bibliographical references and index.
ISBN 0 521 39201 2 (hardback)
1. Quakers – Great Britain – History.
2. Demographic transition – Great Britain.
3. Demographic transition – Ireland.
4. Quakers – Ireland – History.
5. Society of Friends – History.
I. Eversley, David Edward Charles.   II. Title.   III. Series.
DA125.Q34V36   1991
941'.0088286 – dc20 90–21802   CIP

ISBN 0 521 39201 2 hardback

6003615594   C

CE

for
P. F. V. and E. E. E.

Contents

Figures

xii   *List of figures*

Tables

Preface

The technique of family reconstitution, on which this book is based, has been used in various ways since 1915. We first got the idea for our joint project thirty years ago, not suspecting how long it would take to bring it to fruition. Our task has been complex, but we have been fortunate in having a multitude of helpers.

The two of us began independently, and from different points. David Eversley in the early 1960s discovered the Irish family lists and took the first steps towards a reconstitution of the English Quaker population as well; while Richard Vann, approaching demography from the context of Quaker social history, hoped both to refine some crude demographic figures established for two English counties and to extend the sample to an entire region. In 1966 it became apparent that there would be great advantage to combining our efforts, and since April of 1967 our two files have been integrated, though the materials on Ireland, Scotland, Wales, the northern counties of England, London, and the family histories were compiled under the supervision of Eversley, while most of the urban families (from Bristol and Norwich) and those from Southern England were the responsibility of Vann.

Among the collaborators whose help was vital in the completion of our work first mention must go to the ESRC Cambridge Group for the History of Population and Social Structure. In particular, the expertise of E. A. Wrigley on all aspects of family reconstitution and of Roger Schofield on programming and design of tables was in constant demand. Without their assistance, this book in its present form would have been impossible. We cannot fairly implicate them in the evidence or the interpretations we advance here, but we are keenly aware of how much whatever merit our work may have derived from them.

We are also deeply indebted to Michael Martin, who provided a great deal of assistance in placing our findings within the context of English society in the seventeenth and eighteenth centuries. Besides tirelessly searching the published literature, he generously made available many of his own findings, and advised us on the interpretation of ours.

We could scarcely have begun without the help of a large number of volunteers – part of an even larger army of local workers who have made a vital contribution to English historical demography. Some of these, regrettably, did not survive to see the eventual fruit of their labors. The bulk of the work of transferring information from the digests onto family reconstitution forms was done by Jessie Dicks, Hove; the late Jennie Ellinor, Pickering; Sheila Fox, Totteridge; Leslie Johnston, Cheadle; Margaret Kohler, Dorking; Margaret Stone, Ilford; and M. Ingle Wright, London. Also helping us by compiling family reconstitution forms from the digests were the late Eric Follows, Worcester; the late William Marwick, Edinburgh; Kathleen Moore, Birmingham; Stephen Nicholls, Cheadle; the late Lucy O'Brien, Sutton, near Macclesfield; the late Robert Taylor, Moor Park; the late Hubert Wood, Barnard Castle; and Frank Wright, Croydon. Barbara Taylor, then of Birmingham and now of Hong Kong, made up the Irish family reconstitution forms from the microfilms of the family listings.

The entire group of genealogies depended on information supplied by the following people: the late Enid Allen, East Grinstead; the late Mary Artiss, Southampton; Enid Barlow, Birmingham; Agnes Bowman, Scarborough; the late George Braithwaite, Cheltenham; Bowman Brockbank, Wolverhampton; the late Mary Clark, Tunbridge Wells; the late Sarah Clark, Street; the late Norman Collinson, Ipswich; Michael Darby, Birmingham; Hubert Dunning, Wentbridge; the late Henry Dyne, Grays; the late Eric Follows; Joseph Fox, Birmingham; Sheila Fox; Margaret Gayner, Rednal; the late Ronald Gundry, Alderney; the late Elspeth Hodgkin, Darlington; David Impey, Alvechurch; the late Ethel Adair Impey, Birmingham; Ina Lamb, Sibford Ferris; Bridget Lowe, Canterbury; Gwen McGilvray, Letchworth; Edmund Mounsey, Kendal; the late Olive Newton, Newbury; the late Eric Pease, Shaftesbury; John Pierse, Horsham; Ann Rake, Bristol; the late Mary Smith, Edinburgh; Ursula Smithson, Leicester; the late Hilda Sturge, Cambridge; Ioan Thomas, Oundle; Arnold Waterfall, Skipton; the late Evelyn Whiting, Salisbury; G. Reuben Wilson, Bournemouth; and the late Dorothy Wright, Woodford Green.

Agnes Bowman, the late Eric Follows, Margaret Gayner, the late Lucy O'Brien, Peter Robson of London and the late Mary Stansfield of

Reading prepared family reconstitution forms from the genealogical information which we had received.

Preliminary analysis of the information received, including some editing and extracting occupational data, was done by Adrienne Dewell, Christina Olsen, and Bill Quin in Berkeley, California, and the late Jennie Ellinor, Margaret Stone, and Kirstin Wood in England. Margaret Stone also did a good deal of the general editing and (with Margaret Kohler) prepared some of the maps.

The final editing of David Eversley's completed forms was done by the late Edith E. Eversley.

Helping us to transfer information from forms onto paper tapes were Robert Hind and George Moring, then undergraduates at the University of Sussex. We received assistance in computing, methodology, and programming from Mary Toms at the University of Sussex, Rosamund Davis at Cambridge, and Nigel Cox, then of the Computing Centre at the University of Newcastle, as well as the ever-present Roger Schofield and E. A. Wrigley, to whom most of the credit for design of the tables belongs. In the part of the analysis done at the University of Birmingham, Richard Pickvance and Jane Williams assisted in analyzing birth intervals, child mortality, and age at marriage. The special project on causes of death in London was done by Tom Cobb and John Eversley. The late Henry Cadbury of Haverford, Pennsylvania, shared his vast knowledge of Quaker history with us whenever requested, and we are equally grateful to Hugh Barbour of Earlham College for reading an earlier draft and making helpful comments. Late in our work we were assisted and comforted by John Landers, who shared his own work on London demography with us and reassured us that some of our more eccentric ideas were supported by his data as well.

Clare Currey afforded great help in editing the Irish materials. G. Leslie Stephenson of Lisburn kindly gave us access to the Northern Irish family lists still preserved at Lisburn, and Jane Houston transcribed the Lisburn registers for us. Jacqueline Rich and Patricia Camden of the Center for the Humanities at Wesleyan University helped prepare the index, and much else. Preparation of the graphs and figures was much assisted by Janet Morgan and especially by Patricia St. Clair of the Wesleyan University Computing Center and Public Affairs Center Data Lab. From the first family reconstitution form to the last page proof, Patricia Fenn Vann was a constant collaborator. Finally, we are much indebted to the staff of the Friends House Library in London and above all to Edward H. Milligan, whose tranquillity our workers so often interrupted, whose space they so often occupied, and whose knowledge of Quaker history we so often called on.

We were also the beneficiaries of financial support from various institutions. The ESRC Cambridge Group for the History of Population and Social Structure again tops the list, along with its earlier supporter, the Gulbenkian Foundation. Thanks are due to the University of Birmingham for the loan of equipment and for research and typing assistance during the early days of the project; to the Joseph Rowntree Charitable Trust, for assistance with the financing of the computer tape punching operation at the University of Sussex; to the University of Sussex for supplying facilities for this work; to the School of Public Health, University of California, Berkeley, for providing generous research assistance and computing facilities for David Eversley during his visiting professorship there; to the late Olive Goodbody of Dublin, secretary of the historical committee of Ireland Yearly Meeting and keeper of the records at Friends Meeting House, Eustace Street, Dublin; to the National Library of Ireland for microfilming, free of charge, the entire Irish family lists so that they could be analyzed at leisure in Birmingham; and to the American Social Sciences Research Council, the American Council of Learned Societies, the Policy Studies Institute, and Wesleyan University.

It is conventional to absolve all our helpers from any error, and assume that burden ourselves. We do so with a full awareness of the good advice we may not have taken as well as all that from which we did profit.

Introduction

Why a book on the demography of the British and Irish Quakers? And
what kind of book?

We have written this book as a contribution to the social history of
Quakerism and to the history of British and Irish populations from the
mid seventeenth to the late nineteenth centuries. The context for the
former is fairly obvious, but the latter requires some elaboration. We
therefore begin with our larger framework, that of the evolution of
historical demography in the last twenty-five years.

For the generation which spanned World War II, the explanation of
both English and Irish population growth during the century from
1750 to 1850 was fairly clear and uncomplicated, even though there
was a latent contradiction between two parts of the explanation. The
only evidence that scholars had to work with was estimates of the
crude birth and death rates. In England, there was admittedly a rise in
the birth rate, attributed to the decline of apprenticeships, greater
opportunities for employment in industry or industrial by-
employment, and (by some) to the operation of the Poor Laws. All
these were supposed to have allowed workers to marry earlier and
thus (assuming the absence of family limitation) have larger families.
Despite these indications of higher fertility, there was general agreement with the conclusion of G. Talbot Griffith that "the fall in the
death rate is a much more striking movement during this period than
the rise in the birth rate."[1] Griffith thought that the main reasons for
lower mortality were the increased productivity of agriculture resulting from the enclosure movement, which enabled a larger population
to be reliably fed; improvement of sanitary and living conditions in the
towns; a decline in alcohol consumption; and better medical practice
(inoculation against smallpox, safer hospitals, and better midwifery).

[1] G. Talbot Griffith, *Population Problems of the Age of Malthus* (Cambridge, 1926), 128.

1

2   *Introduction*

Griffith, in the chapter of his book devoted to Ireland, betrays some embarrassment about the fact that few of the causes at work in England can have operated with anything like the same force in Ireland, and yet the Irish population during this period apparently rose twice as fast as the English. He endorses the view that potato cultivation made possible extensive subdivision of land-holdings and thus very early marriages. But this made Ireland exceptional.

The tranquillity which had settled over the issue of English population increase in the eighteenth century is well illustrated (just as it was being dissipated) in T. S. Ashton's volume in the series which he edited on the economic history of England. Ashton, who declared himself proud that he could write the volume without using any word ending in "ism" – except, as he was reminded, "baptism"[2] – depicted a society where there was no problem which a rising population might create that could not be solved by human (or more precisely English) ingenuity. The increasing population, Ashton thought, was in the view of "informed opinion" the result of the elimination of plague after 1665 and the lower incidence later of famine and disease as greater supplies of food became available. He also recounted, with a wealth of colorful detail, the depressing effects on population of excessive gin drinking. The only factor increasing fertility which he discussed was the possibility that there was a more perfect marriage market in the eighteenth century; if, as he speculated, the area within which marriage partners were sought was expanding during the eighteenth century, more people would have had the opportunity to marry, because imbalances between the genders on the parish level could be evened out in a larger area.[3]

Without a corresponding increase in productivity, of course, an increased population would have suffered "Asiatic horrors" – the reference here is explicitly to the Irish famine of the 1840s.[4] However, England had not only avoided this fate, but had actually created some homeostatic mechanisms (such as the improvement in food supply, sanitation, medical care, and the widening of marriage horizons) which made increasing industrialization and increasing labor supply into a virtuous circle.

Most of the books on which this serene view of demographic issues rested were published between 1922 and 1926.[5] The evidence they

[2] T. S. Ashton, *An Economic History of England: The 18th Century* (London, 1955), v.
[3] *Ibid.*, 2–9.
[4] T. S. Ashton, *The Industrial Revolution 1760–1830* (London, 1948), 161.
[5] Besides the book of Talbot Griffith cited in n. 1, these were A. M. Carr-Saunders, *The Population Problem* (Oxford, 1922); M. C. Buer, *Health, Wealth and Population in the Early Days of the Industrial Revolution* (London, 1926); M. Dorothy George, *London Life in the*

cited was various series of totals of vital events (from parish registers, bills of mortality, and back projections from the first English census of 1801) supplemented by studies of economic and medical institutions and the writings of contemporaries.

All these authors emphasized – as well they might – the skimpiness of this evidence and the speculative quality of any generalizations that might be drawn from it; but for twenty-five years little more evidence was discovered and no major reinterpretations advanced. When university life was resumed after World War II, however, the consensus about the causes of population growth in the eighteenth century began to break up.

We can, in retrospect, identify three interlocking problems which began to be more and more troublesome. The first, and in a sense the basic one, was that without better techniques of wringing evidence from the vital records of the past, there was no way to move from speculation towards something approaching real knowledge. In particular, the estimates of crude birth and death rates, besides being rough and ready, could never establish whether fertility was really rising or mortality really falling. The reason for this is that crude birth or death rates are sensitive to changes in the age structure of the population as well as to real changes in fertility or mortality. A true rise in fertility would mean that there were more frequent births among women in the age group from 15 to 49; but the crude birth rate might rise even if fertility remained exactly the same, provided there were more women within this age group in the population. Without any means of establishing age-specific fertility or mortality, there was no way to distinguish real effects from artifacts of the changing age structure. Second, the classic problem of the increase in population in the eighteenth century, once the Irish experience was compared with the English, suggested the need for an explanation which was not an *ad hoc* construction for a single country. Finally, as the scope of demographic investigation expanded to take in historical populations as well as those of the developing world, demographers – and politicians – became interested in how a rapid rise in population eventually slows down or even stops. In other words, they were developing the theory of "demographic transition," or the change from a society with high fertility balanced by high mortality to one

XVIII Century (London, 1925); and A. Redford, *Labour Migration in England, 1800–1850* (Manchester, 1926). See the review essay by T. H. Marshall, "The population problem during the Industrial Revolution: a note on the present state of the controversy," *Economic History* 1 (1929), reprinted in *Population in History*, ed. D. V. Glass and D. E. C. Eversley (London, 1965), 247–68.

typical of the industrialized countries today, with historically low levels of both fertility and mortality.

The theory of demographic transition has been stated as follows:

> That mortality and fertility are so related to urbanization and industrialization that low levels of the vital rates are associated with high levels of modernization; and that high levels of the vital rates are associated with low levels of modernization; and further, that medium levels of modernization will serve to depress mortality more rapidly than fertility.[6]

The claim is thus that as modernization begins, mortality declines first, followed by a decline in fertility until both reach "modern" values. The process was well underway in France by the middle of the nineteenth century; in England it became manifest when "The long period of rapid population growth which had lasted unbroken since the late eighteenth century came to an abrupt end in the second decade of the twentieth century."[7] In most discussions, it is the fall in fertility which has appeared to be the key problem. Some scholars proposed theories that fecundability itself had fallen – attributed, rather fancifully, to excessive bicycle riding or affection lavished on poodles, or more plausibly to modern diets and the strains of life in industrial society.[8] In general, though, it appears that modern women should be healthier and better able to conceive and bear children than their forebears; so the reduction in fertility appears to be due largely to deliberate family limitation. Use of contraception is of course widespread in the twentieth century, but deferring the age of marriage was also important in middle-class groups. As N. L. Tranter pointed out, "the English middle classes (and no doubt some skilled lower-class groups too), in their anxiety to grasp the economic and social rewards offered by an industrializing society, had already begun to adopt new and more prudential attitudes towards marriage as early as the 1830s."[9]

As early as 1950 K. H. Connell drew attention to the oddity of giving opposite explanations for similar population increases in England and Ireland. For one thing, the economies of the two were interlocked (Irish grain production had been regulated by act of the English parliament, Ireland was the chief source of immigrants into England). The received wisdom about both countries should be revised, he suggested; and this meant, for the English historians, reconsidering

---

[6] Paul K. Hatt, Nellie Louise Farr, and Eugene Weinstein, "Types of population balance," *American Sociological Review* 20 (1955), 15.
[7] N. L. Tranter, *Population since the Industrial Revolution: The Case of England and Wales* (New York, 1973), 97.
[8] *Ibid.*, 99–100.   [9] *Ibid.*, 104.

the birth rate, and for the Irish, looking again at the role of the death rate.[10]

During the next twenty years of energetic research, historians, economists, sociologists, geographers, and medical doctors produced much new evidence – all of it necessarily partial – and almost as many new theories. The old ones did not die out completely, by any means; for example, David Glass's summary of the question in 1965 concluded that "such evidence as there is at present would lean much more heavily towards lower mortality as an explanation of population growth than towards changes in marriage or fertility."[11] But defenders of this position had considerable difficulty in specifying just what mechanism could produce such a result. Thomas McKeown and R. G. Brown cast great doubt on the theory that medical improvements can have made much difference: surgery and midwifery were scarcely better, if not worse; new medicine had little effect; and hospitals "did no good but . . . positively did harm." Even inoculation for smallpox, they thought, did not have a substantial effect on national mortality trends.[12] But since they were convinced that increase in the birth rate can not have been significant, they fell back on general improvements in the environment as the only remaining possibility – even though there was little positive evidence for these.

The most enthusiastic partisan of the case for reductions in mortality was Peter Razzell, who had the advantage of identifying the mechanism at work: "Inoculation against smallpox could theoretically explain the whole increase in population, and until other explanations are convincingly documented, it is an explanation which must stand as the best one available."[13] On the other hand, the reexamination of the birth rate recommended by Connell was persuading some scholars that the key to the enigma lay there. Like McKeown and Brown, H. J. Habakkuk in 1953 doubted that medical improvements in the eighteenth century can have had much effect in raising the population; but he also questioned that there was a sig-

---

[10] K. H Connell, "Some unsettled problems in English and Irish population history, 1750–1845," *Irish Historical Studies* 7 (1951), reprinted in *Population in Industrialization*, ed. Michael Drake (London, 1969), 30–39.

[11] D. V. Glass, "Introduction," in *Population in History*, 15.

[12] Thomas McKeown and R. G. Brown, "Medical evidence related to English population changes in the eighteenth century," *Population Studies* 9 (1955), 119–41, reprinted in *Population in Industrialization*, 40–72.

[13] P. E. Razzell, "Population change in eighteenth-century England: a reinterpretation," *Economic History Review* 2nd ser. 18 (1965), 312–32, reprinted in *Population in Industrialization*, 128–56.

nificant decline in mortality at all.[14] Instead, he suggested a scenario in which a variety of effects of industrialization and economic growth impinging on a generation rebounding from high mortality from 1725 to 1729 caused the birth rate to rise significantly.

In pre-industrial conditions, spurts of population increase might occur after a peak of mortality. Even when families were not broken up by the death of one of the parents, fertility probably diminished during the unhealthiest time; but afterwards fewer women were anovulatory because of a recent pregnancy. Fertility was also depressed during high mortality by the deferral of marriage; but afterwards there were opportunities for young people, who could succeed to holdings or occupations made vacant by recent deaths, and so could get married. The rise in marriages made possible by earlier succession to properties could create a surge in population that would still be noticeable a generation later. By 1985 some such account as this had become the classical view of the mechanism whereby population recovers from crises such as last took place, in Britain, in 1725–29 and 1740–41.

That there was an increase of births in the 1740s had already been shown in a local study by David Eversley.[15] Building on these data, Habakkuk went on to argue that when this large cohort came to marrying age, it did not encounter the checks that tended to trap pre-industrial populations in a negative feedback loop. Instead, harvests were unusually bounteous, wages tended to resist reduction even though labor was now more abundant, and various diseases took less of a toll. This made it possible for the age at first marriage to fall, which not only allowed women to have more children during their married life – a decline of less than two years in age at first marriage would lead to an addition to the annual growth rate of 0.5 percent, he estimates – but also caused the generational rhythm to speed up.

The evidence that this had something to do with industrialization is drawn mostly from the nineteenth century. In 1821 there was a higher ratio of children to women in the industrial counties, and later in the century a high correlation between the proportion of women employed in industry and marriage rates. Habakkuk also quotes contemporaries like Adam Smith and T. R. Malthus who thought that, in Smith's words, "The demand for men, like that for any other

---

[14] H. J. Habakkuk, "English population in the eighteenth century," *Economic History Review* 2nd ser. 6 (1953), 117–33.

[15] D. Eversley, "A survey of population in an area of Worcestershire from 1660 to 1850 on the basis of parish registers," *Population Studies* 10 (1957), reprinted (in slightly amended form) in *Population in History*, 394–419.

commodity, necessarily regulates the production of men [used generically]." This would suggest that more vigorous economic activity, not merely industrialization, would cause a rise in wages, enabling earlier marriages. Also, shifts in employment from one sector to another could put more people in milieux where early marriage was easier: for example, agricultural laborers could be deprived of their customary rights during enclosure, or no longer be boarded-in by their employers; and cottage industry carried on by members of the family was replaced, increasingly, by the factory.[16]

Although by 1970 there was a stimulating array of competing theories, conclusive evidence seemed almost as hard as ever to acquire. For example, reliable figures about marital fertility were almost nonexistent, so almost all the speculation about fertility had to work from estimates about age at first marriage and what effect changes in it would have on fertility as a whole. No single source was likely to be entirely satisfactory; and so all the following seemed necessary: (1) further aggregative studies to determine exact local, regional, and national population, both by re-examining parish registers and by using some sort of back-projection from the first censuses;[17] (2) local studies to link changes in population size and composition with economic developments – if possible, drawing a national sample of parishes; (3) studies of subgroups of the population for whom age-specific rates might be derived, again with the project to link these with local economic change; (4) analyses of topics bearing on health and nutrition, such as inoculation and vaccination, the workings of hospitals, possible advances in sanitary engineering, and the production and marketing of foodstuffs.[18] Fortunately, for the first three of these new techniques have been worked out which promise for the first time to produce a body of evidence solid and extensive enough to decide between conflicting interpretations.

Despite the skepticism with which the possibility of making accurate estimates of the national population by back-projection from the censuses had been treated, an ambitious and sophisticated attempt has now been completed (which, incidentally, supports the view which Habakkuk expressed thirty-two years earlier).[19] These projec-

---

[16] H. J. Habakkuk, *Population Growth and Economic Development since 1750* (Leicester, 1971), 26–29, 36–41. In this later work Habakkuk did not deny that there was a fall in mortality in the last two or three decades of the eighteenth century.

[17] Glass, "Introduction," 9, is very skeptical about this particular approach.

[18] See Michael Drake's introduction to *Population in Industrialization*, 2. Drake did not foresee the possibility of any accurate national figures.

[19] E. A. Wrigley and R. S. Schofield, *The Population History of England, 1541–1871: A Reconstruction* (Cambridge, Mass., 1981).

8 *Introduction*

tions inevitably require a good deal of weighting the raw data, since they were based on a non-random sample of about 4 percent of the English parishes, with no parishes from London at all.

The technique which makes possible community studies and studies of subgroups of the population is family reconstitution, developed in France in the mid-1950s and introduced to England in two publications of the mid-1960s. In a famous study of Colyton in Devonshire, E. A. Wrigley showed for the first time that substantial variations in marital fertility occurred well before 1800, which might at least in part have been attributable to deliberate family limitation.[20] A year earlier T. H. Hollingsworth had used a kind of family reconstitution (somewhat different in its conventions) to study the demography of the British peerage. Among his significant findings were the first reliable data showing that at least among the peerage mortality did decline in the last part of the eighteenth century.[21]

The relationship of community and subgroup studies to a massive national aggregative study is like that of a close-up to a panorama. The fine details show up much more clearly, though nothing guarantees that the camera has zoomed in on a spot entirely representative of the whole. But of course there is no reason to make only one close-up; as more communities and subgroups are analyzed in fine detail, not only they but also the panorama will make more sense.

The Quakers are eminently suitable for one close-up. They can provide reliable evidence about most of the problems in population history which have been in dispute since World War II. We believe that their registers were probably kept more accurately and completely than the records of any other contemporary group or country. For the first time, an Irish population can be compared in many demographic aspects with an English one – and since the Irish Quakers were genetically English, the differences in the Irish milieu stand out the more sharply. Similarly, the urban Quakers – in London, Bristol, and Norwich – can be contrasted with those in the rest of the country. For the London Quakers, we know not only infant mortality rates and estimated life expectancies, but also what causes of death were given, so it is possible to make some tentative estimates about the age-specific incidence of fatal smallpox and other diseases.

We know the occupations of most of these Quakers. Though few

[20] E. A. Wrigley, "Family limitation in pre-industrial England," *Economic History Review* 2nd ser. 19 (1966), 82–109.
[21] T.H. Hollingsworth, *The Demography of the British Peerage* [Supplement to *Population Studies* 18 (1965)]; slightly revised figures are presented in *Population Studies* 32 (Sept. 1977), 323–49.

Quakers could be found in the industrial labor force, they were very prominent in the ranks of industrial and commercial entrepreneurs, as the names of Darby, Gurney, Lloyd, Fry, and Barclay will testify. We can thus see how a sector of the enterprising bourgeoisie experienced the high fertility of the heroic age of industrialization; and since the prolific family histories of the Quakers extend right through the nineteenth century, we can also see them pass through the demographic transition as they voluntarily reduced the size of their families. At the same time, we can look at the Quakers relatively little touched by the Industrial Revolution, those in Ireland (outside Ulster), in the market towns of the English Home Counties, and the remaining rural areas of East Anglia and the North of England.

Finally, our Quakers are not mere silent entries on a family reconstitution form. They were as industrious in writing about themselves as in every other sphere of their lives. Although these autobiographies are meant to detail their ministries and spiritual experiences, they also yield insights into attitudes towards marriage, family life, and death. Individual members of the British peerage are undoubtedly better known, but there is no population whose records have been reconstituted which contains so many people who can speak to us in their own voices.

For all these reasons, we expected the Quaker records to throw a great deal of light on the outstanding points at issue in historical demography. The following chapters will show to what extent they have done so. At no point, however, did we expect that providing an answer valid for the Quakers alone would entitle us to claim that the changes over time demonstrated here, and the differences between regions, could be extrapolated to the rest of the population. We could not even be certain that Quaker demographic patterns were typical of groups with similar socio-economic characteristics: middle-class tradesmen, people who lived in country towns, or those with some scientific knowledge and abstemious habits.

The most we could claim, if our analysis was successful, would be that we have demonstrated a variety of mechanisms whereby changes in nuptiality, fertility, and mortality could be linked to changes in population size, even though we cannot calculate the number of Quakers alive at any particular time or in any one area as a base for vital statistical rates. But though we cannot conclude that the rest of the population of Britain and Ireland behaved as the Quakers did, if we observe certain demographic patterns among the Quakers, and link these to social and economic changes, there is at least a strong possibility that similar linkages could be found in the population at

large, especially in the "middling classes." This is especially so for the
last part of the eighteenth century and the first half of the nineteenth,
when the assimilation of the Society of Friends to the population in
general probably reached its apogee.

Just as the demography of the Quakers cannot be understood without
a knowledge of their history, Quakerism cannot be fully understood
without a knowledge of their marrying, giving birth, and dying. These
were at the core of their social life; they determined the way that
generations succeeded one another, renewing the life of the society.
None of their "testimonies" – against war, pride, tithes, swearing of
oaths – cost Friends nearly so many members as the insistence that
Quakers should marry only other Quakers; and no effort was more
intense and long-lasting than the care to make every Quaker child a
full member of their holy community. These deep concerns have often
been studied,[22] and at first glance bear no great relationship to
statistical series of fertility rates, infant mortality, mean age at first
marriage, or the like. But, in fact, as we hope to show, the way the
Quakers married, the particular care that they gave their children, and
even the effects of their way of life on their length of life can be shown
only in these demographic series; and they reveal facets of Quaker life
which were previously unknown.

   Thus the student of Quakerism needs to know about their demography – but perhaps not as much about it as we have laid out here. Since
we have written for two sets of readers which are unlikely to overlap
substantially, it may be useful to suggest strategies for reading the
book. We hope that readers with primarily demographic interests
will be able to pass quickly through any historical detail which does
not particularly catch their interest (a stringent measure would be to
start with chapter 3). Similarly, we absolve our readers with a primary
interest in Quaker social history from the task of perusing every single
table – though of course we cannot recommend that they lay down the
book at the end of chapter 2. If we have done our job properly, the
demography will be interpreted by the history, and the history will be
enriched by the demography.

---

[22] See, for example, Arnold Lloyd, *Quaker Social History 1669–1736* (London, 1950);
Elisabeth Isichei, *Victorian Quakerism* (London, 1970); and Richard T. Vann, *The Social
Development of English Quakerism, 1655–1755* (Cambridge, Mass., 1969).

1

The quality of the sources

The study of the demography of the British and Irish Quakers is only made possible by the quality of the records they left behind. It is therefore necessary first to assess the reliability of the sources and establish that their imperfections are not so great as to render our statements about the Quakers speculative. This will be our task in this chapter.

Fortunately, the easiest sources to use were also the most reliable and comprehensive. These were the Irish Quaker family listings and the considerable array of genealogies compiled by descendants of the Quakers. The largest of these, by far, was that devoted to the descendants of Isaac and Rachel Wilson, Friends who lived in Westmorland in the mid eighteenth century, and who now have some 10,000 living descendants.[1] The genealogies thus compiled, especially where they could be supplemented from the registers kept by the Quakers, were suitable for copying straight onto the family reconstitution forms – with the additional advantage that the danger of attributing events to the wrong person was considerably reduced. The family lists seem to have been kept with great faithfulness by the Irish Quakers in addition to the separate chronological record of births, marriages, and burials. These are found in the registers preserved in Dublin immediately following the marriage certificate of a Quaker couple. They show what children were born to the couple and usually which of the children died in childhood – or, if they survived, whom they married. The lists also show the deaths of the parents. They are in effect ready-made family reconstitution forms, and also have almost no risk of mistaken attributions.

Sometimes both the genealogies and the Irish family lists allowed us

[1] R. S. Benson et al., *Descendants of Isaac and Rachel Wilson, Photographic Pedigree* (privately printed, Middlesbrough, 1949), 4 vols.

to go beyond the Quaker registers of births, marriages, and burials. This was particularly true when they showed marriages and births of those who had been disowned – increasingly numerous after 1750. The Lisburn registers consist to a large extent of listings of families where one or both parents had been disowned for at least part of their lives, and thus where the children had no entitlement to membership. These listings suggest that the pastoral concern of meetings still went out to those who had been disowned (but often continued to frequent Friends' meetings), and also that registration was a real concern of meetings and not just of family members. Friends in England also at times compiled such family lists. They can occasionally be found with the original records of births, marriages, and deaths, which the Quakers and other Nonconformists surrendered to the Registrar General under the terms of the Non-parochial Registers Act of 1840. (These registers are now deposited in the Public Record Office.) We examined some of these and concluded that the custom of keeping family lists with the marriage registers was probably not practiced long enough in any part of England to make them a worthwhile source for English Quakerism. Furthermore, the English family lists which we have seen are often much less legible than the original registers and are relatively inaccessible to the researcher, because many registers may have to be produced before we find one that has such lists. For the rest of our English work, therefore, we had to work from the Quaker registers, of births, marriages, and burials. These are like parish registers, but the Quaker material is easier to exploit, because when the registers were surrendered the Society of Friends made digests of them for each of the twenty-six quarterly meetings then in existence. All the entries were arranged alphabetically under initial letters and were put in rough chronological order. The clerks also tabulated all the relevant information in a standardized fashion, as is shown in the photographic reproduction of a page from one of the digested registers (Figure 1.1). The copies of these registers preserved in the Friends House Library provided our third major source. They enormously facilitated the task of filling out the family reconstitution forms, since our workers could work straight from the source to the form, without the intermediate stage of filling out paper slips for each event, as is normally required in parish register work. They could also, by simply going to another drawer in a cabinet, produce the records of a distant area where we might know, or suspect, that a family had moved to or a marriage partner had come from. We did not make a comprehensive national canvass, but our coverage of Southern England was reasonably thorough.

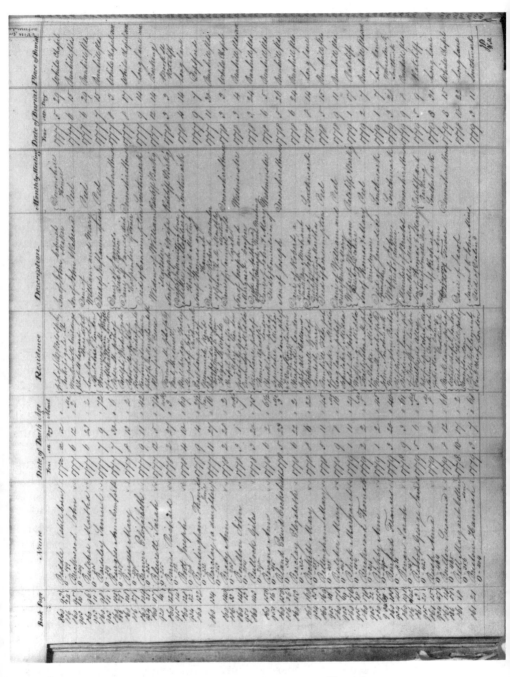

Fig. 1.1 Sample page, London Friends' register of burials.

Besides their ease of exploitation, the Quaker records offer two further advantages. The first arises from the fact that the administrative unit for registration for the Quakers was much larger than the ecclesiastical parish. When Friends met for worship, it was usually in their local communities; but when they met for "the affairs of truth" (church business) they gathered from a considerable distance. Once a month Friends from an area of perhaps a hundred square miles (depending of course on the density of its Quaker population) would meet to oversee the general concerns of Friends – relief for those who were suffering from persecution or poverty, approval of proposals of marriage, granting of "certificates" attesting to the good conduct of those who were traveling or moving to another meeting, maintenance of the property of the meeting, and the discipline of offenders against the testimonies which Friends felt themselves bound to uphold. The monthly meeting thus might embrace a quarter of a small county or a sixth of a larger one. (There were several monthly meetings in London.) Dozens of ecclesiastical parishes would normally be located within the compass of one monthly meeting. By lodging the responsibility of seeing to the affairs of Friends in such a large group, the Quakers diminished the possibility that small and isolated local meetings might become completely negligent in keeping up their registers as well as in more urgent matters. Records of each monthly meeting were then inspected and forwarded to the quarterly meeting, which covered two or three small counties or one large one (London & Middlesex Quarterly Meeting, for example, contained not only the six urban monthly meetings, including Southwark, but also the four rural ones for western Middlesex and, from the beginning of the nineteenth century, the rural monthly meeting for northern Surrey).

The centralized mode of record preservation and the large size of the original unit of registration enhance the chance of keeping in observation a family moving around, even from county to county. We also chose contiguous counties in the South so as to include most migratory families (the great majority of moves in early modern England were short ones, though some families moved quite long distances). It is not families moving away but leaving the Society of Friends which accounts for most breaks in the continuity of the Quaker records.

The other advantage over the parish registers comes from another peculiarity of Quaker usage. They did not practice any ritual of "outward baptism," so their registers record only births. There is thus no need to guess how old babies were when they were baptized, and our calculations of the mortality of children in the first few days of life are relieved of that possible source of inaccuracy. Also the responsibility was on the parent to report the birth of a child, rather than on a vicar to report its baptism. The vicar might take the attitude that it was not his business to report the births of unbaptized babies in his baptismal register, but all births should have been included in a Quaker register of births.

Whether Quaker registration was in practice more thorough cannot be completely determined, but there are ways of making statistical tests which can suggest whether there were areas of systematic underregistration. It is also sometimes possible to cross-check against other Quaker records in which marriages and burials are mentioned, so that we can see whether these were in fact properly recorded. We shall discuss these at their appropriate places; but any discussion of the completeness of the registration must begin with a consideration of the purposes for which the registers were kept in the first place.

Quite early, George Fox exhorted Friends to "buy convenient Books for Registring the Births and Marriages and Burials, as the holy men of God did of old, as you may read through the Scripture; that every one may be ready to give Testimony and Certificate thereof, if need requires, or any be called thereunto."[2] The registers seem to have begun in all parts of England and Ireland before the formal establishment of monthly meetings around 1667. The registration of marriages had an obvious usefulness, since legal record of these might be required if there were disputes over inheritances. Under the Commonwealth Friends were advised to show copies of their marriage certificates to the nearest Justice of the Peace, and they later took legal counsel about the proper form of words to say in their weddings.[3] The Quaker marriage discipline, with its careful inquiry into the consent of the parents and freedom from other engagements as well as its public witnessing of the wedding and signing of the marriage certificate, soon was accepted even by the hostile authorities of Restoration Britain. Even though Quaker marriages were not expressly legitimized until the Marriage Act of 1836, they were repeatedly held valid in the courts (when, for instance, the legitimacy of children was questioned). When the other Nonconformists lost

---

[2] First printed in George Fox, *Friends Fellowship Must Be in the Spirit* (London, 1668), 10. The manuscript, which differs in insignificant ways, is in Register No. 262 of those surrendered to the Registrar General. J. S. Rowntree, "The Friends' registers of births, deaths, and marriages, 1650–1900," *The Friend* new ser. 43 (1903), 53 gives its date as 1659 – apparently from internal evidence, since the manuscript itself is undated.

[3] Arnold Lloyd, *Quaker Social History* (London, 1950), 50; Donald John Steel, *Sources for Nonconformist Genealogy and Family History* (London, 1973), 659.

their right to perform weddings through Hardwicke's Marriage Act of 1753, Quaker weddings were not proscribed.

There was, however, less apparent reason for the registration of births and deaths by the early Quakers. In the first few years of Quakerism there was very little discussion of placing the responsibility for relief of poor Friends with any particular meeting, although everyone agreed that Friends should relieve their own poor and not send them to the parish for relief. It does not seem, therefore, that any right was created by being born into a Friend's family that would require a formal registration of births, although this certainly came to be the case by the eighteenth century.[4] We must therefore attend to Fox's evocation – erroneous as it may be as a piece of history – of the "holy men of God of old" carefully recording their births, marriages, and burials in their "necessary books." The impulse to establish the Quaker system of registration cannot be separated from their fundamental belief that they were recreating, against the false and perverted churches of their day, the true forms of the Christian life. They were determined to withdraw from every aspect of the national church – its sacraments, its hireling ministry, its poor relief, and its parish registers.[5] To each of these Friends posed their alternatives, and this meant an alternative system of registration.

Unfortunately we have only scattered evidence of how the registers were kept in the first century of Quakerism. The marriage register should have been the easiest to keep, since the wedding was a public affair giving rise to a certificate which was supposed to be copied into the register as well. Even though Friends disapproved of funeral pomp, their burials were also often public events, and were generally followed by meetings for worship in which, if the spirit moved, some memorial words about the departed Friend might be said. Also, a burial note was usually issued. The burials of influential Friends were great social occasions, to which visitors from quite a distance might come.[6] Births, however, were more or less private (though more a public occasion than they are today) and there would be no essential reason for the clerk of a monthly meeting to know that they had occurred.

4 For a fuller discussion of the development of the Quaker system of poor relief, see Charles F. Carter, "Unsettled Friends," *Journal of the Friends' Historical Society* 51 (1967), 143–53 and Richard T. Vann, *The Social Development of English Quakerism, 1655–1755* (Cambridge, Mass., 1969), 143–57.
5 An exception to this was probate registration. Friends did appear before the ecclesiastical courts to prove wills, though if they were faithful they did not swear the oath.
6 See, for example, the manuscript Diary of Rebecca Butterfield (in Friends House Library, London) in which the concourse of Friends to funerals provides the chief excitement.

It appears that it was up to the parents to submit a notice of the birth. In Bristol, the mother had this responsibility, and in 1687 the meeting had a woman registrar.[7] Friends in the Southwark Monthly Meeting were particularly conscientious about keeping their registers – they made the only surviving list of their members in 1737, for example – and in their minutes we can get some examples of the procedure for recording births, marriages, and burials. In one of the first minutes (13 March 1666/7) we find them asking "that Freinds hear doe give notise to Freinds to bringe in notes of the days of the birth of their Children with the name and plase of their dwelling of the parents." The request was repeated in 1673 – perhaps a sign that the response had been disappointing. In 1688 there was a regular registrar of births, marriages, and burials, Richard Scoryer, and John Douding was appointed on 28 March 1688 to receive the "papers of Births, Marridges & Burialls" from the meeting and take them to him to be registered. On 27 July Friends attending the Meeting of Twelve and the "person yt Keeps ye Register Book of Marages Births Burialls & Sufferings" were directed to take annually the books to "ye Generall Register att London to bee Compared to See how they Consist." Despite the evidence of such care, it was once again necessary to tighten procedures, and on 5 February 1706/7 it was proposed "that Friends do for the future make two Originall Birth Notes of their Children by the Women Signing both, One to be kept by the Parents, and the other to be Sent to the Monthly Meetings they belong to, in order to be Registred." It is not clear here who "the Women" who were to sign were: the reference could be to mothers, midwives, or the women's monthly meeting, although it seems most likely that the members of the latter were to do the signing. In any case, a more systematic procedure, with witnesses, had now been instituted.

There are no minutes about the registration of marriages, which suggests that they proceeded smoothly. Registration of burials was probably connected with notes which were required for the gravemaker, since on 25 October 1670 John Stuchbury was appointed to have the key of the burial ground and warned "that he observe to bury none but such as he shall have notese for from the Freinds concerned."

Besides manifesting a desire that the registers be as complete and accurate as possible, Southwark Friends intended that they record only the names of those whose behavior was consistent with the high standard of Quaker conduct. They refused to register the births of the children of Arthur Dekens, "hee haveing not walked as becomes a

[7] Lloyd, *Quaker Social History*, 111.

friend professing truth."[8] On 28 December 1691 they warned Friends
who had been married by a priest that they could not be buried in the
burial ground unless they made a public repentance of their action in
good time. Birth and burial notes were queried or refused because the
father had escaped his creditors by taking sanctuary in the Mint, or
failed to frequent meetings, or had been married by a priest, or had
returned from Maryland without a proper certificate from Friends
there, or simply was insufficiently well known to Friends.[9] Sometimes, however, a birth might be registered if only one parent
remained faithful; on 27 April 1709 the meeting agreed to register the
birth of James Harrison's child "only on his Wife's accot: he having
Wholly declin'd and gone out from Friends & Truth as this Meeting is
inform'd."

Southwark Monthly Meeting, and doubtless others whose minutes
we did not search, took their duties conscientiously; but there is much
evidence that in many parts of the country in the first half of the
eighteenth century there were serious shortcomings in registration.
(We speak of course only of the digested registers; it may be that the
English family lists showed the same willingness to record vital events
in disowned families that we encountered in Ireland.) In any case, in
1774 London Yearly Meeting addressed itself to the difficulties and
overhauled the entire registration system, along lines anticipated by
the practices of the more careful monthly meetings.[10] Birth notes,
which perhaps had not been in general use at all,[11] were standardized
and made mandatory, and printed registers were prepared. In every
local meeting one or two persons were appointed to issue birth notes,
account for where they were delivered, and submit them for inspection by the next monthly meeting. Two notes were to be made for each
birth: one given to the parents, and the other copied into the monthly
meeting register and then filed and copied again into the quarterly
meeting register. A similar procedure was employed for burial notes,
which went in the first instance to the grave-maker and then were
again copied twice.

Thus far we have discussed the efficiency of registration of births,
marriages, and burials; but beyond the question whether an event

8 Southwark Monthly Meeting, minute of 15 September 1686.
9 Southwark Monthly Meeting, minutes of 7 December 1709, 6 December 1710, 15
   August 1711, 26 March 1712, 28 January 1712/3, and 30 November 1715. During these
   six years questions of this sort arose several times, but not at all during later periods.
10 In 1774 London Yearly Meeting issued *Directions for a More General Uniformity in
    Keeping Records* and *The Method to be Observed in Recording Marriages, Births, and Burials*.
    The new regulations were to take effect on 1 January, 1776.
11 This is the opinion of Steel: *Sources*, 643, n. 133.

might have failed to be recorded in the first place, there is also the question whether the record once made was safely stored. This is more difficult to determine, since meetings which lost their registers were probably not careful about keeping their minute books; but a good many registers turned up after most of them had been surrendered, which suggests a certain disarray. Also, the loss of some registers can be inferred; there are, for example, very few for Wales.

Even with a highly efficient system of registration, and a perfect preservation of records, there would still be some reasons why the Quaker registers could never record all their vital events. People joined Friends, through convincement, and – with increasing frequency in the eighteenth century – they left, or were disowned. The births of convinced people would of course not have been registered by the Quakers when they occurred, and so cannot figure in age-specific calculations unless their age at death was accurately given (which it almost always was in the later registers) or unless it was retrospectively entered at the time of their convincement, as often happened in the Irish family listings. A more difficult problem is that it is unclear to what extent those who had been disowned would leave further traces in the records. The most common occasion of disownment – it was virtually automatic after 1760 – was marriage by a priest, and such marriages would of course never be in the Quaker registers. On the other hand many of the Irish family lists do include marriages outside the discipline, and such marriages also commonly figure in the genealogies. Furthermore, people who had been disowned might still associate with Friends, and often the births of their children would be registered, although with an indication that they were not members. London Yearly Meeting provided for the registration of births of children of non-members as early as 1767.[12] They were also frequently recorded in Ireland. It seems likely that a substantial minority of all births recorded in the nineteenth century were actually those to non-members. In Yorkshire there were very few such before 1760, but one-fifth of the births between 1760 and 1800 and almost two-fifths of those between 1800 and 1837 were so designated.[13]

We do not have to depend entirely on these designations in the

---

[12] In 1767 London Yearly Meeting declared that "Children born of parents, who have been disowned, ought to be registered, upon application made for that purpose; and in making such registers it should be noted, that those children were born of parents out of unity with us; and that it shall in no wise be esteemed a title to membership." The 1774 directions repeat the admonition to note in the margin or at the bottom of the entry that the child was born to parents not in unity with the Society. We are grateful to Edward Milligan for drawing this to our attention.

[13] Rowntree, "Friends' registers," 53.

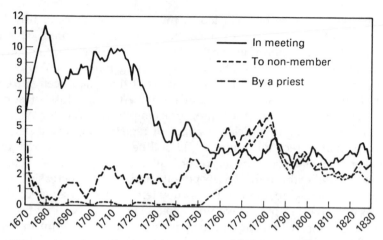

Fig. 1.2 Regular and irregular marriages, Southwark Monthly Meeting.

registers to discover the extent to which the registers are not completely reflecting the vital statistics of Friends. Just as marriages
according to Quaker usage required abundant notice and investigation, all of which showed up in the minutes of the monthly meetings
for business, so these meetings also took notice of Friends who had
breached the discipline by marrying outsiders, or marrying other
Friends in an Anglican ceremony. This means that the minute books
will record most of the irregular marriages as well as those that went
forward in harmony with Friends' testimonies. Monthly meeting
minutes are too voluminous to be read for the whole country, but
some indication of the extent of marriages contrary to discipline can be
gained from the 10,000 pages of minutes kept by Southwark Monthly
Meeting between 1667 and 1840. As Figure 1.2 shows, marriages
according to Quaker form were several times as numerous as irregular
ones until about 1720, when the number of Friends' marriages began
to fall sharply. In 1760 the lines cross and for the first time the average
of marriages by a priest exceeded that of marriages in meeting, as it
continued to do until the end of the 1780s. Even when the average of
marriages according to the discipline climbed above that of irregular
ones, it maintained only a narrow lead through to the end of the
period. Many of the earlier marriages contrary to discipline were to
other Quakers, since even couples who were both Quakers would
want to evade Friends' marriage discipline if their parents were
opposed to the match. In Southwark on 12 May 1742 James Rodgers
"acknowledg'd to have broken the Rules of the Society; But had no

expectation of accomplishing the same any other way." Such engaging candor recognized that parents – even parents who were not themselves Friends – had a virtually unbreakable veto over marriages proposed in meeting.

The extent of underregistration can sometimes be measured directly, when there is an independent source against which the register can be checked. We were able to do this for marriages and burials in parts of Buckinghamshire, in Norfolk, and in Southwark. Where a complete run of minute books survives, the certificate of "clearness" for marriage – which declares that there were no impediments to the wedding's taking place – can be compared with the marriage register. A check of the completeness of monthly meeting minutes in Southwark against the marriage register shows only a handful omitted during the period from 1667 to 1837, and some of these may not have taken place, or may have occurred in meetings outside London. In Buckinghamshire and Norfolk in the early and mid eighteenth century, Friends were less careful: more than half of Norfolk marriages around mid-century, and up to 90 percent of the burials in the Upperside of Buckinghamshire seem to have escaped registration.[14]

Even when checks against other documents are impossible or too tedious to make, there are various internal checks which may reveal underregistration. A widow may remarry even though there is no record of her husband's death, or the daughter of a Quaker couple may marry although there is no record of her birth. Figures which deviate markedly from biological norms may also be suspect, although we cannot usually be sure they are wrong. For example, if more than 20 percent of the marriages of women who marry in their twenties appear to have been childless, it is likely that children were born who were not recorded; if very few babies who died in infancy are recorded as dying within the first week of their lives (the first day of life being the most hazardous that anyone ever experiences) then neo-natal deaths are likely to have been underregistered.

In summary: underregistration certainly occurred in England, and

---

14 Upperside burials were noted in the Diary of Rebecca Butterfield; see Vann, *Social Development*, 161. Further evidence of the incompleteness of the Upperside burial register comes from the parish of Tring (in Hertfordshire, but belonging to Buckinghamshire Quarterly Meeting). There the incumbents regularly noted burials in the Friends' burial ground (all incumbents were supposed to do this, but most did not). Between 1682 and 1747 eighty-four burials were recorded in the parish register as occurring in the "Quakers' burial place," but only forty-four of these are in Friends' registers. Gaps occur in 1698–1709, 1712–15, 1722–25, 1728–31, and 1734–37. See "Burials of Friends from Tring parish register," *Journal of the Friends Historical Society* 31 (1935), 49, quoted in Steel, *Sources*, 628, fn. 88.

was probably considerable for the first half of the eighteenth century
(at least in some areas outside London). Through cross-checking we
can get some ideas of the extent of underregistration of marriages and
burials, but it is much harder to get information about unregistered
births. Everything suggests, however, that these were at least as
common as unregistered marriages or burials. This problem, it should
be noted, only affects the English registers. Quite different procedures
(and, it seems, more thorough ones) were used in the compilation of
the Irish family lists. The genealogies we have used – which are only a
minority of the ones consulted – drew on information passed on in the
family as well as the registers.

Fortunately, even when we must depend on our least perfect source,
the registers, we have ways of greatly mitigating the effects of
underregistration. The technique of family reconstitution, which was
especially designed for work on materials of this sort, can obviate
almost all the problems which arise from the incompleteness of the
historical record. If we were attempting an aggregative study – one
that aimed at showing the total number of Quakers at various times,
and relied on simple counting of the various demographic events – we
would find ourselves in all sorts of difficulties. There was no overall
census of the British Quakers until 1861; the best guess of their
numbers prior to that is given in Figure 1.3. Even if regular censuses
had been taken back to the seventeenth century, they would not have
been particularly useful for demographic purposes (although of
course they would be indicative of the prosperity of Quakerism). The
reason of course is that the population of Quakers was not a closed
one; not only were there the disownments and conversions to which
we have already referred, but besides migrations between Britain and
Ireland, Quakers from both islands went to America. So simply
knowing the change in the number of Friends at various times would
not allow us to decide whether we were measuring a real growth or
decline in the population, through an excess of births over deaths or
vice versa, or just the fluctuations of conversions and emigration.
    Although the Quaker records are quite unsuitable for aggregative
demography, they lend themselves very well to the other major
technique of the historical demographer. Family reconstitution is a
method long known to genealogists, and its application to historical
materials on a large scale was anticipated as long as seventy years
ago;[15] but the era of modern work begins with the pioneering

[15] The earliest example known to Roger Schofield (who kindly supplied this information) is a reconstitution of several Swedish parish registers in a study of fertility

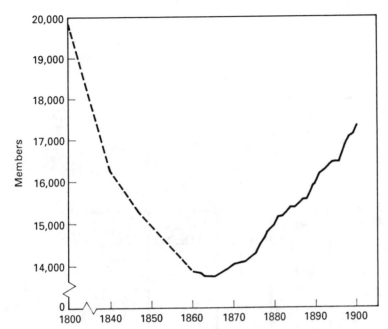

Fig. 1.3 Estimate of English Quaker population before 1861.
Source: Isichei, *Victorian Quakers*, 111.

monographs of Emile Gautier and Louis Henry, *La Population de Crulai, paroisse normande* (Paris, 1958) and of Pierre Goubert, *Beauvais et le Beauvaisis* (Paris, 1959).

In family reconstitution, events are not merely counted, but rather are assigned to the families in which they occurred. If the ages of the various members of these families are known, and if they remain constantly "in observation" – that is, if we can be satisfied that all the pertinent deaths, births, and marriages are still being recorded in the sources, and have been correctly attributed to the appropriate individuals – then age-specific rates of various kinds can be derived. These can give us an understanding of the dynamic of population change which cannot be directly achieved by aggregative methods.[16] We have

reported in 1915 (K. A. Edin, "Studier i svensk fruktsamhetsstatistik," *Ekonomisk Tidskrift* 17 [1915], 251–302). See also C. C. Morrell, "Tudor marriages and infantile mortality," *Journal of State Medicine* 43 (1935), 173–81. Morrell presents data from a kind of reconstitution of the parish registers of North Elmham, Norfolk and Wedmore, Somerset. Another early example, also from Scandinavia, is a study by Hannes Hyrenius of Swedish communities in the eastern Baltic, which was published in 1942.

16 We say "directly" because it is possible to estimate life expectancy, age-specific fertility, and infant mortality (among other things) from aggregative figures, if one

HUSBAND BARCLAY | David

WIFE TAYLOR | Anne

Son Robert BARCLAY, late of Ury (Christian Molleson) SCOTLAND 113

Daughter James TAYLOR & Cheapside

Occupation
husband Citizen & Draper (linen draper)
husband's father Laird

LMX 53v

MARRIAGE 835. 117	solemnized at Bull & Mouth		Marriage		Dates			Age at	Remarriage	LMX 562 of Cheapside
			rank of	age at	marriage 12. 6. 1707	end of union 3.12.1720	length 13 yrs	end of union	8. 8. 1723 FREAME 835.738	
HUSBAND born at Ury Kincardine t.p. SCOTLAND.	residing at Cheapside t.p.	1	24	birth 17.9.1682	burial 1769		38	Widowhood 20 (months)	buried at t.p.
WIFE t.p. Cheapside t.p.		1	18	1689	3.12.1720 (childbed)	31			Bunhill Fields

Age groups	Years married	No. of births	Age of mother	Inter-val (months)	sex	rank	Births date	Burials date	status	age	Marriages date	age	Name(s)	Surname of spouse
15–19					M	1	5. 7. 1708	20.2.1766 consumption	m. 58				James LMX 571	Sarah
20–24					M	2	5. 8. 1709						Robert	
25–29					F	3	25. 8. 1710	16. 2. 1712	—				Christian	
30–34					M	4	11. 1. 1712	17. 1. 1713	—				Robert	
35–39					M	5	10. 1. 1713						Alexander	
40–44					F	6	21. 6. 1714	30.10.1745 consumption	m. 31	9. 10. 1735	21	Elizabeth	BEVAN LMX 298 836.196
45–49					F	7	2. 8. 1715	24. 9. 1731 fits	s. 16	—		Christian	
TOTAL 11					F	8	24. 1. 1717		not looked for			Anne	
boys 5					F	9	29. 11. 1718					Patience	
girls 6					M	10	14. 9. 1719 died	14. 9. 1719	—			Infant boy	
Remarks					F	11	24. 11. 1720	24. 11. 1720	—			Stillborn girl	
						12								
						13								
						14								
						15								

FRF ii 65

Fig. 1.4 Sample family reconstitution form.

already discussed the difficulties in knowing whether fluctuations in totals of births and deaths in parish registers represent genuine changes in vital rates, rather than being the result of migration or

relies on specimen life tables and other techniques of statistical adjustment. This has been done by E. A. Wrigley and Roger Schofield in the *Population History of England, 1541–1871: A Reconstruction* (Cambridge, Mass., 1981). It is also possible to estimate a base population from family-reconstitution materials, as is done in Allan Sharlin, "Methods for estimating population total, age distribution and vital rates in family reconstitution studies," *Population Studies* 32 (1978), 511–21.

differing degrees of underregistration. Furthermore, even if we can establish *that* changes in the total population were taking place, this would not necessarily tell us *why* these changes were occurring. If there were, for example, more births, the explanation could be that women were marrying earlier, or that more women were getting married, or that married women were having babies closer together – or any combination of these. An increase in mortality might be the result of an epidemic or famine, but it also might be produced simply by a change in the age structure of the population: since young children were most vulnerable to disease, the more of them there were in the population, the more mortality would tend to rise.[17] Also, the same number of deaths will have a quite different impact on the future of a population if it is concentrated among the young rather than the old.

Family reconstitution is obviously more laborious than counting totals of baptisms, marriages, and burials, which even in a large parish can be done in a few hours. Each entry in a parish register has to be copied on a separate slip of paper and the slips, alphabetized and finally assigned to families, are in turn transcribed on a "family reconstitution form."[18] Figure 1.4 shows what a family reconstitution form looks like when all relevant events recorded in the registers have been transcribed. Computations are then made on the intervals between the events shown on the form. If all data were known – which hardly ever happens – we would know how old the bride and groom were when they married, how old the mother was when she had each of her children, what the infant and child mortality rate of the children was, and at what ages the parents died.

The form reproduced as Figure 1.4 is unusually complete; but even it has a number of gaps. If we were counting events, these lacunae would undermine the accuracy of our totals. In family-reconstitution work, we have ways to address this difficulty. Since so few forms will have every date, it is obviously essential to have some rules for knowing what to do with forms which give some dates but not all. The basic rule is to include all forms which give evidence of at least one hard fact: that is, a usable interval, such as an age at marriage even if

---

[17] An assessment of the weaknesses as well as the advantages of the aggregative method is given in David Eversley, "Exploitation of Anglican parish registers by aggregative analysis," in *An Introduction to English Historical Demography*, ed. E. A. Wrigley (London, 1966), 44–95. See also Roger Schofield, "Historical demography: some possibilities and some limitations," *Transactions of the Royal Historical Society* 5th ser. 21 (1971), 119–32.

[18] A fuller description of the process of family reconstitution from parish registers and criteria for which parishes it is suitable can be found in *Introduction to English Historical Demography*, ed. Wrigley, ch. 4.

there were no children recorded, or intervals between the early births
even if the couple passed out of observation shortly after the marriage.
   The concept of "being in observation" clearly needs to be refined.
Let us take the most usual case, when a couple shows up in the
registers as parents with no prior record of their birth or marriage. We
cannot use this form as evidence of age at marriage, nor, since the ages
of the parents and the date of marriage are unknown, can we treat it as
evidence for fertility calculations. It can be used, however, in the
calculation of infant mortality, for as long as there continue to be
entries relating to this family which assure us that it is still in
observation. Nevertheless we must be careful not to let our definition
of "being in observation" bias the figures. Usually when a family
passes out of observation the last recorded date is that of the birth or
death of a child. If we allow the set of families in observation for the
purposes of determining infant mortality to include those for whom
the last evidence is of the death of a child, we would give an upward
bias to mortality rates.[19] The same would be true of fertility rates if the
last date were the birth of a child. When we know the date of marriage
but not the age of either partner, we obviously cannot use the form for
any age-specific calculations, but we can use it to determine birth
intervals between marriage and the first and subsequent births (what
demographers call "parity-specific" rates). This means, in short, that
families are not just "in observation"or out of it; they are usually in
observation for some purposes and not for others.
   Even when dates were not supplied by the registers, the situation is
not hopeless. There were often forms where certain dates, though not
known exactly, could easily be inferred. Some of the Quaker burial
registers gave ages at death; after the reform of the registration system
in 1774, almost all did so. These at first sight look like estimates –
"aged about 73," and the like – but with true Quaker scrupulosity the
clerks reckoned people were exactly 73 only on their birthdays, and so
unless they chanced to die on that birthday, their age at death was
only "about 73." When the ages at death given in the registers could be
checked against the birth register, they proved remarkably accurate.
Another safe inference could often be made when it was obvious
where a child fitted into the order of births within a family. It was
particularly easy to infer the approximate date of birth of infants who
died very early. We were able to use these inferred years of birth

[19] The effect of the rules on being in observation on the establishment of accurate rates
   of infant mortality is discussed (with reference to work of parish registers, where the
   problem of growing delay in baptism arises) by E. A. Wrigley and R. S. Schofield in
   "English population history from family reconstitution: summary results 1600–1799,"
   Population Studies 37 (1983), 175–77.

without treating them as though they were exact by using a code for the computer. An inferred date would be entered as something like 0–0–1712* while an exact date would be entered as 3–11–1712. The asterisk and the fact that zeroes rather than positive numbers were used for the months signaled the computer to exclude these dates from tables where we wanted exact dates and to include them if approximate dates would suffice.

An illustration will show how this works. Suppose an Irish family list gives all the children born to William and Anne Pim, but by year of birth only, without the month and day they were born. We can still make statements about the couple's total fertility and age-specific fertility in maternal five-year age groups; but obviously these entries could not be used to compute birth intervals, because we could, in extreme cases, be wrong by eleven months either way if we assumed that children born in 1720 and 1722 were born twenty-four months apart. They could be thirteen months apart if their exact dates of birth were 15 December 1720 and 15 January 1721/2, or thirty-five months apart if they were born 15 January 1719/20 and 15 December 1722 respectively.

In summary, each item of information can be classified and used only for the appropriate calculations. In general, our practice has been to use only the exact information; when we include also approximations, this will be specially noted. When dates based on estimates and interpolations are included, the results seldom change much, suggesting our method of estimating is sound. We could thus use a form for what it told us or for what we could infer from it, and nothing more; and we did not trouble ourselves further with forms which told us nothing.

Since every piece of information is used according to its precision and degree of reliability, it follows that there will be different numbers of cases in the various tables. In some we have information about virtually all the Quakers, and for others the restrictions are so stringent as to reduce the numbers greatly – at times so much so that it is hard to get results which can be used to make reliable statements about differences. For Britain and Ireland, of the almost 13,000 forms originally compiled by the various workers, almost 2,000 were found to refer to the same families, although almost always supplying different information about them. (In almost every case the overlap was between forms from the registers and those from the genealogies.) The supplementary information was copied onto the more completed form, and the other – or occasionally the other two – discarded. This reduced the number to around 12,000; but almost 4,000 of these failed the test of providing information about at least one interval. These, presumably, were the ones most affected by the underregistration we have been discussing. The remaining 8,000 found their way into the final analysis, supplemented by almost 400 family lists from Lisburn which were analyzed by hand calculator. For the whole of Ireland 2,900 family reconstitution forms were compiled, but only 1,600, a little over half, could be used for most of the calculations, and only about one-fifth for the computation of age-specific fertility. Since it was hard to find out when the parents of the first generation of Quaker children were born, fewer than one-quarter of the births to families formed before 1700 could be used for age-specific fertility calculations even in London, and the figure was lower still elsewhere (only one-eighth of the Irish births were usable for this first cohort). The situation improves markedly in the first half of the eighteenth century, where 40 percent or more of the English births are generally included and more than a quarter of the Irish; in the later eighteenth century around 70 percent of the Southern English and London births are included in age-specific fertility tables, along with about half of those from the genealogies and Northern English and Scottish areas, while the Irish slipped to below one-fifth. For the final half-century, about half of the English births figure in the age-specific fertility tables, but only about one-sixth of the Irish ones.

The price we pay for discarding forms with incomplete evidence is of course contracting the size of our sample. It may be that the families about whom too little information survives to enter our calculations differed in some systematic way from those which were more fully recorded. While we cannot muster any evidence to disprove this hypothesis, neither can we see any way in which the forms rejected differed, except as to their completeness, from those accepted. It also appears that all family-reconstitution studies will suffer from this same difficulty – if it is one. For example, let us consider thirteen English parishes whose registers have been analyzed by the ESRC Cambridge Group for the History of Population and Social Structure. In only a few are age-specific fertility calculations for the early nineteenth century possible at all, and for the period from 1650 to 1800 only 16 percent of the legitimate live births figure in age-specific fertility calculations, as against 45 percent of the English Quaker births. Notwithstanding this, the fecundability of these Anglican women as calculated in a different manner, from the distribution of birth intervals, seemed indis-tinguishable from that of those excluded from age-specific fertility calculations.[20]

[20] Wrigley and Schofield, "English population history," 158. Of course there was an undetermined number of women in these parishes for whom birth intervals could not be calculated either, so it cannot be known whether *their* fertility was very similar to that of women whose age-specific fertility could be established.

Thus far we have been discussing what we might call the raw materials: that is, the sources just as any researcher might read them in the archives. We also have to establish that we have represented these sources correctly. The possibilities for incorrect representation obviously arise because of the number of operations through which each piece of data must go. Before we saw it, everything in the registers (a birth or burial entry, for example) had already been copied twice: first into the monthly and quarterly meeting registers, and then again into the digests made from 1840 to 1842. Very few errors, however, seem to have been introduced by these transcriptions; the digested copies were checked for their accuracy by two clerks at the time, and we seldom found it necessary to consult the originals in the Public Record Office. The family lists are of course original sources, which had not been transcribed before we saw them.

The family reconstitution forms from the registers were compiled in Friends House, London, but the Irish family lists were microfilmed and the forms made up from the microfilms – which were, inevitably, slightly less legible than the originals. The next step was the editing: rejection of unreliable material, developing conventions for making the best guesses for reliable but undated inferred events, making sure that these were coded properly so that the computer could count them as appropriate, and cross-allocating events from one record to another in cases of duplication. Editing was supposed to detect any errors made in compiling family reconstitution forms from the registers, and did detect manifest absurdities, but since there were some people with the same names alive in the same area at the same time, some events were undoubtedly attributed to the wrong families. We see no reason to think there was any systematic error here, so that these few mistaken allocations should not affect the averages.

Any researcher with enough time to spend could carry a project through the stages we have described so far. Next, however, came the preparation of the materials for computer analysis. Each form, with its identifying number designating its place of origin, was punched onto paper tape – the fourth transcription for the materials from the registers, and one which had the same possibilities for the introduction of error as the earlier ones. This process involves no very expensive equipment but a great deal of trained labor. The paper tape was then fed onto magnetic tape for computer storage and access.[21]

21 In our project this process was more adventurous than it usually is, since we had to change computers and conversion codes had to be written so that the material originally intended for the KDF9 computer in Newcastle-upon-Tyne, which had a memory of only 16K, could be handled by a larger and newer IBM computer at Cambridge.

Of course the data, even if they found their way in perfect accuracy into the computer's memory bank, would simply lie there inert without the development of analytical programs which were to produce the eventual tabulations. This was the crucial step, without which we historians could have done very little; and it was entirely the contribution of Roger Schofield and his colleagues of the ESRC Cambridge Group for the History of Population and Social Structure. We were of course consulted as to our own particular needs, but all the actual work was theirs, and some idea of its magnitude can be gained from the fact that several hundred separate commands to the computer are involved just in the calculation of age-specific fertility rates. If there is the slightest breakdown in the logical chain, the program fails. Each program thus had to be tested, often a large number of times, since in the early stages of running the information through the machines the process would come to a premature end; and even when a complete run to print-out took place, the resulting tables might turn out on first inspection to contain nonsense. So the wearisome process of "de-bugging" the programs went on, until the experts were finally satisfied.

Even then there is no guarantee that the historian can accept what is printed out, for the final stages of this long process involve a dialogue between the historian and the programmer. Some safeguards against error can be built into the program; for example, the computer can be instructed not to accept a birth ascribed to a mother less than 15 or more than 50 years old; or one which followed by seven months or less a previous birth to the same woman; or one apparently occurring after the recorded death of the mother, or more than ten months after the death of the father. (Despite our precautions, we blush to confess that at least one example of each of these prodigies was found in our input.) The danger, however, is not so much the impossible as the improbable which might nevertheless turn out to be correct. In the last analysis it must be the historian's judgment whether to accept an average number of 11 births to all couples married in Mountmellick between 1700 and 1724, and of 2.3 to those married at the same time in Moate; or whether to believe infant mortality rates of almost 400 per 1,000 live births – as we found in a manual computation for London, which finally stood up as substantially correct – or conversely, a figure as low as 20 per 1,000 in a rural part of Ireland. A mistake in the calculations can still produce a result which is barely plausible, and only a great deal of care, experience, and repetition can lead to a high degree of confidence in the results. When accounts of some 50,000 events are transcribed three or four times, some errors are bound to creep in; but we believe that no *systematic* errors were made, and that random errors will largely cancel one another out. If cumulative errors have nevertheless been made, we hope that they will be swamped by the large number of accurate data. Our confidence level is thus high, but we of course must leave it to our readers to decide whether to extend their confidence to what we have found.

2

Characteristics of the sample

This chapter deals with two questions: how representative of the British and Irish Quakers as a whole our sample was, and how representative of the population as a whole the British and Irish Quakers were.

The three main sources which we used, digested registers, family lists (in Ireland), and genealogies, need to be discussed in turn in order to answer the first question. Both of us contributed something to the work on the registers, starting independently and adopting somewhat different procedures (though eventually harmonizing our methods). David Eversley included all usable Irish and Scottish families, but for the English registers adopted a sampling procedure. Families where the surname of the bridegroom or father began with the letter "B" – usually from 10 to 15 percent of the whole – were reconstituted by volunteers from the following Quarterly Meeting registers: London & Middlesex, Westmorland, and Yorkshire. For several smaller meetings, a larger sample was obtained by including families whose surnames began with either "B" or "S": these were Cheshire, Sussex & Surrey, and Hereford, Worcester & Wales. Sampling of this sort was not used by Richard Vann, who supervised the compilation of family reconstitution forms for every family formed between 1655 and 1840 for which a birth or marriage was recorded in the registers for the following Monthly and Quarterly Meetings: Bedfordshire & Hertfordshire, Berkshire & Oxfordshire, Bristol, Buckinghamshire, Cambridgeshire & Huntingdonshire, and Norfolk (with Norwich treated separately). With the exception of Bristol, chosen because it was at the time a relatively large metropolitan area, these make up a contiguous area stretching from the Thames Valley eastward to the North Sea. It was hoped that this contiguity would make it easier to trace families who had moved around. As the map (Figure 2.1) shows, all the English areas we worked on, except Hereford, Worcester & Wales,

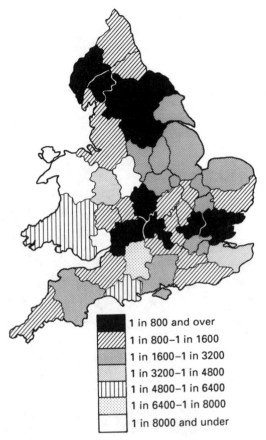

1 in 800 and over
1 in 800–1 in 1600
1 in 1600–1 in 3200
1 in 3200–1 in 4800
1 in 4800–1 in 6400
1 in 6400–1 in 8000
1 in 8000 and under

Fig. 2.1 Distribution of the Society of Friends in England in 1851, propor-
tionate to the general population.
Source: Isichei, *Victorian Quakers*, 170.

had a relatively heavy Quaker population when the first comprehensive religious census was taken in 1851. We can compare this
with estimates of the density of the Quaker population in the first
decade of the eighteenth century (Figure 2.2). These show Bristol as
the only place with more than 5 percent of the population Quaker; but
London and Middlesex, Hertfordshire, Bedfordshire, Huntingdonshire, and Westmorland, among the counties we worked on, also had
among the heaviest concentration of Quakers, and there were good
numbers of Friends in Norfolk, Buckinghamshire, Berkshire, and
Oxfordshire.

The characteristics which made a register desirable to work on –
other than the willingness of some volunteer to take it on – were

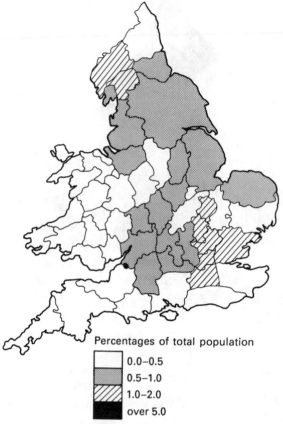

Percentages of total population

	0.0–0.5
	0.5–1.0
	1.0–2.0
	over 5.0

Fig. 2.2 Distribution of English Quakers, 1700–1709.

mostly those pieces of information which made the reconstitution easier and more certain. In particular, it helped greatly if we knew from the marriage register who the parents of the couple were and whether it was the first marriage for the two. We also preferred registers where the age at death was given at the time of burial, especially since these estimated ages turned out to be so accurate. Finally, information about the occupation of the bridegroom was valuable, not only for its obvious assistance in placing Quakers within the social structure of England, but also as further assistance in distinguishing between people with the same names.

Table 2.1 compares the meetings we chose with some other quarterly meetings, showing that in general we selected the most informative records with which to work. Our aim was to accumulate

Table 2.1. *Comparison of data supplied by quarterly meeting registers*

Quarterly Meeting	Number of marriages to 1837	% of grooms' occupations given	% brides' marriage rank given	Parents' name given	Age at death given
Beds. & Herts.	*450*	50	5	1700–	1700–
Berks. & Oxon.	*1,008*	80	55	*Usually throughout*	*Scattered until 1750*
Bristol & Somerset	1,583	85[a]	15[a]	1760–	1780–
Buckinghamshire	474	67	42	1680–	1775–
Cambs. & Hunts.	334	31	28	1720–	1775–
Cheshire & Staffs.	673	63	53	1760–	1700–
Derby & Notts.	587	35	5	1750–	1775–
Devon	310	41	8	1760–	*Scattered throughout*
Durham	551	34	3	1670–	*Scattered until 1775*
Essex	831	50	18	1700–	*About half throughout*
Lincolnshire	521	44	16	1770–	1775–
London & Middlesex	*4,600*	92	20	1680–	1670–
Norfolk & Norwich	844	58	55	1695–	*Norwich 1700– Norfolk 1790–*
Northampton	351	22	3	1770–	1775–
Suffolk	355	48	40	1680–	1760–
Surrey & Sussex	*871*	72	35	1680–	1760–
Warwick, Leicester, Rutland	870	56	8	1760–; but some from 1680	1785–
Western	*847*	39	6	1770–	1775–
Westmorland	*1,088*	25	7	1760–	1777–
Yorkshire	*3,994*	45	11	1760–	1770–

Note: [a] Percentage for Bristol only.
Italicized meetings included in our sample.

as many data as our resources would allow, so that we could break them down by both period and place. When we wanted to date some development more accurately, we treated all the English and Irish Quakers together, making a group big enough to divide into twenty-five-year cohorts and still leave large enough numbers to have some reasonable level of confidence in the resulting tables. When we compare areas, larger (fifty-year) cohorts are used.

For our geographical subdivisions we constructed five groups. Ireland is obviously a natural geographical subdivision, but in turn (even before its twentieth-century political division) falls into two different areas. The province of Ulster (roughly equivalent to modern Northern Ireland) is joined to the heavily populated part of the three southern provinces (now the Republic of Ireland) by a narrow corridor at Newry and Dundalk, where there were few Friends. The Northern Irish Friends differed not so much in origins as in subsequent economic development from the Southern ones. Their environment consisted partly of the native Irish Catholics, but increasingly of the Presbyterian (and later some Church of Ireland and Methodist) settlers who mostly came from Scotland in Cromwell's time, as did Friends themselves. As will be explained, this led to rather different social developments in Northern and Southern Ireland. Although the Dublin Yearly Meeting still covers the whole of Ireland, Ulster Friends have tended to keep themselves (and, as it happens, their records) rather apart from the Southern ones.

For Britain we used the line between the mouth of the Severn and the mouth of the Humber that has so often been an important demarcation line in English history. We call the families to the north and west of the Humber–Severn line our "Northern" ones and those to the south and east "Southern." After the middle of the eighteenth century much of the Quaker population lived in the various market towns; but we wished to distinguish them from the families who lived in Norwich, Bristol, and London. These latter we aggregated as "urban" – for the computer it had the Dickensian name of "Quaktown." For some purposes the families from London were tabulated separately. Finally, all the families included in the gene-alogies – most of whom, particularly up to 1800, lived in the north and west – were treated as a distinct group because of the possibility that systematic biases had occurred in compiling these sources. The three pie graphs (Figure 2.3) show the composition of the English sub-groups. It should be pointed out that quarterly meetings, although named for counties, did not exactly coincide with the modern bound-aries of the counties; a good part of southern Northamptonshire, for

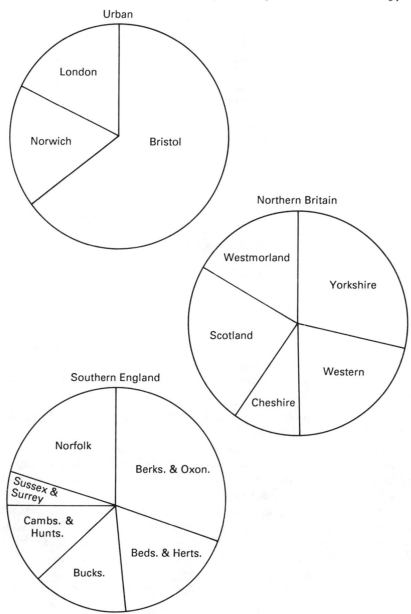

Fig. 2.3 Distribution by monthly and quarterly meetings within areas.

Table 2.2. *First marriages by decennial periods, Irish Quakers (except Lisburn)*

1630–39	2
1640–49	10
1650–59	21
1660–69	38
1670–79	82
1680–89	112
1690–99	119
1700–09	119
1710–19	117
1720–29	82
1730–39	87
1740–49	78
1750–59	78
1760–69	55
1770–79	66
1780–89	54
1790–99	42
1800–09	35
1810–19	25
1820–29	19
Later	89
Total	1,330

example, was included in Buckinghamshire Quarterly Meeting, and Southwark Monthly Meeting was part of London & Middlesex Quarterly Meeting, not Sussex & Surrey. Still, most quarterly meetings were close enough to the boundaries of the counties for which they are named to give a rough approximation of the areas for which we have compiled evidence.

We estimate that we have usable data for between one-fifth and one-quarter of the English, Welsh, and Scottish Quakers. The basis for this estimate is that between 1650 and 1849 there were 27,467 marriages registered among the English Quakers.[1] We have 6,209, or 22.5 percent, on our forms.

All the surviving Irish family lists were transcribed, but it is less easy to estimate what percentage of the total Irish Quaker membership was comprehended in them. As in England, it is impossible to establish with any precision what the membership was in the eighteenth

[1] John Stephenson Rowntree, "Some lessons of the Friends' registration figures," *The Friend* new ser. 43 (1903), 72.

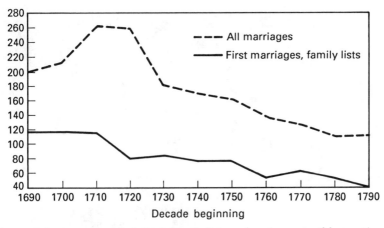

Fig. 2.4 Marriages recorded, Irish family lists and various monthly meetings.

century. Isabel Grubb, a leading student of Irish Quakerism, inclines to a low estimate; she believes that even at the height of Quaker population in Ireland there were not more than 750 Quaker households.[2] This would suggest a population no greater than 5,000, and probably rather smaller. The number of Quaker marriages in Ireland, as Table 2.2 will show, fell quite sharply from about 1720 onwards, which suggests that the total population must have begun to decline in the latter eighteenth century. A fairly careful estimate put the number of Irish Friends in 1830 at 3,500; on the other hand, Thomas Shillitoe thought there were as many as 6,000 in 1812.[3] A count of marriages in seven of the largest Irish monthly meetings, based on the minutes supplemented by the registers of marriages, is represented graphically in Figure 2.4. This can be compared with the total number of first marriages recorded on the family lists we were able to use. To estimate what percentage of marriages were recorded on the family lists, we have to make allowance for the rest of the monthly meeting registers on the one hand and the fact that we are comparing first marriages with all marriages on the other. A reasonable guess is that the *usable*

---

[2] Isabel Grubb, *Quakers in Ireland, 1654–1900* (London, 1927), 89.

[3] John Thurnam, *Observations and Essays on the Statistics of Insanity* (London, 1845), 178. In order to estimate the incidence of "insanity" among the Quakers (almost all of whom were treated at The Mount, near York), Thurnam had to estimate the total Quaker population. The English estimate was made by a back-projection from the estimate made in 1840 by J. S. Rowntree, which had showed a population of 16,227, using the sums of vital events in the Quaker registers. So far as we can tell, Thurnam was the first to use these registers for demographic purposes in any systematic way. Thomas Shillitoe's estimate for the Irish Quaker population may be found in Edward Wakefield, *An Account of Ireland, Statistical and Political* (London, 1812), II, 809.

Fig. 2.5 Leading monthly meetings, Irish Quakers.

family lists represent from one-third to two-fifths of all the Irish Friends, with coverage somewhat more comprehensive in the seventeenth century than later. This sample is surely large enough to be representative of the Irish Quakers, unless there is something unknown to us which systematically precluded some kinds of families from figuring in the family lists. Unfortunately, the decline in numbers in the early nineteenth century means that for the calculations with very stringent criteria for inclusion we are not able to muster many families, rendering the resulting figures vulnerable to wide swings caused by a very few extreme values. We are thus tantalized by the results for the important period in Irish population history just before the Great Famine of the 1840s. Our Irish materials do however throw

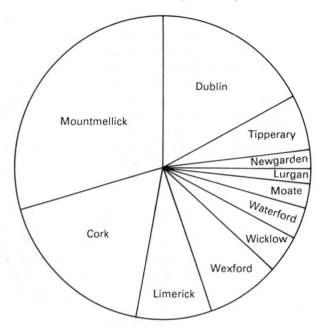

Fig. 2.6 Distribution of Irish Friends, by monthly meeting.

significant light on the population in the late seventeenth and eighteenth centuries.

The meetings of Irish Quakers are shown on the map (Figure 2.5) but they figure quite differently in the composition of our sample (Figure 2.6). The meetings in the west of Ireland contributed very little compared to those in the east and the central areas, especially the most heavily represented in our lists, Mountmellick. Dublin meeting was the largest in Ireland, but some of the Friends in that meeting did not live in the city itself, which was why – even though eighteenth-century Dublin was considerably larger than Norwich and Bristol – we left it with the Irish group instead of transferring it to the urban one.

The final source of data was the genealogies. Because of the decline in the number of Friends, which probably began early in the eighteenth century and had certainly become quite marked by 1800 (Figure 1.3) we wanted additional sources for the forty years before the first comprehensive census of the kingdom in 1841; if possible these might even enable us to extend our study into the latter part of the nineteenth century. This was made possible by the considerable number of genealogies which various descendants of Quaker families have compiled. We have already mentioned the very large number of descendants of Isaac and Rachel Wilson of Kendal in Westmorland. Their family history is unlike the usual genealogy, since it is not a tracing of descent backwards from one or more people now alive to more and more generations in the past, doubling the number of ancestors – if it is complete – with each generation. It is rather an attempt to give an account of a complete descent group, including those who died without issue. It therefore grows larger with each generation, and also avoids the tendency which makes most gene-alogies a biased source for historical demography, which is leaving out of account those who are not in direct line of filiation to someone now alive. (This obviously would give an infertile couple no chance of appearing in the sample.)[4]

Still, it is likely that a small degree of bias affects the genealogies, insofar as they depend on memories or family records. The ratio of male to female births recorded in the genealogies is 112:100, which is the highest of our five subdivisions and about 7 percent higher than the normal ratio. Given the general cultural preference for male children, it is plausible to explain this by unrecorded births of girls who died young. Whereas this bias understates fertility (and infant mortality) there is probably also a small one which overstates it. Families with a large number of children in the eighteenth century are more likely to have had descendants who have gone to the trouble of compiling a genealogy. They simply have more presently alive, so even if the propensity to commit genealogy were randomly distribu-ted, there would be a higher chance of a genealogist turning up among these descendants. Furthermore, large and complex families probably arouse a genealogist's curiosity more often than ones without wide-spread kinship ramifications. However, the fact that most of the families in the genealogies came from descent groups removes the chief source of possible bias, and the other two would largely cancel one another out.

A good many of the descendants of Isaac and Rachel Wilson left Friends. The other genealogies also record a good many marriages which took place outside Friends' meetings. Most of the families included in the genealogies lived in the north of England, and surprisingly few lived in the largest cities. The comparative scarcity of families from the south of England in the genealogies suggests that the great Quaker dynasties were mostly in the north, while families in the

---

[4] Louis Henry and T. H. Hollingsworth discuss the use of genealogies for historical demography in *Annales de démographie historique* (1984), 45–54 concluding that despite the problems of representativeness, work from descending genealogies is likely to be more reliable than that reconstituting parish registers.

south were more likely to marry out and lose their distinctive Quaker identity. Some of the southern families also were in areas where the reconstitution from the registers had been carried out (for example, the Harrises and Lambs of Oxfordshire and the Baxes of Sussex). Since we worked with the rule of retaining the more complete form, regardless of its provenance, some records of these families are in the genealogies and some in the "Southern English" grouping.

The boundaries between our groups are thus not completely tidy, and there were times when we ignored them altogether. Thus, in order to produce cohorts of a more even size we have generally added the families from the genealogies to those in the "northern" sample, and we have also at times made assertions about the entire set of families, English and Irish alike, in the interests of more precise dating. When we did this, of course, we had to beware the risk of committing a fallacy of composition. Suppose we argued that there had been a general fall in fertility without noticing that fewer and fewer of the high-fertility Irish families were figuring in the sample. The appearance of lower fertility could have come even when the fertility in all subgroups remained exactly the same, just because there were now more of the less fertile families included. This makes it important to specify the relative size of the different subgroups throughout the period, as is done in Table 2.3. This shows that the families in the southern counties were the most numerous up to 1800, ranging from more than two-fifths to about a third of the total. The Irish families remain a pretty constant one-sixth to one-fifth of the total and the urban ones average about 30 percent. The northern counties and Scotland never supply as much as 10 percent of the whole. The great change is in the representation of the genealogies, which make up only 3 percent in the seventeenth century but, as one would expect where descent groups are being traced in an expanding population, roughly double with each new fifty-year period until they make up two-fifths of the whole sample by the first half of the nineteenth century.

In summary, then, our sample of the English Quakers is drawn mainly from areas where the Quakers were particularly strong: London and the large cities of Bristol and Norwich, the Home Counties and East Anglia, and the cradle of the movement in West-morland and Yorkshire. The Midlands would appear to be the area most seriously underrepresented. The numbers from the northern counties and Scotland are small, as are those from the genealogies until about 1750; the Irish, although all available family lists were analyzed, also show small numbers for some calculations after 1800. We have no reason to believe, however, that we have systematically

Table 2.3 Distribution of all marriages, by area and cohort

	Urban		Southern England		Ireland		Northern Britain		Genealogies		Cohort total
	No.	% of cohort	No.	% of cohort	No.	% of cohort	No.	% of cohort	No.	% of cohort	
1650–99	615	28.9	885	41.6	379	17.8	182	8.6	66	3.1	2,127
1700–49	763	31.5	849	35.0	486	20.0	173	7.1	154	6.4	2,425
1750–99	453	26.3	560	32.5	301	17.5	146	8.5	262	15.2	1,722
1800–49	202	16.7	303	25.0	114	9.4	77	6.3	517	42.6	1,213
1850–99									459		459
1900–49									134		134
Total	2,033	25.1	2,597	32.1	1,280	15.8	578	7.2	1,592	19.7	8,080

excluded any subgroup among the Quakers, nor that the smaller numbers who can be included in the age-specific calculations are not representative of the wider group.[5]

One of the standard dilemmas facing historical demographers has been that the most precise technique, family reconstitution, has seemed to be suitable only to groupings which were so small and isolated, like geographical enclaves or social elites, that genetic and other peculiarities were likely to play a disproportionate part in their demographic experience. Thus the question whether the British and Irish Quakers were representative of the population as a whole, though very complex, must be faced. On one view, we are dealing with a closed and endogamous sect so separated from the rest of society that it would share few if any of its norms and values, and might even differ significantly in its genetic make-up. This would mean that its demography would be worth studying chiefly as a sample of what peculiarities might develop in conditions of extreme isolation. The British Quakers would then be comparable to such groups as the Amish and the Hutterites, whose demography is interesting precisely because these sects offer almost laboratory conditions of certain kinds.[6] On another view,

[5] The general problem of the representativeness of samples of course arises in all historical demography before the national censuses, and indeed in most historical work. Parishes suitable for reconstitution may be untypical, and even in a suitable parish, the age of marriage of up to two-thirds of the brides may not be known, so all the age-specific calculations will represent no more than one-third of the women (presumably those from families which did not move). However, it appears that in practice the difficulties caused by the unrepresentativeness of the reconstitutable families may not be very great; see E. A. Wrigley and R. S. Schofield, "English population history from family reconstitution: summary results 1600–1799," *Population Studies* 37 (1983), 157–84 and Louis Henry, "Mobilité et fécondité d'après les fiches de famille," *Annales de démographie historique* (1976), 279–302. The representativeness of parish register family reconstitution studies has been studied, from various angles, by Roger Schofield, "Representativeness and family reconstitution," *Annales de démographie historique* (1972), 121–25; P. Thestrup, "Methodological problems in Danish family reconstitution," *Scandinavian Economic History Review* 20 (1972), 1–26; David Levine, "The reliability of parochial registration and the representativeness of family reconstitution," *Population Studies* 30 (1976), 107–22; and R. A. P. Finlay, "The accuracy of the London parish registers, 1580–1653," *Population Studies* 32 (1978), 95–112. See also *An Introduction to English Historical Demography*, ed. E. A. Wrigley (London, 1966), 110–11.

[6] See such studies as Julia A. Erickson, *et al.*, "Fertility patterns and trends among the old order Amish," *Population Studies* 33 (1979), 255–76; Joseph W. Eaton and Albert J. Mayer, *Man's Capacity to Reproduce: The Demography of a Unique Population* (Glencoe, Ill., 1954) and "The social biology of very high fertility among the Hutterites," *Human Biology* 25 (1953), 206–64. The methodological value of studying small and more or less self-contained cultures is of course well known to anthropologists; some broader consequences are set out by David Eversley in "The validity of family and group statistics as indicators of secular population trends," in *Population Growth and the Brain Drain*, ed. F. Bechhofer (Edinburgh, 1969), 179–95.

the Quakers, despite some cherished peculiarities, associated sufficiently with their compatriots to share their basic attitudes towards
such things as the timing of family formation and limitation of fertility.
If this was so, then any peculiarities of their demography might simply
be traced to their particular social position; they might perhaps be a
"leading sector" like the Genevan bourgeoisie or the British peerage in
foreshadowing developments which would subsequently show up in
the society at large.

To arbitrate between these two points of view we need to know as
precisely as possible what position the Quakers had in the social order
and to what extent they were a closed group. We also need to consider
the peculiarities of the Quaker lifestyle and the effects these may have
had on their demographic behavior. To understand all of these, a brief
review of Quaker history is desirable.

Quakerism was almost entirely an English phenomenon, and
indeed has never spread much beyond the boundaries of English
settlement, whether it be in the British Isles, America, or Africa. This
means that it was always somewhat exotic to the indigenous populations in Ireland, Scotland, and Wales. The Scots provided
Quakerism with its only systematic theologian – a service which the
Scottish temperament and educational system was well suited to
provide – but Quakerism never gained much of a foothold there. In
Ireland there came to be a thriving Quaker movement, but it was
almost entirely confined to English settlers, many of whom had come
to the country with the Cromwellian armies. A few had come to
Ireland already converted by the first English Quaker preachers, but
many more – especially Independents and Baptists, but also a good
number of Anglicans – joined with Friends as the result of the work of
traveling ministers, both British and Irish, who felt impelled to spread
the Quaker message wherever they thought it might be heard.[7]

These early Quakers in Ireland were intensely conscious of their
English identity. Those already converted in England brought with
them the strict customs and practices prevalent in the early years of
English Quakerism, and often adhered to them even after their
co-religionists in England had to some extent abandoned them.[8] In

[7] John Rutty, *A History of the Rise and Progress of the People Called Quakers in Ireland, from
the Year 1653 to 1700*, 4th edn (London, 1811), 72ff.; William C. Braithwaite, *The
Beginnings of Quakerism*, 2nd edn revised by Henry J. Cadbury (Cambridge, 1955),
210–23; Grubb, *Quakers in Ireland*, 20–30, 36–39. See also T. C. Barnard, *Cromwellian
Ireland: English Government in Ireland* (Oxford, 1955).

[8] Grubb, *Quakers in Ireland*, 85; John Stephenson Rowntree, *Quakerism, Past and Present*
(London, 1859), ch. 6, 117ff. and ch. 7, 144ff. In the last part of the eighteenth century
many Irish Friends sympathized with currents of religious liberalism which were
counter to the growing Evangelical mood, and there was a schism which further

both islands the Quakers regarded themselves as people who had, in the words of one of their favorite scriptural texts, heeded the call to "come ye out from among them, and be separate." This separateness, on the one hand, guarded them from the vain customs of the world and the danger of lapsing back into outworn "outward" worship. On the other, they cultivated an intense cohesion, strengthening themselves against the waves of persecution directed at them first by the Protectorate and then by the restored Stuart monarchy. There was much inquiring about the health and safety of Friends, and their state was reported to monthly and quarterly meetings and, in England, to the London assembly which is still known, 300 years later, as the Meeting for Sufferings.[9]

The Society was organized for mutual help, and although many Quakers were generally charitable when they could afford to be, their early eleemosynary activities were necessarily confined to their own ranks.[10] (It was this responsibility for mutual help which eventually led to tighter definitions of the conditions and location of membership, and also to the practice of requiring "certificates" so that Friends could have evidence of the character – and solvency – of those from other areas who settled among them.)

In Ireland, as we have already seen, the Quakers were not evenly dispersed throughout the country, but rather were thickly settled in a few areas. The initial concentrations can be described as falling into four distinct groups: the early Ulster Monthly Meetings of Grange, Ballyhagan (later called Richhill), Lurgan, and Lisburn; the richer agricultural areas in central Leinster (Mountmellick with its important centers at Edenderry, Newgarden, and Moate, some of which became separate monthly meetings); the isolated small urban centers like Wicklow and Carlow; and the major coastal trading cities (Dublin,

reduced their numbers. See Rufus M. Jones, *The Later Periods of Quakerism* (London, 1921), I, 295–99 and Grubb, *Quakers in Ireland*, 117–19.
[9] Richard T. Vann, *The Social Development of English Quakerism, 1655–1755* (Cambridge, Mass., 1969), 91, 101; Olive C. Goodbody, *Guide to Irish Quaker Records 1654–1680*, with contributions on Northern Irish records by B. C. Hutton (Dublin, 1967), 6ff. for the method of recording sufferings and other important events in monthly meetings, and the transmission of those records to the National Meeting at Dublin from 1669. It is not clear at what stage these details began to be regularly reported to London. See also E. H. Milligan, *Britannica on Quakerism* (London, 1965), 6, and Abraham Fuller and Thomas Holme, *A Compendious View of Some Extraordinary Sufferings of the People Call'd Quakers in the Kingdom of Ireland* (n.p., 1731), 2 vols.
[10] Rutty, *Rise and Progress*, 118–19; Arnold Lloyd, *Quaker Social History 1669–1738* (London, 1950), ch. 3, 32–47 and 116; Isabel Grubb, "Social conditions in Ireland in the seventeenth and eighteenth centuries as illustrated by early Quaker records" (London University MA Thesis, 1916), 31; George R. Chapman, compiler, *The History of Ballyhagan and Richhill Meetings, 1654–1793–1979* (Richhill, 1979); Vann, *Social Development* 41, 101–2, 143–53.

Cork, Waterford, and Limerick).[11] One of the few defects of the Irish
family lists is that they lack occupational information, so we are unable
to give a proper quantitative analysis; but the literary evidence suggests that the first Irish Quakers were engaged mostly in agriculture,
though some were in the linen trade and other trading ventures. But
Quakers were well placed to move into the linen trade, which rapidly
expanded in the 1680s, and very soon they began to mix occupations
like milling and later manufacturing with agriculture, while persecution over not paying tithes further discouraged them from continuing
as farmers.[12] By the mid eighteenth century most Irish Quakers were
artisans, shop-keepers, merchants, and professional people.[13] Very
few, if any, were common laborers, and few men were in receipt of
relief. Few, also, were identified as gentry, although this may be partly
because Friends objected to giving themselves social airs. In the earliest period the sums seized for non-payment of tithes and other fines
levied on them suggest that some were well-to-do even at that date,
and by the mid eighteenth century the general level of wealth had
increased. Some Quaker manufacturers became household names,
like Jacobs the biscuit-makers, and in 1780 Arthur Young declared
them the only wealthy traders in Ireland.[14]

[11] For the geographical distribution and number of meetings (there were fifty-three in
1701), see Grubb, "Social conditions," 21.
[12] Liam Kennedy in *An Economic History of Ulster 1820–1940*, ed. Kennedy and
Ollerenshaw (Manchester, 1985), 1.
[13] For the largest collection of material on Irish Quaker occupations, see *Abstracts of Wills*
in Irish Historical Manuscripts Commission, *Church Records*, ed. P. B. Eustace and
O. C. Goodbody (Dublin, 1957) and Goodbody, *Guide to Irish Quaker Records*, "List of
documents held at Eustace Street." Altogether these sources do not provide information on the occupations of more than about 200 men, and even if we could
overcome other difficulties in interpreting them, this would not be enough for
breakdowns into periods or localities. There is some incidental information in
Wakefield, *Account of Ireland*, I, 707; II, 171; 594–95; 602; 606–8; 624–25; 734, 774.
[14] Young makes this remark in the context of criticizing the tendency of Irish business-
men to withdraw from trade and set themselves up (or try to pass) as minor gentry;
but "Many quakers who are, (take them for all in all) the most sensible class of people
in the kingdom, are exceptions to this folly; and mark the consequence, they are the
only wealthy traders in the island." (*A Tour in Ireland* [London, 1780], II, 344). See also
L. M. Cullen, *An Economic History of Ireland since 1660* (London, 1972), 60, 146.
Barnard, *Cromwellian Ireland*, 112, records that in Cork in 1683 it was said that "the
Quakers were the town's greatest traders." In 1779 Arthur Young noted that the
Catholic population spun wool, but that their employers, and indeed the sole
organizers of the worsted trade, were Quakers of Clonmell, Carrick, Bandon, etc. See
Arthur Young's Tour in Ireland, ed. A. W. Hutton (London, 1846), II, 65. For Quaker
business in general see David H. Pratt, *English Quakers and the First Industrial
Revolution: A Study of the Quaker Community in Four Industrial Counties – Lancashire,
York, Warwick, and Gloucester, 1750–1830* (New York, 1985); Paul H. Emden, *Quakers in
Commerce: A Record of Business Achievement* (London, 1940); Arthur Raistrick, *Quakers
in Science and Industry, being an Account of the Quaker Contributions to Science and Industry
during the 17th and 18th Centuries* (London, 1950). For a full account of the Quakers in

Such records as survive point to the trade in linen, salt, and timber as opportunities for Friends in commerce, but they also entered rural industries like tannery in some numbers. There were also many grocers and drapers. In the absence of an organized banking system, some Quaker families – as in England – were bankers, or at least money-lenders, and were often able to help members of their extended families with credit at crucial times. The richer Quakers, however, are bound to predominate in the literary evidence, and we must not ignore those who fared relatively poorly. Some Ulster Friends, in particular, could not cope with the adverse conditions of the Restoration, and despite the caution which the Quakers enjoined upon traders, went under (especially in the 1720s, when in one year alone there were twenty-four certificates of removal to Pennsylvania, Rhode Island, and Virginia after a particularly dead time of trade).[15]

One of the most important Irish Quaker meetings was Mountmellick, in Queen's County (the modern county of Laoighis) in beautiful and fertile countryside some 50 miles southwest of Dublin. Some of the famous names in the annals of Irish Friends belonged to this meeting: Gershon Boate, formerly of Crutched Friars in the City of London, by origin from the Low Countries and onetime physician to Charles I; William Edmundson from Westmorland, who is usually regarded as the father of Irish Quakerism; the Goodbodys, originally from Yorkshire and still prominent in the twentieth century; the Strangmans; the Penningtons[16] (some of whom moved back to Cumberland in 1713, and who included Miles Pennington, the schoolmaster at Edenderry for some time); and others of note.[17] Most of them came from Northern Britain, though there were also some from London and the Southeast. Many were Cromwellian soldiers, and one or two are designated by the hated appellation "planter," which simply denotes that they were given land in lieu of back pay. The experience of many

the Ulster linen industry, see W. H. Crawford, "Drapers and bleachers in the early Ulster linen industry," in *Négoce et industrie en France et en Irlande aux XVIIIe et XIXe siècles*, ed. L. M. Cullen and P. Butel (Paris, 1980), pp. 113–19; and Crawford, "The origins of the linen industry in North Armagh and the Lagan Valley," *Ulster Folklife* 17 (1971). For Quaker prosperity, see Grubb, "Social conditions," 9–10 for footnote to Robert Barclay's *Inner Life of the Religious Societies of the Commonwealth* (London, 1876), 167, 491, and Eustace and Goodbody, *Abstracts of Wills*.

15 A. C. Myers, *Immigration of the Irish Quakers into Pennsylvania, 1682–1750, with Their Early History in Ireland* (Swarthmore, Pa., 1902), ch. 2.

16 For Miles Pennington, see MOU 2104. (These numbers refer to individual family reconstitution forms, which are accessible, with the shelfmark "Temporary Manuscripts," in the Friends' House Library in London.)

17 For details on all these families, see Goodbody, *Guide to Irish Quaker Records* and Goodbody and Eustace, *Abstracts of Wills*. Forms for the Strangmans are WAT 25–30 and 32–33.

was like that of Thomas Holme, who "was born at Monciston in Lancashire, married Sarah Craft at Tewkesbury in 1649" and "came into
Ireland a member of the Army, and his lot for his arrears falling in the
County of Wexford has there settled his outward abode in the year
1655."[18] We may assume from the fact that so few are identified by
occupational names that most of them were farmers. In the Mountmellick meeting there was an occasional disownment, and even more often
people passed out of observation by going to Pennsylvania, where they
are distinguishable in accounts of the population there.[19] In general,
however, this is the most representative meeting of the rural type, as
Cork or Dublin would be for a preponderantly urban group.

Cork was the largest urban settlement outside Dublin, the second
most important Irish administrative, trading, and shipping center. Its
population at the end of the eighteenth century was about 80,000.[20]
The Quakers there were for the most part Irish-born, though also of
English stock. Their numbers become important only in the
eighteenth century. The Peets, Penroses, and some other descendants
of William Edmundson are most easily identified in Irish (and English)
social and economic history. Only one family with an Irish surname is
encountered more than fleetingly, the Doyles.[21] Unlike Dublin, Cork
migration patterns show few links to England in either direction,
though it was one of the main sources of emigrants to Pennsylvania.
Possibly this was because of local shipping connections to the Dela-
ware region, but more likely the successive waves of migration are
associated with fluctuations in local trading prosperity. Some Cork
Friends also went to Australia, Canada, and other areas of the North
American colonies, and later to the United States.

In Dublin the records show the usual mixture of English-born
Quakers and later Irish-born converts, coming from Protestant immigrants with the single exception of one Patrick Nailan, who married in
1690. One of the peculiarities of Dublin was the frequency with which
women born in England came to the city to marry Irish-born Friends.
The families most frequently encountered in Dublin are again the
Goodbodys, the Yorkshire Braithwaites, the Barringtons (originally
from County Durham, now an important family in the administration
of the Republic and long since lost to the Society of Friends), and the

---

[18] See WEX 2. He had ten children born in Wexford.
[19] These can often be located again in Myers, *Immigration of the Irish Quakers.*
[20] L. A. Clarkson, "Irish population revisited, 1687–1821," in *Irish Population, Economy,
and Society: Essays in Honour of the Late K. H. Connell,* ed. J. M. Goldstrom and L. A.
Clarkson (Oxford, 1981), 32.
[21] For the Doyles, see CK 236, 237 and WAT 45.

Grubbs.[22] Once again information about occupations is lacking, and the description of their residences is not full enough to warrant any inference beyond that many of them lived in rural surroundings near the city.

An even more clearly marked pattern of mixed rural and urban settlement can be seen in the meetings in market towns like Limerick, Waterford, Tipperary, Wicklow, and Wexford. Here again a very infrequent Irish surname can be found. Wexford and Waterford are distinctive in having a relatively large proportion of settlers from the West of England, no doubt in large part because the shipping route was clearly the shortest available. As in England, most of the villages and rural settlements which figured prominently in early Irish Quaker history, and which produced such well-known families as the Strangmans, Pims, Clibborns, and Fullers, ceased to have much importance later, if the number of surviving marriages can be taken as a reliable guide.[23]

In summary, the Irish Quakers, from all the available historical background material, would appear to be a population as sharply distinguished from the rest of Irish society as they could have been without living in a separate territory with a self-sufficient economy. They intermarried very little with the native population (and much with the English Quakers); nor did they mingle much, except for commercial purposes, with the Ulster Presbyterians or the landed gentry of the Anglo-Irish ruling class. Though we venture only briefly and circumspectly into the complex world of Irish politics, it would appear here again that the Quakers were isolated. Some notable early converts, like the Clibborns, came from the ruling class, but they were effectively isolated from it by the persecutions – which of course were committed by the same men who were exploiting the Irish peasantry.[24] The Quakers were far from making common cause with the Catholics, but at least the latter had no reason to view them as part of the landed establishment. Insofar as the Quakers entered into rela-

---

[22] Tipperary has twenty-four Grubb forms (out of 143) with some marriages as late as 1873, showing intermarriage with well-known English Quaker families, such as the Southalls and the Lloyds, and with the Jacobs (for whom see WAT 25–30 and 32–33). Of course no general rules can be derived from the experience of one wealthy family. See also Geoffrey B. W. Grubb, *The Grubbs of Tipperary: Studies in Heredity and Character* (Cork, 1972) and Eustace and Goodbody, *Abstracts of Wills*.

[23] On some of these smaller meetings, see Chapman, *Ballyhagan and Richhill Meetings*; Rutty, *Rise and Progress*, 108, 148–49, 190, 318; Grubb, *Quakers in Ireland*, 27–28, 42, 70, 72. The Fullers intermarried with the Boates and with the Clibborns; see Eustace and Goodbody, *Abstracts of Wills*, 24.

[24] Henry Cromwell in 1656 saw the Quakers as "our most considerable enemy" (Barnard, *Cromwellian Ireland*, 109). See also Grubb, "Social conditions," 22ff.

tions with the Catholics at all, which was probably very little, it was as employers; and though they paid low wages, at least they did not receive rents, not to mention tithes. Too, there were occasional philanthropic employers, like the Richardsons, who in 1847 built a village (which still stands) for their workers at Bessbrook.[25] But even here the benevolent gesture arose naturally out of the Quaker tradition of philanthropy rather than springing from any deep understanding of, much less sympathy with, the alien culture of their workers. Also, Friends had little occasion to associate with other Nonconformists, who – except for the Presbyterian linen manufacturers of the North – did not figure very prominently in the Irish economic scene.[26]

In the early nineteenth century it was said to be difficult sometimes to distinguish an English Quaker brewer or banker from his Unitarian or even Anglican rivals.[27] Contemporary journals by Irish Friends, or English Friends who visited Ireland, are full of complaints about the worldliness which had crept into Irish Quakerism; but it seems nevertheless that in Ireland distinction from "the world's people" was quite a bit easier to make; nor did the Irish Quakers make the sort of contribution to the wider society – as scientists, social reformers, political radicals, members of parliament, or as local sheriffs and magistrates – made by some of the English Friends.

After we had completed the computer analysis of the English and Irish Quaker meeting records shown in our main tabulations, we discovered that with the exception of a few records relating to Lisburn and Lurgan, most of the Northern Irish Quaker registers had never been deposited in Dublin. They are still kept in the Meeting House at Lisburn, some in bad condition. These were being repaired in the Northern Ireland Public Record Office, and therefore some of the registers (notably Grange and Ballyhagan/Richhill) were not fully available for inspection.

We think it worthwhile to present a brief analysis of this additional material in the light of what we already know about the rest of the Irish Quakers. In all, just over 400 records of marriages were found for the period 1650 to 1849, of which about 30 were immediately discarded as being too defective for any analysis at all. This left records of 179 marriages for Lurgan Monthly Meeting, 78 for Grange, 63 for Ballyhagan (later Richhill), and 59 for Lisburn, besides those found in Dublin.

25 Thomas Adams, compiler, *Bessbrook: A Record of Industry in a Northern Ireland Village Community and of a Social Experiment, 1845–1945* (Bessbrook, 1945); Grubb, *Quakers in Ireland*, 143.
26 Cullen, *Economic History of Ireland*, 60, 146; Grubb, *Quakers in Ireland*, 95.
27 Isichei, *Victorian Quakers*, 144–65; see also the works of Raistrick and Emden cited above.

Table 2.4 *Mean family size (children ever born), Ulster Quakers*

	All		Lurgan only	
Period	Mean	*n*	Mean	*n*
1650–99	6.6	52	6.6	52
1700–49	6.6	83	7.8	49
1750–99	6.6	182	7.1	57
1800–49	4.3	28	4.4	8

Note: For some families, completed family size was larger than shown here, since there are indications that some migrated to another area in the British Isles, emigrated to America, or were disowned. The age at marriage is unknown in most cases.

Whereas in our main analysis we excluded a number of records, for reasons explained in chapter 1, in this later exercise we considered all marriages for which there was a date and a record of children or evidence like a date of death for one of the parents to explain the absence of any children. We excluded those where the rules of the Society in relation to the parent(s) being in membership provide an explanation of why no children could be recorded.

Because of the stringent criteria employed in the main analysis, we had only 120 families for all of Ireland from 1650 to 1849 whose completed family size could be measured. Those results are presented in Table 4.3; they are at any rate not incompatible with those which follow (Table 2.4), which are based on 345 families. Lurgan shows more of a change over time, including a rise in fertility in the early eighteenth century. The apparent fall from the first to the second half of the eighteenth century is found in Table 4.3 only for the 25–29 age-at-marriage cohort. We cannot explain why it should have occurred in the area of Lurgan Monthly Meeting, but the numbers are large enough to give us some confidence that the phenomenon is real.

Of the original 408 recorded marriages, at least 105 involved one or both spouses from one of 10 prominent families in the linen trade, like the Greer/Greeves, Sintons, Malcolmsons, Nicholsons, Richardsons, and Christys. This is probably an underestimate, since in about a third of all records the maiden name of the mother is not given. There are also few records from the prominent Richardson family, though that family lived mostly in Lurgan Monthly Meeting, for which records are generally good.

These couples from the linen-trade elite had marginally larger families (5.9 as against 5.8 on average) but this is not a significant difference.[28] More of these affluent families passed out of observation, because more of them left the Society of Friends. There is no evidence of family limitation (even that which might be achieved by delaying marriage) and like all the Irish Quakers, they had considerably more children than the English. Thus they did not experience the relatively low fertility of the first half of the eighteenth century nor the sharp rise in the second half. Although a decline can be seen after 1800, the number of cases is too small to warrant any firm conclusions.

Material relating to the daily lives of the Irish Quakers is much scarcer than for their English counterparts.[29] The standard histories of the Quakers in Ireland[30] do not say much about occupations, lifestyles, or even their environment. Biographies and autobiographies of the Irish Friends are not as plentiful as those of English Quakers, and they tend, even more than is the case in England, to concentrate heavily on their lives as members of the Society; in some cases on their charitable deeds; and on their travels in the ministry. Some attention is given to their families and perhaps a little to the houses and households they occupied – without, however, giving much of a clue of the wealth they may have accumulated. The biographies, as in England, are heavily biased towards the "Public Friends," or ministers in the Society, and thus towards the better-off, those with resources and leisure to engage in public affairs, or travel, and write books or pamphlets. (Biographies of the rest of the population would be biased in a similar way, but a higher proportion of Friends were the subjects of biographies, which is probably as much a function of their social class and income as of the virtually universal literacy and careful recording practices of Friends.) Fewer Irish Friends led public lives, were involved in reform move-

---

[28] It is possible that the Richardsons, if we had their complete records, would show lower fertility. They were the only family that lived in a grander style, and became an important part of the public life of Ireland (they furnished two of the four Quaker Members of Parliament returned for Ireland in the nineteenth century; see C. Pell-Smith, *James Nicholson Richardson of Bessbrook* [London, 1925], especially chs. 3 and 4).

[29] J. N. Richardson of Bessbrook and his sisters wrote in 1882 a volume of bad but funny verses, *The Quakri at Lurgan and Grange* (n.p., 1899) which recounts the goings-on at the quarterly meeting at Grange. By this time important Quakers came to Grange by railway rather than coach and horses, and were given to simple amusement, simple food, and rustic sports. There is no Northern Irish equivalent to Mary Leadbeater's *Annals of Ballitore*, written between 1766 and 1824 (republished, ed. John McKenna, Athy, 1986) which was the account by a schoolmaster's daughter of life in a Kildare village 30 miles southwest of Dublin, including the relations of Friends to their neighbors, servants, and personages of importance. The level of affluence may be gauged from a single detail; at the end of the eighteenth century "All the parlours had earthen floors" (p. 28). Later some Friends laid boards and "listing" (bordered) carpets, and others put down stone flags.

[30] Besides Rutty's history, which is actually a revision of Thomas Wright's original, and the works by Isabel Grubb already cited, see *Friends in Ireland*, ed. M. A. Hodgkins (Dublin, 1910).

ments, established charities, or even played much of a role in the Society of Friends at large, so not as many evoked biographies. Deaths of Friends were systematically recorded in the *Annual Monitor*,[31] which covered notable lives of those who had died "in Great Britain and Ireland," but the obituaries in these volumes make only the vaguest references to social and economic matters. It is fair to say that the more important Friends, especially those "in affluence," received the longest notices, but they never mention how they had made their fortunes, and the fact that their marriages were frequently prudently dynastic and contracted in search of business capital and connections can only be inferred from checking on the wife's pedigree. The obituaries are instead testimonies to the grace of God.

There is, as in England, ample material in the monthly meeting records relating to individual Friends, but it does not enable us to say much about them except as regards personal conduct. If they came to the notice of the monthly meeting (apart from certificates of removal, approval of marriages, and the like) it was most often in a negative way: threatened or actual disownment, for a stated cause. But whether the cause was some kind of moral misconduct, business negligence, or even insolvency, we seldom have any indications of their social or economic status.

In the Lisburn registers, the names of Quaker abodes are given, and these are, as far as we can still identify them, modest houses: bourgeois rather than workers' cottages, to be sure. Most of the families would have had servants, and many of them horses, but not an ostentatious lifestyle, and one lived outside the public world.

Unfortunately for our purposes "place of residence" has little meaning as such in Ireland. The "townland," within the much larger parish, is almost invariably the address; but this does not tell us whether the Friend is a tenant or an owner, whether he farms land or is an artisan or trader, whether an employer or employee. Where, in the records we have examined, a trade is stated, we have – as in England – no idea whether a "linen-bleacher" is the owner of a works, or a waged or dependent worker. As we know from other sources, it is most probably the former; but even then we do not know, from Friends' sources, whether the undertaking was a substantial one. From the standard Irish economic histories, and from monographs on the linen industry in particular, we can derive some information about the undertakings[32] at a particular point in time; but this does not yet

---

31 *Annual Monitor . . . or Obituary of Members of the Society of Friends in Great Britain and Ireland* (established in 1813; titles and publishers vary).
32 See C. Gill, *The Rise of the Irish Linen Industry* (Oxford, 1925); E. R. R. Green, *The Lagan Valley, 1800–1850* (London, 1949) and *The Industrial Archaeology of County Down*

tell us whether the family under review was, in 1780 or 1820, affluent, just comfortable, or even in financial difficulties.

Outside the manufacturing families (who were very much concentrated in Ulster), most Friends were either in rural occupations or traders in the cities, notably Dublin. As time went on, especially in the nineteenth century, urban concentration increased. Even here the evidence is too scanty to allow us to make accurate assessments of wealth, income, or lifestyle. Many of the most important settlements, such as Mountmellick and Edenderry, are in small towns serving a rural hinterland. Most individuals, especially in the south, would still have had some land even if their main income was derived from trading, craft-type production, financial dealings, or (in the later period) professional avocations. This leaves, as the only major reliable source of information, wills and probate inventories. There are a good many of them, some of which have now been printed (see fn. 12). These usually reveal a Friend's position at the end of life. There are, however, severe limitations to this source. First, the position of the family at the death of the father (for the vast majority of wills are those of men) does not necessarily indicate what it was at the point in their lives when they married and took decisions (if any) as to their family size. The longer men lived, the less likely their inventories are to reflect what they had owned several decades earlier. What the wills can tell us is the general level of affluence (or otherwise) prevailing in the Quaker population – at least in relation to particular periods or areas, and by comparison with the English Quakers. They tell us nothing about how well off Friends were in comparison with the rest of the Irish middle-class population.

With this statement we are of course excluding, straightaway, the great mass of the Irish population from our comparison. Whatever Friends were, they were not impoverished peasants. We have found none who were subject to eviction or rack-renting or the other evils of Irish landlordism so familiar in mainstream Irish history. When Friends emigrated to America, as many did, it was sometimes as a result of decay of trade, but they did not emigrate as paupers, and their motive was to find a better living, not to escape persecution or intolerable hardships in Ireland. Much emigration was probably

(Belfast, 1963), especially 21–27; and Cullen, *Economic History*, 59ff. Cullen points out (p. 60) that the role of the Huguenots in the Irish linen trade has been much exaggerated, and that the Quakers in fact played the predominant part in the seventeenth and early decades of the eighteenth century. In fact, the predominance of the Quakers continued well into the nineteenth century, and even later.

related to family size and relative economic growth rates; if there were too many children to make a reasonable living on the family farm, or in the family business, then those who could not find alternative land or exercise a profitable local trade would emigrate. The difficulty is to know what individuals might regard as "reasonable." Friends' land-holdings, where we know anything about them, were not so small as to preclude subdivision *per se* (assuming that was legally possible) but such a process might well leave them with too meager a standard of living by their own lights.

We are therefore left with the usual general statement that the Irish Quakers were "middle class," meaning that they were neither peasants nor laborers nor aristocratic landowners. They might, however, be petty artisans, or very substantial manufacturers. The difficulty is to determine where, within this middle spectrum, any one family belonged at a particular time. This issue will only matter to us, of course, if we assume that living standards influence mortality levels, or lead to a conscious decision as to the desired family size. Though we can formulate the question, the available sources provide no definite answer. The four cohorts of Friends' marriages from the Lurgan registers (Table 2.4) do not allow valid intergenerational comparisons. They do suggest that family size was much the same among wealthy linen-traders as among the rest of the Quaker popu-lation. To subdivide the Irish Friends further, into urban and rural, or north and south, would lead to still smaller groupings and thus invalidate any attempted comparison of mortality, fertility, or age at marriage.

There are, it is true, the overall time-trends: greater urbanization; a greater degree of affluence, at least within the large family groupings about which we have some information; and more Friends entering the professions. Undoubtedly these developments are in some way related to the long-term decline in fertility, as well as the greater expectation of life at all ages. But that much can be said about any population anywhere, and the changes cannot be tied, in any one cohort, to identifiable subgroups within this small population.

In what is now the Irish Republic, Friends were grouped in meetings which roughly correspond to common economic activities. Dublin and its immediate vicinity, by the end of the eighteenth century, was wholly urbanized – its population was reckoned at almost 200,000 at the end of the eighteenth century[33] – so that virtually all male Friends there were traders, manufacturers, or (later) pro-

---

[33] Clarkson, "Irish population revisited," 32.

fessionals. In Cork and Waterford this was also true, so far as we know, though some of the particular meetings within these monthly meetings were more rural. It is only in the Mountmellick and Edenderry areas, and the rest of the Irish Midlands settlements, that we can at least at first assume a predominantly agricultural economy. As these last meetings were numerically the most important in the earliest periods, while some of them all but died out towards the end, we should be able to produce an urban–rural differential at least for the two earliest cohorts, but in fact we have not been able to find any such marked differences as those which obtain, with regard to infant and child mortality, between London and Middlesex and the Southern rural English Quaker population (see chapter 5). But then London mortality was quite exceptional, and though Dublin was frequently described as "unhealthy" in Irish literature, it cannot have rivalled London in this respect.

The Northern Irish Quakers also have common economic characteristics. The Ulster meetings were dominated by the linen trade, since linen-manufacturing families form a far higher proportion of all Friends than do manufacturers of any sort in the south of Ireland. Although their residential patterns would be termed "rural" in the modern sense, the nature of the mill settlements, especially in the Bann Valley, was much nearer a modern urban pattern. (This was true, of course, of the early water-driven mill complexes of the Industrial Revolution in England.) Because the linen industry expanded through most of the eighteenth and nineteenth centuries, and did not begin to decline until the 1870s, the economic opportunities, even of larger families, were in all probability less restricted than was the case in the south of the country. Urbanization did take place, but Belfast never assumed the importance to Ulster Friends that Dublin, with Cork and Waterford, did in the South. Moreover, the few families who engaged in various aspects of the linen industry intermarried frequently and, one must assume, had easier access to capital for trading.

This can be illustrated from the records of the Greers (or Greeves) family, who, with their immediate relations, form the backbone of Ulster Quakerism. They did intermarry with southern Irish Quakers, but not to any great extent. In the nineteenth century, a far higher proportion married out of the Society, and became allied to Presbyterian and Church of Ireland families and were therefore disowned, or resigned even before marriage.

Although the family lists, even more than in the South, tend to record such marriages, and their progeny, even after disownment, we are faced with the usual bias: we know more about those who stayed within the Society and those who remained in Ulster than those who emigrated. Extensive research has been carried out on the Greers and their relations,[34] so we are better informed about their lifestyle and occupations than is the case in the South.

There is one final aspect of the Northern Irish Quakers which deserves mention. The Southern Irish Friends had two principal origins. The majority came from Northern English stock, mainly from Cumberland, Westmorland, and northern Lancashire (the cradle of Quakerism itself) and others from Northumberland and north Yorkshire. The rest came mainly from Southwestern England. Those from the North went principally to Dublin and the midlands counties, the others to Waterford and Cork. A somewhat oversimplified model in terms of the shortest shipping routes seems to account for this pattern. Tradition had it that the Northern Irish Friends came, to a much larger extent, from the Southwest of Scotland. A number of factors might have lent plausibility to this theory: the greater proximity of the Galloway coast to Belfast and the existence of the Scottish linen trade. Principally, however, the reason for this belief must lie in the dominance of the Greer (or Greeves) family, who were generally believed to be descended from Scottish landowning stock. In addition, northern Irish Protestants were Scots by origin, and Presbyterians to boot, so what could be more plausible?

However, on closer examination, it turns out that the Greers (at least those who first appear in the Friends' registers from the 1650s onwards) did not come from Scotland; they came from Cumberland. When the Greers (or Greeves) came to occupy an influential position in Ulster society, they began to look for respectable, and if possible, aristocratic origins; and since the names Grieves, Grierson, and the like were common in Scotland, genealogists sought to establish a link (which possibly did exist) between these families and the Greers who were in Ireland before the Cromwellian settlement. All the evidence for the main body of Greers, however, points to their descent from James and Mary Greer, who came from "Rock nexe Annick" (or Arrick) in Cumberland.[35]

[34] The Greer (or Greeves) family records are to be found in unpublished manuscripts deposited in the Linenhall Library, Belfast. See: Greeves, J. R. H., Manuscript Pedigrees and Notes, 6 vols., MS 678.8.12. MS 11; Pedigree Maps (N 18873); Greeves Family Notes, 929.1 GREE. Greeves MS 24 includes wills of Ballyhagan Monthly Meeting copied from originals in Lisburn Meeting House and Grange Monthly Meeting Family Records, *ibid.*, vol. 6. (For these, see also G. R. Chapman, *An Historical Sketch of Grange Meeting* [1950], N. 10427.)
[35] The attempt to identify this town with Alnwick in Northumberland is, in our view, misguided. We are indebted to Col. J. R. H. Greeves of Altona, Belfast, for the loan of

Moreover, our examination of all marriages contracted under the rules of the Society in the first cohort (to 1699) produced only two cases of Scottish migrants. The vast majority of the rest came from the traditional center of Quakerism in Northwest England; after all, the crossing from Morecambe Bay was more accessible to them than that from Stranraer or the Clyde. It is true that in the eighteenth-century registers there appear some distinctive Scottish names, more so than in the South, and one must assume that these were convinced Friends drawn from the Presbyterian settlers.

When Irish Friends did leave the Society through marrying out, they seem to have married descendants from other Quaker families, Northern or Southern, who had already been disowned.

In the North, Protestant fertility, while lower than that of the Catholic population, seems to have been higher than that of the English (church and Nonconformist) population as far back as records go, and this is still the case. While the very high fertility of the Southern Irish Friends might be related in some way to that of the Catholics around them, we could equally ascribe the large average family size of their Northern co-religionists to a similar environmental influence. There is, however, no good reason why there should be such an influence.

The Greers are so well documented that a closer look at them will reveal important trends in Northern Irish Quakerism. In the seventeenth century they were clearly still agriculturalists, mostly in the Lisburn and Dungannon area. However, by 1700 some were clearly engaged in spinning and weaving: mostly flax, but also wool. Looms begin to figure in their inventories and distraint for tithes was made in quantities of yarn. By 1710, we find them as linen drapers at Lurgan, which means that they acted as middlemen between producers and Belfast merchants. By the time of Henry Greer of Lurgan (born in 1716) they were clearly rich; he possessed extensive tracts of land, some of which he had bought from the great families of the area. In 1766 Henry for his second wife married one of the Pims of Kings County, one of the wealthiest of the Southern Quaker families. With that generation, we come across a complex system of dynastic marriages, both within and outside the Society of Friends. A granddaughter married an Anglican clergyman, another a Malcolmson, a Friend who was a banker already related by marriage to Anglican gentry. One of their sons in turn married the daughter of the High Sheriff of Antrim. John,

manuscript material and personal information, as well as to G. L. Stephenson of Lisburn for access to Quaker records deposited at Lisburn Meeting House.

Henry's only son, was also a linen draper, and the first of the family to live in what can only be described as a country house, if not a palatial one. (It had a name, which was a sign of status; those who had modest houses in their townlands do not record the names of their dwellings.) John Greer eventually became Inspector General of the Linen Trade in Ulster.

We need not follow the descent in detail. Wills, property settlements, descriptions in the registers, monthly meeting minutes of disownment, and records of the Irish linen trade in general show the Greer family as prosperous. Some of them were very rich, and they were certainly part of the Protestant establishment of Ulster. What proportion of the descendants of the first Greers remained Friends at any one time we cannot calculate. Probably the majority had gone out of the Society by the third quarter of the eighteenth century, but enough of them remained for the name Greer still to occur more frequently than any other in the registers. Again, whether those who remained were slightly less well off than those who left is a matter of conjecture. Within the Society, the network of Greers, together with their close relatives, the Malcolmsons, Christys, Richardsons, Sintons, and others, constitute the social top tier.[36] As a general rule, the higher the social rank of any Greer, the more likely he or she was to marry out, to acquire property and business connections in Dublin (or marry someone who had them) and to produce daughters and sons who would marry into the Church and the militia. By 1830, Joseph Greer, born in 1795 in the sixth generation from the original immigrants and owner of the Grange (or Grange McGregor) in the townland of that name in County Tyrone, was a major in the Tyrone militia, a justice of the peace for County Tyrone and County Armagh, Grand Master of the Grand Lodge in Tyrone, a Deputy Lieutenant for County Tyrone, and – by his death in 1862 – a Freeman of Dublin. He may be taken as representative of the extreme swing away from the simple way of his ancestors, and from the persecution of the 1670s and 1680s, to complete social prominence and an expansive lifestyle. However, even the Grange was not a mansion; it does not compare with the properties owned by that time by the great English Quaker families, the bankers, ironmasters, food and chemical manufacturers, shipbuilders, and so on.

To recount this ascent to the ranks of the gentry is not, however, to

---

[36] See Cullen, *Economic History*, 146; M. A. B. Hobson, *Memoirs of Six Generations* (Belfast, 1947); Adams, *Bessbrook*; J. M. Richardson, *Six Generations of Friends in Ireland* (1893); and pedigrees of families in the Greeves MS., especially vols. 3 and 6, which contain the descents of all the Quaker linen dynasties.

describe the typical Ulster Friends family. Those Greers who remained faithful to Friends' testimonies may have actually had greater assets, since ostentatious lifestyles led quite a number of Greer descendants into financial difficulties. There are a number of cases where cousins who had remained Friends reacquired property from those who had left the Society, when the latter were in such straits.

The larger Greer/Greeves pedigree (which includes those who left Friends) shows that the general pattern of marriage, the types of business in which they engaged, and their residences were much the same whether the individual was still a Friend or not. No manufactures other than linen play any large role; even when daughters married at a distance, it was mostly within the industry. Malcolmson, Sinton, Richardson, and Christy are the names which appear most often – some of them literally household names. Many of them changed from manufacture to trade, and eventually to banking, and these then allied themselves to other Quaker or Quaker-related Southern Irish mercantile dynasties. Some in each generation went to America, and there was a strong trading (and marital) link to Bristol Quakers. But by and large the genealogies show the extensive network remaining in one part of Ireland, one industry, and one lifestyle. This seems to justify treating the Greers and their relations (which means more than half of Ulster Friends) as a single sub-population. Out of the 400-odd marriage records inspected, roughly a third relate to the Greers and to the dozen families with which they intermarried most frequently. This is probably an underestimate because in many family lists the former name of the wife is not given, and in only a few cases do the lists record the names of the spouses of all the children of the marriage. A closer study of record linkages would probably establish that nearer half the total of Ulster Friends, certainly in the latter two-thirds of the eighteenth century, were closely allied to the Greers. This is possibly important genetically, but much more so economically, since the Greers and the other leading textile firms had such diverse interests in manufactures and trading that they could both employ one another's sons and, if required, reinforce their capital structures through exchange of marriage portions. We have not analyzed the few extant marriage settlements in detail, but at least those of the Greers show the importance of this form of finance, and the history of individual mills demonstrates how closely the enterprises were kept within the family system.

Since, as we shall show, large families remained the norm in this population, the question arises of how they coped with the problem of maintaining all their offspring in a moderately affluent lifestyle. If there was money for a dowry, the daughters could be married off; otherwise they had to remain spinsters. The sons had a variety of choices. America provided one outlet. As long as the linen industry throve (as it did throughout the period under discussion) there was room for more than one son in the main business. Where this was not the case, fathers purchased leases for them – of other textile undertakings, of shops, or of farm holdings. The wills of the sons thus provided for suggest that they retained a moderate lifestyle. Decency rather than luxury was the watchword. They had a servant or two; they had some non-essential furniture; most of them had horses. They sent their children to Friends' schools, where fees were as moderate as the living was spartan. Many lived in premises above their shops or offices. In general, if they remained in this lifestyle, they married others of the same class and survived as Friends of the middle or at worst lower-middle class. Those with higher aspirations often failed in business; or if they succeeded, they tended to leave the Society.

Only some such mechanisms can explain the network which lies behind the family records. As long as this system worked (and it did through 1850) there would be no reason for applying Malthusian or any other form of family limitation. Marriage ages are no different from those in the South, and do not appear to rise; and birth intervals remain somewhere above the biological minimum typical of fairly normal lactation. They would neither have used wet-nurses in that stratum of society nor, one must assume, unduly prolonged lactation. We then get, in the larger families, the usual longer intervals until reproduction ceased.

In summary: the Northern Irish Quakers had a distinctive lifestyle. Almost from the beginning they were industrial and commercial in their occupations rather than agricultural. They lived in dispersed settlements, in townlands set in a mostly rural environment, but close to the larger centers of population in the east of the province. They were moderately well off, but lived quietly and unostentatiously. They managed to provide for their children in one way or another. Neither famine nor economic crises are reflected in the demographic data. Those who reached the peaks of affluence mostly left the Society, but even they did not have visibly smaller families. Once the linen industry declined, they must have shared the experience of the whole of the Ulster economy. More of them emigrated; more turned to professional occupations; more of them moved into Greater Belfast. Far more left Friends even when the rules of disownment were no longer so strictly enforced. In time, their demographic pattern showed significant changes – bearing in mind that even middle-class fertility in

Ireland, certainly Catholic but even Protestant, remained above the English levels. The explanations for this difference in regimen have so far escaped the analysts of Irish demography, so we are unlikely to find a separate explanation for Friends; but it is clear that, as in the North, their behavior is more like that of the population around them and less like that of their co-religionists in England. If we find no early desire for a smaller family, such as that which we observe in England, this may be explained in terms of the modest lifestyle ambitions which the Friends shared with their Protestant middle-class neighbors. If children constituted no burden when they were young, and there was no great difficulty in finding a place for them later in society, there was no great economic incentive for restriction. We know that land and houses were cheap to rent (and land prices very low); we also know that servants, especially Catholic girls, were paid even less than in England. Horses and their keep required no great expenditure. A reasonably comfortable lifestyle, therefore, imposed no burdens. Much later, when industrial decline set in, and when Ireland as a whole was to an increasing extent impoverished, even in its middle ranks, as compared to England, smaller families made their appearance, though even then family limitation did not (until recently at any rate) have such drastic effects as in England. So the national differences remain.

It is important to note that the Irish Quakers did not go so far as the Hutterites, the Old Order Amish, and the Mormons (up until around 1880)[37] in trying to preserve their sectarian purity by setting up a closed farming economy on lands in which they were the dominant, or even the only, settlers. (They did not even attempt to do this where they had the chance, in parts of Pennsylvania and New Jersey.) But except for the commercial interactions that were necessary to their life, they seem to have kept themselves as much apart as they could. Thus, to all initial appearances, their demography was *in* Ireland, but scarcely *of* it. It does not necessarily bear any more relationship to the demography of the Catholic peasantry than that of the Hutterites does to the Chicano harvest workers of California. What it does provide is a sort of benchmark. Although many statisticians center their attention on the norm or most frequent case and regard the extremes as the oddities that demand explanation, an equally approved technique is that of the surveyor who takes his measurement with respect to sea level, or the highest peak in the district. On many demographic measures (though not all) the Irish Quakers achieve that peak; their

---

[37] Mark Skolnick, *et al.*, "Mormon demographic history: nuptiality and fertility of once-married couples," *Population Studies* 32 (1978), 5–19.

fertility, in particular, is the maximum which could be achieved, in the periods and places to which we refer, given the income, environment, and the personal habits of individuals and families.

When we turn from Ireland, where the population history of the country before the 1841 census is very obscure and there are substantial gaps in our knowledge of Quaker history, to England, the first impression is of an almost dazzling flood of light. Although there are still many unresolved puzzles about the development of population – puzzles which indeed make this book worth attempting – there are at least sources which should allow us eventually to resolve them, and there is no shortage of informed hypotheses to be tested. The English Quakers wrote prolifically about themselves, and have been written about almost as copiously. Now in the making of many books there is not always wisdom, and it would be a bold person who would claim that the – or even a – definitive work on English Quakerism has yet been written; but the main lines of the study which we require as background to our demographic materials seem well enough understood.

English Quakerism has been characterized as a sort of "wild Puritanism." Almost all its early adherents had grown up in Puritan parishes and many had passed through some, or sometimes all, of the other churches which had sprung up in the growing religious fervor and decaying ecclesiastical discipline of the English Revolution. Though Presbyterians, Congregationalists, and Baptists recoiled in horror at what seemed to be these apostates from their doctrines, they were in fact developing relentlessly some of the logic of Puritanism in the direction of a new form of faith and church government.[38]

The earliest Quaker traveling preachers came from the North of England, especially Westmorland, northern Lancashire, and the West Riding of Yorkshire, but they found groups awaiting their message in many parts of Eastern and Southern England. The proclamation of the Quaker message, in an atmosphere made more concentrated and expectant by the discipline of silence, evoked the sort of emotional power seen also in later revival meetings, and provided enemies with their scornful nickname for the new movement. The early Friends chose dramatic means to bring their ideas to others; they often interrupted the parish priest in the course of the service, and some felt

---

[38] An earlier generation of Friends had thought of themselves as heavily influenced in the beginning by the continental mysticism. This is a theme developed by Rufus Jones in his *Studies in Mystical Religion* (London, 1909), and *Spiritual Reformers in the Sixteenth and Seventeenth Centuries* (London, 1914). The interpretation given here derives chiefly from the pioneering work of Geoffrey Nuttall, *The Holy Spirit in Puritan Faith and Experience* (Oxford, 1946).

called upon to cast off their clothes and testify as an emblem of *nuda veritas*. Because their experience of the indwelling Truth was so intense, they felt no need to rely on the words of the Bible, which in any case they suspected of having been corrupted in the passage of time. They believed also in perfection in this life – a dangerous opening towards antinomianism, their adversaries thought – and their language was often suffused with apocalyptic hope that this definitive reformation of the church would usher in the last days. (In an ill-judged attempt to symbolize this, James Nayler rode into Bristol in a manner which seemed to suggest a deliberate parallel with Christ's last entry into Jerusalem.) Finally, Friends held their duty to the Truth to override conventional obligations to their families; children left their fathers' churches and even stood with their hats on in their fathers' presence. Wives left their husbands and even traveled on preaching missions with male Friends. It is not surprising that this seemed to represent a threat to social order, already precariously balanced after revolutionary upheavals.

It took a generation of persecution on the one hand and suffering on the other before any accommodation between Quakers and the state was reached. It came not as true religious freedom, but as toleration – a license to differ in some respects from the Established Church. Toleration also best expresses the relationship between Friends and English society after the downfall of the Stuarts had put an end to any prospects of an absolute monarchy or an all-inclusive national church. The Quakers could no longer be put in jail for attending their meetings or fined for not coming to Anglican services; but they still refused to support the state church with their tithes and church rates, and so the now ritualized distraints, seizures of goods, and meticulous recording of these events continued.[39] The Quakers might be esteemed for their contributions to the national wealth, in an age which was learning to compute and value that, but they were still kept out of the universities – no great loss, if Gibbon's account of eighteenth-century Oxford is recalled – and out of the professions, with the important exception of science and medicine. For their part, Friends manifested as much eagerness to leave the state alone as to be left alone by it. While they still labored under legal disabilities Friends had shown a precocious talent for organizing mass petitions and putting pressure on members of parliament;[40] but in the long and quiet years of toleration Quaker

---

[39] Richard T. Vann, "Friends' sufferings – collected and recollected," *Quaker History* 61 (1972), 24–35.
[40] Norman C. Hunt, *Two Early Political Associations: The Quakers and the Dissenting Deputies in the Age of Sir Robert Walpole* (Oxford, 1961).

piety was dominated by a fear of "the creature" – the danger that in the bustle of merely human striving the divine intimations might be missed. Even when they sensed a withering in Truth's prosperity in the mid eighteenth century and instituted a revival of discipline in 1760, it was still from concern that Friends were becoming too much entangled in the world. Also, though the flow of converts from the outside never entirely ceased,[41] it clearly was relatively uncommon for someone to come into the Society of Friends, and the future of Quakerism was seen to rest with the children.[42] The revival of discipline was aimed in large part at refurbishing the idea that the family was the true cell of the church. Unfortunately for the hopes of the elders, an even more stringent enforcement of the rules against marrying out or by a priest went along with the revival of discipline, with consequences for the membership totals which we have already mentioned.

By the end of the century the Augustan calm was leaving the Society of Friends as it was leaving England. Reverberations of the Evangelical revival associated especially with the name of John Wesley were being heard more and more loudly in Friends' meetings.[43] Social and political activism, too, had revived with the struggle for prison reform and the abolition of the slave trade, in both of which Friends took a leading part. Both these currents in Quakerism bore Friends away from their self-absorption and towards a hesitant cooperation with other political allies and even other churches. But while the evangelically minded were reaching outwards towards their fellow evangelicals in other churches, there was also a movement on the part of many towards a relaxation of the traditional customs of dress and speech. Those who married outside the society had obviously drifted from the old rigorous standards; but even those who did not were, as we have seen, moving closer to the amusements and fashions of thinking characteristic of their social class. As early as the eighteenth century we begin to hear of "wet Quakers," and by the end of the century it is clear that, especially

---

[41] We have made an analysis of the reports on the "prosperity of Truth" which every quarterly meeting was supposed to return to the queries addressed them annually by London Yearly Meeting. Bearing in mind Friends' caution not to overstate the truth, the reports of "some appearance of convincement" which some areas show in most years suggests converts were not a rarity; on the other hand, other areas tend to bewail the low state of their meetings. No quantitative treatment is possible even if it were feasible to read all the relevant minute books, because there were no formal minutes recording admission of a person into membership through convincement until very late in the eighteenth century.

[42] Richard T. Vann, "Nurture and conversion in early Quakerism," *Journal of Marriage and the Family* 31 (1969), 639–43, and more generally in *Social Development of English Quakerism*.

[43] An excellent treatment of this theme may be found in David Swift, *Joseph John Gurney: Banker, Reformer, Quaker* (Middletown, Conn., 1962).

in the South but also among the successful manufacturers and traders
of the North, strict Quaker observance was either compromised or had
lapsed entirely. (Hannah Chapman Backhouse, who was brought up
in the wealthy Gurney family of "gay Quakers," as she called them,
became a "grave Quaker," [that is, obedient to the plainness testi-
monies] as her religious convictions deepened.)[44]

It would appear that the Quaker population was more closed the
longer the movement went on, since it was being steadily diminished
by disownments which were not counter-balanced by conversions
from other churches. (Our sample, since it includes some non-
members, does not fully reflect this trend, and therefore does not completely represent any genetic or behavioral peculiarities that English
Friends might have exhibited.) As it diminished in numbers, the
Society of Friends became markedly more concentrated, both geo-
graphically and occupationally, than it had been in the earliest period.
The geographical contraction can be seen most clearly in the long list of
discontinued meetings, starting as early as the 1720s, which is preserved in the Friends' House Library.[45] Similarly, in the first few years
of the movement, under the Commonwealth, quite a few members of
gentry families had at least briefly cast their lot with Friends; and
indeed the success of the movement to some extent depended on the
protection for its adherents that a husband or father with territorial
political influence could give. On the other hand, a good many of the
earliest Friends were drawn from artisans, small shopkeepers, and
peasant proprietors. Quakerism, however, did not appeal to the totally
landless or the totally unskilled laborer, who are very much underrepresented. There are also regional variations of some importance; for
example, Warwickshire, where – probably not coincidentally –
Quakerism had a hard time establishing itself, had very few Friends of
social prominence and considerably more of humble means than
seems to have been the case in Buckinghamshire or Norfolk.[46]

The registers of marriages, beginning about 1660, provide a source
suitable for quantitative investigation of Quaker occupational distri-

[44] On this see *Extracts from the Journal and Letters of Hannah Chapman Backhouse* (London, 1858).
[45] The "Guide to meeting records" in the Friends' House Library includes notices of discontinued meetings.
[46] There is now a considerable literature on the social status of the first generation of English Quakers: see Alan Cole, "The social origins of the early Friends," *Journal of the Friends Historical Society* 48 (1957), 99–118; Richard T. Vann, "Quakerism and the social structure in the interregnum," *Past and Present* no. 43 (1969), 71–91, with a debate with Judith Hurwich in *ibid.*, no. 48 (1970), 155–64; Judith Hurwich, "Dissent and Catholicism in English society: a study of Warwickshire, 1660–1720," *Journal of British Studies* 16 (1976), 24–58; and A. Anderson, "The social origins of the early Quakers," *Quaker History* 68 (1979), 33–40. The latest contribution is by Barry Reay

bution; but it is subject to some limitations. In the first place, bride-grooms are not representative of the entire group in the earliest period, because many converts, including some socially prestigious Friends, were already married, and quite a few of them melted away once persecutions under the restored Stuarts began. This difficulty ceases to be troublesome after around 1675. Even in those registers where the bridegrooms' occupations are stated with great regularity, the occupational names are not always informative. A "hus-bandman" could be an agricultural worker, a smallholder, or – by the end of the seventeenth century – a yeoman.[47] A draper could be the proprietor of a substantial business or one of his former apprentices. Terminology generally lagged behind real social change; the Gurneys of Norwich were still being described as "worsted weavers" even in the late eighteenth century, when they had become financiers and were among the richest families in the city. A good many Quakers were apothecaries; in the provinces an apothecary in 1730 was "essentially a shopkeeper who at times practiced medicine," but by 1800 they "had largely abandoned the drug trade altogether and were engaged in almost full-time practice of medicine."[48] Sometimes two different occupations are given, and it is unclear which is primary and which secondary; also, of course, Quakers often managed to improve their position substantially after the first mar-riage. It is common to have some of the engineers in the North of England described only as artisans when they first appear in the marriage registers. Finally, the registers may have systematically declined to use "gentleman" as an occupational description, and thus understated the representation of the top end of the social spectrum.

Thus, ideally, records of sufferings, wills, manorial records, quarter sessions presentments, and such sources should be searched and the resulting information added to that gathered from the marriage

---

(*Journal of Interdisciplinary History* 11 [1980–81], 55–72), and *The Quakers and the English Revolution* (New York, 1985) which though generally supporting Vann's methods claims that he overstated the gentry and upper bourgeois element through sampling error.

47 Vann, in *Social Development of English Quakerism*, 63–66, concluded that by the end of the seventeenth century the words "husbandman" and "yeoman" no longer had meanings precise enough to be usable at all, and attempted to use the word "yeoman" only for independent proprietors who could be shown to have owned at least 20 acres of land. This however takes no account of regional variations in the fertility and accessibility of land; 20 acres of rich arable is obviously worth a great deal more than 20 acres of stony upland, as was pointed out by Margaret Spufford in *Contrasting Communities* (Cambridge, 1974), 306.

48 Joseph Kett, "Provincial medical practice in England 1730–1815," *Journal of the History of Medicine and Allied Sciences* 19 (1964), 18.

Friends in life and death

Table 2.5 *Occupational distribution, English Quaker bridegrooms,*
1650–1849

Occupational group	Rural England							
	1650–99		1700–49		1750–99		1800–49	
	n	%	n	%	n	%	n	%
Agriculture	97	29.5	94	23.2	104	20.8	23	9.0
Textiles	74	22.5	70	17.2	66	13.2	23	9.0
Draper, mercer, clothier, woolman, woolstapler	28	8.5	38	9.4	40	8.0	14	5.5
Weavers	23	7.0	13	3.2	9	1.8	1	0.4
Tailors	11	3.3	4	1.0	5	1.0	1	0.4
Food	38	11.6	100	24.6	138	27.7	46	18.0
Grocers	3	0.9	14	3.4	39	7.8	24	9.4
Brewer, distiller, maltster	11	3.3	20	4.9	17	3.4	3	1.2
Mealman, miller, flourman, corn chandler	23	7.0	43	10.6	48	9.6	13	5.1
Leather	26	7.9	45	11.1	29	5.8	6	2.3
Shoemakers	15	4.6	26	6.4	13	2.6		
Tanners	6	1.8	8	2.0	8	1.6	2	0.8
Professional, clerical, gentry	22	6.7	29	7.1	72	14.4	87	34.0
Gentlemen	3	0.9	4	1.0	3	0.6	7	2.7
Merchants	7	2.1	9	2.2	24	4.8	9	3.5
Physicians, schoolmasters	11	3.3	12	3.0	12	2.4	18	7.0
Bookkeepers, accountants, clerks					17	3.4	38	14.8
Commerce	120	36.5	217	53.4	271	54.3	106	41.4
Wholesale (including drapers, grocers)	76	23.1	131	32.3	180	36.1	75	29.3
Retail	44	13.4	86	21.2	91	18.2	31	12.1
Artisans	99	30.1	71	17.5	68	13.6	35	13.7
Carpenters	8	2.4	4	1.0	5	1.0		
Blacksmiths	6	1.8	2	0.5	2	0.4		
Clockmakers	2	0.6	6	1.5	3	0.6		
Wheelwrights	6	1.8	2	0.5	4	0.8	1	0.4
Totals	329		406		499		256	

Table 2.5. (*cont.*)

	Urban							
Occupational group	1650–99		1700–49		1750–99		1800–49	
	n	%	n	%	n	%	n	%
Agriculture	4	1.4	9	3.6	4	2.1	1	5.0
Textiles	110	38.1	79	31.7	32	16.8	4	20.0
Draper, mercer, clothier, woolman, woolstapler	13	4.5	19	6.6	16	8.4	4	20.0
Weavers	44	15.2	24	9.6				
Woolcombers	23	8.0	12	4.8	2	1.1		
Tailors	10	3.5	2	0.8	5	2.6		
Food	48	16.6	54	21.7	36	18.9	5	25.0
Grocers	9	3.1	12	4.8	15	7.9		
Brewer, distiller, maltster	8	2.8	12	4.8	1	0.5		
Mealman, miller, corn chandler	6	2.1	7	2.8	7	3.7	2	10.0
Bakers	7	2.4	11	4.4	4	2.1		
Leather	31	10.7	10	4.0	21	11.1	1	5.0
Shoemakers	22	7.6	6	2.4	5	2.6		
Tanners	1	0.3	2	0.8	5	2.6	1	5.0
Professional, clerical, gentry	13	4.5	38	15.3	32	16.8	2	10.0
Merchants	6	2.1	24	9.6	9	4.7		
Physicians, schoolmasters	5	1.7	7	2.8	9	4.7		
Bookkeepers, accountants, clerks	2	0.7	5	2.0	10	5.3	2	10.0
Commerce	130	45.0	125	50.2	107	56.3	15	75.0
Wholesale (including drapers, grocers)	65	22.5	80	32.1	62	32.6	10	50.0
Retail	65	22.5	45	18.1	45	23.7	5	25.0
Artisans	149	51.6	102	41.0	57	30.0	2	10.0
Carpenters	14	4.8	2	0.8	5	2.6		
Coopers	10	3.5			2	1.1		
Totals	289		249		190		20	

Notes: Occupations are of bridegrooms whose age at marriage was known. Cohorts are by years of birth, rather than years at which married, so the "1700–49" cohort includes many people who did not marry until after 1750.

"Total" is the number of bridegrooms; but many occupational groups are listed more than once. "Merchants" are included both under "Professional" and "Wholesale trade"; workers in textiles, food, and leather trades are also listed again under wholesale or retail trade or as artisans. Grocers, brewers, distillers, maltsters, mealmen, millers, flourmen, and corn merchants are listed as wholesalers, along with cheesemakers, vintners, and salters. Butchers, bakers, and tobacconists are listed as retailers. Drapers, mercers, woolstaplers or woolfactors, and tanners are considered wholesalers; hosiers, hatters, tailors, glovers, and shoemakers are also considered artisans.

registers before a completely reliable judgment can be made. This, however, is too exhausting a task for 8,000 families, and Table 2.5, based entirely on analysis of the marriage registers, is unlikely to be seriously misleading, especially for the later periods.

It is not easy to make comparisons with the distribution of occupations within England as a whole, not least because the same difficulties we have described beset any work with other samples of the whole population.[49] Nevertheless it seems that the percentage of Friends engaged in agriculture, even in the first century, was somewhat below that in the population as a whole, while those engaged in commerce were certainly well above the national average.[50] The line between commerce and artisanship is difficult to draw, since many shoemakers and tailors kept a small shop and sold their products directly to the public. It also is difficult to tell whether "grocers" kept shops and sold in small quantities to the public, or were "dealers in gross," as the etymology of the word suggests. "Mercers" and "drapers" also might be shopkeepers, but usually these words, in the eighteenth century, at least, described entrepreneurs in the putting-out of cloth to be woven. Examination of the wills of self-styled "drapers" and "grocers" suggests that most of them were in fact in the wholesale trades, at least before 1750, but that the word increasingly came to describe small shopkeepers in the nineteenth century. So to the various ambiguities of these words at any one time we must add the problem of shifts in meaning, proceeding at an undetermined rate (and with strong regional variations) throughout our period. All these caveats may make anything but the most cautious inference from Table 2.5 hazardous; but it would appear that a distinctive feature of the Quaker occupational structure is the prominence of wholesale traders, and later of professional men. In Bristol, where according

---

[49] For a discussion of difficulties in occupational classification in the period of the national census, see Alan Armstrong, *Stability and Change in an English County Town* [York, 1801–51] (London, 1974), 14–15, 29.

[50] The Quakers' occupational distribution appears to be more unlike that of the general population if we accept the picture which Gregory King gave of English occupational distribution. King estimated that in 1696 families engaged in agriculture were 62 percent of the economically productive population of England, while shopkeeper, merchant, and tradesman families together were only 12 percent. Recently, however, Peter Lindert, in "English occupations, 1670–1811," *Journal of Economic History* 40 (1980), 685–712, has argued that King's England was "just London and a vast, poor agricultural hinterland" (707). Although these comments refer specifically to King's earlier 1688 estimates, the same biases which led him to underestimate numbers in commerce, manufacturing trades, building, and mining trades and to overestimate numbers in agriculture can be found in his later estimates as well. King's calculations are conveniently reproduced in Peter Laslett, *The World We Have Lost* 2nd edn (New York, 1973), 36–37.

to city directory estimates only about 1 percent of the population were Quakers in 1793–94, 10 percent of the physicians and surgeons, 11 percent of the apothecaries, 13 percent of the glass makers, 18 percent of the distillers, a quarter of the soap boilers, and a third of the tanners and of the ironmasters were Friends.[51] Even though the estimate of Friends in the total population is almost certainly too low, this dramatically shows where Quakers were found in the economy. At roughly the same time in Manchester, 9 percent of the dyers were Quakers and in Leeds they were prominent in tanning, brewing, and paper-making. All these industries, as David Pratt points out, are dependent on chemistry.[52]

The most striking difference between Friends and the rest of society, however, is the virtually complete absence, not only of paupers, but also of persons called only "labourers." (The absence of servants in the marriage registers is predictable, since manservants had to have established an independent occupation before marrying; but literary evidence suggests that only adolescent Friends were servants.) If we may judge by the hearth tax returns of the 1660s and 1670s, from one-quarter to one-third of all English heads of households were in occasional or regular receipt of poor relief. The number of Friends in such circumstances can be roughly estimated from the minute books, and can very seldom have exceeded 5 percent of the membership, even in London; it was probably closer to 1 percent in the southern parts of England. There were almost no Quaker agricultural laborers, and all the evidence suggests that few of them were wage laborers (although some professional men were salaried). This means that real-wage series have markedly less import for Quaker demographic behavior than for the population as a whole.

When the relative wealth of Friends was first reliably estimated, in 1863, it was high indeed – perhaps ten times as high as the national average.[53] No such figures, of course, are available for the middle of the seventeenth century, but it seems unlikely that the differential would have been nearly so great. This at least is a plausible inference from the changes in occupational distribution shown in Table 2.5. In the countryside, about 30 percent of those born before 1700 were engaged in agriculture and another 30 percent were artisans. About twice as many were engaged in the textile trades as the food trades,

51 Pratt, *Quakers and the First Industrial Revolution*, 64–65.
52 *Ibid.*, 58–59.
53 Isichei, *Victorian Quakers*, 166 estimated Friends' *per capita* income in 1863 was £182, when the average annual wage (which of course often had to support three or four people) was only £50.

and just over a third were in commerce at either wholesale or retail level (or often both). Over the next 150 years there was a steady decline in the numbers in agriculture, textiles, and artisanal pursuits. Quaker involvement in food trades, on the other hand, grew substantially, especially in the first half of the eighteenth century, when the Quakers began that specialization in the wholesale grain trade which was to win them the loathing of William Cobbett. While the number of artisans was declining, the number of tradesmen was rising; but from 1750 on the most dramatic development was the growth in the professions, which as a percentage of the whole doubled and then doubled again. The Quakers, in particular, were key agents in the bureaucratization of business; their all but universal literacy and reputation for honesty made them excellent candidates to take over the keeping of books and rationalization of inventory control which the early Industrial Revolution was promoting.

In Bristol, Norwich, and London similar changes could be seen, although with a different rhythm. The dramatic increase in professions came a bit earlier, and there was nothing like such a pronounced rise in the numbers dealing in food. The most striking change, undoubtedly, was the fact that Quakers ceased to be worsted weavers and woolcombers. Almost a quarter of all urban Quakers born before 1700 had followed one of these trades; a hundred years later barely 1 percent did so. One explanation of this certainly lies in the decline of the worsted industry in Norwich and Norfolk, where most of these worsted weavers lived; but it is also of a piece with the tendency of Friends who were themselves manual workers (the shoemakers are another good example) to be able to set up their sons as tradesmen; their grandsons would perhaps be clerks or schoolmasters.

Although we know more about the occupational structure of the Society of Friends in England than in Ireland, the question for this book still remains whether we know enough about their lifestyle, and especially their standards of consumption, to be able to associate changes in reproductive behavior with standards of living – actual or expected. Within the wide spectrum of the Quaker "middle class" there must have been many shades of Quaker gray in a young man's views about the proper age to marry, or a couple's consideration of limiting their family size. They need hardly have been trying to emulate the gentry and aristocracy, as the Gurneys and Frys were undoubtedly doing, to have these issues arise.

Furthermore, decisions about timing of marriage and family size must have appeared in a different light north of the Humber. This is not fully brought out in our tabulations, because we grouped together the Northern British Friends with those whom we traced from the genealogies. While this procedure can be justified by the fact that most of the families in the genealogies did come from the northern counties, where the Society of Friends originated, it is also true that with few exceptions the families reconstituted from the genealogies moved southwards as they became richer. This southward move betokens worldly ambitions which made it unlikely they would preserve the lifestyle of the fells and moorlands; yet they still figure in the "Northern British" cohorts along with those who were left behind in the North, who would be more likely to engage in rural pursuits or practice trades and professions in small provincial towns where the demands of society were not great.

As Table 2.3 shows, the families reconstituted from our sampling procedure for Northern Britain are after 1750 outnumbered by those reconstructed from the genealogies, resulting in a bias towards families in better circumstances, many of whom now lived in the Southern counties and a good many of whom were no longer in the Society of Friends. Since in the North as elsewhere there was increasing disownment and an even higher rate of emigration to the South of England and to America, by 1800 relatively few families remain in the sample based on the first letter of the surname.

It is thus possible that the decline in marital fertility after 1800 is more regionally localized than our tables in chapter 4 suggest. It is at least possible that the Northern Friends were in their daily lives not unlike those in Ireland, especially in Ulster. We have already seen that the two groups were closely connected, in that the majority of Northern Irish Friends originated in Cumberland, Westmorland, Lancashire, and Yorkshire.

Thus the picture of rising Quaker affluence may also be skewed by a bias towards the southern population and its records. One of the consequences of the southward drift we have been discussing is that most Quaker historians live and work in the South of England, and the great repository of records is in London.

A recent publication by David Bower and John Knight helps redress the balance by throwing light on the daily lives of Northern Friends whose deaths were not recorded in the *Annual Monitor*, whose journals (if they kept any) were never published, and who have never been the subjects of biographies.

The work lists the surviving houses once inhabited by Friends, and

gives photographs of a few of them. We may safely assume that only
the better built and more important houses survive; but even this
biased sample shows how simply many Friends lived. There is little
"carriage trade" in these annals, except for a handful of nationally
prominent families. "Midhope Hall," the home of John Woodhouse,
has no manorial pretensions beyond its slightly grandiose name.
"Strines," which the photograph shows to be little better than a
wooden shack, was the home of Henry Dickinson, who was said to be
in "lowish circumstances."[54] Henry Dickinson had eight children
between 1738 and 1762, and his much more affluent contemporary
and kinsman Edward had seven. In the early nineteenth century, both
sets of Dickinson offspring had smaller families.

Further light on the way of life of the Northern Friends is shed by an
account of the life of Robert Robinson of Countersett in Wensleydale
and some of his descendants.[55] Although Robinson was a substantial
yeoman and Countersett (which only much later was styled a "Hall")
was a solid gentleman's house, the family's lifestyle was very simple at
least until the mid eighteenth century. Later Robinsons were found in
the professions and business interests, including brewing. John Robinson, born in 1750, became a physician in Bradford; he and his
children lived in grander houses. His son John, a fourth-generation
Quaker, was styled an "esquire" by 1820; he had a very large family
and no occupation is listed, indicating that by this time he had
ascended into the ranks of the gentry. In 1820, also, Robinsons were
marrying in church; by 1850 few if any of the descendants of Robert
Robinson remained in the Society of Friends.

Family records speak of substantial estates probated, a library of
books and manuscripts and (by 1775) a legacy of table silver. Greater
numbers of indoor servants are mentioned, but also mortgages, debts,
auctions, and emigration to Australia. Their story is thus one of
transition from a life of simplicity and arduous upland farming to
professional status, urban life, and a turning away from Quakerism.
But, significantly, their marriages and family sizes seem not to have
been affected by this transition. Their family tree[56] shows that the first
Richard Robinson and his wife Margaret, who were married around
1651, had ten children, with only one boy and one girl recorded as
marrying. (Two brothers and one sister certainly attained adult life,
but did not marry; there are references to mental illnesses afflicting

<hr>

[54] David Bower and John Knight, _Plain Country Friends: The Quakers of Wooldale, High
Flatts and Midhope_ (Wooldale, 1987), 25.
[55] David S. Hall, _Richard Robinson of Countersett 1628–1693 and the Quakers of Wensleydale_
(York, 1989).
[56] _Ibid._, vii–viii.

members of all generations.) Only one male child in each generation seems to have married; the majority of offspring died adult but unmarried. There were four live births in the period from 1700 to 1749; five in the next half-century; and thirteen from 1800 to 1849 (from at least two marriages). So the Robinsons are a family experiencing important changes in occupation, residence, lifestyle, and religious practice which did not reduce the fertility of those who did marry, nor increase the propensity of male adults to marry, long past the stage when one might have guessed that the danger of fragmentation of the family holding would restrain men from founding families. It is useful to be reminded of the diversity that may be comprehended in a single social category, and of the wide disparities which undoubtedly existed throughout the period we are studying.

These 200 years are those of the Industrial and Agrarian Revolutions: a time of high rates of migration, of rapid change in occupations. Against the background of a rising secular trend in real incomes for those above the level of wage workers, they were also centuries of marked economic cycles. New fortunes were created (and Friends had more than their share of them) and new urban pauper classes, true proletarians and lumpenproletariat, came to take their place beside the traditional rural poor. Each crisis or "panic" in the business cycle brought the need for modest economies in affluent households and desperation for the poor. For those in the middle (where most Quakers found themselves), who had followed the same or similar trades and enjoyed a comparable standard of living for several generations, there arose the hope, and eventually the expectation, that they could better themselves in their own lifetime, by acquiring skills, by working harder, by moving to where the opportunities were, whether in Coalbrookdale, in London, or in America.

In this climate, we must assume that even in a group which started off as a congregation of saints and martyrs rather more worldly calculations would gain ground among some, though hardly among all. We shall see in the following chapters whether demographic changes are connected with these economic and social structural changes. At the outset, though, it seems likely that the Northern English and Northern Irish Friends, who are underrepresented in our sample, clung to a simpler lifestyle even until the late eighteenth century, and possibly to a concomitantly higher level of fertility even when mortality began to fall. In this respect they may well represent a different stage of the "demographic transition" from that exhibited by the Southern English and urban Quakers.

We can now return to the question of how representative the British Quakers were. They were of course not a scientifically drawn random sample of the whole population, and therefore in a trivial sense not like it. It seems, however, that a scientifically drawn sample will not meet the peculiar requirements for successful family reconstitution, so we will have to give up the other advantages of this approach if we insist on perfect representativeness. The more significant contrast is with other subgroups, whether defined topographically or by some other means of social selection which could produce religious, occupational, or genealogical stratification. Examples of studies of topographically defined subgroups are Saville's on the South Hams area of Devonshire, T. E. Smith's work on the Cocos or Keeling Islanders, and Stycos' investigations in Puerto Rico, which are respectively, subgroups of the population of England, Malaysia, and of the West Indies.[57] Sometimes these subgroups may themselves have very large populations, as is true of the Taiwanese subgroup of the Chinese population studied by Freedman.[58] The social subgroup may be compact and self-segregated, like the Hutterites, Mormons, and Mennonites, who have already been mentioned; or it may be an elite, either local (the Genevan bourgeoisie) or national (the British peerage).[59] The English and Irish Quakers were a dispersed, self-selected group, formed along religious lines though heavily clustering in certain parts of the economy and social structure. They were not a closed population, like that of an island, though comparatively few were converted after 1700 and endogamy was enforced throughout the period with which we are concerned. Thus, although they were not a genetically isolated group, the Irish Quakers around 1850, in particular, were, to a much greater degree than the general population, the descendants of a fairly small group of people six or seven generations previously.

The Quaker population in all probability deviated somewhat from the demographic behavior of "average" English people. So do the various subgroups in the population today, reminding us that, useful as the statistical notion of an average is, we do not meet all that many

[57] See J. Saville, *Rural Depopulation in England and Wales, 1851–1951* (London, 1957); T. E. Smith, "The Cocos-Keeling Islands: a demographic laboratory," *Population Studies* 14 (1960), 94–130; J. M. Stycos, *Family and Fertility in Puerto Rico* (New York, 1955).

[58] R. Freedman *et al.*, "Fertility trends in Taiwan, tradition and change," *Population Studies* 16 (1963), 219–36.

[59] Louis Henry, *Anciennes familles genevoises, étude démographique, XVIᵉ–XXᵉ siècles* (Paris, 1956); T. H. Hollingsworth, *The Demography of the British Peerage* (Supplement to *Population Studies* 18, 1965).

"average" English people now. Furthermore, it is not clear whether the deviations that might have been exhibited by the Quaker population would affect the three fundamental demographic rates with equal force. There is good reason from what is known of their history to expect that their marriage patterns might differ sharply from those of the wider society, since their marriage customs and social position were so distinctive. Quite possibly their fertility, too, might be markedly different. It has been argued that mortality rates of a reconstituted subset of the population are more likely to approximate those of the rest of the population than either marital or fertility ones.[60] For this reason we might expect Quaker mortality to be more like that of the population as a whole. This, at least, would be a real test of how "typical" they were. Finally, there are advantages as well as pitfalls in studying well-defined subgroups. It may be that the best way to study a population as a whole is to build up a picture from the intensive study of more and more subgroups. Valuable as it is to obtain figures about national demographic rates, populations in advanced societies are segmented and the national averages are made up of the distinctive behavior of these subgroups. Anthropologists are seldom reproached for having studied tiny isolated groups and neglecting the whole populations of advanced nations; and we claim some of the same virtues for the study of the British and Irish Quakers. But now, having followed Sir Lewis Namier's maxim for all historical study to "find out who the guys were," we can turn directly to the demographic issues.

[60] Allan Sharlin, "Methods for estimating population total, age distribution and vital rates in family reconstitution studies," *Population Studies* 32 (1978), 511–21, at 512. Sharlin is thinking about possible differences between the stable part of the population and those who moved about.

3

Marriage according to Truth

Of all the activities that demographers study, marriage is the most embedded in culture. It is therefore the most variable among human communities. Just before World War II over half the women aged over 29 in Ireland, Sweden, and Finland had not yet married and more than a quarter of them were destined never to do so. At the same time in Korea, 98 percent of teen-aged women were already brides, and only 1 in 1,000 failed to marry before the age of 50.[1]

To the historical demographer, especially in the last few years, patterns of marriage behavior or nuptiality have come to be of absorbing interest. For English society as a whole, fertility within marriage does not offer much change to explain; it seems to have stayed pretty much the same from the sixteenth century to around 1825. Mortality did change; but some of the change seems to lie more in the history of microbes, in that variations in their virulence, rather than in what humans could do about them, apparently account for some of the difference in death rates. Nuptiality is thus the arena where there is significant change resulting entirely from human agency.

Furthermore, changes in nuptiality are now believed to be the key to the great increase in the population of England after 1750.[2] Most of this increase was the result of a greater number of births; but because marital fertility did not change much (and illegitimate births were not

[1] Figures for Korea, Sweden, and Finland are for 1930; those for Ireland for 1941, in Ruth B. Dixon, "Late marriage and non-marriage as demographic responses: are they similar?" *Population Studies* 32 (1978), 450–51.

[2] See E. A. Wrigley, "Marriage, fertility, and population growth in eighteenth-century England," in *Marriage and Society: Studies in the Social History of Marriage*, ed. R. B. Outhwaite (New York, 1982), 137–85; David R. Weir, "Better never than late: celibacy and age at marriage in English cohort fertility, 1541–1871," *Journal of Family History* 9 (1984), 340–54; and Roger Schofield, "English marriage patterns revisited," *Journal of Family History* 10 (1985), 2–20.

numerous enough to make a substantial difference) almost all the change in the birth rate came from increases in the proportions ever marrying and reductions in the ages at which they married.

Changes in the level of real wages and in the housing of servants in husbandry (most of whom were no longer lodged with their employers in the latter eighteenth century) are thought to have been largely responsible for these trends. Most Quaker men were not waged workers, and almost none were servants in husbandry; so one would not only expect a different pattern of nuptiality, but also require a distinctive conceptual framework to explain it.

Sexual drives can find many outlets. In a functional interpretation, it is the task of cultural institutions, above all marriage, to harness these drives and direct them towards heterosexual intercourse so that society can reproduce itself in the next generation. Marriage fixes responsibility for providing the resources needed by a helpless infant and a nursing woman, so that there will be enough workers (and fighters) in the next generation. If population begins to press heavily on resources, a change in the timing and incidence of marriage is one way to adjust population to the means to support it. It is open to social groups to control fertility directly, as by contraception or induced abortion, or even to kill off "excessive" members, as in the infanticide and geronticide practiced by some gathering and hunting cultures. These methods, however, may arouse moral repulsion, and some (like effective contraceptive devices) require a fairly high level of technical expertise. Customs that delay and obstruct or hasten and facilitate marriage, on the other hand, can be fitted into a harmonious or at least coherent cultural whole. (Of course there can only be room to allow earlier and more general marriages if, as in Northwest Europe at least since the Reformation, marriage usually takes place well after puberty and quite a few people never marry. Social customs of early and almost universal marriage, such as are found in Eastern Europe, give no such flexibility.)[3]

In a society becoming industrialized, such as Britain during the period we are studying, there is an intricate relationship between capital accumulation and demand for and supply of labor on the one hand and the age at which people can marry – if they can marry at all – on the other. To consider only the economic variables: a middle-class couple, when deciding to marry, must take into account the costs of children, possibly including the "human capital" required for apprenticeships or prolonged education as well as the outlays for food,

---

[3] J. Hajnal, "European marriage patterns in perspective," in *Population in History*, ed. D. V. Glass and D. E. C. Eversley (London, 1965), 101–43.

clothing, and shelter; the possible supplements to the father's income which can be contributed at some times by the mother and the children; and the standard of living they were brought up to expect. The costs of children fall heavily on the couple in the first few years of marriage, when the mother (if she ever worked for wages) is likely to have to forego any possible earnings, the children are too young to earn, and – in the Western European marriage pattern, at least – the new family's resources are already depleted from the expenses of setting up a new household. If there are to be apprenticeship premiums or extensive education, a second period of high expense will be encountered in late adolescence. The timing of these squeezes on resources has to be fitted to the income which the family can expect over the duration of the marriage.[4] Thus people might marry very soon after puberty if they were already earning almost as much as they could ever expect to earn (a fairly typical situation for wage laborers) and if they could quickly turn their children into economic assets. On the other hand, if a peasant's son had to await his father's death to inherit a tenancy, or if a tradesman had to wait for the capital to set up on his own, marriage would be postponed. When children required expensive educations or dowries and could not be put to work in early childhood, there was a further incentive to delay marriage as one way to limit the economic burdens of such costly children.

There are some difficulties in applying an analysis of this sort to the Quakers of the early modern period. We have no direct way of computing what a child might have cost, or what opportunities there were for putting children to work.[5] It is probably safe to assume that

[4] This framework of analysis rests on Valerie Kincade Oppenheimer, *Work and the Family: A Study in Social Demography* (New York, 1982), especially chs. 1 and 9.

[5] See Alan Macfarlane, *The Family Life of Ralph Josselin* (London, 1970), 36 and 41 for the curve of Josselin's income over his lifetime and 44–51 for estimates of the costs of children in the seventeenth century. Dowries and apprenticeship premiums were especially onerous. Macfarlane makes no attempt to assign a monetary value to labor performed without compensation by the children, and presumably they did not work for wages outside the home. Using survey data from such places as India, Egypt, the Philippines, and Guatemala, demographers have devoted a good deal of energy to modeling and estimating the economic costs and benefits of various family sizes in modern peasant economies. Eva Mueller, for example, estimates that a peasant family with only two children would produce more than it consumed until the husband was 65 and the wife 62; but with more children, the family would be in deficit in the earlier part of their married life, although somewhat better off later ("The economic value of children in peasant agriculture," in *Population and Development*, ed. Ronald G. Ridker [Baltimore, 1976], 143). She thinks that the maximum strain for such a family would be between the tenth and seventeenth years of the marriage. Peter Lindert finds that more children might be a net economic benefit (to the master, of course) in conditions of American slavery, and also perhaps in Java and Nepal, but probably not in the Philippines ("Child costs and economic development," in *Population and Economic Change in Developing Countries*, ed. Richard Easterlin [Chicago, 1980], 45–48). That our

wives did not work for wages, but we can only guess at the earnings curve over the lifetime of the Quakers. We also do not know to what degree deliberate control of fertility within marriage would allow for earlier marriages without increasing the eventual family size.

Furthermore, this model is a purely economic one, although it does not depend on the assumption that all behavior is rationally directed towards the end of maximizing income. (It might be the case that a marriage pattern could be like the behavioral adaptation of an animal which confers an advantage in the struggle for existence even though not consciously designed to do so.)[6] In fact, it is difficult to find economic causes for the European transition to lower fertility, suggesting that cultural considerations must have played a very important role in persuading people to have smaller families.[7] Above all, since our subjects are Quakers, we must not lose sight of the fact that to them, marriage must be a part of the religious life.

In virtually every culture marriage has been celebrated with religious rituals. It is therefore not surprising that the Quakers, aspiring to build a purified religious community, should have reached a distinctive conception of marriage and a set of rituals which embodied it. The purpose of this chapter is to examine the demographic consequences of this Quaker way of marriage and to see how it distinguished Friends from the society around them.

Marriage in the Church of England, the Quakers believed, shared in the corruption of the degenerate world against which they testified. It had been perverted by the hireling clergy into an opportunity to exact money from the people. Thus the first impulse of the Quakers was to expel the clergy from the role in the marriage ceremony which they had, through greed, usurped. The Quaker couple was not married by a priest, or by anybody else. In Friends' usage the couple married each other; only the presence of faithful witnesses, not ordained ones, was required to attest to a valid marriage. (As Friends were quick to point out, the priest is only a witness even in Anglican or Catholic weddings). The conscientious priest, of course, counseled the prospective bride and groom and made sure that there was no canonical obstacle to their union. The Quakers passed this responsibility to the meetings for the conduct of church affairs. Where the Church of England simply

Quaker families would have made the same computation (even supposing that they could have) cannot be known, but seems doubtful.
[6] Oppenheimer, *Work and the Family*, 357.
[7] John Cleland and Christopher Wilson, "Demand theories of the fertility transition: an iconoclastic view," *Population Studies* 41 (1987), 5–30.

forbade bigamous marriages or unions with close kin, however, the
Quakers, sharing the high value that the Puritans put on the com-
patibility of the marriage partners, believed that in addition it was
essential not to be "unequally yoked" – that is, married to "people of
the world."[8]

As the monthly meetings developed a full-fledged discipline, candidates for marriage had to go through a lengthy procedure before their
marriage in meeting could be approved. If there was a woman's
monthly meeting, its approval had first to be obtained before the
matter was laid before the men's monthly meeting. The consent of
both the bride's and the groom's parents was required; the meetings
had to be satisfied that both parties were clear of any engagements to
other parties; and if it were a remarriage, Friends demanded some
assurance that the rights of any children by the previous marriages
would be protected. None of these ideas were unique to Friends, but
by developing the discipline through the monthly meetings they made
the enforcement of them much more reliable.

The influence of Quaker values can be seen in the seasonal distribution of weddings. In parishes which still kept to the traditional
prohibition of marriages during Lent and Advent, which passed into
Anglican usage from the Middle Ages, there were relatively fewer
weddings in December or March. The Quakers had a testimony
against the observance of such outward forms, and so did not avoid
times when weddings had traditionally been prohibited (Figure 3.1).
Although March and December usually saw fewer Quaker weddings
than the average month, the pattern of avoidance was not so extreme
as in Anglican parishes. One small but revealing index of increasing
Quaker conformity to the customs of the world around them is that
avoidance of March and December became increasingly common after
1750. In fact, as Figure 3.2 shows, the over-all shape of the curves for
Quakers and Anglicans is similar, but – even though far more
Anglican marriages are included – the peaks and troughs in the
Anglican parishes are considerably more pronounced.

One reason for this is doubtless the relative concentration of
Quakers in non-agricultural work, especially in the later periods. In
rural England October and November were the peak months for
marriages in grain-producing areas, since the harvest had been
gathered and servants in husbandry were released from their con-

[8] Those already married before their conversion to Quakerism were not required to
divorce their spouses even if these remained in "the world." Divorce was in fact
almost unknown among Quakers before the present century; see Thomas Clarkson, *A
Portraiture of Quakerism* (London, 1806), II, 4.

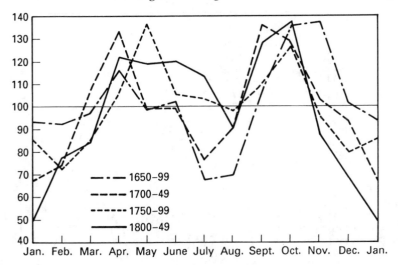

Fig. 3.1 Seasonality of English Quaker weddings.

tracts on Michaelmas (29 September). In pastoral areas the peak tended to be in the late spring and early summer, since intensive care for young animals was no longer necessary by then. Although non-agricultural work may have had more seasonal peaks then than now, it certainly was less seasonal than agriculture.[9] But the Quaker pattern also reflects their consistent position that no time of the year is intrinsically more holy than any other.

What we most need to know is the motives which led Friends to get married; but these can seldom be directly discovered, especially since there is little private correspondence which has survived from any period before about 1750 and Friends wrote no imaginative literature. Though the motives for an individual marriage must remain obscure, the statistical pattern of Friends' marriages is much easier to establish; in fact we have reliable data for almost exactly half the Quakers we

[9] The best study of seasonality of marriage in rural England is Ann Kussmaul, "Time and space, hoofs and grain: the seasonality of marriage in England," *Journal of Interdisciplinary History* 15 (1985), 755–99. Kussmaul has taken the data assembled in E. A. Wrigley and R. S. Schofield, *The Population History of England, 1541–1871: A Reconstruction* (Cambridge, Mass., 1981), 298–305 and removed the market towns so as to leave as purely rural a sample as possible. As late as 1843 it was still said that Lent and Christmas were having an effect on seasonality of marriages, but the main influence was said to be that in the late autumn agricultural wages had all been paid; see *Fifth Annual Report of the Registrar General* (2nd. edn, London, 1843), 4–5. See also David Cressy, "The seasonality of marriage in Old and New England," *Journal of Interdisciplinary History* 16 (1985), 1–21.

86 *Friends in life and death*

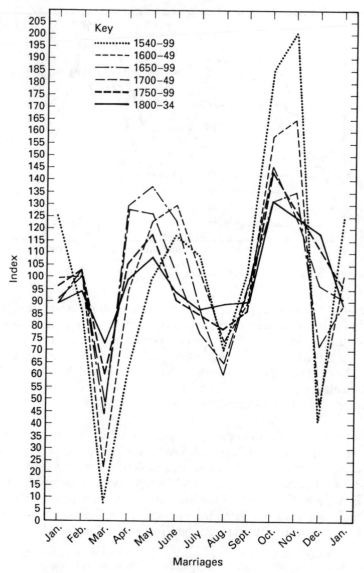

Fig. 3.2 Seasonality of weddings, 404 English parishes.
Source: Wrigley and Schofield, *Population History of England*, 299.

have studied. From these we can hope to establish the general conditions in which marriages were contracted and the relationships between nuptiality and fertility and mortality.

The overall pattern of Quaker marriages is revealed by Table 3.1.

Table 3.1   *Ages at marriage, all British and Irish Quakers (known remarriages excluded)*

Cohort	n	Median	Mean	s.d.	5% Conf level	Mode
Men						
1675–99	376	27.3	28.28	6.25	0.63	27
1700–24	571	26.8	28.15	6.61	0.54	24
1725–49	480	27.6	29.15	6.39	0.57	25
1750–74	517	27.6	29.56	7.20	0.62	24
1775–99	509	28.0	29.40	6.97	0.61	24
1800–24	442	28.2	29.57	6.50	0.61	29
1825–49	366	29.4	31.30	7.87	0.81	26
Women						
1675–99	437	24.0	25.29	6.72	0.63	21
1700–24	614	24.5	26.06	6.30	0.50	22
1725–49	564	24.9	26.75	7.05	0.58	24
1750–74	526	26.0	27.56	6.88	0.59	23
1775–99	551	25.7	27.73	7.68	0.64	22
1800–24	446	25.7	27.45	6.46	0.60	24
1825–49	337	26.7	28.77	7.45	0.80	24, 25

Two features are immediately apparent. The first is that even in the seventeenth century, ages at marriage were higher than they are today; and the second is that they increased more or less steadily throughout this period. The increase from the last half of the seventeenth century to the first half of the eighteenth may not be significant, since it is to some – probably small – degree the result of a "truncation effect." (This means that to the extent that we depend on births entered in the Quaker registers to give us the ages at which people married during this half-century, only people young enough to have been born after registration started can figure in the sample; this source leaves out people born before the registers began to be kept.) For most of our sample we can infer an accurate date of birth from an age given at death, which substantially mitigates the truncation effect; but it is still necessary to note its existence.

The seventeenth-century Quaker figures present few surprises to students of the pre-industrial populations of Europe. As far as we can tell, they were close to those of the rest of the English population, and they conform to the configuration which has been familiar since John Hajnal's famous article contrasting European with other marriage patterns.[10] In what Hajnal called the "European" pattern – actually

[10] Hajnal, "European marriage patterns."

Friends in life and death

Table 3.2 *Men's ages at marriage, by regions*

Cohort	n	Median	Mean	s.d.	5% Conf. level	Mode
Ireland						
1650–99	158	26.6	27.02	4.90	0.76	27
1700–49	231	27.1	27.91	5.37	0.69	27
1750–99	111	28.0	28.87	6.24	1.16	28
1800–49	63	28.9	29.19	4.52	1.12	29
Southern England						
1650–99	139	28.2	28.95	6.38	1.06	24
1700–49	388	27.2	28.70	6.80	0.68	25, 27
1750–99	399	28.3	30.25	7.27	0.71	24
1800–49	211	29.4	31.63	8.51	1.15	25
Northern Britain						
1650–99	27	27.8	28.79	6.23	2.35	30
1700–49	76	29.0	31.11	7.78	1.75	28
1750–99	89	30.1	31.25	8.73	1.81	23
1800–49	55	33.1	36.12	10.96	2.90	25, 33
Urban						
1650–99	109	28.3	29.75	7.54	1.41	23
1700–49	261	26.7	27.93	5.64	0.68	24
1750–99	229	26.4	28.47	6.98	0.90	24
1800–49	107	28.0	29.83	7.66	1.45	23
Genealogies						
1650–99	20	25.0	26.09	5.54	2.43	24
1700–49	95	27.8	29.78	8.32	1.67	27
1750–99	198	27.6	28.65	6.08	0.85	29
1800–49	380	28.4	29.52	6.00	0.60	29
1850–99	330	28.4	30.04	6.50	0.70	24

Note: Known remarriages and dates inaccurate by more than one year excluded.

West European, since it obtained for most of Europe north and west of a line from Trieste to Leningrad – most women married in their mid to late twenties, thus losing several years of opportunity for child-bearing when their natural fertility would have been at its highest. (These elevated ages at first marriage generally went along with low rates of bastardy.) A fairly large proportion of women – certainly over 10 percent – never married at all. (As we shall see, the percentage of women who were never married among the earliest Quakers seems a little lower than this.)

The steady rise in ages at marriage is more surprising. Of the measures given in Table 3.1, the median age at first marriage for men is

Table 3.3   *Women's ages at marriage, by regions*

Cohort	n	Median	Mean	s.d.	5% Conf. level	Mode
Ireland						
1650–99	131	21.9	23.09	5.02	0.86	20, 21
1700–49	237	23.0	23.95	4.81	0.61	22
1750–99	119	24.0	25.18	6.08	1.09	23
1800–49	53	24.9	25.39	4.94	1.22	22
Southern England						
1650–99	169	24.7	25.73	6.12	0.97	21
1700–49	415	25.4	27.05	6.85	0.66	23
1750–99	434	26.6	28.42	7.63	0.72	26
1800–49	252	28.1	29.63	7.75	0.96	28
Northern Britain						
1650–99	25	23.5	25.89	11.51	4.51	25
1700–49	85	25.1	26.35	5.03	1.07	23
1750–99	96	26.3	28.25	6.89	1.38	23
1800–49	62	27.8	30.10	8.68	2.16	24, 27, 28
Urban						
1650–99	141	24.8	26.35	7.35	1.21	21, 24
1700–49	363	25.6	27.54	7.70	0.79	24
1750–99	270	25.9	27.86	7.15	0.85	23
1800–49	104	26.9	28.46	7.08	1.36	24
Genealogies						
1650–99	18	22.6	25.05	8.99	4.15	22, 23
1700–49	78	23.7	24.98	4.76	1.06	20
1750–99	158	25.0	26.66	7.25	1.13	23, 24, 25, 28
1800–49	312	25.2	26.60	5.53	0.61	24
1850–99	301	26.0	27.40	6.06	0.69	24

Note: Known remarriages and dates inaccurate by more than one year excluded.

perhaps the best indicator. It rises slowly but – except for the early eighteenth century – steadily from 1675 onwards, making the only sharp jump in the last twenty-five years. By 1850 it was two years higher than it had been in the late seventeenth century. A similar rising tendency can be seen in the median age for women, except that the sharpest jump occurs in the mid eighteenth century. In all, the median age at first marriage for women rose almost three years. A similar pattern can be found in the means, although these were always higher and rose a bit more.

While it presents the general picture, Table 3.1 conceals regional variations which demand explanation. These are visible in Table 3.2

and 3.3. Regional differences within England are discernible, but not especially pronounced; there is a clear, but small tendency for women in Northern England and Scotland to marry earlier than those in the South, where marriage seems to have been delayed longer than anywhere else.[11] The most remarkable difference, however, is between Ireland and Britain. The Irish men married at slightly lower ages than those in Britain, whereas women there consistently married earlier than their British counterparts, and often by an average of two years or more.

To begin an explanation of these findings it is necessary to go beyond single measures, such as means and medians. Perhaps the most revealing perspective on Quaker marriage patterns can be gained when the ages of both partners are known and can be broken down by quinquennial periods, as is done in Table 3.4. This shows again that ages at first marriage during the first century were relatively stable; for example, in both half-centuries exactly 55 percent of the women married before reaching age 25. Almost a third of the men married before that age. At the higher ages, only a fifth to a quarter of the men married after age 30 in the late seventeenth century and 30 percent in the early eighteenth.

What looks like a distinctive Quaker pattern begins to emerge in the second half of the eighteenth century, when the age at first marriage of both men and women began to rise, although less markedly in the cities than in the countryside. For women, the most noteworthy change was the sharp decline in those marrying under the age of 20. Before 1750 more than one-eighth of all Quaker brides had been under this age; by the first part of the nineteenth century, fewer than 1 in 20 married so young. At the same time there was an increase in those marrying aged 30 or more; more than a quarter of all Quaker women married after their thirtieth birthday in the period from 1800 to 1849. Very few Quaker men had ever married before the age of 20, and fewer and fewer did so even before the age of 25 (31.7 percent as against 22 percent at the two ends of our period). During the same time span the number of men marrying aged 30 or over increased to 42 percent of the whole.

These figures contrast sharply with those of the Irish Quakers,

[11] There is one small piece of evidence to support the view that ages at first marriage after 1700 might have been lower in the North of England, at least for women; see the comparison of Methley in Yorkshire with fifteen other parishes reconstituted by workers with the ESRC Cambridge Group in Minoru Yasumoto, "Industrialization and demographic change in a Yorkshire parish," *Local Population Studies* no. 27 (1981), 12. On the other hand, studies by John Krause, cited in n. 23, indicate the opposite.

Table 3.4 *Husband's age at marriage by wife's age at marriage, British Quakers (%)*

Wife's age				Husband's age			
1650–99							
	<20	20–24	25–29	30–34	35–39	⩾40	All
<20	1.7	8.3	1.7	1.7	—	—	13.3
20–24	—	15.8	12.5	11.7	0.8	0.8	41.7
25–29	—	5.0	8.3	4.2	2.5	2.5	22.5
30–34	—	2.5	6.7	1.7	2.5	2.5	15.8
35–39	—	—	0.8	0.8	0.8	0.8	3.3
⩾40	—	—	—	2.5	—	0.8	3.3
All	1.7	31.7	30.0	22.5	6.7	7.5	*n* 120
1700–49							
<20	0.4	7.3	3.5	1.4	—	—	12.6
20–24	0.8	12.6	18.7	7.3	1.6	1.2	42.4
25–29	—	5.9	10.6	5.1	2.0	1.4	25.0
30–34	0.2	2.6	4.5	3.9	1.2	1.4	13.8
35–39	—	0.4	1.4	1.0	0.2	1.2	4.3
⩾40	—	0.2	0.2	—	0.2	1.2	1.8
All	1.4	29.1	38.9	18.7	5.3	6.5	*n* 491
1750–99							
<20	0.3	2.4	3.2	1.1	0.4	0.1	7.6
20–24	0.4	15.9	12.6	6.6	1.9	1.0	38.4
25–29	0.1	8.5	11.0	7.4	2.9	1.4	31.4
30–34	0.1	1.9	4.0	2.7	2.4	1.7	12.9
35–39	—	0.4	1.1	1.0	1.3	1.1	5.0
⩾40	—	—	0.7	0.6	0.4	3.0	4.7
All	1.0	29.1	32.7	19.5	9.3	8.4	*n* 698
1800–49							
<20	—	1.1	2.2	0.4	0.2	—	3.8
20–24	0.2	13.2	16.5	6.6	1.3	0.2	37.9
25–29	—	6.2	13.6	6.6	2.7	2.6	31.7
30–34	—	1.3	2.7	5.9	2.4	2.4	14.7
35–39	—	—	0.9	1.6	1.6	1.6	5.9
⩾40	—	0.2	—	0.9	0.9	4.0	6.0
All	0.2	22.0	35.9	22.0	9.2	10.8	*n* 546

Note: Known remarriages and dates inaccurate by more than one year excluded.

Table 3.5 *Husband's age at marriage by wife's age at marriage, Irish Quakers (%)*

Wife's age	Husband's age							
	<20	20–24	25–29	30–34	35–39	≥40	All	
1650–99								
<20	1.2	15.5	9.5	—	1.2	—	27.4	
20–24	1.2	11.9	22.6	9.5	—	—	45.2	
25–29	—	10.7	8.3	1.2	1.2	—	21.4	
30–34	—	—	1.2	—	1.2	—	2.4	
35–39	—	—	2.4	1.2	—	—	3.6	
≥40	—	—	—	—	—	—	—	
All	2.4	38.1	44.0	11.9	3.6	—		*n* 84
1700–49								
<20	0.8	5.4	11.5	3.8	0.8	—	22.3	
20–24	—	18.5	19.2	6.2	3.8	0.8	48.5	
25–29	—	3.8	12.3	3.1	—	—	19.2	
30–34	—	1.5	3.1	2.3	1.5	—	8.5	
35–39	—	—	—	—	0.8	—	0.8	
≥40	—	—	—	—	—	0.8	0.8	
All	0.8	29.2	46.1	15.4	6.9	1.6		*n* 130
1750–99								
<20	1.8	19.6	1.8	1.8	1.8	—	26.8	
20–24	—	8.9	17.9	3.6	—	1.8	32.1	
25–29	—	3.6	17.9	1.8	5.4	—	28.6	
30–34	—	1.8	—	1.8	1.8	—	5.4	
35–39	—	—	3.6	—	—	3.6	7.1	
≥40	—	—	—	—	—	—	—	
All	1.8	33.9	41.1	8.9	8.9	5.4		*n* 56
1800–49								
<20	—	7.4	3.7	—	—	—	11.1	
20–24	—	7.4	22.2	11.1	3.7	—	44.4	
25–29	—	3.7	22.2	7.4	3.7	—	37.0	
30–34	—	—	—	3.7	—	—	3.7	
35–39	—	—	—	3.7	—	—	3.7	
≥40	—	—	—	—	—	—	—	
All	—	18.5	48.1	25.9	7.4	—		*n* 27

Note: Known remarriages and dates inaccurate by more than one year excluded.

shown in Table 3.5. Before 1750, almost three-quarters of the women
who married did so before the age of 25, and even in the early
nineteenth century there were still more than half who married that
early. More than twice as many Irish as English Quaker brides
married while still in their teens, while marriage after age 30 was
uncommon: at no time did more than 1 in 8 wait so late. The Irish
bridegrooms were closer to the English pattern, but still showed a
propensity to marry somewhat earlier. More than four-fifths married
before the age of 30 in the seventeenth century, and three-quarters
of them did so in the eighteenth century. A trend to later marriages
for men does not show up markedly until the nineteenth century,
when a quarter of bridegrooms were aged 30 to 34. In Ireland the
ages at first marriage of men and women tended to move sympathetically through time, but with a substantially greater gap than in
England: the mean in Ireland was always four to five years higher
for men than for women.

Data about the Irish population are sparse, with almost nothing
suitable for quantitative evaluation before about 1780. Almost all that
survive relate to the Protestant population. This is a situation which
invites speculation, and students of Irish population have not been
reluctant to indulge; but most of them believe that a pattern of early
marriages was typical of Ireland during the late seventeenth and
eighteenth centuries.[12] Two family reconstitutions from Church of
Ireland parish registers have been done, for Coleraine and Blaris in
Ulster; the registers are not of good quality and the sample is of course
minute, but the mean ages at first marriage for women were only 18 to
19 in Blaris in the seventeenth century and 21 or 22 in Coleraine from
1820 to 1840. Similar results for Antrim, also in Ulster, can be
obtained from the enumerators' handbooks for the 1851 Irish census,
which escaped the 1921 fire which devastated the Irish Public Record
Office. In Antrim in the early nineteenth century women married in
their early twenties and men in their mid-twenties. It is important to
note that these later Ulster figures may be influenced, in the direction

[12] See L. A. Clarkson, "Marriage and fertility in nineteenth-century Ireland," in
Marriage and Society, ed. Outhwaite, 237–55 and "Irish population revisited, 1687–
1821," in *Irish Population, Economy, and Society: Essays in Honour of the Late K. H.
Connell*, ed. J. M. Goldstrom and L. A. Clarkson (Oxford, 1981), 13–35; Cormac Ó
Gráda, "The population of Ireland 1700–1900: a survey," *Annales de démographie
historique* (1979); Joel Mokyr and Cormac Ó Gráda, "New developments in Irish
population history, 1700–1850," *Economic History Review* 2nd ser. 37 (1984), 473–88;
and L. M. Cullen, "Population growth and diet, 1600–1850," in *Population, Economy,
and Society*, ed. Goldstrom and Clarkson, 89–112.

of lower ages at first marriage, by the "proto-industrial" development of linen-spinning in the province.[13]

The reasons why the Irish Quakers married earlier than the English may be the same as those which generally led Irish men and women to marry earlier. Arthur Young in 1780 described Ireland as favorably situated to increase population for the following reasons: (1) there was no poor law, so that people could move to wherever their industry would thrive; (2) housing was much easier to come by: "The cabbins of the poor Irish being such apparently miserable habitations, is another very evident encouragement to population" because whereas in England people would not marry until they get a house, which would cost £25 to £50 to build, and thus "half the life, and all the vigour and youth of a man and woman are passed, before they can save such a sum: and when they have got it, so burthensome are poor to a parish, that it is twenty to one if they get permission to erect their cottage," in Ireland "the young couple pass not their youth in celibacy for want of a nest to produce their young in"; (3) "the generality of footmen and maids, in gentlemen's families, are married, a circumstance we very rarely see in England"; (4) children were not burdensome to the Irish, who reckoned their happiness proportional to the size of their families (presumably in part because they helped bring in wages, or at least labored on the family allotment); and (5) since potatoes, the staple diet of the peasantry, produced the maximum nourishment per acre of land, families could feed their families adequately without having to buy any food.[14]

These considerations, of course, pertain to peasant families; but some English visitors thought that even upper-class women married a good deal earlier than in England. According to Edward Wakefield, writing in 1812, such women commonly married between ages 16 and 19, because there was no need for them to get a house; after a wedding trip in which they visited various of their friends, they moved in with one set of parents once the wife became pregnant. Even after they got a house, Wakefield added, the couple only went deeper and deeper into debt.[15]

[13] Eric L. Almquist, "Pre-famine Ireland and the theory of European proto-industrialization," *Journal of Economic History* 39 (1979), 709; W. Macafee and V. Morgan, "Population in Ulster, 1660–1760," in *Plantation to Partition: Essays in Ulster History in Honour of J. L. McCracken* (Belfast, 1981), 46–63 and "Irish population in the pre-famine period: evidence from County Antrim," *Economic History Review* 2nd. ser. 37 (1984), 182–96; Valerie Morgan, "The Church of Ireland registers of St Patrick's, Coleraine as a source for the study of a local pre-famine population," *Ulster Folklife* 19 (1973), 56–67.
[14] Arthur Young, *A Tour in Ireland* (London, 1780), II, 196–98.
[15] Edward Wakefield, *An Account of Ireland Statistical and Political* (London, 1812), II, 798–99.

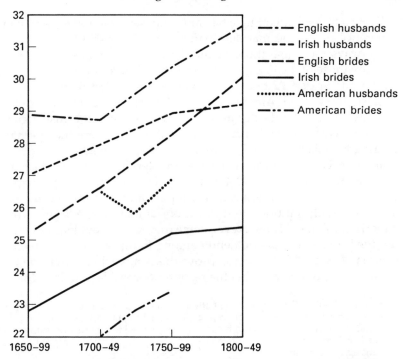

Fig. 3.3 Mean age at first marriage, Irish, rural English, and (middle colony) American Quakers.

It would be rash to base our judgment of actual demographic facts on these impressionistic accounts by English visitors, but it is likely that they were alert to some cultural patterns. How far these were shared by the Protestant population – for example, whether Quaker newly-weds lived with their parents for a while rather than waiting to set up households of their own at the time of their marriage – is impossible to know. Of course almost all the Irish Protestants were richer than the Catholic peasantry. Sir William Petty dramatized this in the late seventeenth century in his estimate that there would be no repetition of the Irish rebellion of the 1640s since "the British Protestants and Church have 3/4 of all the Lands; 5/6 of all the Housing; 9/10 of all the Housing in wall'd Towns, and Places of strength and 2/3 of the Foreign Trade," not to mention the fact that "6 of 8 of all the *Irish* lived in a brutish nasty Condition, as in Cabins, with neither Chimney, Door, Stairs nor Windows; feed chiefly upon Milk and Potatoes, whereby their Spirits are not dispos'd for War."[16]

16 "Political anatomy of Ireland," in *The Economic Writings of Sir William Petty*, ed. Charles Henry Hull (Cambridge, 1899), I, 156.

Being a transplanted English community seems to have made some difference, since the marriage patterns of the Irish Quakers are in some ways more like those of the American colonial Quakers than they are those of the English. As Figure 3.3 shows, this was especially true of the brides. Although the average age at first marriage of the English, Irish, and American colonial Quaker women all rose at roughly the same rate during the period studied, the Irish figures remained closer to the American colonial ones.[17] Were they perhaps sharing a similar "colonial" experience? Robert Wells has suggested that there is a "colonial" marriage and fertility pattern which fits roughly half-way between the two poles of Hajnal's typology.[18] Evidence of such a pattern can be seen in Quebec in the seventeenth and eighteenth centuries, and in various studies of the British North American colonies. There is even some fragmentary evidence suggesting the same sort of phenomenon among Europeans in seventeenth-century Mexico.[19] But what can prove this is more than a coincidence? An obvious possibility is that the resources available in Ireland for the

[17] Robert V. Wells, "Quaker marriage patterns in a colonial perspective," *William and Mary Quarterly* 3rd ser. 29 (1972), 415–42. As Wells has not provided calculations of confidence level with respect to his means, and since his cohorts are clearly quite small, it is possible that the differences in average age at first marriage are not statistically significant.

[18] Wells, "Quaker marriage patterns," 429–30.

[19] For colonial Mexico (reconstitution of a parish in Guadalajara), see Thomas Calvo, "Familles mexicaines au XVIIᵉ siècle: une tentative de reconstitution," *Annales de démographie historique* (1984), 149–74. For Quebec, Jacques Henripin, *La Population canadienne au début du XVIIIᵉ siècle: nuptialité, fécondité, mortalité infantile* (Paris, 1954) and George Sabagh, "The fertility of French–Canadian women during the seventeenth century," *American Journal of Sociology* 47 (1942), 680–89. There is a burgeoning literature on the demography of the North American British colonies. See, among others, John Demos, "Notes on life in Plymouth colony," *William and Mary Quarterly* 3rd ser. 22 (1965), 246–86 and "Families in colonial Bristol, Rhode Island: an exercise in historical demography," *ibid.* 3rd ser. 25 (1968); Wells, "Quaker marriage patterns" and "Family size and fertility control in eighteenth-century America: a study of Quaker families," *Population Studies* 25 (1971), 73–82; Philip Greven, *Four Generations: Population, Land, and Family in Colonial Andover, Massachusetts* (Ithaca, 1970); Robert Higgs and H. Louis Stettler, "Colonial New England demography: a sampling approach," *William and Mary Quarterly* 3rd ser. 27 (1970), 282–94; J. Potter, "The growth of population in America, 1700–1860," in *Population in History*, ed. Glass and Eversley, 631–88; J. Houdaille, "Démographie de la Nouvelle Angleterre aux XVIIᵉ et XVIIIᵉ siècles," *Population* 26 (1971), 963–66; Kenneth Lockridge, "The population of Dedham, Mass., 1636–1736," *Economic History Review* 2nd ser. 19 (1966), 318–44; Nancy Osterud and J. Fulton, "Family limitation and age at marriage: fertility decline in Sturbridge, Massachusetts, 1730–1850," *Population Studies* 30 (1976), 481–94; Helena Temkin-Greener and A. C. Swedlund, "Fertility transition in the Connecticut Valley: 1740–1850," *Population Studies* 32 (1978), 27–41; Louise Kantrow, "Philadelphia gentry: fertility and family limitation among an American aristocracy," *Population Studies* 34 (1980), 21–30; and Daniel Scott Smith, "'The demographic history of Colonial New England," *Journal of Economic History* 32 (1972), 165–183.

English settlers there to exploit were in some way comparable to those in the virgin lands of the North American colonies, and that these made it possible to marry and start families earlier. That the English settlers – and we must remember that roughly as many English migrated to Ireland as to the American colonies during the seventeenth century – occupied a privileged place in the Irish economy is clear. In the late seventeenth century, after Catholic landowners had been dispossessed, there seems to have been an abundance of land relative to prospective tenant farmers, and the rapidly growing and highly volatile population of Blaris at that time exhibits considerable similarities to that of the British North American colonies.[20] This, however, leaves unexplained why the age at first marriage of Quaker men – and like all "Malthusian" explanations of nuptiality this one applies chiefly to men – would rise from 1750 onwards. We do not know whether the intensity of or opportunities for exploitation in Ireland were slackening off then, but the Irish Quakers seem to have been increasingly successful commercially at this time, and would not have needed to delay marriages purely because of lowered real incomes. Furthermore, such evidence as we have for early nineteenth-century Ireland suggests that it was the exploited – peasants and laborers – rather than the exploiters who were most likely to marry early.[21] From the 1830s, however, ages at first marriage of Irish Catholics rose steadily (eventually to reach heights unmatched anywhere else in Europe); the Irish Quaker marriages of which we have record after 1850 – a number too small for reliable statistical treatment – hint at a continuation of their trend towards higher ages at marriage.

Some of the same problems confront us in interpreting the English Quaker pattern of high and rising ages at first marriage. Data about the general English population are relatively profuse, but not all of the same tendency. There is not even a consensus on such a basic question

[20] Macafee and Morgan, "Population in Ulster," 56; Clarkson, "Marriage and fertility," 239–40.
[21] The mean age at marriage of working-class women in Limerick from 1822 to 1839 was 21.1; that of men was 26.2, according to figures gathered by a doctor living there at the time; see Ó Gráda, "Population of Ireland," 286. Since all marriages were averaged, the age at first marriage would have been slightly lower. The Poor Inquiry of the 1830s gave a figure of 22 for the average age at first marriage of laborers; since the national average was given in the census of 1841 as 26 for males, it looks as though those in higher social strata were already delaying marriage and looking for a "match." See Joseph Lee, "Marriage and population in pre-famine Ireland," *Economic History Review* 2nd ser. 21 (1968), 283–84 and K. H. Connell, *The Population of Ireland, 1750–1845* (London, 1950) and, for a contrasting minority view, Michael Drake, "Marriage and population growth in Ireland, 1750–1845," *Economic History Review* 2nd ser. 16 (1963–64), 301–13.

as whether men's ages at first marriage fell or remained about the same during the eighteenth century. One reason for this disagreement is that some studies of nuptiality use family-reconstitution methods, whereas others rely on aggregations based on allegations for marriage licenses. The family reconstitution studies are limited either to individual parishes or to distinctive social groups like the peerage or the Quakers. Furthermore, not all the family reconstitution studies are comparable, or even usable; one, of three Lancashire parishes, yielded fewer than 300 families and insufficient data for any time series.[22] On the other hand, marriage licenses were not taken out by everyone who married, and if different strata of the population were using them at different times – a possibility which cannot be excluded – then changes over time which they might show may simply be consequences of the different composition of the group using them. Also, some studies using marriage license allegations have compared different regions, leaving open the possibility that apparent changes over time are simply enduring regional variations. For these reasons the family reconstitution results are the more trustworthy.[23]

[22] David J. Loschky and Donald F. Krier, "Income and family size in three eighteenth-century Lancashire parishes: a reconstitution study," *Journal of Economic History* 29 (1969), 429–48. The ages at first marriage which this study found look rather similar to the Quaker figures for Northern England and Scotland in the eighteenth century, especially in such occupational categories as tradesmen and farmers, which were strongly represented in the Quaker community; but some of the occupational groupings in the Loschky–Krier study are minute and so not much reliance can be placed on their results.

[23] It nevertheless may be appropriate to present evidence which is based on other methods. In a national compilation done by Peter Razzell, based almost entirely on marriage license allegations, no pattern of change over time was discerned. Comparing regional samples for different periods from 1615–21 to 1796–99, Razzell concluded that the mean age at marriage for spinsters always stayed within a range from 23.76 to 24.9 years. Razzell's sample is somewhat biased by the fact that marriage by license was generally used by people of some means, and there is also a possibility that allegations for marriage licenses have a systematic tendency to understate ages, since they depend on the bride's statement of how old she was, and these statements by people over 25 may not always be trustworthy. Even if they did not understate their ages out of vanity, it is by no means clear that all people knew their ages. (See Peter Razzell, "Population change in eighteenth-century England: a reinterpretation," *Economic History Review* 2nd ser. 18 [1965], 312–22.)

At the other extreme, John Krause claimed that in "three southern agricultural areas" (not further specified) there was a dramatic fall in average age at first marriage, from around 27 for women between 1700 and 1750 to averages of 20, 22, and 25 by 1801–12. Of nine parishes which he studied for the last quarter of the eighteenth century, age at first marriage was between 24.6 and 25.8 in all but two; Ardingley in Sussex had a mean age at first marriage of only 20.9, while Penrith in Cumberland had one of 27 (John T. Krause, "Some neglected factors in the English Industrial Revolution," *Journal of Economic History* 19 [1959], 531; and "Some aspects of population change, 1690–1790," in *Land, Labour and Population in the Industrial Revolution: Essays Presented to J. D. Chambers*, ed. E. L. Jones and G. E. Mingay

Most family reconstitution studies of parishes thus far published show declines in age at first marriage after 1750. In the most comprehensive recent summary, Michael Flinn concludes that prior to 1750 the mean age at first marriage for women (based on studies of around 43 parishes) was 25; it rose to 25.3 (in around 17 parishes) from 1740 to 1790, and then fell to 24.2 (also from around 17 parishes) from 1780 to 1820. He presents no comparable figures for men.[24] For thirteen parishes scattered throughout a variety of rural, market-town, and industrializing parishes in England reconstituted by co-workers with the ESRC Cambridge Group, the means show a decline from 28.1 to 27.2 years for men between 1600 and 1749, and then a more dramatic decrease to 25.7 for the last half of the eighteenth century. For women there was little change in the three cohorts before 1750 – the figures were 25.6, 26.2, and 25.4 – but then a considerable fall to 24.0 in the last half of the eighteenth century.[25] A different

[London, 1967], 187–205). Krause bases his opinion that age at marriage was "obviously relatively late" around 1700 on seven community listings made between 1695 and 1705, which all show that the majority of women were married no earlier than age 25–29; in three half or more did not marry until age 30–34. Figures for the late eighteenth century came from Bridekirk, Carlisle, Penrith, and Newton Reigny and Skelton in Cumberland; Gisburn and Liston-in-Craven in Yorkshire; Shap, Westmorland; Ardingley, Sussex; and Branscombe, Devon ("Aspects," 202, 205).

The best discussions of the reliability of marriage bonds and allegations is in R. B. Outhwaite, "Age at marriage in England from the late seventeenth to the nineteenth century," *Transactions of the Royal Historical Society* 5th ser. 23 (1973), 62–70. Comparison of the ages of women married by license and by banns in eighteenth-century Warwickshire showed that after 1745–49 those married by license were consistently slightly older than those married by banns, suggesting that if they were understating their ages, it was to a modest extent (J. M. Martin, "Marriage and economic stress in the Felden of Warwickshire during the eighteenth century," *Population Studies* 31 [1977], 529). Confronted with a variety of findings from a variety of methods, Outhwaite has reduced himself to nescience on the subject of ages at first marriage. He cautions against attempts to make any time series or to derive anything like a national mean age at first marriage from an accumulation of local samples; nor, in his view, should ages derived from marriage allegations be compared to those from family reconstitutions. With appropriate reticence, he introduces his own findings, compiled from examining around 11,000 marriage bonds and allegations, only in a footnote; they show mean ages at first marriage for bachelors around 26, with a dip of about a year in the period 1801–10, whereas the comparable figure for spinsters ranged between 23.1 and 23.5 in the early and mid-eighteenth century, falling to 22.3 for Sussex and 23.8 for Leicestershire in the first decade of the nineteenth century.

24 Michael W. Flinn, *The European Demographic System* (Baltimore, 1981), 124–27. Katherine Gaskin, "Age at first marriage in Europe before 1850," *Journal of Family History* 3 (1978), 23–26 summarizes findings about both genders.

25 E. A. Wrigley and R. S. Schofield, "English population history from family reconstitution: summary results 1600–1799," *Population Studies* 37 (1983), 157–84. This article also contains a variety of other measures of ages at first marriage of both men and women on pp. 161–68. In their *Population History of England*, 255, they present, much less completely, data from twelve parishes for the period 1800–49. They show men marrying at an average age of 25.3 and women at 23.4, so the decline in ages at

computation, adding a cohort centered on 1816 (calculated by back projection from the 1851 English census) showed means (for both sexes in the cohort) of 24.10 and 23.63 in the latter eighteenth century, but 25.54 in the 1816 cohort.[26] It seems unlikely that these figures will not stand up, since, in the absence of increases in marital fertility in the population as a whole, there could not have been such a rise in births if age at marriage had not declined at the same time that more people were able to be married.

Our material is suitable for comparison with family reconstitution studies on English parishes done with the same methods and conventions. Table 3.6 shows the distribution of ages at first marriage in thirteen of the parishes which have been so studied. A comparison with the Southern English and urban Quaker brides and bridegrooms, given in Table 3.7, shows that in the period before 1700 slightly more Quaker women married for the first time at a lower age; whereas 53 percent of the Southern English and 52 percent of the urban ones had married before the age of 25, only 48 percent of the brides in these thirteen parishes were already married by that age. Quaker men in the late seventeenth century, on the other hand, seem to have married later than the bridegrooms in these parishes. Not until age 28 were the majority of male Quakers married, whereas the figure for the parishes was two years lower. In the first half of the eighteenth century the difference between marriage patterns of Quaker brides and those in these parishes was very narrow; ages at first marriage for both had increased, but those of the Quakers had increased more. The differences in ages at first marriage among men also declined, although the Quakers still married at a slightly later age.

The dramatic divergence of Quaker experience began after 1750. In the last half of the eighteenth century Quaker brides for the first time married significantly later than those from the thirteen parishes. Over half of the Southern Quaker women and 49 percent of the urban ones were still unmarried at age 25. Meanwhile the women in the thirteen parishes were moving decisively towards earlier marriage; half of them were married before the age of 23. Furthermore, the same tendency now appeared in the ages of first marriage for men; the age at

marriage seems to have continued; but to avoid a bias in favor of lower ages at first marriage, both the earliest and latest years in a series had to be discounted; and since no parish reconstitution went past 1837 and some stopped around 1812, most of the marriages in the "1800–49" cohort actually took place early in the nineteenth century. It should be noted that in the book, means of means of the twelve parishes are presented; in the article, all family reconstitution forms from the thirteen parishes are pooled, so that each community no longer has an equal weight and means from the big ones, like Banbury and Gainsborough, can swamp the smallest parishes.

[26] Schofield, "English marriage patterns revisited," 9.

Table 3.6   *Ages at first marriage in 13 English parishes (pooled data)*

	Under 18	18	19	20	21	22	23	24	25	26	27	28	29	30	31	32	33	34	35–9	Over 40
Men																				
1650–99	8	5	22	40	49	58	84	96	90	72	65	64	53	42	42	33	32	23	67	55
1700–49	6	10	23	46	68	86	84	91	88	74	68	61	54	39	36	22	20	18	60	46
1750–99	7	17	42	76	114	113	106	91	79	60	52	40	32	28	25	19	12	10	46	31
Cumulative																				
1650–99	1	1	3	7	12	18	27	36	45	52	59	65	71	75	79	82	85	88	94	100
1700–49	1	2	4	8	15	24	32	41	50	58	64	70	76	80	83	85	88	89	95	100
1750–99	1	2	7	14	26	37	47	57	64	70	76	80	83	86	88	90	91	92	97	100
Women																				
1650–99	40	25	49	57	64	90	70	85	63	62	60	56	32	38	32	22	34	23	68	30
1700–49	39	35	53	74	74	84	86	76	72	60	57	51	42	36	29	22	22	18	48	22
1750–99	51	58	74	104	113	99	78	72	57	48	48	36	27	24	22	16	13	12	31	17
Cumulative																				
1650–99	4	6	11	17	23	32	39	48	54	60	66	72	75	79	82	84	88	90	97	100
1700–49	4	7	13	20	27	34	41	48	56	64	70	74	78	83	86	89	91	93	98	100
1750–99	5	11	18	29	40	50	58	65	71	75	80	84	86	89	91	93	94	95	98	100

Notes: Numbers of men are 1,706 for the 1650–99 cohort, 2,407 for the 1700–49 one, and 4,220 for the last one. Numbers of women are 1,962 for the first cohort, 2,998 for the second one, and 5,098 for the third one. The parishes are Birstall, Methley, Gainsborough, Gedling, Shepshed, Bottesford, Alcester, Banbury, Campton with Shefford and Southill, Terling, Aldenham, Hartland, and Colyton.

Source: E. A. Wrigley and R. S. Schofield, "English population history from family reconstitution: summary results 1600–1799," *Population Studies* 37 (1983), Table 3, p. 164. Distributions are rates per 1,000; the cumulative figures are rounded off.

which more than half of them were married was 25 for the urban Quaker men and 27 for the Southern English ones, but 24 for the men in the thirteen parishes. In the first half of the nineteenth century, the age at first marriage of urban Quaker brides did not change much, while that of the Southern English ones continued to rise. Both urban and Southern Quaker bridegrooms were also marrying later and later. The contrast can best be seen in graphic form, as in Figure 3.4, which shows the curve in the cumulative marriage figures moving steadily to the right along the age axis for the Quakers and to the left for the parochial sample.

A direct comparison of the Quakers with the entire English population first becomes possible after the beginning of civil registration. By 1841, both Quaker men and women were undoubtedly marrying at considerably later ages than the population as a whole. English Quaker brides in the second quarter of the nineteenth century

Table 3.7(a)   *Distribution of age at first marriage, urban Quakers*

	Under 18	18	19	20	21	22	23	24	25	26	27	28	29	30	31	32	33	34	35–9	Over 40	N
Men																					
1650–99	9	0	18	9	28	64	92	55	73	55	73	64	55	46	73	55	55	28	64	83	109
1700–49	0	0	8	31	61	57	84	100	73	130	61	65	65	27	38	27	50	31	19	38	261
1750–99	4	0	9	17	66	61	87	118	109	70	52	87	31	39	44	22	31	9	70	74	229
1800–49	0	0	0	0	47	37	103	84	65	75	84	47	84	47	56	56	37	47	47	84	107
Cumulative																					
1650–99	1	1	3	4	6	13	22	28	35	40	48	54	60	64	72	77	83	85	92	100	
1700–49	0	0	1	4	10	16	24	34	41	54	61	67	74	76	80	83	88	91	96	100	
1750–99	0	0	1	3	10	16	24	36	47	54	59	68	71	75	79	82	85	86	93	100	
1800–49	0	0	0	0	5	8	19	27	34	41	50	54	63	67	73	79	82	87	92	100	
Women																					
1650–99	43	64	50	85	99	50	28	99	71	78	21	14	35	43	43	28	21	13	64	50	141
1700–49	19	39	63	74	52	74	63	77	69	50	52	25	39	50	36	33	17	11	80	77	363
1750–99	7	26	37	41	44	100	107	70	74	37	55	52	44	33	63	30	30	7	81	59	270
1800–49	0	0	10	29	77	77	67	115	48	87	77	58	48	29	87	29	38	0	48	77	104
Cumulative																					
1650–99	4	11	16	24	34	39	42	52	59	67	69	70	74	78	82	85	87	89	95	100	
1700–49	2	6	12	20	25	32	39	46	53	58	63	66	70	75	78	82	83	84	92	100	
1750–99	1	3	7	11	16	26	36	43	51	54	60	65	70	73	79	82	85	86	94	100	
1800–49	0	0	1	4	12	19	26	38	42	51	59	64	69	72	81	84	88	88	92	100	

Table 3.7(b)   *Distribution of age at first marriage (Southern English Quakers)*

	Under 18	18	19	20	21	22	23	24	25	26	27	28	29	30	31	32	33	34	35–9	Over 40	N
Men																					
1650–99	7	14	29	36	22	36	79	101	50	50	65	65	65	58	43	36	43	50	86	65	139
1700–49	5	10	13	21	46	75	75	70	90	77	90	57	44	46	46	41	28	31	72	62	388
1750–99	0	3	0	13	30	53	68	95	88	55	73	63	45	63	40	30	43	23	125	93	399
1800–49	0	0	0	0	38	47	52	62	85	76	52	62	66	38	52	38	43	28	123	137	211
Cumulative																					
1650–99	1	2	5	9	11	14	22	32	37	42	49	55	62	68	72	76	80	85	94	100	
1700–49	1	2	3	5	10	17	24	31	40	48	57	63	67	72	77	81	84	87	94	100	
1750–99	0	0	0	2	5	10	17	26	35	40	48	54	58	65	69	72	76	78	91	100	
1800–49	0	0	0	0	4	9	14	20	28	36	41	47	54	58	63	67	71	74	86	100	
Women																					
1650–99	41	49	49	73	81	89	81	65	98	73	49	57	24	57	24	8	8	8	49	16	123
1700–49	19	25	65	74	53	84	102	84	62	65	50	31	56	53	19	15	19	9	68	50	323
1750–99	8	8	45	61	67	89	81	56	45	95	56	61	47	28	28	17	19	36	53	100	359
1800–49	0	13	4	26	57	61	70	66	57	57	66	88	48	66	35	31	39	9	88	118	228
Cumulative																					
1650–99	4	9	14	21	29	38	46	53	63	70	75	80	83	89	91	92	93	93	98	100	
1700–49	2	4	11	18	24	32	42	50	57	63	68	71	77	82	84	85	87	88	95	100	
1750–99	1	2	6	12	19	28	36	42	46	55	61	67	72	75	77	79	81	85	90	100	
1800–49	0	1	2	4	10	16	23	30	36	41	48	57	61	68	71	75	79	79	88	100	

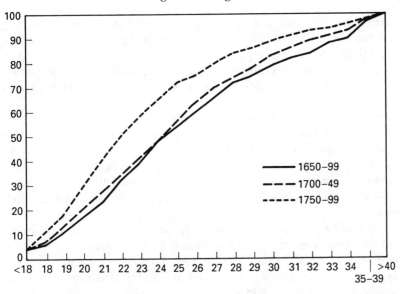

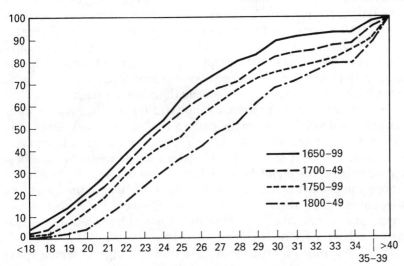

Fig. 3.4 Percentage of women ever married cumulated by age at first marriage, Southern England Quakers and 13 English parishes.

married, on the average, at around 29, with the highest figures coming from Southern England, whereas the average age at first marriage for all English women was 24.3. For men the disparity was comparable: the English Quakers entered matrimony aged about 31.5 years, on average, whereas the figure for the general population was exactly six years lower.[27]

Therefore, unless the family reconstitution studies are unrepresentative, we are justified in claiming that as early as 1750 the English Quakers began going counter to the national tendency by entering marriage at ever-increasing ages. Though we cannot make comparisons with the general population of Ireland, the Irish Quakers were also, though at a less accelerated pace, marrying later in their lives.

In this behavior the English Quakers can be usefully compared with that of other elite groups, the British peerage and *haut bourgeois* families of Geneva. Table 3.8 shows the comparison with the "secondary universe" of peers, as studied by T. H. Hollingsworth. The experience of peers' children and the Quakers suggests that the national trend towards a lower age at first marriage conceals a countervailing one on the part of at least some privileged groups towards higher ages. A reasonable guess is that wage laborers and those in at least occasional receipt of poor relief, who made up the great majority of the population, were marrying earlier; those who lived on salaries, rents, or profits were delaying marriage.

Yet any broader comparison, as shown in Figure 3.5, makes it clear how unusual was the marriage pattern of Quaker wives. Until 1725 they married at about the same age as the Genevan *haute bourgeoisie*, both groups marrying considerably later than all the noble families. But once again the anomaly is the further rise in age at first marriage among the Quaker brides, at the same time that that of the Genevans was plunging. By the 1825–50 cohort the Quakers are almost off the chart, almost four years later than the British nobility and more than six years later than the Genevan *bourgeoises*.

In the seventeenth century the size of the bourgeois families was increasing faster than the economic opportunities which Geneva could provide. The result was substantial emigration; but those fewer potential husbands who stayed in Geneva were marrying at somewhat younger ages, and came to prefer brides even younger.[28] In the

---

[27] *Fourth Annual Report of the Registrar General* (London, 1842), 9. These means are based on 13,683 marriages of bachelors and 14,311 of spinsters.

[28] Louis Henry, *Anciennes familles genevoises, étude démographique, XVIe–XXe siècles* (Paris, 1956), 63–66.

Table 3.8 *Mean ages at marriage (all marriages), Quakers and peers' children*

	Quakers								Peers' children		
	Southern England		Northern Britain		Urban		Ireland				
	M	F	M	F	M	F	M	F		M	F
1650–99	29.77	26.15	28.22	25.54	32.49	28.05	28.22	23.54	1650–74	30.33	23.75
									1674–99	30.83	24.08
1700–40	29.61	27.95	30.94	25.87	31.65	28.94	29.76	24.13	1700–24	32.75	24.75
									1725–49	32.25	25.25
1750–99	31.52	28.75	31.33	27.37	30.81	28.63	29.81	25.38	1750–74	32.5	25.08
									1775–99	32.42	26.33
1800–49	32.58	30.16	31.25	27.3	30.86	28.77	30.2	25.8	1800–24	33.92	26.25
									1825–49	33.58	26.5

Source: Data for children of peers from T. H. Hollingsworth, *The Demography of the British Peerage* (Supplement to *Population Studies*, vol. 18, no. 2, 1965, Table 2, p. 11).

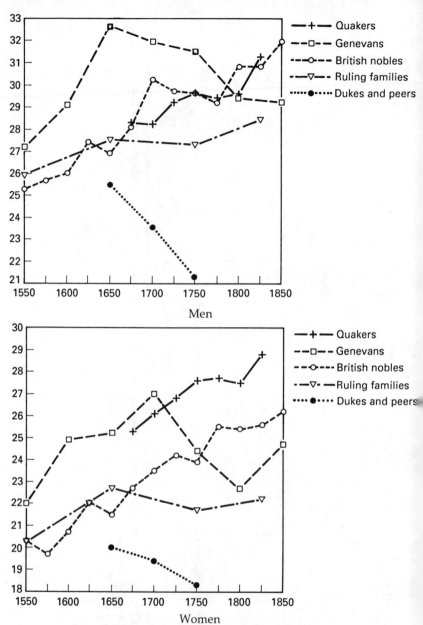

Fig. 3.5 Mean ages at first marriage, British and Irish Quaker men and women and other groups.

Sources: Henry, *Anciennes familles genevoises*, 55; Hollingsworth, *Demography*, 26–27; Louis Henry and C. Lévy, "Ducs et pairs sous l'Ancien Régime," *Population* 15e année (1960), 813; for European ruling families, Sigismund Peller, "Studies on mortality since the Renaissance," *Bulletin of the History of Medicine* 13 (1943), 427–61; *ibid.* 16 (1944), 362–81; *ibid.* 21 (1947), 51–101 and "Mortality, past and future," *Population Studies* 1 (1948), 405–56.

first half of the nineteenth century there was a development something like we noticed in Quaker families; as the age at first marriage of
men declined slightly, that of women rose significantly. The disparity
in their ages was thus considerably reduced, although it was still
almost five years. As with the Quakers, a growing degree of emotional
closeness may have accompanied this growing closeness in the ages of
spouses.[29]

While the marriage pattern of Quaker women is quite distinctive,
that of men is not; it is barely distinguishable on our graph from that of
the British nobility. This is of course significant, and it is tempting to
explain it by "the general possibility that in every era age at marriage
rises with social class."[30] This is a serviceable explanation for the rise in
age at first marriage of Quaker men after 1750, and the late marriages
of both peers' sons and Quaker men in the nineteenth century can be
plausibly attributed to their relatively high social positions. But the
explanation breaks down completely for the period from 1675 to 1750,
when men in the general population were marrying at about the same
age as the Quakers or the peers' sons.[31] It may be hard to accept that a
powerful cultural norm about the proper age for men to marry was
accepted by these diverse social groups in pre-industrial England; but
this at the very least seems more persuasive than an explanation based
on social stratification.

In the English population as a whole, fertility was maintained at a
relatively low level prior to 1750 not through fluctuations in the age at
marriage, but chiefly in the proportions who ever married.[32] Unfortunately figures about this important aspect of nuptiality are difficult to
derive from family reconstitution studies, but we can make an estimate in a somewhat indirect way by considering the marital status of
those who died after attaining the age of fifty. Those still single after
that age can be taken to have been definitively celibate. The figures are
subject to question because of the number of unknowns; and even if
this were not so high, this is still not the ideal way to measure
definitive celibacy, because, among other things, mortality is usually

---

[29] Greater intimacy in aristocratic families is suggested, on other grounds, by Randolph
Trumbach in *The Rise of the Egalitarian Family: Aristocratic Kinship and Domestic Relations
in Eighteenth-Century England* (New York, 1978).

[30] T. H. Hollingsworth, *The Demography of the British Peerage* (Supplement to *Population
Studies* 18 [1965]), 13.

[31] Hollingsworth was not aware of the convergence of ages at first marriage throughout
English society, since the data for the general population come from family-
reconstitution studies completed after he published his work.

[32] J. A. Goldstone, "The demographic revolution in England: a re-examination,"
Population Studies 40 (1986), 5–33, and articles by Weir and Schofield cited in n. 2.

Friends in life and death

Table 3.9   *Definitive celibacy (% dying unmarried aged 50 or over)*

	SOUTHERN ENGLAND				NORTHERN BRITAIN			
	Males		Females		Males		Females	
	%	n	%	n	%	n	%	n
1700–49	1.6	171(26.3)	3.0	149(11.4)	1.5	114(43.0)	0	43(20.9)
1750–99	3.3	445(31.5)	14.9	356(9.2)	5.1	289(39.1)	7.2	212(27.8)
1800–49	0.7	422(28.0)	23.3	428(5.6)	8.5	421(35.9)	17.9	311(35.7)
	URBAN				IRELAND			
1700–49	1.2	209(19.1)	3.5	199(14.1)	5.0	121(33.9)	1.9	69(21.7)
1750–99	2.7	285(22.5)	14.7	308(11.7)	9.7	188(28.7)	15.1	172(26.7)
1800–49	0.9	289(24.2)	20.0	291(5.5)	28.4	131(38.2)	24.7	137(45.9)

Note: *n* is the total number of burials for that birth cohort where the exact age at death is known and is over 50. The figure in parentheses following it is the percentage of that figure whose marital status at death is unknown. The percentage figure for "definitive celibacy," in the first column, is the percentage of persons with known marital status who are known to have been single at the time of their deaths.

higher among the celibate than the married. But in the absence of a census it is the best we can do.[33] Though we must take the figures with caution, the trend, as epitomized in Table 3.9, is very striking for women; the figures for men, however, must be a considerable understatement, since there is no evidence of a sex imbalance severe enough to allow fewer than 1 percent of the men to remain unmarried while more than 20 percent of the women were celibate. It was much less usual to identify men by marital status in the burial registers, and so the "unknowns" must conceal a substantial number of bachelors. The Irish family lists and the genealogies included in the sample for Northern Britain are in this respect a better source than the registers, and doubtless give a more accurate picture of the extent of male celibacy.

There was an extremely low rate of celibacy among women who died between 1700 and 1749, but this rose dramatically to around 20 percent for those dying in the first half of the nineteenth century. At the same time the proportion of women unmarried at age 50 among the daughters of peers was very similar: 202 and 238 per 1,000 for

---

[33] This method for estimating the extent of definitive celibacy was used by Louis Henry and Jacques Houdaille in "Célibat et âge au mariage aux XVIIIe et XIXe siècles en France," *Population* 33 (1978), 43–84. Their sources were less informative than the Quaker registers; the marital status at death was unknown for 18 percent of the women and 55 percent of the men.

1800–24 and 1825–49. The comparable figures were 201 and 178 for sons of peers. Although the Quakers and the peers had comparable celibacy rates at this time, that of the peers had been high since the seventeenth century; the proportion for both men and women had been over 200 since the cohort born between 1675 and 1699.[34] Here again, therefore, the Quakers were arriving at a pattern of long standing among noble families. From the late sixteenth through the mid seventeenth centuries, estimates show that roughly similar figures for definitive celibacy obtained in the population as a whole; but from the cohort centered on 1666 there was a dramatic rise in the proportions ever marrying. Until 1840 it never fell below about seven-eighths of the population, and most of the time after that more than nine-tenths of the general population married at some time during their lives.[35]

Fertility can also be curtailed, of course, by the premature death of one partner. A reasonable idea of the frequency of such deaths can be obtained from Table 3.10. In the last column is a percentage of those marriages which lasted until the wife was at least 40 years old, which is an average time for the birth of a last child even in "completed" families (see Table 4.7). (Since our age-groups at marriage are quinquennial, and our duration-of-marriage figures are also arranged in quinquennial groups, a marriage which lasted until the wife was least 40 might have lasted until she was 49.) The only group where premature death was seriously curtailing fertility was the urban wives married in the seventeenth century, where the minimum figure for marriages lasting until the wife's fortieth year was only 35 percent. (The explanation for this seems to be the unusual age disparity between wives and husbands in urban marriages in the late seventeenth century. As Table 3.16 shows, almost half the marriages were between partners separated by more than five years.) Whenever the percentage of marriages lasting until the wife's fortieth year rose to three-quarters or more, as was often the case after 1750, we are justified in saying that fertility was relatively unaffected by the premature death of one of the marriage partners.

Furthermore, the effects of such mortality could be mitigated by the remarriage of the surviving spouse. The magnitude of this effect is shown in Table 3.11. Except in Northern England and Scotland, the percentage of remarriages was always lower in the early nineteenth century than it had been in the late seventeenth, reflecting the increased duration of marriages on the one hand and the generally decreased propensity to marry at all.

[34] Hollingsworth, *Demography*, 20.   [35] Schofield, "English marriage patterns," 10.

Table 3.10 Duration of marriages, all marriage ranks

Wife's age at marriage	1650–99			1700–49			1750–99			1800–49		
	n	Mean	% lasting to wife age ≥40	n	Mean	% lasting to wife age ≥40	n	Mean	% lasting to wife age ≥40	n	Mean	% lasting to wife age ≥40
20–24												
Southern England	39	26.1	66.7	118	25.5	60.2	153	28.1	63.4	45	30.1	64.4
Northern Britain	16	29.0	75.0	57	31.6	77.2	76	28.5	65.8	107	33.5	78.5
Urban	40	17.5	35.0	89	22.5	57.3	65	24.5	53.8	20	26.4	65.0
Ireland	24	23.7	54.2	63	23.2	52.4	23	26.2	56.5	10	26.1	60.0
25–29												
Southern England	29	26.2	69.0	83	27.3	72.3	136	28.4	79.4	60	26.6	75.0
Northern Britain	6	28.2	83.3	23	25.2	73.9	58	27.2	72.4	83	29.0	74.7
Urban	21	22.6	61.9	70	20.1	57.1	68	26.2	73.5	27	28.7	74.1
Ireland	15	25.6	60.0	21	32.2	85.7	14	30.8	85.7	11	23.3	63.6
30–34												
Southern England	17	24.5	76.5	54	24.5	75.9	63	24.5	79.4	27	26.2	81.5
Northern Britain	3	38.1	100.0	16	22.4	75.0	17	28.8	88.2	39	28.4	79.5
Urban	21	27.0	90.5	48	19.2	70.8	36	26.4	80.6	14	19.0	71.4
Ireland	8	31.3	87.5	11	22.4	72.7	6	22.5	50.0	2	27.8	100.0

Table 3.11 *Percentage of all marriages which were remarriages*

	URBAN		SOUTHERN ENGLAND		NORTHERN BRITAIN		IRELAND	
	M	F	M	F	M	F	M	F
1650–99	20.4	11.3	10.9	4.5	9.6	None	12.2	8.0
1700–49	21.6	11.5	8.9	6.1	10.9	2.4	13.5	2.5
1750–99	17.6	6.3	9.1	4.0	10.3	1.9	7.5	4.0
1800–49	8.5	4.6	6.6	3.4	10.5	1.8	8.7	1.9

There are a number of possible explanations for the rise in the age at first marriage of Quakers and the apparently associated increase in definitive celibacy. Although it is the effect of delayed marriage upon women which is of primary demographic importance, the explanations of variation in age at marriage which are usually advanced have to do with aspects of the occupational structure and the effect of economic factors during the life cycle. Thus they pertain chiefly to men. It is to these that we shall first turn.

One possibility is that as the occupational distribution within the Society of Friends changed, the average age at first marriage for men rose because occupational groups which traditionally married late came to be more heavily represented. A test of this argument requires that we look at marriage patterns within the various occupational groups during our period – bearing in mind the difficulties in allocating occupations to larger groupings that we discussed in chapter 2. Fortunately there are a lot of data about the ages at which men in different occupations married, and we have been able to make use of some work by our volunteers as well as our own. The results are shown in Table 3.12. As Table 2.5 showed, the main changes in occupational distribution from the middle of the seventeenth to the middle of the nineteenth centuries were a decline in the number of men engaged in agriculture and artisans (and perhaps a move from retail into wholesale trade, although this is more questionable). Fewer Quakers engaged in textile or leather production. On the other hand, professional men became considerably more prominent after 1750, and selling goods, whether on the retail or wholesale level, became much more important for Quakers than making them. If artisans or yeomen and husbandmen married early throughout our period, and professional men or wholesalers married late, then the increasing age at marriage of Quaker men would probably be just a compositional effect. What Table 3.12 shows, however, is that for those bridegrooms

Table 3.12 Ages at marriage by occupational groups, English Quakers

Occupation	1650–99			1700–49			1750–99			1800–49		
	n	Mean	Median	n	Mean	Median	n	Mean	Median	n	Mean	Median
Urban												
Men												
All	289	28.8	27.7	249	28.8	27.6	190	28.2	27.4	20	27.0	27.5
Textiles	110	27.5	26.4	79	28.1	27.4	32	27.5	26.6	4	26.0	27.0
Food	48	27.9	27.4	54	27.9	27.0	36	27.2	26.5	5	27.4	26.5
Leather	31	31.0	29.7	10	27.2	25.5	21	30.5	29.5	1	25.0	
Professional & clerical	13	29.0	28.5	38	29.8	28.4	32	27.8	27.0	2	26.5	
Wholesale trade	65	27.4	26.9	80	27.9	27.2	62	28.4	26.8	10	26.6	26.5
Retail trade	65	29.7	28.7	45	28.6	27.5	45	28.0	28.4	5	27.2	27.5
Artisans	149	28.4	27.7	102	28.0	27.0	57	28.5	27.2	2	29.0	
Rural												
Men												
All	329	30.1	29.2	406	30.1	28.8	499	30.1	29.0	256	29.3	28.7
Textiles	74	28.0	27.6	70	28.7	27.0	66	29.6	29.5	23	31.1	30.5
Food	38	30.7	28.0	100	29.8	26.9	138	30.8	30.0	46	29.1	28.5
Leather	26	30.2	29.0	45	29.1	28.8	29	28.8	27.7	6	29.5	30.0
Professional, clerical	22	32.5	31.0	29	31.3	31.3	72	31.0	29.2	87	29.0	28.0
Wholesale trade	76	29.2	27.2	131	29.9	27.8	180	30.4	29.8	75	29.7	28.6
Retail trade	44	30.6	31.0	86	29.1	27.0	91	29.6	28.4	31	29.5	28.7
Artisans	99	29.4	28.6	71	30.8	28.4	68	29.3	28.4	35	29.5	29.7
Agriculture	97	31.1	30.4	94	31.0	30.7	104	31.0	29.7	23	28.3	29.2

Fathers' occupation	1650–99			1700–49			1750–99			1800–49		
	n	Mean	Median	n	Mean	Median	n	Mean	Median	n	Mean	Median
Urban												
Women												
All	70	26.0	23.6	90	26.8	26.0	76	25.5	25.2	10	24.2	24.5
Textiles	15	25.6	22.3	33	26.8	25.5	13	25.7	26.5			
Food	11	32.0	25.7	15	27.4	25.6	17	25.8	26.3	2	24.0	
Leather	5	27.8	28.5	7	27.3	28.3	7	23.1	23.5			
Professional, clerical	11	24.0	22.5	26	28.6	27.0	15	26.2	24.7	3	26.7	28.3
Wholesale trade	27	28.3	25.7	37	27.7	25.5	26	25.9	25.5	4	24.8	25.5
Retail trade	7	30.7	28.5	16	26.2	26.5	14	24.1	24.5	1	22.0	
Artisans	22	24.8	22.0	36	26.7	26.6	25	25.6	25.5	1	21.0	
Rural												
Women												
All	109	26.5	25.8	179	27.0	26.2	246	28.0	26.2	151	26.9	26.7
Textiles	23	25.8	24.3	17	27.9	27.4	29	28.4	26.3	15	26.8	26.6
Food	28	25.2	25.4	42	25.7	25.5	83	28.2	27.5	40	27.3	27.4
Leather	10	22.8	22.5	11	26.4	25.7	11	30.8	24.7			
Professional clerical	5	27.4	28.5	11	23.2	24.3	30	24.8	25.0	38	27.2	27.0
Wholesale trade	37	24.3	23.5	57	25.9	25.4	93	27.6	26.4	46	26.8	27.0
Retail trade	17	27.1	27.3	29	29.1	28.5	35	28.1	26.8	20	27.1	26.7
Artisans	18	29.9	30.4	32	27.4	25.0	37	30.0	28.3	28	26.5	26.6
Agriculture	32	26.4	25.5	49	27.3	26.6	53	27.8	25.6	27	26.1	26.3

Notes: Cohorted by year of birth. Occupational groupings are as in Table 2.5.

whose occupations we know, the mean age at first marriage remained remarkably stable, not changing at all before 1800 outside the cities and in the cities showing a very gradual tendency to fall after 1750. This means that the rise in the age at first marriage which we find among the entire Quaker group must be concentrated among those whose occupations are unknown. It also appears that differences among the occupational groups are rather small. To some extent this is because some occupations have been put with two different groups, but even those classified in only one group, such as agricultural or professional workers, are consistently within a year of the mean. While textile workers were regularly below the mean, food workers usually were as well, while artisans showed no consistent pattern of deviation. Those engaged in agriculture married on average a year later than the mean for all with known occupations until the nineteenth century, when their mean age at first marriage was a year lower than the overall average. A similar pattern emerges for professional men; before 1750 they tended to marry a bit later, but as they became more numerous in the nineteenth century their average age at first marriage slipped below that for the whole sample.

In the population as a whole, it might be thought there is a more straightforward relationship between occupational groupings and ages at marriage, and indeed these have shown up in studies of individual parishes. For example, in three eighteenth-century Lancashire parishes, farmers and their wives married distinctly later than laborers, craftsmen, and the poor. In Ashford, Kent, from 1840 to 1865 the wives of laborers consistently married at earlier ages than the wives of retailers. But it is not clear whether these variations are more than local, especially since some of the occupational groups are very small. The largest study yet done suggests that whatever the effect on the ages at marriage of men, occupational differences were not noticeable in the age at first marriage of wives. In Nottinghamshire from 1701 to 1770, out of 1,410 brides, divided into occupational groupings of farmers and yeomen, husbandmen, laborers and servants, artisans and tradesmen, and gentlemen, the means were within a half year of 24 except for the laborers and servants, where the mean was 25.[36]

---

[36] P. E. Razzell, "Population growth and economic change in eighteenth- and early nineteenth-century England and Ireland," in *Land, Labour and Population*, ed. Jones and Mingay, 262. It is not clear whether the occupations referred to are those of the brides' fathers or husbands. For the Nottinghamshire study, see Martin, "Marriage and economic stress"; R. E. Jones "Population and agrarian change in an eighteenth-century Shropshire parish," *Local Population Studies* no. 1 (1968), 16; Loschky and Krier, "Income and family size"; and Carol G. Pearce, "Expanding families: some

It looks therefore as though the common fact of being Quakers had more to do with the age of marriage than the particular occupation which was followed; but before giving up any attempt to link age at marriage with the social structure we should consider another hypothesis which associates rise in age at first marriage with increased longevity in the parental generation. The linking mechanism is inheritance, required to set up the children in an independent household. If we assume that marriage ensues immediately upon inheritance, the children's age at the time of inheritance, and hence marriage, would be the number of years the parents lived after the child was born.[37] Our tables express this as the parents' life expectancy at the age when the child was born. (This assumes that fathers would not make *inter vivos* settlements to compensate children for the inconvenience of their delayed deaths.) An inheritance pattern which delayed children's marriages in this fashion would tend to stabilize the population, since longer life expectancy would automatically result in lower fertility. If, on the other hand, *inter vivos* settlements were common, the population would tend to rise.[38]

This hypothesis looks plausible when applied to the Quaker data, since there was a considerable increase in longevity at the same time the age at first marriage was rising in some parts of England. Since more men married between the ages of 25 and 29 than in any other quinquennium, their experience is the best single indicator of this. It is epitomized in Table 3.13. In Southern England, and also in the families represented in the genealogies, there was an over-all improvement in male life expectancy at this age: it went from 28.9 to 35.4 in Southern England and from 35.7 to 43.5 in the genealogies. In neither group was there an uninterrupted increase, but in both the sharpest rise was in the early eighteenth century, which saw more improvement than the 100 years after 1750. On the other hand, there was a steady *decline* in male life expectancy for this age group in Ireland, and two of the last three cohorts in the cities also showed a lower life expectancy than in the late seventeenth century. In the last cohort of Irish Quakers, however, the figures for life expectancy are deceptively lower because of a "truncation effect": no comprehensive search for deaths after 1837 was made, and so those who died before that date predominate in the

aspects of fertility in a mid Victorian community," *Local Population Studies* no. 10 (1973), 29.
[37] G. Ohlin, "Mortality, marriage, and growth in pre-industrial populations," *Population Studies* 14 (1961), 190–97.
[38] See E. A. Wrigley, "Fertility strategy for the individual and the group," in *Historical Studies in Changing Fertility*, ed. Charles Tilly (Princeton, 1978), 135–54 for a very thorough theoretical study of this relationship.

Table 3.13   *Expectation of life of adults aged 25–29, known dates of death only*

Area		1650–99	1700–49	1750–99	1800–49	1850–99
Ireland	M	34.1	33.9	32.7	NA	NA
	F	27.4	29.9	31.2	29.1	NA
Southern	M	28.9	32.9	37.0	35.4	NA
England	F	24.5	30.1	33.9	33.4	NA
Family	M	35.7	40.8	39.5	43.5	40.4
histories	F	34.7	35.7	36.4	35.9	36.7
Urban	M	29.8	28.1	33.0	27.1	NA
	F	25.7	26.7	30.6	32.1	NA

figures which were used to calculate life expectancy. But for the urban Quakers, at least, there is no plausible connection between life expectancy and age at marriage, since their later ages at marriage were associated with life expectancies in the parental generation which were on the whole lower. In the rest of England, it is possible that there was such a connection. It is difficult to be sure, partly because our cohorts are too long to make it easy to match up generations. One way to approach the question, however, is to look at the age at which children of different rank orders of birth could marry. The relevant figures are given in Table 3.14.

This tests the hypothesis about the relationship between parental life expectancy and age at marriage as follows: if nobody could marry until their father's death, and then the resources of the parental generation were made available to all the children,[39] one would expect that the older children in a family could marry at roughly the same time as the younger ones; therefore ages at first marriage should decline significantly as one went further down the rank order of birth. No such effect is consistently seen. If it were going to show up, it should have been among the Southern English men in the period from 1750 to 1800, when paternal longevity was certainly increasing; but, instead, the gap between the ages at marriage of the first and second sons actually declined as compared to the previous half-century, and the third and fourth sons married, on average, older than the first-born.

It is also obvious from inspecting Table 3.13 that the life expectancies

[39] In making their wills, Thomas Clarkson reports, the Quakers "are not apt to raise up an eldest son to the detriment of the rest of their offspring" (*Portraiture of Quakerism*, III, 273).

Table 3.14 *Mean age of children at marriage, by sex and birth rank*

		1		2		3		4		5		6		≥7	
		n	Mean	n	Mean	n	Mean	n	Mean	n	Mean	n	Mean	n	Mean
Ireland															
Males	1650–99	17	27.3	16	26.1	17	26.2	9	26.4	10	26.5	3	24.8	12	27.4
	1700–49	21	29.2	21	29.6	17	26.8	14	29.6	9	27.0	8	29.5	23	30.4
	1750–99	13	27.6	11	28.6	8	28.2	9	30.4	3	25.3	7	29.5	15	24.8
	1800–49	3	32.5	8	32.5	4	30.2	3	31.0	2	30.3	3	26.9	7	31.8
Females	1650–99	37	21.8	27	23.8	15	22.3	15	24.8	8	22.1	8	26.8	9	21.9
	1700–49	33	23.7	23	24.8	16	25.2	11	25.7	11	24.1	8	24.6	26	26.8
	1750–99	15	27.5	15	25.0	7	26.3	8	22.1	6	25.6	4	23.5	—	
	1800–49	5	25.8	6	27.8	2	23.3	7	27.2	1	23.2	3	29.1	11	28.3
Southern England															
Males	1650–99	41	27.8	21	30.2	18	26.4	10	28.2	6	21.4	3	27.0	4	30.6
	1700–49	40	28.9	27	27.1	18	27.5	16	31.5	10	30.8	9	29.2	12	25.7
	1750–99	32	29.7	26	28.7	15	30.5	22	30.3	14	28.0	6	28.7	12	31.2
	1800–49	5	27.2	2	26.2	2	31.1	1	30.8	4	27.5	—		1	26.7
Females	1650–99	48	25.5	43	26.6	27	27.1	27	28.4	9	26.1	8	26.9	8	27.4
	1700–49	48	26.4	40	28.9	32	27.6	29	26.1	21	29.4	5	27.9	16	28.5
	1750–99	32	27.3	35	28.4	22	28.6	16	31.1	9	25.2	5	30.0	18	28.8
	1800–49	7	24.6	6	23.9	9	26.1	7	26.2	2	24.7	4	27.9	10	26.6
Northern Britain															
Males	1650–99	22	32.7	17	29.5	12	30.5	7	28.9	7	28.8	4	24.6	12	27.8
	1700–49	39	31.7	33	28.9	22	29.0	20	28.2	14	31.7	14	30.2	12	30.7
	1750–99	64	28.9	48	29.8	53	30.5	31	30.4	23	30.7	17	27.9	42	31.8
	1800–49	125	29.4	90	29.8	74	29.2	64	29.1	47	30.0	46	29.1	97	29.0
Females	1650–99	18	24.9	14	25.7	12	23.9	12	28.4	9	27.1	4	26.1	10	31.6
	1700–49	26	26.6	30	25.9	23	29.5	17	25.9	16	25.9	9	26.0	15	29.1
	1750–99	50	24.2	61	26.4	37	28.3	37	27.3	22	27.3	26	29.2	33	32.3
	1800–49	90	27.3	75	26.7	57	26.1	50	28.5	35	29.7	28	28.3	76	27.7
Urban															
Males	1650–99	18	26.6	17	29.3	8	27.3	7	23.5	4	22.0	2	24.8	3	28.4
	1700–49	23	29.1	26	26.3	17	28.5	13	26.4	10	24.5	8	29.7	13	29.6
	1750–99	25	26.1	16	27.5	14	28.6	10	26.1	9	26.7	2	28.3	12	30.3
	1800–49	4	23.5	1	20.8	2	25.0	3	27.1	1	24.7	3	25.6	3	25.6
Females	1650–99	27	26.6	17	22.6	21	24.4	14	27.5	11	29.6	5	29.2	8	26.3
	1700–49	37	26.4	24	27.2	18	28.3	19	24.0	7	24.7	17	25.6	23	26.3
	1750–99	21	27.7	21	25.9	22	28.1	13	27.2	11	24.6	6	27.0	12	27.6
	1800–49	2	25.8	3	23.9	2	24.9	6	30.5	1	27.2	1	25.7	4	25.2

at this age are almost always higher than the average ages at first marriage. Thus the link between longevity and age at marriage, although plausible, does not appear to be behind the rising age at first marriage of the British and Irish Quakers. Furthermore, there is abundant literary evidence of marriage settlements enabling children to marry long before their fathers' deaths. A good many such settlements survive for the Northern Irish Quakers, and the biographies and autobiographies of English Friends suggest the practice was common there as well.

A third possible explanation, even more difficult to put to a direct test, is that postponement of marriage by both genders was a classic "Malthusian" response, mediated by their shared religious values and common life, to the increased marital fertility and lowered infant mortality experienced by Friends after 1750.

When T. R. Malthus wrote his first *Essay on the Principle of Population*, which appeared in 1798, he drew the evidence for the central propositions of the book not from official statistics (which were not available), but from his observations of the conduct of the people among whom he lived. The behavior patterns he describes bear such a striking resemblance to those which we may infer from the data relating to the Quakers that it seems worthwhile to sketch, briefly, Malthus's framework.[40]

In his first *Essay*, Malthus admitted to only three categories of factors inhibiting population growth: vice, misery, and moral restraint. We need not say much about the first two. "Vice," we may assume from the context and later comments, included abortion, contraception, infanticide, prostitution, homosexual practices, and perhaps masturbation. "Misery" meant famines and epidemics. These were, in the Malthusian vocabulary, the positive checks. The only way to insure that human beings were not driven to vice, and not subject to misery, was to allow the operation of the "preventive check" – that is, moral restraint. In its original form this meant, for a man, waiting until he had sufficient capital and income to support a family before he married and practicing perfect chastity until that time.

Through the five subsequent editions of the *Essay*, Malthus's position scarcely changed, except that in later writings he was realistic enough to admit that there was such as thing as "prudential restraint"; but whether this meant simply later marriage from prudential motives without, necessarily, complete abstinence, or whether it might have

[40] The analysis of the Malthusian framework is drawn mostly from D. E. C. Eversley, *Social Theories of Fertility and the Malthusian Debate* (Oxford, 1959), especially chs. 3, 4, and 9.

included a tacit acknowledgment that reproduction might in some way be limited within marriage by one method or another, we do not know for certain.[41]

What does matter is his first statement of how the preventive check worked:

The preventive check appears to operate in some degree through all the ranks of society in England. There are some men, even in the highest rank, who are prevented from marrying by the idea of the expences that they must retrench, and the fancied pleasures that they must deprive themselves of, on the supposition of having a family. These considerations are certainly trivial; but a preventive foresight of this kind has objects of much greater weight for its contemplation as we go lower.

A man of liberal education, but with an income only just sufficient to enable him to associate in the rank of gentlemen, must feel absolutely certain, that if he marries and has a family, he shall be obliged, if he mixes at all in society, to rank himself with moderate farmers, and the lower class of tradesmen. The woman that a man of education would naturally make the object of his choice, would be one brought up in the same tastes and sentiments with himself, and used to the familiar intercourse of a society totally different from that to which she must be reduced by that marriage. Can a man consent to place the object of his affections in a situation so discordant, probably, to her tastes and inclinations? Two or three steps of descent in society, particularly at this round of the ladder, where education ends, and ignorance begins, will not be considered by the generality of people, as a fancied and chimerical, but a real and essential evil. If society be held desireable, it surely must be free, equal, and reciprocal society, where benefits are conferred as well as received; and not such as the dependant finds with his patron, or the poor with the rich.

These considerations undoubtedly prevent a great number in this rank of life from following the bent of their inclinations in an early attachment. Others, guided either by a stronger passion, or a weaker judgment, break through these restraints; and it would be hard indeed, if the gratification of so delightful a passion as virtuous love, did not, sometimes, more than counterbalance all its attendant evils. But I fear it must be owned, that the more general consequences of such marriages, are rather calculated to justify, than to repress, the forebodings of the prudent.

The sons of tradesmen and farmers are exhorted not to marry, and generally find it necessary to pursue this advice, till they are settled in some business, or farm, that may enable them to support a family. These events may not, perhaps occur till they are far advanced in life. The scarcity of farms is a very general complaint in England. And the competition in every kind of business is so great, that it is not possible that all should be successful.[42]

Let us remember the time and the place: the passage is expanded, but never modified, from the first edition in 1798 to Malthus's death in 1834.

41 Eversley, *Social Theories*, 245–46.
42 Thomas Robert Malthus, *An Essay on the Principle of Population, As It Affects the Future Improvement of Society* (London, 1798), 63ff.

Malthus was born in Surrey, educated at Warrington Academy (a dissenting academy where he may well have encountered Quakers), and at Cambridge. After a short period as a curate, again in Surrey, he spent most of the rest of his life in Hertfordshire, where he taught at an Anglican school, but in a locality where Quakers (mostly business-men) were numerous. In their conduct, these affluent Hertfordshire Quakers were mostly indistinguishable from other families of the same social milieu in that period, as we may infer from their diaries, their biographies, and by looking at the houses where they lived.[43]

We should note that Malthus is writing about a fairly narrow social stratum in this passage, which is followed by another on "the labourer who earns eighteen pence a day" – a member of a quite different group, though also credited with the ability to exercise moral restraint. He is not speaking of the very rich landowners or the peerage. If, as we believe, he has caught the essence of the Quaker lifestyle, the question for us is whether this analysis applies only to Friends in the Home Counties. Were the "statesmen" of Westmorland, or the rural Irish Quakers, different in their habits? Was there (if we may use Nassau Senior's tripartite division of all consumption into necessities, decen-cies, and luxuries) less pressure on them to conform to the notions of "decency" in their lifestyle?

The post-Malthusian and anti-Malthusian literature is full of criti-cisms of other parts of his writings: his arithmetic and geometric ratios, his doubts about the perfectibility of the human race. Nowhere, however, is there any challenge of what we might call his political economy of marriage. What his most fervent followers (like Harriet Martineau) stressed was that pauperism, where it occurred, was mostly due to the imprudent and profligate habits of the working population.[44] Family size and age at marriage were invariably used as indicators of these moral deficiencies.

Some writers claimed that Malthus was demanding an impossibly high standard of morality from the population. He never quite gave up

---

[43] The lifestyle of the Quakers of the later period has not been specifically chronicled. See Richard T. Vann, *The Social Development of English Quakerism 1655–1755* (Cam-bridge, Mass., 1969), especially ch. 5, for an account of the traditional lifestyle. The best approach to knowing how the Southern Quakers lived at the turn of the nineteenth century may be found in Clarkson's *Portraiture of Quakerism* and in the biographies and journals of Friends (for a listing of the ones we read, see the bibliography). Such works as *Life of William Allen, with Selections from His Correspon-dence* (3 vols.: London, 1846) give a good picture of the social life of the leading Quaker business families of the period. Families like the Gurneys of Norwich, who produced Hannah Chapman Backhouse, were somewhat higher in the social scale.
[44] Harriet Martineau, *Illustrations of Political Economy* (9 vols.: London, 1832–34), especially *Weal and Woe in Garveloch*.

that demand, but in later editions "prudence" became much more prominent than "morals." Unfortunately he never spelled out exactly what distinguished the prudent man from the moral man. In practice, the Quaker population could fit either description; their discipline was designed to hold them to a high moral standard, and they were certainly prudent. Therefore the only question we cannot answer is precisely the one on which Malthus himself was vague, and which did not surface until the neo-Malthusian movement of the later nineteenth century: once married, did Friends still limit the number of children they produced? In the evidence we present below, and in chapter 4, we shall try to weigh the balance of probabilities. However, the first component of the classic Malthusian prescription, that a man should not marry, and would not marry, until he could support a wife and family in the style to which he and she were accustomed, is demonstrated in the age at marriage statistics, and also in the illustrations we can derive from the journals and autobiographies of the Quakers.

One of these gives a rare account of a Quaker courtship in the late eighteenth century. Catherine Phillips, the eventual bride, describes William Phillips as the agent to a copper company; he was also "considerably older than myself [so] that none of these circumstances could of themselves make a connection with him desirable."[45] She was already over 40 when they met; but both were very cautious, lest they marry outside God's will; and the wedding eventually took place in 1772, when the bride was 45.

Joseph Oxley also had to delay his marriage; as he explains, his eventual wife's family "were people of greater property in the world than I expected or thought of, and that might probably be some objection." Although Oxley does not say so, his worldly prospects had doubtless improved by the time he finally won the consent of the bride's family and their monthly meeting for the match.[46]

It is worth emphasizing that Malthus's "prudential restraint" did not require the fear of absolute destitution as a goad. We have mentioned already that there is no reason to believe that the real incomes of the Quakers were falling, or that they were in any danger of starvation through being over-burdened by children. Still, the increasing family size brought on by higher fertility and lower infant mortality would pose problems in families which needed to provide

---

[45] *Memoirs of the Life of Catherine Phillips* (London, 1797), 207–15.
[46] *Some Account of the Life of Joseph Pike: Also, a Journal of the Life and Gospel Labours of Joseph Oxley*, ed. John Barclay (London, 1837), 199, 217, 247; David H. Pratt, *English Quakers and the First Industrial Revolution: A Study of the Quaker Community in Four Industrial Counties – Lancashire, York, Warwick, and Gloucester, 1750–1830* (New York, 1985), 77–86.

dowries for their daughters and capital sums to set up sons in business or a profession, and more and more Friends were going into such occupations. If children could not bring in any income and if hundreds or even thousands of pounds had to be laid out for them in late adolescence, parents would have to have much higher incomes later in their married life, which perhaps could not be reasonably anticipated. The most reliable, and most morally acceptable, way to have smaller families, and thus to have fewer such expenses, would be to delay marriage.

Furthermore, there were positive advantages in concentrating capital if an advantageous marriage could eventually be worked out. This can be seen most dramatically among Quaker bankers; fully half of the banking families were connected by marriage with other banking families, and intermarriages between them and great wholesale traders in wool, cloth, iron, corn, tea, and wine assisted in the founding of branches. About a quarter of all country banks at the start of the Industrial Revolution were Quaker firms.[47] There was some slight check to the process in that the Quaker discipline did not allow marriage to cousins,[48] but there was nevertheless a dense network of relatives among the Quaker upper bourgeoisie.

Some of this need not have been, and indeed almost certainly was not, a matter for naked calculation of economic advantage. Although Catherine Phillips was undoubtedly more pious than most Quakers, her story only exhibits in emphatic form tendencies to which all Friends were subject. In fact, everything suggests the strong cultural determination of the age at marriage among the Quakers; unmediated economic and purely demographic factors were important, but hardly decisive. Specifically, in their marriage discipline Friends possessed an instrument which always had the effect of imposing at least a short delay on marriages, since the requisite permissions, certificates, and approvals by the various meetings prevented any hasty weddings. The strict requirements of parents' consent would prevent couples from launching out without an agreement from their parents that it

[47] Pratt, *English Quakers*, 73–77.
[48] For cousin marriages, see Arnold Lloyd, *Quaker Social History 1669–1738* (London, 1950), ch. 4, especially 58–59. In view of this prohibition it is interesting to note that oral tradition in the Society of Friends had it, as a joke, that they always intermarried, partly for financial reasons. In fact an analysis of over 1,000 marriages in the four-volume *Descendants of Isaac and Rachel Wilson of Kendal* by R. S. Benson *et al.* (Middlesbrough, 1949) showed only about 2 percent of all marriages took place between people who were second cousins or nearer kin; of these, there were only four cases of first-cousin marriages (among those who remained in membership; perhaps there were others who made such marriages and were disowned in consequence).

was time to transfer resources to the new generation. Further, the requirement that Friends marry only other Friends, enforced by the disownment of those who married outside the society, had the effect over the years of narrowing the horizons of those who wished to select their spouses in accordance with Friends' teaching (recall Figure 1.3). In the rural areas, in particular, the number of Friends steadily declined from the first part of the eighteenth century until about 1860.[49] As more and more Quaker women moved into the country towns and cities, they faced the familiar difficulties with which urbanization confronts the desire to get married – particularly the unfavorable ratio of men to women characteristic of most early modern cities.

As variety in choice of spouses declined, especially in areas where there were only a few Quaker families, a correspondingly greater temptation to marry outside meeting could be expected. Furthermore, some spotty but suggestive evidence indicates that such marriages were likely to be at an earlier age than the means of marriages approved by the meeting; in other words, the regulations for approval of marriages were delaying them. In the early eighteenth century in Buckinghamshire and Norfolk marriages contrary to Quaker order (which more often than not were marriages to other Quakers which had not been approved by the parents concerned) occurred at an earlier age; and those marriages within the genealogies which we know were solemnized outside meeting also occurred on average earlier in life.[50]

Even though these scattered data cannot be said to be statistically conclusive, they all point in the same direction: the Quaker marriage discipline itself was one cause of the rising age at first marriage. Those who wished to marry earlier than the norms of the Society of Friends allowed sometimes had to do so by violating the rules controlling marriage.

Quaker women found themselves particularly affected by the cultural patterns which Friends were developing. It appears that before 1750 they were on the whole more obedient to the discipline; men were more likely to be disowned or leave Friends for one reason or another than women.[51] Furthermore, men were considerably more

---

49 The best evidence of this is the list of monthly meetings in the Friends House Library, London. From around 1730 there is a steady contraction as more and more rural meetings were discontinued.

50 See Vann, *Social Development*, 187. Only a dozen marriages in the genealogies allow a comparison of ages at marriage inside and outside meeting.

51 The records of Southwark Monthly Meeting show both one of the causes and a likely consequence of such an imbalance. Prior to 1750 in the Southwark Monthly Meeting

Table 3.15   *Sex ratio at burial, all British and Irish Quakers except those who died aged under 20 years (men:100 women)*

	Southern England		Northern Britain		Genealogy		Urban		All England		Ireland	
	R	n	R	n	R	n	R	n	R	n	R	n
1700–49	97	694	122	173	125	146	102	733	103	1746	116	430
1750–99	104	742	111	192	113	269	89	553	101	1756	105	481
1800–49	97	589	136	186	105	497	86	363	100	1635	85	318

Note: *n* is the number of men buried.

likely to emigrate from England than women. However, after 1750 women were apparently more likely to break the rules by marrying non-Quakers. Despite this greater propensity to be disowned, there nevertheless came to be an increasing preponderance of women within the membership of the Society of Friends. By 1840 there were 120 women to every 100 men.[52] This trend shows up clearly in Table 3.15, which once again uses sex distributions at death in lieu of a census.

It would thus appear that Quaker women after 1750, particularly those in London, were in something of a "marriage squeeze," in competition for a decreasing number of Quaker men.[53] The fact that

more men than women were disciplined for infractions of the marriage discipline; but from 1750 to 1799 almost half again as many women as men (122 against 86) were disciplined for these reasons. Infractions seem to have been less common (or discipline was more slack) after 1800, and the two genders were equally likely to be involved in disciplinary proceedings.

[52] John Thurnam, *Observations and Essays on the Statistics of Insanity* (London, 1845), Appendix II, xix.

[53] The term "marriage squeeze" seems to have been invented by Paul C. Glick, David M. Heer, and John C. Beresford in their "Family formation and family composition: trends and prospects," in *Sourcebook in Marriage and the Family*, ed. Marvin B. Sussman (New York, 1963), 38. Much of the thinking about it, however, has been done by Louis Henry, see especially "Nuptiality," *Theoretical Population Biology* 3 (1972), 136–52; "Schéma d'évolution des mariages après de grandes variations des naissances," *Population* 30 (1975), 759–80; "Perturbations de la nuptialité résultant de la guerre 1914–1918," *ibid.*, 21 (1966), 273–32; and "Schémas de nuptialité: déséquilibre des sexes et âge au mariage," *ibid.* 24 (1969), 1067–122 (and a similar article on celibacy, *ibid.*, 457–86). See also Gerhard Mackenroth, *Bevölkerungslehre: Theorie, Soziologie und Statistik der Bevölkerung* (Berlin, 1953), 17–19. The subject first came to the attention of demographers because of the enormous loss of male lives in World War I, and unfortunately for our purposes they started from census materials and a known imbalance between the genders and then tried to work out the demographic consequences of this. H. V. Muhsam, "The marriage squeeze," *Demography* 11 (1974), 291–99 points out the great variety of reasons whereby a theoretical freedom to marry anyone of the opposite gender is abridged; but he also says (295) that a marriage squeeze may lead to more, about the expected number, or fewer marriages.

women's ages at first marriage rose faster than men's, that definitive celibacy seems to have been higher for women, and probably also the fact that proportionately more women married non-Quakers after 1750[54] are likely consequences of this squeeze.

For men, of course, the surplus of available brides, in the absence of other considerations, might have caused the average age at first marriage to decline, but this effect was apparently over-ridden by the expectation that a bridegroom should be able to provide for what looked like being a larger family, even if the full rise in fertility was mitigated by a delay in marriage. It also appears that one of the cultural values influencing Quaker marriages was a preference for marrying someone nearer one's own age. It is this which may explain what Table 3.1 has already shown: that the direction of changes in men's and women's ages at marriage was almost always the same, and though the gap between the two widened and narrowed in a somewhat irregular way, it was generally less at the end of our period than at the beginning.

A more thorough explanation of this can be seen in Table 3.16, which shows that the ages at first marriage of men and women may have drawn closer together than the means themselves indicate. The sums of the last four columns in this table might be called an "age disparity index": that is, the percentage of persons marrying for the first time who were more than five years apart in age. In all four areas there was – with one trifling exception – an uninterrupted decline in this index. The most dramatic example is the English cities, where 47.8 percent of those marrying were separated by more than five years in the late seventeenth century but only 34.2 percent in the early nineteenth. The values for the other areas were roughly the same in the late seventeenth century – in fact in Northern England and Scotland more than half of the couples had at least a five-year age disparity – and declined to around 40 percent in the first half of the nineteenth century.

This obviously makes it extremely hazardous to infer from a high definitive celibacy rate or a rise in ages at first marriage that there was necessarily a marriage squeeze.

54 At least if the statistics from Southwark Monthly Meeting (see n. 51) are representative. They coincide with what Friends themselves thought; Thomas Clarkson was told that "the number of the women who are disowned for marrying out of the Society far exceeds the number of the men who are disowned on the same account" (*Portraiture of Quakerism*, II, 23). His explanation for this is the greater desirability of Quaker women, on account of their education, prudence, and sobriety, which led a good many "men of the world" to pay court to them. He also contrasted the garb and peculiar manners of Quaker men, which would likely make them relatively unattractive to non-Quaker women, with the attire (considered "neat and elegant") and the demure manners of Quaker women.

Table 3.16   *Relationship between husbands' and wives' ages at first marriage*

Time	Husband older		5–9 years older		>10 years older		Wife 5–9 older		>10 years older	
	n	%	*n*	%	*n*	%	*n*	%	*n*	%
Ireland										
1650–99	48	75.0	17	26.6	8	12.5	7	10.0		
1700–49	55	76.4	21	29.2	9	12.5	4	6.9		
1750–99	35	81.4	13	30.2	4	9.3	2	7.4		
1800–49	22	81.5	8	29.6	2	7.4	1	3.7		
Southern England										
1650–99	29	65.9	12	27.3	8	18.2	1	2.3		
1700–49	123	72.4	40	23.5	19	11.2	9	5.3	6	3.5
1750–99	195	69.6	60	21.4	35	12.5	21	7.5	12	4.3
1800–49	105	62.5	26	15.5	14	14.9	15	8.9	5	3.0
Northern Britain										
1650–99	17	77.3	10	45.5	1	4.5	1	4.5		
1700–49	74	78.7	29	30.9	15	16.0	7	7.4		
1750–99	131	70.1	43	23.0	21	11.2	12	6.4	2	1.1
1800–49	218	75.2	68	23.4	36	12.4	12	4.1	2	0.7
1850–99	157	75.1	54	25.8	25	12.0	4	1.9		
Urban										
1650–99	49	73.1	14	20.9	12	17.9	3	4.5	3	4.5
1700–49	142	68.9	46	22.3	17	8.3	19	9.2	4	1.9
1750–99	138	60.8	42	18.5	21	9.3	17	7.5	4	1.8
1800–49	65	58.6	16	14.4	7	6.3	11	9.9	4	3.6

Note: Known remarriages of men are excluded; for women, the age is known to be that of the first marriage. Families from the genealogies are aggregated with those from Northern England, and make up the entire 1850–99 cohort.

Declines of this sort are associated with greater longevity in adults (discussed in chapter 5). When many were cut off in young adulthood, men would tend to remarry considerably younger women, and propertied widows would have a good chance, if they wished, of marrying a younger man. As such catastrophes became less common, ages at marriage moved closer together: a sign of the modern "intimate family."[55]

Table 3.16 reminds us also that among the Quakers marriage to an older woman was not at all uncommon. This was especially so in Southern England and in the cities, where by the early nineteenth century around two-fifths of the brides were older than their husbands. In a significant number of such cases (over 10 percent in the

[55] This is the argument of Arthur E. Imhof, "From the old mortality pattern to the new: implications of a radical change from the sixteenth to the twentieth century," *Bulletin of the History of Medicine* 59 (1985), 1–29.

last cohort) the bride was five or more years older. It is no surprise to find a considerable number of older wives; this, along with a fairly small age gap between spouses, has been taken to be one of the characteristics of the northwestern European marriage pattern.[56] But nowhere in northwestern Europe were as many as 40 percent of wives older than their husbands; among colonial American Quakers, the comparable figure was only 10 percent.[57] The increasing number of men marrying women older than themselves (in Southern England and the cities) is also associated with the decreasing age disparity between marriage partners, since the age at first marriage of women rose more steeply than that of men. Faced with a greater choice of prospective brides, those Quaker men who remained faithful to the testimonies about marriage did not seize the chance to marry younger women, but instead increasingly chose those roughly their own age, or even somewhat older ones. They seem to have preferred greater congruity in experience to whatever delights of the flesh which might be supplied by younger women.[58]

These later ages at marriage of British Quaker wives, as we have seen, were associated with a rise in definitive celibacy: a "marriage squeeze" arising from the disproportionate number of women Friends. In Geneva, there was a similar "marriage squeeze" – Louis Henry goes so far as to call it a "crisis of nuptiality" – which was most intense throughout the eighteenth century. Almost 30 percent of Genevan bourgeois women born between 1700 and 1750, and more than 30 percent in the following half-century, never married. Even in the fifty-year periods on either side, a quarter of the women remained celibate. Oddly, however, the Genevan crisis had no uniform relationship to ages at first marriage. Although both definitive celibacy and age at first marriage were high prior to around 1750, the chances of ever marrying became even lower for Genevan bourgeois women after 1750; but those who did marry did so at an increasingly lower age.[59]
    The trend of ages at first marriage for the British Quakers was almost the same as that for the wives and sisters of the British nobility, although consistently three or four years later. The British nobility,

---

[56] Peter Laslett, *Family Life and Illicit Love in Earlier Generations: Essays in Historical Sociology* (New York, 1977), 26–28. See also James Matthew Gallman, "Relative ages of colonial marriages," *Journal of Interdisciplinary History* 14 (1984), 609–17.

[57] Wells, "Marriage patterns," 415–42.

[58] Clarkson, *Portraiture of Quakerism* (III, 302) makes a point of extolling the companionable nature of Quaker marriages, and the fact that wives and husbands were together in society much more than was customary in the world at large.

[59] Henry, *Anciennes familles genevoises*, 52.

too, had a high level of definitive celibacy, and, as with the British Quakers, age at first marriage rose sympathetically with levels of definitive celibacy.

These suggestions must remain hypotheses as long as some of our statistical measures are indirect and we lack first-hand information about the actual matrimonial strategies of eighteenth- and nineteenth-century Friends. But should our string of hypotheses prove correct, it would be a striking confirmation of the Weber thesis, since religious values at first blush remote from economic concerns, such as the need to preserve religious harmony within the family, would turn out to have advantageous economic and demographic consequences, in promoting capital accumulation and limiting the dispersal of resources that would have occurred if the rise in marital fertility and decline in infant mortality had not been counter-balanced in any way. The exact line between pious and prudent behavior is always difficult to draw in the Puritan tradition, and perhaps never more so than when we try to explain Quaker marriage patterns. But it seems clear that although the Quakers could not consider marriage and child-bearing as purely, or even primarily, matters of economic calculation, their cultural life and religious beliefs worked towards a "rational" – even if unconsciously rational – demographic response.

4

The fruitfulness of the faithful

Just as Quaker marriages were distinctive, so were their patterns of child-bearing after marriage. In fact, investigation of their fertility produced some of our most surprising findings; but before we give these, we should briefly explain how we measured fertility.

As is usual among demographers, we focus on women and count, in various ways, the number of children which married women bore. With the Quakers, the emphasis on married women is justified by the fact that marital fertility was virtually the total fertility. Although there is no record of any illegitimate births in Friends' registers, since mothers of bastards would have been promptly disowned, there is no reason to believe that illegitimate births amount to more than a minute fraction of the total births to Quaker women.[1]

Fertility, to Anglo-Saxon demographers, is measured in the number of live births. It would obviously be desirable to know more about fecundity, or the capacity to conceive; but this would require knowledge of how often conceptions occurred as well as the frequency of live births, and while the latter can be counted, there is no way to tell how many pregnancies ended in miscarriages. Even stillbirths are not included in our figures, which express fertility only in terms of live births.

Live births can be measured in a number of different ways, each of which illuminates a different aspect of Quaker reproductive behavior. The three basic measures are: family size, age-specific fertility rates, and intergenesic intervals. All require some preliminary explanation.

"Family size" states how many children were ever born in a given family. It must not be confused with a measurement of household

---

[1] Only two came to the attention of Southwark Monthly Meeting during the 180 years covered by our study, and none have been mentioned in the records of any other monthly meeting we have searched.

size, which would specify how many children were living in a family at a given time. The latter, of course is the proper measure of how the family's fertility was experienced; but it is the whole record of a woman's fertility, without regard to the subsequent fate of her offspring, that interests us at the moment. "Completed family size" states how many live births there were in unions where the mother remained married (and in observation) until her 45th birthday. (Although women sometimes bore children after the age of 45, this was so uncommon that this age is conventionally taken to be the one at which women's reproductive career is over.) When we can compare women who married at the same ages, completed family size is a pure measure of fertility, since we have excluded all cases where the woman's child-bearing career was cut short by death. Because of this exclusion, however, the number of cases for "completed family size" is smaller than for any other measure of fertility – in some cohorts, too small to justify complete reliance on the findings.

Many more women's experience can be analyzed if the measure is age-specific fertility. Here we count live births within successive five-year age periods, once again comparing women of the same ages. Should a union be ended prematurely by the death of one of the spouses, or if for some reason the family passes out of observation, data concerning fertility completed up to that time can still be used. Age-specific fertility is expressed as the number of births per year in a particular age-group per 1,000 years lived by women within that age group.

A family is "in observation" as long as further demographic events pertaining to it are still being recorded. Here, however, we have to be careful not to introduce a bias. Suppose the last event recorded is the birth of a child. We could include the interval before the last birth, but when measuring age-specific fertility, we cannot allow the last event showing the family is still in observation to be the birth of yet another child, since this would obviously introduce a bias towards overstating fertility. For this reason for many fertility calculations it is a death or remarriage which terminates the period of being in observation; for mortality calculations, it is usually a birth.

The final fertility measure is relatively straightforward: the average number of months between births of different ranks. This measure can be useful even when we do not know the age of the mother, as long as we know when she married and the order in which the births occurred. This therefore can allow a still further expansion of the numbers measured. However, birth intervals are obviously germane only to families that are still producing children; one which stops early or has no children at all cannot have its particular experience caught by this measure.

While there is a value in having measures which apply to many cases, the most interesting findings often come when we know both the age at marriage and the intergenesic intervals. This is particularly important when we were trying to find out whether couples were deliberately limiting the size of their families. Women's fecundity naturally declines with age; but if women of the same age who already have several children stop or markedly slow the pace of child-bearing, while their exact contemporaries with fewer children keep on having them at the same rate, deliberate fertility control is the probable explanation.

To some degree family size, age-specific fertility, and intergenesic intervals can be translated into one another. If all married women space their births exactly two years apart, the age-specific fertility rate will be exactly 500, whereas a rate of 333 means that the average interval between births was three years for women in that age-group. Age-specific fertility rates for successive five-year periods can be summed and, when multiplied by five, give a notional figure for total marital fertility (children ever born). The figure is deceptively high, since to achieve that family size a woman would have to marry exactly at 20 and bear children at the average rate all through her reproductive span; but it is still useful for comparing areas and periods.

For analytical purposes it is best to start with a measure of fertility alone for women of comparable ages, and to be as precise as possible about the timing of change. Our strategy will be to get a picture of age-specific fertility of the entire British and Irish Quaker populations – bearing in mind its different composition in the various time-periods (Table 2.3). This is given by Table 4.1.

The range of variation between periods here is striking. The highest rates are from 15 to 30 percent greater than the lowest, while the range of figures for total fertility is about 20 percent. As for the trend, there are two possible interpretations. If we consider only the first century, there appears to have been an oscillating pattern. Fertility was relatively low in the late seventeenth century, particularly for women between their twentieth and twenty-fifth years. It rose slightly in the first quarter of the eighteenth century, but then fell to an even lower level in the second quarter. Then there was another rise, a bit stronger than the one in the first quarter of the century. These oscillations suggest that the Quakers may have shared in the

Table 4.1   *Age-specific marital fertility rates, all British and Irish Quakers*

Wife's age period	1675–99	1700–24	1725–49	1750–74	1775–99	1800–24	1825–49
<20	440 (84)	329 (85)	310 (116)	354 (65)	367 (49)	200 (21)	313 (16)
20–24	415 (646)	423 (826	422 (798)	463 (655)	491 (635)	467 (481)	429 (211)
25–29	423 (1,092)	437 (1,493)	405 (1,561)	439 (1,522)	477 (1,521)	437 (1,234)	448 (766)
30–34	369 (1,214)	380 (1,643)	343 (1,848)	373 (1,885)	421 (1,780)	410 (1,575)	393 (992)
35–39	277 (1,075)	282 (1,578)	263 (1,723)	287 (1,853)	313 (1,660)	329 (1,481)	299 (922)
40–44	144 (890)	132 (1,313)	126 (1,465)	142 (1,700)	146 (1,476)	173 (1,226)	132 (808)
45–49	33 (796)	30 (1,084)	17 (1,319)	21 (1,489)	29 (1,330)	23 (1,108)	18 (759)
Total marital fertility (sum of 20–49 × 5)	8.31	8.43	7.88	8.63	9.39	9.20	8.60

Notes: Women married at all ages under 50 are included, but those married under age 20 have been omitted from total fertility calculations because of the extreme rarity of cases. Figures in parentheses represent the number of women years lived on which the rate is calculated, and thus show the size of the sample included.

demography of a society where the "negative feedback" effect limiting the expansion of resources had not been overcome.[2]

There is, however, another way to interpret the trend from 1650 to 1750, which is to see it as a long, although uneven, rise in fertility, with a temporary drop in the second quarter of the eighteenth century. This interpretation is much more plausible when the figures after 1750 are taken into account; for our picture of fluctuations around a mean value changes radically after 1750. The rise in fertility from 1750 to 1774 was not only in itself much more dramatic than that of fifty years earlier (a 9.5 as against a 2 percent rise in total marital fertility); it assumes further significance from the fact that it was followed not by another fall but by a further 9 percent rise, attaining its peak in the last quarter of the eighteenth century. We believe that some degree of conscious

[2] On this see E. A. Wrigley, *Population and History* (London, 1969), 53–59.

fertility control may account for the slight decline in total marital fertility in the next quarter century and the somewhat sharper fall from 1825 to 1849; but even then the level was almost as high as it had been in 1750–74, and higher than it had been before 1750. Here again, the Quaker experience is comparable to the general take-off in population which occurred throughout Europe in the last half of the eighteenth century.

The decline in fertility after 1825, perhaps foreshadowed by the slighter decline after 1800, seems to mark the beginning of the "demographic transition" for the British and Irish Quakers. It can be clearly seen in the figures after 1850. But their fertility curves are somewhat different from the traditional idea of the "demographic transition." Before 1850 their population, instead of maintaining a high level of fertility which could be considered "natural" and then slowly decreasing in response to lowered mortality, oscillated for the century before 1750 around a level which looks lower than other examples of "natural fertility." Most of our Quaker figures for marital fertility, for example, are slightly to somewhat lower than the averages of thirty-eight family reconstitution studies, mostly from France, which were chosen by Daniel Scott Smith so as to exclude parishes where family limitation appears to have been in use.[3] Only in one of the seven quarter-centuries do our figures surpass the (mostly eighteenth-century) ones summarized by Smith.

The fertility experience of the Quakers is placed in a broader context in Table 4.2. Unfortunately, the most significant comparisons are difficult or impossible to make. The most useful would be with the rest of the Irish population, but there are no directly comparable figures prior to the 1851 census. At that time marital fertility in Ireland was 21 percent higher than in England; an estimate of the crude birth rate in the two countries going back to 1822 shows the Irish one as consistently higher, though by less of a margin.[4] It seems probable that marital fertility was comparably high in the eighteenth century, but there is little evidence one way or the other.[5]

Results from twenty-six family-reconstitution studies of various English parishes have been published, but only thirteen cover the

3 Daniel Scott Smith, "A homeostatic demographic regime," in *Population Patterns in the Past*, ed. Ronald Demos Lee (New York, 1977), 23.
4 Joel Mokyr and Cormac Ó. Gráda, "New developments in Irish population history, 1700–1850," *Economic History Review* 2nd ser. 37 (1984), 479; Phelim P. Boyle and Cormac Ó Gráda, "Fertility trends, excess mortality, and the Great Irish Famine," *Demography* 23 (1986), 550.
5 Mokyr and Ó Gráda, "New developments," 480; Boyle and Ó Gráda, "Fertility trends," 543.

Friends in life and death

Table 4.2 *Comparison of fertility, British and Irish Quakers, French Catholics, Québecois, and English parishes (all ages at marriage)*

Area and period	Wife's age period					
	20–24	25–29	30–34	35–39	40–44	Total
Irish Quakers						
1650–99	443	438	421	360	192	9.27
1700–49	488	460	442	343	154	9.44
1750–99	598	502	470	426	204	11.00
1800–49	514	445	437	366	167	9.65
Urban Quakers						
1650–99	401	445	372	277	128	8.12
1700–49	405	396	356	250	115	7.61
1750–99	444	463	418	303	149	8.89
1800–49	518	498	460	319	152	9.74
Remaining British Quakers						
1650–99	385	371	327	249	154	7.43
1700–49	389	414	332	260	129	7.62
1750–99	461	450	379	283	137	8.55
1800–49	437	432	391	314	157	8.66
13 English Parishes						
1650–99	409	364	306	248	126	7.27
1700–49	415	364	306	238	126	7.29
1750–99	423	356	289	237	133	7.19
4 English Parishes, 1780–1820	427	361	318	261	162	7.65
Quebec, c. 1700	522	522	512	495	NA	10.26
30 French Parishes, 18th century	475	453	402	318	157	9.03
91 French parishes, pre–1750	467	445	401	325	168	9.03
73 French parishes, 1749–90	496	459	400	309	148	9.06
45 French parishes, 1789–1820	458	383	329	245	120	7.68

Sources: For the thirteen English parishes (pooled data) see E. A. Wrigley and R. S. Schofield, "English population history from family reconstitution: summary results," *Population Studies* 37 (1983), 169. For the four English parishes from 1780 to 1820, see Michael W. Flinn, *The European Demographic System, 1500–1820* (Baltimore, 1981), 103–7. The larger samples of French parishes also come from this source. Data from Quebec are from Jacques Henripin, *La Population canadienne au début du XVIIIᵉ siècle: nuptialité, fécondité, mortalité infantile* (Paris, 1974), 65. The sample of thirty eighteenth-century parishes, chosen to exclude those where family limitation was apparently being practiced, is from Daniel Scott Smith, "A homeostatic demographic regime," in *Population Patterns in the Past*, ed. Ronald Demos Lee (New York, 1977), 23. We have excluded the five German, one Flemish, and one Danish parishes and also the reconstitution study of the Genevan bourgeoisie which Smith included. For nine of his thirty parishes the reconstitution began in the seventeenth century (there are very few French parish registers before 1650) and one parish, Coulommiers, was studied only for the period 1670–95.

period after 1750, and not all of these use the same cohorts or measures.[6] We are somewhat better informed about France, where more than a hundred studies have been published; but there we are limited in chronological range by the comparatively late starting date of the French parochial registers. The excellent sources for the early population of French Canada provide a further point of comparison and, it seems, show how high fertility can go.

Figures for twenty-six English parishes, out of some 10,000, and not chosen randomly, cannot be fully representative; even 100 parishes, considering that France had a population several times as large as England's, are a minute and non-random sample. Nevertheless these data do tend to confirm what we know from studies using aggregative and other methods. In particular, until about 1780 English marital fertility appears to have lagged consistently behind that of France. At most age periods the French figures were 15 to 25 percent higher than in the English parishes. The French Canadian, in turn, are consistently higher than the French – or even the Irish Quaker. It is particularly remarkable that French Canadian women were almost as fertile in the age period 35–39 as they had been in their early twenties; none of these other groups of women maintained anything like the same fertility levels after fifteen years.

Marital fertility in the English population as a whole, besides lagging consistently behind that of the French or Québecois, also

---

6 The most comprehensive data derived from family reconstitution on fertility in the general English population are contained in C. Wilson, "Natural fertility in pre-industrial England 1600–1799," *Population Studies* 38 (1984), 225–40. Wilson adds the results of two parish reconstitutions to the thirteen cited in E. A. Wrigley and R. S. Schofield, "English population history from family reconstitution: summary results 1600–1799," *Population Studies* 37 (1983), 157–84. Fertility measures for three parishes were published by David Levine in *Family Formation in an Age of Nascent Capitalism* (New York, 1977). These were Terling, Bottesford, and Shepshed. Other published studies used in Michael Flinn's summaries, besides the inevitable Colyton, are for parishes in the Forest of Arden (V. Skipp, *Crisis and Development: An Ecological Case-Study of the Forest of Arden, 1570–1674*, Cambridge, 1978) and for Moreton Say, Shropshire, 1690–1840 (R. E. Jones, "Population and agrarian change in an eighteenth-century Shropshire parish," *Local Population Studies* no. 1 [1968], 6–29). Besides these, see studies of Chesham, Buckinghamshire (Dorothy McLaren, "Nature's contraceptive: wet-nursing and prolonged lactation: the case of Chesham, Bucks. 1578–1601," *Medical History* 23 [1979], 426–41); Charlton-on-Otmoor (C. F. Küchemann, A. J. Boyce, and G. A. Harrison, "A demographic and genetic study of a group of Oxfordshire villages," *Human Biology* 39 [1967], 251–76); and three parishes in the Lonsdale hundred of Lancashire, Over Kellet, Gressingham, and Claughton (David J. Loschky and Donald F. Krier, "Income and family size in three eighteenth-century Lancashire parishes: a reconstitution study," *Journal of Economic History* 29 [1969], 429–48). Like Jones, these authors made no chronological divisions within their sample and were interested chiefly in possible relationships between wealth and social rank and fertility.

changed very little; figures from the English parish registers show almost no rise in age-specific fertility before 1800. There was in fact a very small decline in the last half of the eighteenth century. On the other hand, the marital fertility of the English Quakers, which prior to 1750 (apart from the urban ones) had been about the same as in the sample of twenty-six, now became unmistakably higher.

The new picture of English population history emerging from the aggregative studies of E. A. Wrigley and Roger Schofield emphasizes that the main element in the rise of population after 1750 was an increase in the birth rate; but since they find no rise in age-specific marital fertility, they argue that in the population as a whole, the chief mechanism promoting higher fertility was an earlier age at marriage (with a small contribution being made by a higher illegitimate birth rate).[7] Prior to 1750 the British (but not the Irish) Quakers fit the picture of pre-industrial England as a "low-fertility" society. After 1750, however, we see a fairly steep rise in marital fertility, which even after it began to decline still stayed at a somewhat higher level than earlier. From 1750 on, too, the fertility of the British and Irish Quakers became steadily higher than that in the French parishes. But while the Quaker population, like that of England as a whole, experienced a rising birth rate, it was in other respects quite different; ages at marriage were also rising, and there were no illegitimate births to augment the totals. The Quaker experience shows that a number of different tributaries fed the swelling stream of population in the eighteenth century. Among the Quakers, at least, higher fertility was achieved not by earlier marriages or by higher proportions marrying but by a faster pace of child-bearing after a somewhat delayed marriage.

This then suggests one striking problem: why did this segment of the British and Irish population experience such markedly higher fertility after 1750? And when we go from our composite picture of all Quakers to the regional break-down, another problem in interpretation arises. To begin again with the measure of pure fertility, let us consider the experience of women who married between age 20 and 34 – by far the

[7] The germ of this interpretation can already be seen in E. A. Wrigley's famous article "Family limitation in pre-industrial England," *Economic History Review* 2nd ser. 19 (1966), 82–109. For a good short statement of the argument see Wrigley, "The growth of population in eighteenth-century England: a conundrum resolved," *Past and Present* 98 (1983), 121–50. It is more thoroughly developed in Wrigley and R. S. Schofield, *The Population History of England, 1541–1871: A Reconstruction* (Cambridge, Mass., 1981), especially 236–48. Family limitation, however, receives very little attention in this book. The same argument, though supported with less proficient demographic technique, may be found in Levine, *Family Formation*, 95–98.

Table 4.3   *Family size, completed families only, all marriage ranks*

Wives' age at marriage	1650–99			1700–49			1750–99			1800–49		
	n	Mean	s.d.	n	Mean	s.d.	n	Mean	s.d.	n	Mean	s.d.
Ireland												
20–24	13	7.8	3.7	31	7.9	3.1	10	8.7	4.0	5	6.4	2.8
25–29	8	5.0	1.1	17	6.9	2.3	11	6.6	3.3	7	5.7	3.9
30–34	7	5.3	1.8	6	4.2	2.5	3	6.7	1.2	2	4.5	0.7
Southern England												
20–24	25	4.5	2.8	64	5.9	3.0	90	6.6	3.8	28	6.0	3.7
25–29	17	5.5	2.8	56	4.8	3.2	99	5.1	3.1	39	5.5	3.1
30–34	13	4.0	2.7	39	4.0	2.3	48	2.9	2.5	20	4.0	2.4
Northern England												
20–24	9	7.6	NA	42	6.4	NA	47	8.1	NA	80	6.8	NA
25–29	5	6.2	NA	16	5.0	NA	39	6.2	NA	59	6.2	NA
30–34	3	4.3	NA	11	4.3	NA	15	4.1	NA	28	4.4	NA
Urban												
20–24	14	6.1	4.0	45	6.3	4.2	35	6.8	3.8	11	7.6	4.2
25–29	12	4.4	3.9	35	4.1	3.4	46	6.5	3.0	20	5.8	3.2
30–34	19	3.8	2.4	30	3.6	2.0	25	4.3	2.6	10	3.6	2.1

majority of Quaker women – and who remained alive and in observation until age 45. This is given in terms of completed family size in Table 4.3 and in age-specific fertility rates in Table 4.4.

As one might expect, the variations here are even more marked than in the aggregate figures. The highest figure among the four time periods is seldom less than 20 percent higher than the lowest, and quite often much more. When numbers are smaller, variations are bound to be greater; but by no means all variation is explainable in this way. Even our largest subdivision, Southern England, shows fluctuations of more than a third in the fertility rates of women married between ages 30 and 34.

Not only are there considerable differences over time; the differences between the various areas are even more impressive. The eye-catching figure is certainly the Irish one. Some of their fertility rates exceed even those of the Hutterites, who have long served as the standard for unrestrained and enthusiastic fertility (though Québecois women of the late seventeenth century in fact deserve this title). The highest fertility rate ever attained by a five-year age group of Hutterite wives was 501, which shows the extraordinary character of the rates

Table 4.4 Age-specific fertility rates, all marriage ranks

Wife's age period	Wife's age at marriage											
	20–24				25–29				30–34			
	I	II	III	IV	I	II	III	IV	I	II	III	IV
Southern England												
20–24	353 (133)	389 (337)	440 (421)	417 (143)								
25–29	365 (203)	432 (618)	438 (792)	437 (300)	404 (114)	419 (301)	419 (432)	391 (198)				
30–34	263 (175)	313 (511)	344 (694)	340 (259)	377 (154)	364 (453)	398 (704)	416 (351)	311 (61)	378 (185)	401 (172)	425 (105)
35–39	177 (141)	203 (438)	247 (584)	279 (204)	240 (129)	272 (375)	261 (612)	280 (304)	384 (73)	366 (273)	296 (301)	404 (141)
40–44	31 (128)	81 (360)	103 (496)	99 (151)	200 (100)	136 (308)	131 (535)	178 (214)	227 (66)	193 (212)	123 (253)	161 (118)
45–49	0 (103)	3 (301)	17 (414)	7 (134)	12 (85)	15 (260)	18 (450)	16 (185)	36 (56)	26 (192)	34 (237)	0 (100)
Total	5.94	7.09	7.94	7.89	6.16	6.03	6.13	6.40	4.79	4.81	4.27	4.95
Northern Britain												
20–24	506 (38)	434 (166)	502 (213)	425 (287)								
25–29	414 (70)	442 (337)	518 (454)	450 (675)	500 (20)	400 (95)	481 (212)	419 (322)				
30–34	385 (65)	323 (316)	401 (384)	363 (592)	320 (25)	420 (150)	434 (318)	430 (481)	444 (9)	388 (67)	414 (58)	438 (162)
35–39	323 (65)	236 (263)	318 (318)	264 (518)	280 (25)	301 (113)	338 (260)	352 (372)	267 (15)	360 (75)	371 (89)	422 (211)
40–44	123 (57)	138 (225)	167 (251)	129 (442)	280 (25)	129 (85)	192 (213)	179 (313)	333 (15)	193 (57)	187 (80)	191 (157)

Ireland

20–24	467 (180)	481 (260)	561 (98)	487 (39)								
25–29	454 (251)	468 (425)	500 (172)	411 (90)	412 (102)	508 (128)	476 (63)	491 (53)				
30–34	401 (212)	449 (321)	368 (144)	373 (83)	456 (171)	506 (180)	593 (123)	443 (70)	486 (37)	429 (49)	452 (31)	429 (8)
35–39	345 (145)	336 (271)	377 (106)	375 (56)	355 (124)	365 (148)	461 (89)	268 (41)	418 (55)	371 (70)	594 (32)	400 (15)
40–44	125 (72)	121 (182)	208 (72)	69 (29)	182 (66)	202 (99)	141 (64)	171 (35)	279 (43)	200 (45)	471 (17)	400 (10)
45–49	46 (65)	15 (136)	23 (43)	0 (25)	44 (45)	49 (81)	57 (53)	86 (35)	86 (35)	0 (27)	0 (15)	0 (8)
Total	9.19	9.34	10.18	8.57	7.24	8.15	8.64	7.29	6.34	5.00	7.58	6.14

Urban

20–24	404 (109)	393 (243)	449 (196)	521 (73)								
25–29	445 (173)	405 (439)	462 (383)	511 (141)	457 (94)	377 (207)	509 (214)	474 (97)				
30–34	308 (117)	311 (366)	395 (314)	407 (123)	424 (118)	353 (309)	455 (355)	516 (157)	416 (77)	451 (182)	448 (125)	464 (57)
35–39	167 (90)	205 (307)	236 (233)	281 (96)	259 (85)	227 (247)	337 (306)	375 (157)	376 (101)	353 (221)	323 (161)	315 (73)
40–44	90 (78)	129 (249)	126 (183)	169 (71)	104 (67)	107 (196)	192 (250)	171 (128)	168 (95)	123 (171)	144 (139)	117 (60)
45–49	0 (65)	0 (196)	0 (150)	43 (46)	33 (60)	13 (158)	19 (214)	0 (111)	22 (91)	48 (126)	18 (112)	0 (50)
Total	7.07	7.21	8.34	9.66	6.38	5.38	7.56	7.65	4.91	4.87	4.66	4.48

Note: The four cohorts are indicated by Roman numerals: I, 1650–99; II, 1700–49; III, 1750–99; IV, 1800–49. Numbers in parentheses are women-years lived.

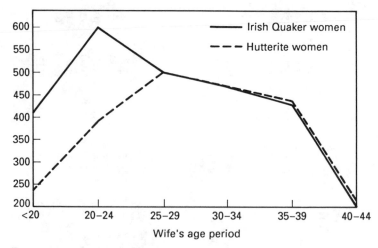

Fig. 4.1 Marital fertility, Irish Quaker women and Hutterite women.
Source: Eaton and Mayer, "Social Biology," 206–64.

over 560 reached in three age-groups in the latter half of the eighteenth century in Ireland (Table 4.4). As Figure 4.1 shows, Irish Quaker wives during this half-century exceeded the levels of fertility of the Hutterites during the quinquennium when Hutterite fertility was at its height. Irish wives, apparently so similar genetically and sociologically to the British, in some age-groups achieved fertility half as great again as that of the Southern English. Explaining this is our second great problem.

Despite this picture of diversity, there were some unmistakable trends as well. For one thing, the ranking among the various areas remained quite stable. Until 1800 the Irish had the highest fertility, followed by the Northern English and Scottish (whose numbers were very small in the first cohort, and whose rates later may have been slightly inflated by a bias towards more fertile families in the genealogies). Then came the urban families, and finally the consistently less fertile Southern English. After 1800 the picture changed somewhat; the urban families and those from Northern England and Scotland (including the genealogies) spurted ahead, while the Irish declined somewhat. Even more important is the high fertility in the period 1750–99, which is marked in almost every cohort and age-group. These tables leave little doubt that in both Britain and Ireland Quakers experienced a strong rise in fertility in the last half of the eighteenth century that did not play itself out until well into the nineteenth century.

Table 4.5 *Comparison of fertility, British, Irish, and American colonial Quakers*

Wife's age period	Ireland		Urban		Rest of Britain		American colonies		
	1700–49	1750–99	1700–49	1750–99	1700–49	1750–99	Wives born by 1730	Wives born 1731–55	Wives born 1756–85
<20	386	410	405	235	197	350	443	446	347
20–24	488	598	405	444	389	461	466	408	351
25–29	460	502	396	463	414	450	423	410	346
30–34	442	470	356	418	332	379	402	326	275
35–39	343	426	250	303	260	283	324	228	215
40–44	154	204	115	149	129	137	147	171	101
Total (20–44 × 5)	9.43	11.00	7.61	8.88	7.62	8.55	8.81	7.71	6.44

Note: Figures for the British and Irish Quakers are for all marriage ranks, all ages at marriage, and date of end of marriage known and unknown.

Source: Figures for the American colonial Quakers are from Robert V. Wells, "Family size and fertility control in eighteenth-century America: a study of Quaker families," *Population Studies* 25 (1971), 76.

The rise in population after 1750 and the differences between British and Irish Quaker fertility become even more intriguing when we contrast them with the experience of Quakers in the American colonies, since the British and Irish Quakers seem to have been unlike the American Quakers. These latter, it appears, are an exception to the conventional picture of much higher fertility in the American colonies. As Table 4.5 demonstrates, the colonial American Quakers (at least those in a sample taken mostly from Pennsylvania, New Jersey, and New York) did have higher fertility during the first half of the eighteenth century than the English Quakers, although they fell somewhat short of the levels of the formidable Irish. In the latter half of the century, however, American Quaker fertility began to fall, just at the time when that of the English and Irish was rising. By 1800 English fertility was almost a third as high again as the American, and even higher in the cities and in Ireland.

We must remember that we are measuring age-specific fertility only, not total family sizes; because of their lower ages at marriage the actual size of the American Quaker families was still slightly higher than that of the English. (In the absence of figures on American infant mortality, we do not know how many children ever born survived to adulthood; if American infant mortality was lower than English, then the experienced size of their families would have been proportionately larger.) Nevertheless, this divergence in fertility rates between American and British and Irish Quakers raises a number of intriguing questions. Robert Wells, who has compiled the American figures, argues that the decline was owing to the adoption of deliberate family limitation beginning about the time of the American Revolution. What circumstances, however, induced the American Quakers to limit the size of their families just when the English Quakers were having substantially larger ones? And, if we suppose that both communities were pressed to cope with these larger family sizes, why did the Americans have recourse to family limitation, while the English (at this period, at least) apparently did not do so to any great extent, but rather acted so as to mitigate the effects of rising fertility and declining infant mortality through later marriages? If the American fertility in the late eighteenth century was lowered through conscious policy, was the same thing true of the late seventeenth- and early eighteenth-century English fertility, or that of the early nineteenth century? Finally, returning to the hypothesized "colonial marriage pattern" which seems to be shared by the Irish and American Quaker colonists, what accounts for the fact that American fertility never came up to the Irish levels, not to mention that it was only about 60 percent of it at the end of the eighteenth century?

Thus the central issue in the interpretation of Quaker fertility is how it could vary so much at different times and in different places among people of exactly the same ages, especially when the populations were genetically similar, had a common lifestyle, and were concentrated in a relatively narrow social stratum.

There is, of course, one answer, which we might call the null hypothesis. This would be that these are just random variations, to be expected in a relatively small population divided into fifty-year cohorts such as the one with which we are dealing. We have been constantly aware of this possibility, but we have decided consistently to propose our best hypotheses, rather than invoking chance.[8]

Another answer, which also dissolves the problem, would be to attribute the apparently low fertility of the Southern English Quakers (in particular) to a mirage caused by underregistration of their births. That there was some underregistration, particularly in the early eighteenth century, we have already seen; but we have also seen how the technique of family reconstitution can cope with such difficulties. Since it was babies who lived only a few days who were most likely to be omitted, we have deferred our principal discussion of the problem of underregistration until chapter 5; but to anticipate our argument there, we do not believe that the fertility figures can have been much affected by underregistration. So we think the phenomena to be explained are real ones.

It may be helpful to begin by raising the most general question: why should fertility differ among *any* human populations? One, or all, of the following may be reasons why one population is less fertile: (1)

---

[8] Wilson, "Natural fertility," 226, argues that "the smaller the number of cases studied, the greater the likelihood that random components will dominate the systematic . . . . [T]he breaking up of our data into the component local data sets greatly increases the variability which can be expected in the analysis." He nevertheless treats local variations as worth investigating, and so presents data about individual parishes, but without dividing them into fifty-year temporal cohorts. He grants that if disaggregation into these cohorts is done, in certain parishes at certain times there is some evidence of family limitation. But, with specific reference to Colyton: "When examining the whole reconstitution, however, the impact of this period of apparent fertility control is counterbalanced by natural fertility at other times, and no over-all evidence of family limitation is found" (240). Few historians will be happy to see differences in time so cavalierly treated; Wilson gives no reason, for example, why all the parishes could not be taken together and the pooled figures divided into time cohorts. This procedure would allow us to test the hypothesis that differences between the early and the late eighteenth centuries were at least as important as differences between Banbury or Gainsborough and Colyton.

more women never marry (and do not have children out of wedlock); (2) women marry later, and thus have less time to bear children (when their fecundity is also lower); (3) sterile unions are more common; (4) birth intervals are longer for the fecund couples; (5) women stop having children earlier in life (because they or their husbands die, or for other reasons).[9] The fourth and fifth of these reasons may have purely physiological causes, but they also may be the result of efforts at family limitation.

The effects on fertility of variations in the frequency or age at marriage or of interruptions of the union by death are discussed in chapters 3 and 5; so we shall concentrate here on sterile unions, birth intervals, and early termination of child-bearing.

Louis Henry, the founder of modern historical demography, has distinguished "non-Malthusian" from "Malthusian" systems. Within the "non-Malthusian" are regimes of "natural" fertility, when no effort to limit the number of children born is being made, and those which he called "pre-Malthusian," in which, although there was no conscious effort to limit births, certain customs such as taboos on intercourse during nursing would lead to wider spacing of births and thus smaller families. All developed countries and a few developing ones, such as China, have "Malthusian" regimes, where there is conscious and widespread family limitation.[10] Of course these will produce many fewer children than those without conscious fertility control; but there is room for great variations in fertility even among populations where "natural" or "pre-Malthusian" fertility is the rule. Consider, for example, the Amish and the Hutterites, religious sects with a similarly pastoral and secluded lifestyle and similar values (which did not include conscious control of fertility). The average Hutterite woman bears 9.5 children, while the average Amish woman bears only 6.3 children.[11] Henry found that fertility levels among thirteen populations which he considered not to practice family limitation varied quite markedly; and these variations are difficult for an historian to explain, since levels of natural fertility seem to bear little or no relation to objectively measurable socio-economic characteristics.[12] Our problem, though, is to decide whether the differences

---

[9] See the discussion in Kingsley David and Judith Blake, "Social structure and fertility," *Economic Development and Cultural Change* 4 (1956), 211–35.

[10] Louis Henry, "La Fécondité des mariages au Japon," *Population* 8e année (1953), 718–19.

[11] J. Bongaarts, "Does malnutrition affect fecundity? A summary of evidence," *Science* 208 (1980), 564.

[12] Fertility at age 25 was 1.72 times higher in the most fertile than in the least fertile of these populations, and total fertility was 1.76 times higher (Louis Henry, "Some data on natural fertility," *Eugenics Quarterly* 8 [1961], 88). John Cleland and Christopher

Table 4.6 *Sterility of Quaker marriages*

Wife's age at marriage	1650–99		1700–49		1750–99		1800–49	
	No.	%	No.	%	No.	%	No.	%
Southern England								
<20	10	0	29	17.1	19	5.3	2	50.0
20–24	34	8.8	83	6.0	96	8.3	39	10.3
25–29	25	8.0	61	13.1	97	12.4	42	9.5
30–34	13	15.3	37	2.7	42	33.3	17	17.6
35–39	7	14.3	18	27.8	18	38.9	10	40.0
40–44	3	66.7	4	50.0	12	66.7	11	90.9
All	92	10.9	232	11.7	284	17.6	110	23.7
Northern Britain								
<20	4	25.0	10	0	10	0	5	0
20–24	14	7.1	62	1.6	80	1.2	15	26.7
25–29	6	0	29	3.4	60	5.0	71	4.2
30–34	3	0	15	0	21	14.3	36	5.6
35–39	1	0	5	20.0	14	14.3	10	40.0
40–44	0	0	2	50.0	4	50.0	4	75.0
All	28	7.2	123	3.3	189	5.9	141	11.4
Urban								
<20	12	0	19	10.5	9	22.2	1	0
20–24	22	4.5	70	14.3	56	7.1	21	4.8
25–29	18	22.2	43	18.6	49	20.4	20	10.0
30–34	18	11.1	35	8.6	25	8.0	9	0
35–39	6	0	18	50.0	22	31.8	2	50.0
40–44	2	0	9	77.8	5	80.0	3	66.7
All	78	9.0	194	20.1	166	17.5	56	10.8
Ireland								
<20	25	12.0	27	3.7	17	5.9	3	0
20–24	40	2.5	66	0	31	6.5	15	0
25–29	24	0	32	3.1	22	4.5	11	9.1
30–34	6	0	11	9.1	2	0	1	0
35–39	4	0	0	0	5	20.0	0	0
40–44	0	0	3	66.7	1	0	1	0
All	99	4.1	139	3.6	78	6.5	31	3.3

between British and Irish fertility generally, and between pre-1750 and post-1750 fertility levels, were variations among populations with "natural" fertility, or whether they resulted from family limitation.

We had best start where there is at least some reasonably reliable evidence. If we assume, as seems warranted, that only a negligible number of couples desired to have no children at all (and could practice family limitation with total success), one measure of fecundity is the extent of definitive or "primary" sterility – where the couple remained childless throughout their marriage. If it is widespread, the general level of fertility will in all likelihood be low. Our findings are shown in Table 4.6. It comes as no surprise that this table shows definitive sterility was higher in those areas, and at those times, where fertility in general lagged; but the difference is not nearly enough to account for the observed variation in fertility.

Another possibility, not much mentioned in the demographic literature, is that it was the different fecundity of husbands which explains at least part of the variation. Although men are still capable of procreating at greater ages than women, their capacity to father a child also declines with age; therefore a woman marrying an older man will be less fertile than if she had married a younger one. This is clearly shown by Table 4.7, where, at most ages of the wife, her fertility is greater with a younger husband. As will be recalled from Table 3.1, there was a greater tendency for Quaker women to marry older men after 1750; but most of the fertility advantage of younger men was manifested before that time, and so the effect of the rising age of the husband was negligible after 1750.

Since the percentages of marriages definitively sterile is too small to account for the observed differences in fertility, the other possibilities to be investigated must be longer birth intervals (such as might be achieved by a "spacing" strategy of family limitation) or an earlier termination of the child-bearing career (the possible result of a "stopping" strategy).[13] To consider birth intervals first: it is useful to break down an interval after a birth into its component parts. Immediately after giving birth, a woman typically has a period of amenorrhea which lasts for two months even among women who do not nurse their babies. Prolonged lactation, it has been estimated, can extend

Wilson, "Demand theories of the fertility transition: an iconoclastic view," *Population Studies* 41 (1987), 16 point out the difficulties of correlating different levels of marital fertility with objectively measurable socio-economic characteristics.

[13] John Knodel, "Starting, stopping, and spacing during the early stages of the fertility transition: the experience of German village populations in the 18th and 19th centuries," *Demography* 24 (1987), 143 gives a good account of these different strategies.

this interval to as long as eleven months – though, as we shall see, this estimate is controversial. After this the menstrual cycles resume, but typically the first two are without ovulation. Once ovulation has resumed the time required for a new conception may be estimated at something like five months. Some of these pregnancies, however, will end in miscarriages; an average based on entire modern populations suggests that another three months can be added to reflect fetal mortality. Finally, a pregnancy carried to term lasts nine months. When these are added up, an average birth interval when the mother does not nurse the baby would last twenty-one months; and an interval of thirty or even thirty-six months, extended by prolonged lactation, would be perfectly reasonable even in a situation of "natural" or "pre-Malthusian" fertility.[14]

Some lengths within the birth interval are largely invariant, such as the nine months required to carry a baby to term. There will usually be at least two months without menstruation just after the birth and probably two anovulatory cycles when menstruation resumes. Most variations, therefore, appear to be when amenorrhea after the birth is extended, in the length of time required for conception after ovulation has resumed, and in the incidence of fetal mortality. These three are where family limitation has a chance to operate: by extending nursing with a view to prolonging amenorrhea; by abstaining from intercourse or using contraceptives after ovulation has begun; or by inducing abortion.

We can now look in particular at the periods of low fertility among the English Quakers to try to determine whether family limitation or a variation in a regime of natural fertility is the most likely explanation.

Direct evidence about nursing, frequency of intercourse, and contraceptive (or abortifacient) practices is unfortunately very difficult to come by. We can, however, dismiss the possibility that contraceptive devices or abortifacient techniques were in use among the Quakers. All contemporary references to contraceptive techniques associate them not with prudent wives but with dissolute single women. We find it hard to imagine our Quaker men and matrons employing the clumsy condoms and pessaries of the time, not to mention inducing

---

[14] We follow the analysis in Robert G. Potter, "Birth intervals: structure and change," *Population Studies* 17 (1963), 155–56. John Bongaarts, "Why high birth rates are so low," *Population and Development Review* 1 (1975), 289–96 also considers a thirty-month birth interval typical of populations with natural fertility, but he thinks that only half of the fertilized ova ever mature and are born alive, and so includes a five-month interval associated with the conception and subsequent intrauterine death of a fetus.

Table 4.7 Age-specific fertility of wives, by husbands' age

Wife's age period		Southern England				Northern Britain			
		1650–99	1700–49	1750–99	1800–49	1650–99	1700–49	1750–99	1800–49
20–24	Husband 0–9 yrs younger	250 (1)	380 (8)	500 (11)	357 (5)	1000 (3)	667 (6)	550 (20)	381 (8)
	Husband 0–9 yrs older	366 (22)	380 (86)	424 (106)	370 (23)	500 (11)	430 (49)	466 (76)	457 (111)
25–29	Husband 0–9 yrs younger	482 (14)	366 (40)	438 (71)	457 (43)	500 (5)	500 (23)	495 (53)	450 (149)
	Husband 0–9 yrs older	432 (35)	446 (166)	398 (213)	379 (63)	420 (21)	409 (96)	481 (194)	432 (268)
30–34	Husband 0–9 yrs younger	388 (21)	338 (66)	353 (103)	341 (55)	471 (8)	341 (82)	385 (69)	393 (94)
	Husband 0–9 yrs older	336 (34)	315 (110)	357 (224)	312 (66)	326 (15)	373 (91)	416 (174)	397 (271)
35–39	Husband 0–9 yrs younger	333 (21)	306 (69)	253 (77)	244 (42)	320 (8)	333 (27)	257 (45)	339 (92)
	Husband 0–9 yrs older	220 (22)	215 (65)	240 (149)	295 (62)	244 (11)	274 (57)	336 (126)	304 (190)
40–44	Husband 0–9 yrs younger	223 (15)	123 (25)	110 (33)	135 (20)	316 (6)	138 (65)	154 (24)	158 (39)
	Husband 0–9 yrs older	131 (14)	107 (28)	101 (56)	141 (23)	156 (7)	141 (26)	183 (59)	144 (82)

		Ireland				Urban			
20–24	Husband 0–9 yrs younger	571 (4)	600 (3)	428 (3)	0	0	333 (4)	434 (10)	333 (3)
	Husband 0–9 yrs older	431 (73)	481 (80)	673 (33)	606 (20)	344 (31)	392 (89)	426 (84)	440 (26)
25–29	Husband 0–9 yrs younger	363 (16)	482 (28)	437 (7)	500 (2)	571 (20)	449 (40)	479 (69)	415 (22)
	Husband 0–9 yrs older	430 (87)	456 (106)	473 (45)	550 (38)	511 (66)	417 (161)	437 (169)	398 (49)
30–34	Husband 0–9 yrs younger	406 (26)	471 (41)	428 (12)	285 (4)	562 (36)	405 (84)	425 (114)	420 (45)
	Husband 0–9 yrs older	370 (74)	466 (208)	428 (42)	453 (34)	347 (41)	325 (129)	380 (156)	391 (63)
35–39	Husband 0–9 yrs younger	470 (24)	300 (27)	517 (15)	90 (1)	425 (34)	327 (80)	289 (88)	279 (36)
	Husband 0–9 yrs older	348 (53)	360 (67)	397 (31)	333 (17)	231 (28)	240 (86)	238 (95)	342 (49)
40–44	Husband 0–9 yrs younger	181 (6)	116 (7)	200 (3)	0 ( )	225 (16)	171 (38)	167 (49)	141 (18)
	Husband 0–9 yrs older	175 (13)	140 (20)	166 (9)	200 (8)	113 (3)	103 (34)	79 (29)	156 (18)

abortions.[15] The argument that there was family limitation must therefore consist of inferences about patterns of nursing and sexual relations from the demographic series themselves.

Demographers are quite accustomed to making such inferences about the behavior of people about whom they know little beyond the bare vital statistics, and they have worked out a series of techniques for dealing with the difficulties which obviously arise. We shall apply these techniques in turn to the British and Irish Quakers.

The classic tests for family limitation in a given population were developed in France – fittingly so, since it was in France that family limitation first became widespread. These are basically tests for family limitation through stopping child-bearing; that is, they depend on the assumption that if family limitation is intended, parents will not employ any "Malthusian'" techniques until they reach or come close to the target size for their family. Once these techniques were used, fertility would be low, and there would be a long interval – four years or more – between the births of the next-to-last and last child. (Even after the decision to stop having children was made, a child was sometimes born, because, aside from abstinence, methods of contraception were rather unreliable, and of course couples occasionally changed their minds). Such a pattern is in contrast to a "spacing" one such as is typical of modern professional families, where a couple marries but delays having the first child for several years or widely spaces the first two pregnancies. The classic tests for family limitation also depend on the assumption that in its absence married women of the same age would have the same fertility no matter how long they had been married or how many children they had previously borne; in other words, unless family limitation was being practiced, only ageing would lead to declining fertility.

These assumptions suggest that the following would be signs of family limitation in a pre-industrial population: with a successful "stopping" strategy, in completed families those women who married earlier would have had their last children considerably earlier in life than those who married later; and intervals before ultimate and penultimate births would be substantially longer than before other births among these early-marrying women. This latter phenomenon is also consistent with a "spacing" strategy; but this strategy might also be employed at the very beginning of married life, whereas the way to detect a stopping pattern is to look at the age- and duration-specific marital fertility of women aged 35 and over. If it is significantly higher

[15] R. R. Kuczynski, "British demographers' opinions on fertility, 1660 to 1760," in *Political Arithmetic*, ed. L. A. Hogben (New York, 1938), 283–327.

Table 4.8 *Wives' age at birth of last child, by age at marriage (completed families only)*

Period	Wife married at age	Urban		Southern England		Northern Britain		Ireland	
		n	Mean age	n	Mean age	n	Mean age	n	Mean age
1650–99	<30	24	37.5	45	37.0	15	40.1	24	42.7
	≥30	25	40.9	24	43.1	5	43.5	7	42.8
1700–49	<30	83	37.4	132	37.1	65	38.4	65	39.1
	≥30	42	41.2	58	41.3	14	42.1	7	42.2
1750–99	<30	87	38.6	194	37.8	88	39.9	28	38.0
	≥30	42	41.2	66	41.7	25	41.1	8	43.2
1800–49	<30	31	38.6	64	39.1	150	39.5	11	40.6
	≥30	14	39.5	31	40.4	38	42.5	1	42.4
1850–99	<30					74	38.0		
	≥30					25	40.2		

Note: Dates inaccurate by more than one year have been excluded. Figures for the 1850–99 cohort are entirely from the genealogies.

among women who married late than among those who married early, family limitation may be inferred.

We have compiled three tables which explore whether any signs of family limitation by stopping are to be found among the British and Irish Quakers. The first, Table 4.8, shows the ages at which women in completed families bore their last children. In the Southern English counties in the late seventeenth century, this average age was only 37 for women who had married before the age of 30. In contrast, women married after the age of 30 bore their last children at an average age of just over 43. By the first part of the nineteenth century the picture had changed, since the gap was now only from 39.1 to 40.4 years – not a significant difference. Similar patterns, though not quite so striking, can be seen in the urban families: significant differences through 1800, but not in the final cohort. The pattern in Ireland and Northern England and Scotland is less easy to interpret, partly because the number of families in some groups is so low; but in general this particular indicator of family limitation suggests that some families were using a stopping strategy in the seventeenth century, particularly in Southern England. At the same time, the differences in the ages at which the last children were borne persisted right into the time of considerably rising overall fertility; in fact there was a gap of more than five years in Ireland at a time when their overall fertility was extraordinarily high. This suggests that family limitation might be employed even after a large number of children had already been born – or else that fecundity might be severely impaired after several previous pregnancies.

We can now turn to the intervals between the births of penultimate and last children, to see if there are any signs of an excessive lengthening of this interval such as was supposed to characterize family limitation in other early modern populations.[16] The relevant data are set forth in Table 4.9. As this table indicates, there were only two instances where the interval before the last birth was remarkably longer than the averages for the other intergenesic intervals. These were once again the seventeenth-century cohorts for the Irish and Southern English families. The interval before the last birth was also

---

[16] Henry, "Natural fertility," 81–91. This criterion itself has been challenged. N. F. R. Crafts and N. J. Ireland, in a simulation study, suggest that as family-limitation methods become increasingly effective, the average interval before the last birth will decline rather than rising, since the last, unintended, birth would be less likely to occur. There is, however, no reason to think that methods of family limitation were improving in this period; certainly no better apparatus was introduced. See "The role of simulation techniques in the theory and observation of family formation," *Population Studies* 29 (1975), 90–91.

Table 4.9 Birth intervals, by birth rank, for wives married under age 34 (families with at least four birth events)

Cohort	n	0–1	n	1–2	n	2–3	n	3–4	n	All later	n	Penult	n	Ult.
Urban														
1650–99	120	17.8	106	22.6	85	24.7	71	25.0	185	25.2	37	26.7	34	36.5
1700–49	282	17.5	236	24.5	194	24.1	150	25.7	376	25.4	72	31.4	68	36.4
1750–99	217	17.0	184	21.2	157	21.9	136	21.6	425	24.8	78	27.0	72	33.4
1800–49	100	17.7	90	19.1	78	21.8	66	23.1	195	27.1	25	28.2	24	30.1
Southern England														
1650–99	110	21.2	96	27.8	76	27.0	58	31.5	137	30.5	34	31.1	34	47.6
1700–49	279	20.8	231	30.5	189	26.3	159	27.6	359	28.4	75	27.5	75	38.8
1750–99	283	20.3	253	23.8	210	25.7	173	27.7	511	25.0	101	27.2	98	35.4
1800–49	129	19.2	114	21.0	96	26.4	83	27.8	214	28.2	34	27.0	34	34.3
Ireland														
1650–99	122	14.5	115	23.3	103	24.4	94	26.5	311	35.0	23	33.1	24	65.6
1700–49	204	16.0	193	23.3	173	25.7	149	25.2	465	25.7	60	29.3	61	37.8
1750–99	101	16.0	96	20.5	85	20.5	76	22.4	298	24.2	26	24.0	25	30.8
1800–49	42	16.1	37	22.9	34	24.9	33	26.6	87	23.7	9	23.9	10	34.4
Northern Britain														
1650–99	32	11.9	28	21.3	24	27.7	23	40.8	68	30.0	17	34.6	16	40.5
1700–49	121	18.8	107	26.8	90	28.3	80	29.4	219	30.0	45	33.1	44	45.5
1750–99	176	14.5	162	22.0	137	25.8	121	25.3	418	25.9	71	27.3	71	33.4
1800–49	263	20.2	230	25.0	210	25.5	184	27.4	533	27.8	112	28.7	115	39.5

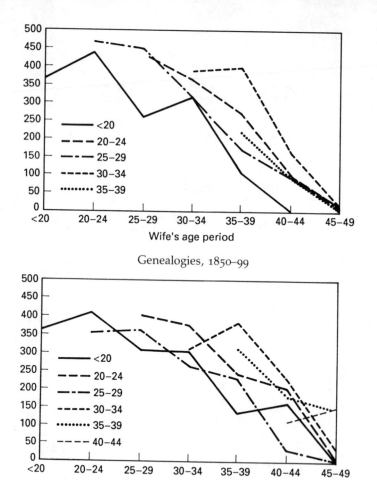

Genealogies, 1850–99

Southern England, 1650–99

Fig. 4.2 Age-specific fertility, by ages at marriage, selected ages and periods.

quite a bit longer for the urban families of the seventeenth century, though the difference is not so dramatic as in either Ireland or Southern England. So here again it appears that family limitation was being practiced in the seventeenth century, although there is less support for this theory from the last two intergenesic intervals found in the eighteenth and early nineteenth centuries. On the other hand, John Landers' study of Peel and Southwark Monthly Meetings in London has shown that there birth intervals of over forty-eight months became quite a bit more common after 1750.[17]

[17] John Landers, "Some problems in the historical demography of London, 1675–1825," (Cambridge University PhD thesis, 1984), 179–80.

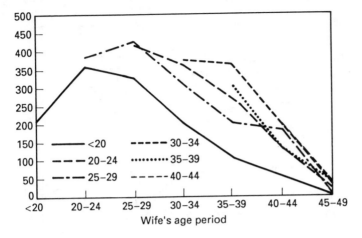

Southern England, 1700–49

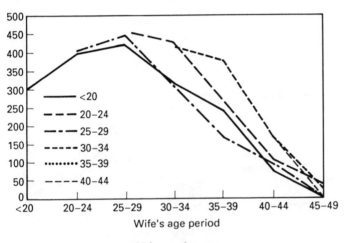

Urban, 1650–99

We also made use of a more recently developed statistical test designed to reveal the existence of family limitation. Devised by Ansley Coale and T. James Trussell, it yielded inconclusive results, discussed at more length in the Appendix (pp. 178ff). There is one more way to compare the fertility at the same ages of women married early and those married later. This is best done graphically, as in Figure 4.2, which shows the period in each area where there is the greatest difference between the fertility of early and late marriers. This in turn can be compared with graphs from two populations where family limitation through stopping was almost certainly being employed (Figure 4.3, p. 172). The visual image to look for is a concave curve of the lines representing marriage at an earlier age and a wide gap up and down the vertical lines, indicating that women more

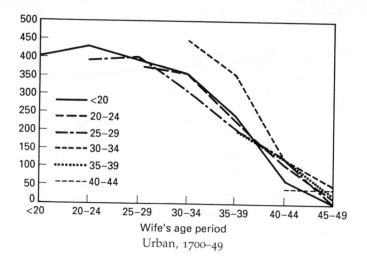

Wife's age period

Urban, 1700–49

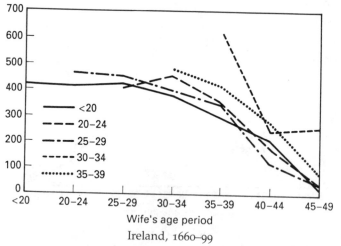

Wife's age period

Ireland, 1660–99

recently married are having considerably more children than those of the same age who had married earlier.[18]

None of the graphs for the British and Irish Quakers shows anything like such a neat pattern. Not only does fertility occasionally seem to rise in the later age periods – and not just in the 25–29 one which is discussed in the Appendix. There are also few of the great gaps which would signal us that widespread fertility control through early cessation of child-bearing was being practiced. It is significant that the widest gaps and the most nearly concave lines (though not without their anomalies) are to be found in the genealogies in the latter

[18] A word should be said about the erratic course of most of the "under 20" lines; there were so few Quaker women who married this early that random variations are very noticeable in this group.

part of the nineteenth century, when contraception had become fairly common, at least in the business and professional classes where the Quakers were heavily clustered.[19] The Southern English pattern in the early eighteenth century comes closest to the genealogies 150 years later, while the Irish in the late seventeenth century – even though this is the period in which it looks most likely that family limitation may have been tried – is an example of the robustly convex curves that typify populations without conscious fertility control.

This is why it is important to recall the French provenance of the tests we have been discussing. When the transition to fertility control occurred in France, there was a dramatic shift away from the high fertility which, as we have seen, characterized most of the *ancien régime*. English populations at the same time show few such convex curves; but neither are their concave ones very dramatic. And we should remember that while the English Quakers show considerably lower fertility than the Irish ones, there is no evidence that it was ever lower than that of the English population generally.

As might be expected, these several tests do not all yield the same answers; and there is the further difficulty that the tests are better able to detect stopping than spacing, which can be mistaken for an underlying low fecundity.[20] Although the evidence for family limitation in the seventeenth century, especially in Southern England, seems strong, it is not quite conclusive. There may have been some Quakers practicing family limitation in the eighteenth century, but it probably was not widespread. Still, it may have been enough to account for at least part of the difference between the fertility rates of English and Irish Quakers.

It is noteworthy that in the areas of low fertility longer intervals were just as characteristic of the early as of the late births within a family. This can be seen from Table 4.10. The peculiarly low fertility in Southern England shows up again; almost without exception the average interval is longer there, sometimes by as much as five or six months. But the birth intervals earlier in the marriage are just as strikingly longer as the later ones. For example, the interval between

19 On this see J. A. Banks, *Prosperity and Parenthood: A Study of Family Planning among the Victorian Middle Classes* (London, 1954) and Judah Matras, "Social strategies of family formation: data for British female cohorts born 1831–1906," *Population Studies* 19 (1965), 167–81.
20 John Knodel, "Espacement des naissances et planification familiale; une critique de la méthode Dupâquier-Lachiver," *Annales: Economies, Sociétés, Civilisations* 36e année (1981), 474. The "Dupâquier-Lachiver method," which measures the percentage of birth intervals of more than forty-eight months, is set forth in Dupâquier and Lachiver, "Sur les débuts de la contraception en France ou les deux malthusianismes," *Annales: Economies, Sociétés, Civilisations* 24e année" (1969), 1391–406.

Table 4.10 *Birth intervals, all British and Irish Quakers, by rank order of births and wives' age at marriage*

	IRELAND							
	1650–99		1700–49		1750–99		1800–49	
Rank	Int.	% change	Int.	% change	Int.	% change	Int.	% change
All ages at marriage								
0–1	14.4 (128)	8.8	15.9 (205)	10.4 10.6	16.1 (110)	1.3 16.3	16.0 (43)	−0.6 14.7
1–2	23.2 (120)	8.9	23.3 (193)	0.4 14.9	20.4 (102)	−12.4 12.8	22.9 (38)	8.1 11.1
2–3	24.2 (106)	9.2	25.6 (173)	5.8 18.2	20.3 (89)	−20.7 7.8	24.7 (35)	21.7 10.9
3–4	26.2 (97)	10.6	25.1 (149)	−4.2 10.0	22.8 (78)	−9.2 15.3	26.3 (34)	15.4 13.1
4–5+	35.2 (317)	73.7	25.7 (465)	−27.0 13.6	24.1 (300)	−6.2 16.2	23.6 (87)	−2.1 11.5
% of Births								
Rank ≥5	41.3		39.2		44.2		36.7	
Those married at ≤24 years								
0–1	14.2		16.5	16.2	16.7	1.2	16.5	−1.2
1–2	23.5		23.7	0.8	21.3	−10.1	24.4	14.6
2–3	24.3		25.1	3.3	20.1	−20.0	26.0	29.4
3–4	25.7		25.7	–	22.0	−14.4	27.3	24.1
4–5+	36.4		25.4	−27.5	23.5	−7.5	22.9	−2.6
Those married at 25–34 years								
0–1	15.2		14.8	−2.6	14.9	0.7	15.5	4.0
1–2	22.7		22.5	−0.9	19.2	−14.7	20.9	−8.9
2–3	24.7		27.0	9.3	21.1	−21.9	23.5	11.4
3–4	28.1		24.0	−14.6	23.0	−4.2	25.6	11.3
4–5+	29.7		26.8	−9.8	26.1	−2.6	25.3	−3.1

SOUTHERN ENGLAND

Rank	1650–99 Int.	1650–99 % change	1700–49 Int.	1700–49 % change	1750–99 Int.	1750–99 % change	1800–49 Int.	1800–49 % change
All ages at marriage								
0–1	20.9	21.7	20.7	−1.0	20.1	−2.9	19.4	−3.5
	(116)		(308)	18.7	(307)	20.3	(143)	17.7
1–2	28.4	16.4	30.3	6.7	23.8	−21.5	21.9	−8.0
	(101)		(248)	78.3	(264)	18.4	(123)	11.4
2–3	27.4	19.7	26.1	−4.7	25.9	−0.8	26.3	1.5
	(81)		(195)	18.9	(218)	15.9	(99)	20.1
3–4	31.4	28.6	27.5	−12.4	27.6	0.4	27.6	−
	(60)		(161)	17.2	(175)	18.0	(84)	18.4
4–5+	30.8	18.2	28.4	−7.8	24.9	−12.3	28.3	13.7
	(139)		(362)	16.8	(511)	14.0	(215)	16.7
% of Births Rank ⩾5	28.0		28.4		34.6		32.4	
Those married at ⩽24 years								
0–1	19.6		22.6	1.53	21.1	−6.8	20.7	−1.9
1–2	27.9		23.6	−15.4	25.1	6.3	22.0	−12.3
2–3	28.0		26.6	−5.0	25.2	−5.3	25.1	−0.3
3–4	31.5		27.6	−12.4	25.8	−6.5	32.2	24.8
4–5+	32.7		29.0	−11.3	25.4	−12.4	29.9	17.7
Those married at 25–34 years								
0–1	23.0		19.0	−17.4	19.6	3.2	18.1	−7.7
1–2	27.6		38.4	39.1	22.5	−41.4	20.3	−9.8
2–3	25.6		25.9	1.2	26.3	1.5	27.5	4.4
3–4	31.5		27.6	−12.4	29.8	8.0	23.9	−19.8
4–5+	26.6		27.4	3.0	24.3	−11.3	26.2	7.8

Table 4.10 (cont.)

NORTHERN BRITAIN

Rank	1650–99 Int.	1650–99 % change	1700–49 Int.	1700–49 % change	1750–99 Int.	1750–99 % change	1800–49 Int.	1800–49 % change
All ages at marriage								
0–1	13.0 (35)		18.4 (127)	41.5	15.2 (191)	−17.4	20.1 (278)	32.2
1–2	21.7 (30)		26.5 (111)	22.1	22.1 (170)	−16.6	24.8 (239)	12.2
2–3	27.9 (26)		28.4 (93)	1.8	25.8 (141)	−9.2	25.5 (217)	−1.2
3–4	39.6 (24)		28.9 (82)	−27.0	25.2 (124)	−12.8	27.1 (187)	7.5
4–5+	29.9 (68)		29.5 (228)	−1.3	25.9 (419)	−12.2	27.7 (535)	6.9
% of Births								
Rank ≥	37.2		35.6		40.1		37.3	
Those married at ≤24 years								
0–1	11.4		19.7	72.8	13.4	−32.0	22.8	70.1
1–2	20.5		25.5	24.4	23.6	−7.5	26.8	13.6
2–3	27.5		27.9	1.5	25.2	−9.6	25.4	0.8
3–4	33.0		29.9	−9.4	23.4	−21.7	27.7	18.4
4–5+	29.8		29.7	−0.3	25.9	−12.8	27.8	7.3
Those married at 25–34 years								
0–1	12.9		17.6	36.4	15.7	−10.8	17.5	11.5
1–2	22.6		28.7	27.0	22.1	−23.0	22.9	3.6
2–3	28.1		29.0	3.2	26.7	−7.9	25.6	−4.1
3–4	58.7		28.3	−51.8	27.7	−2.1	27.0	−2.6

Rank	1650–99 Int.	1650–99 % change	1700–49 Int.	1700–49 % change	1750–99 Int.	1750–99 % change	1800–49 Int.	1800–49 % change
All ages at marriage								
0–1	17.4 (130)	14.1	17.9 (307)	2.9, 16.8	16.7 (242)	−6.7, 19.4	17.7 (108)	6.0, 14.1
1–2	23.3 (113)	15.3	24.7 (249)	6.0, 16.9	21.5 (199)	−13.0, 16.6	19.2 (96)	−10.7, 7.6
2–3	24.6 (88)	18.8	23.9 (202)	−2.8, 17.3	22.2 (165)	−7.1, 9.6	22.0 (80)	−0.9, 9.8
3–4	24.7 (72)	12.9	25.4 (153)	2.8, 17.2	21.8 (142)	−14.2, 10.2	23.1 (66)	6.0, 11.7
4–5+	25.1 (187)	13.1	25.3 (377)	0.8, 16.3	24.8 (426)	−2.0, 14.6	27.0 (195)	8.1, 14.3
% of Births Rank ≥5	31.7		29.3		36.3		35.8	
Those married at ≤24 years								
0–1	18.5		18.7	1.1	18.1	−3.2	14.6	−19.3
1–2	25.2		23.2	−7.9	21.6	−6.9	19.0	−12.0
2–3	29.4		24.4	−17.0	20.8	−14.8	22.2	6.7
3–4	23.2		26.7	15.1	20.3	−24.0	21.9	7.9
4–5+	24.6		25.4	3.3	24.1	−5.1	29.5	22.4
Those married at 25–34 years								
0–1	17.1		16.2	−8.5	15.8	−2.5	20.0	26.6
1–2	20.1		26.0	29.4	20.7	−20.4	19.1	−7.7
2–3	21.1		23.8	12.8	23.1	−2.9	21.4	−7.4
3–4	26.4		24.4	−7.6	23.2	−4.9	24.4	5.2
4–5	25.9		25.5	−1.5	26.1	2.4	24.1	−7.7

marriage and first birth was, on average, 14.2 months in Ireland and 19.6 months in Southern England for those married under the age of 25 in 1650–99. Since prenuptial pregnancies were negligible and there can have been no difference in nursing practices because there was no previous child, we either have here the first known example of family limitation at the beginning of a marriage in pre-industrial Europe, or else a large "natural" fertility variation whose cause cannot yet be fully explained.

The first possibility seems to us more likely. The assumption that efforts at family limitation would begin only after the target family had almost been achieved is only an assumption; because it has been built into most of our statistical tests, it cannot be tested by them. If, as we think likely, the Quakers were unusually prudent and foresighted about things of this world, they might well have wished to start spacing their child-bearing from the beginning of their marriages. As John Landers has written about the two London meetings, the intervals between marriage and the first birth display "some unusual periods, suggestive of artificial prolongation."[21] This supposition gains support from the strong element of "this-worldly asceticism" in the Quaker ethic and mentality. It is unlikely that they made much use of *coitus interruptus*, and even less so of the contraceptive devices available at the time; but periodic abstinence from intercourse could demonstrate a freedom from fleshly concerns while at the same time helping to see that all children born could be adequately loved and provided for. It is significant in this respect that some of the early Quakers made a virtue of complete chastity, and that the marriage of George Fox and Margaret Fell when she was too old to have children was specifically justified as a spiritual union, not one whose aim was simply procreation. In fact, Quaker thought tended to glorify love between men and women as spiritual and inward; it was much more difficult for Quaker writers to come to terms with a physical manifestation of such abstract love. Once marriage when there is no chance of children can be valued, a crucial mental boundary has been crossed that can eventually lead to the sanctioning of sex without reproduction.[22]

---

21 Landers, "Some problems," 141.
22 In the seventeenth century several married Quakers in New England were said to have abstained from sexual intercourse for up to four years (Swarthmore MSS. in the Friends' House Library, iv, 107–8, quoted in Barry Reay, *The Quakers and the English Revolution* [New York, 1985], 36). The manuscripts go on to say that "some weare besids them selves about it" (quoted in Jacques Tual, "Les Quakers en Angleterre: naissance et origines d'un mouvement, 1649–1700: illuminisme et révolution [Doctorat d'Etat es Lettres, Université de Paris III, 1986], 993). On Quaker thought about marriage, see Tual's article "Sexual equality and conjugal harmony: the way to

There may also have been a physiological reason for some of the differences between Irish and Southern English Quaker fertility. We speculate that fertility in Southern England before 1750 was shadowed by morbidity and mortality – that women there were unable to carry as many pregnancies to term, and that these more frequent miscarriages lengthened the intergenesic intervals. Direct evidence for this is impossible to gain, because miscarriages were not recorded, and even stillbirths, which might be an index of fetal health, were seriously underregistered.[23] Nevertheless, all modern studies show a direct relationship between the general level of infant mortality and perinatal deaths (those occurring during delivery, or in the first few days of life). It seems reasonable to suppose that as infant mortality falls, as it did after 1750, so will fetal mortality; therefore the decline in infant mortality in the latter part of the eighteenth century is probably also a part of the explanation of the rise of fertility at the same time, since there were presumably fewer miscarriages.

This effect would be even more marked if the market towns of Southern England were afflicted with the same unsanitary water and food supplies that caused so many deaths from gastrointestinal diseases in London, as discussed in chapter 5. One of the effects of chronic intestinal disorders is inability to carry pregnancies through to a live birth; so if there were in the eighteenth century the same reduction of the incidence of such diseases as is indicated in the London bills of mortality there should have been fewer miscarriages (and shorter intergenesic intervals) in the South of England after 1700.

Thus far we have been reviewing the evidence for family limitation,

celestial bliss. A view of early Quaker matrimony," *Journal of the Friends' Historical Society* 55 (1988), 161–74; for the marriage of George Fox and Margaret Fell, see Richard T. Vann, *The Social Development of English Quakerism, 1655–1755* (Cambridge, Mass., 1969), 182 and Barbara Ritter Dailey, "The husbands of Margaret Fell: an essay on religious metaphor and social change," *Seventeenth Century* 2 (1987), 55–71.

23 Only ten of the twenty-six quarterly meetings (including six of the ones we worked on) recorded stillbirths at all. Even those which did record them obviously did so irregularly. In the entire set of registers there were 155 stillbirths of boys and only 30 of girls recorded for members, whereas there were only 8 male stillbirths and 26 female ones to non-members. In Sweden, where stillbirths were meticulously recorded, and which had a demographic regime similar to England's, stillbirths between 1751 and 1850 comprised 2.8 percent of all birth events; in modern populations stillbirths are about 2 percent of the number of live births (Roger Schofield, "Did the mothers really die? Three centuries of maternal mortality in 'The World We Have Lost'," in *The World We Have Gained: Histories of Population and Social Structure* [Oxford, 1986], 237; Henri Leridon, *Natalité, saisons et conjoncture économique* [Paris, 1973], 17) so there should have been not less than about 2,600 stillbirths, and probably between 3,500 and 4,000. This means that at most one in twelve was recorded. Even though male stillbirths are more likely to occur than female ones, there were unlikely to have been three times as many.

bearing in mind the possibility that at times target families were quite high, so that the Irish, for example, could have been restricting their fertility late in their married lives after producing a comparatively large family earlier. This, together with the effects of higher morbidity and mortality in Southern England (especially if gastrointestinal diseases were particularly significant there) seems the best explanation why the Southern English population, so similar in other ways to the Irish, did not have nearly such high fertility, and why its fertility increased markedly after 1750. But some of the evidence, as we have seen, is difficult to interpret, and not all of it supports the theory which generally seems the best. It requires, in any case, a careful examination of the other possible explanations, and it is to these alternatives that we now turn.

While statistical inferences about conscious control of human fertility are not always conclusive, statistical techniques for examining other variations in "natural" fertility are even less developed, and we encounter the same lack of direct or literary evidence to account for the observed wide differences.

There are, of course, a number of possible explanations for variations in natural fertility – in fact, as usual, the more difficult it is to find evidence, the more hypotheses abound. For example, subfecundity, rather ironically, can be genetically transmitted, so that some populations may have a genetic make-up predisposing them to have fewer children. Levels of nutrition may affect the age at which menstruation begins, and some research, though contradicted by other studies, seems to show that inadequately nourished women find it more difficult to ovulate or become pregnant, and that the pregnancies which do occur are more likely to end in miscarriage.[24]

[24] The weight and age of the mother also have some effect (though it may be a slight one) on the speed with which she resumes menstruating. A study of women in Boston who gave birth in August and September 1963 found that the mean duration of amenorrhea was two months in women who did not breast-feed and five to six months for mothers who breast-fed for more than half a year. But women in modern Boston, unlike many in past populations, are well nourished, and this may make them start ovulating again quicker. As Rose Frisch has pointed out, four months of nursing takes an extra 120,000 calories from the mother, whereas the whole of pregnancy requires only 50,000 calories. It would seem women without adequate food would find it difficult to resume reproductive life while suffering such a drain on her caloric reserves; yet a study of lactation of women in modern Bangladesh did not find a very strong relationship between body weight of the mother and amenorrhea during lactation. On this see E. J. Salber, M. Feinlaub, and B. MacMahon, "The duration of post-partum amenorrhea," *American Journal of Epidemiology* 82 (1965), 347–58; Frisch, "Demographic implications," 18; and Sandra L. Huffman, A. K. M. Alauddin Chowdhury, and Zenas M. Sykes, "Lactation and fertility in rural Bangladesh," *Population Studies* 34 (1980), 337–47.

Vitamin E deficiencies are known to impair fertility, but it is not clear how common these were in the past, or even how we could detect them.

Besides these reasons why women may be less likely to conceive or carry a pregnancy through to a live birth, lactation inhibits the next conception; a change in nursing patterns (most obviously, if mothers decide to nurse their babies themselves rather than employing wet-nurses) can thus result in a considerable difference in fertility levels, even though some nursing mothers do become pregnant. It is this which operates one of the many homeostatic mechanisms which we find in regimes of "natural fertility": high infant mortality evokes higher fertility, because the death of the suckling infant stops lactation, and so the mother is ready to conceive again sooner.

Besides these physiological explanations there are many which point to cultural practices. In some cultures nursing continues for more than two years, and there can be a taboo on sexual intercourse with a nursing mother (or a superstition that her milk would be ruined if she were sexually active). Galen had required that no nursing woman have sexual intercourse, though it appears that this prohibition was not observed in Britain.[25] Such customs and beliefs, although they have the effect of reducing the number of conceptions, are still regarded as consistent with natural fertility, since they are not adopted for that conscious purpose.

Even without the benefit of taboo, superstition, or what passed for expert medical opinion, the frequency of intercourse is quite variable. For one thing, it is age-specific, declining the older one gets. In modern populations, coital frequency has been estimated as half at age forty what it was at age twenty, and some authorities believe that the decline is a function not of age but of the duration of the marriage.[26] This probably was true in the past as well, although there is no way to tell. In areas where there was a great deal of seasonal migration, married couples might be separated a good part of the year.

We also should not let the unmeasurable become the invisible, and thereupon assume it was the non-existent. Heterosexual genital inter-

Thomas McKeown and J. R. Gibson, in "A note on menstruation and conception during lactation," *Journal of Obstetrics and Gynaecology of the British Empire* 61 (1954), 824–26 deny that there is any relationship at all between nursing and amenorrhea; but this opinion seems to rest on ignoring the intensivity of nursing required to inhibit menstruation.

25 Valerie Fildes, *Breasts, Bottles and Babies: A History of Infant Feeding* (Edinburgh, 1986), 60–64, 105.

26 W. H. James, "The causes of the decline in fecundability with age," *Social Biology* 26 (1979), 330–34; C. Tietze, "Probability of conception resulting from a single unprotected coitus," *Fertility and Sterility* 11 (1960), 485–88.

course is not always the preferred outlet for sexual drives.[27] It would be astonishing if there were no homosexual Quakers. We cannot estimate their numbers, much less guess why these numbers may have changed over time or whether there were proportionally more in England than in Ireland; but this does not mean they were not there.

Some of these possible explanations of differences in natural fertility almost certainly do not apply to the Quakers. As we demonstrated in chapter 2, the genetic make-up of the English and of the Irish Quaker populations was very similar. Nor do we find any explanation based on nutritional levels any more convincing than one based on genetic differences. While the effect of a true famine could be devastating, it is less clear that moderate, chronic undernourishment had much effect on fertility.[28] Even if it did, there is no evidence of malnutrition among the Quakers. The English Friends do not show high mortality in years of dearth and in fact we have no reason to believe they were significantly worse nourished than the Irish, much less that they suffered in famines. If there was any difference, it probably was the English who were better fed.

We may be on firmer ground with the known link between lactation and fertility variations. How likely is it that differences in nursing customs can explain the low Southern English fertility before 1750?

Nursing undoubtedly delays resumption of menstruation, although the precise relationship between them is not yet entirely understood. It appears that it is not just the duration, but also the intensity, of breast-feeding that determines when menstruation will resume. Once the mother begins to wean the baby, or introduces supplemental food, the level of prolactin she secretes may decline below the threshold which had prevented the hormones initiating menstruation from

---

[27] We are indebted to Henry Abelove for raising this point.

[28] See Emanuel LeRoy Ladurie, "L'Aménorrhée de famine (XVIIe–XXe siècles)," *Annales: Economies, Sociétés, Civilisations* 24ᵉ année (1969), 1589–1601. Besides the article by Bongaarts cited in n. 11, see Rose Frisch, "Nutrition, fatness and fertility: the effect of food intake on reproductive ability," in H. W. Mosley, ed., *Nutrition and Human Reproduction* (New York, 1978), 91–122. A recent article by Jane Menken, James Trussell, and Susan Watkins, "The nutrition fertility link: an evaluation of the evidence," *Journal of Interdisciplinary History* 11 (1981), 425–41 reviews the controversy and finds that despite its simplicity and plausibility the proposed linkage is not well supported by studies done thus far. It is worth quoting their skeptical and rather despondent conclusion (441): "The difficulties in obtaining information on these factors are enormous and we are not sanguine that the historian, however diligent, will be able to marshal convincing evidence. Yet, to accept nutrition as the primary explanation of fertility differences simply because the truth is difficult (or perhaps impossible) to discover is a retreat to adoption of a simplistic and convenient hypothesis which has yet to be substantiated." Unfortunately their candidate to explain natural fertility variations, frequency of intercourse, is equally difficult to get information about, and subject to many of the same doubts.

operating. An attempt to construct a model schedule for the effects of lactation suggests that it is in the period from ten to twenty months after giving birth that lactation would do the most to prevent a further conception; after twenty months and earlier than ten it would be less significant.[29] So although ovulation has a chance of recurring after a few months, especially if supplementary food is given to the child, a population where the mothers regularly nursed for a year or more, and children received no supplementary food, would have higher birth intervals (for all births past the first, of course) than one where women regularly had immediate recourse to wet-nurses (or to hand-feeding of some kind).[30]

But how shall we determine whether mothers in the seventeenth or eighteenth centuries nursed their babies, and if so, for how long? We can seldom get reliable literary evidence, so perforce most studies have focused on cases where the mother could not have been nursing, because her child had died (and assuming she did not herself have employment as a wet-nurse for somebody else's child). Thus among the extremely fertile Québecois women who lived around 1700, Jacques Henripin found that when a baby lived only a few days, the next birth followed on average 19.3 months later; when it lived for one to six months, the next interval was 18.3 months. Survival up to eleven months increased the interval to 23.6 months, and it was on average 25 months when the previous child survived for more than a year.[31] In Crulai, the differences were more dramatic; when a child died before the end of the first year, the interval to the next birth was nine months shorter (20.7 as against 29.4 months). Gautier and Henry assumed – perhaps rashly – that since this was a small rural parish in a pre-industrial population, almost all the mothers nursed their babies.[32] In

[29] R. J. Lesthaeghe and H. J. Page, "The post-partum non-susceptible period: development and application of model schedules," *Population Studies* 34 (1980), 165.

[30] See J.-P. Habicht, Julie Davanzo, W. P. Butz, and Linda Myers, "The contraceptive role of breastfeeding," *Population Studies* 39 (1985), 213–32; John Knodel and Etienne van de Walle, "Breast feeding, fertility and infant mortality: an analysis of some early German data," *Population Studies* 21 (1967), 124; P. W. Howie, A. S. McNeilly, M. J. Houston, A. Cook, and H. Boyle, "Effect of supplementary food on suckling patterns and ovarian activity during lactation," *British Medical Journal* 283 (1981), 757–59; B. A. Gross and C. J. Eastman, "Prolactin secretion during prolonged lactational amenorrhoea," *Australian & New Zealand Journal of Obstetrics and Gynaecology* 19 (1979), 95–99; and M. R. Duchen and A. S. McNeilly, "Hyperprolactinaemia and long-term lactational amenorrhoea," *Clinical Endocrinology* 12 (1980), 621–27.

[31] Jacques Henripin, "La Fécondité des ménages canadiens au début du XVIIIe siècle," *Population* 9e année (1954), 61–84.

[32] Louis Henry and Emile Gautier, *La Population de Crulai, paroisse normande* (Paris, 1959), 153. Even if the assumption that almost all mothers nursed their babies is valid, the causal chain might be reversed: that is, an early pregnancy could interrupt lactation, and thus the infant, deprived of its best source of nourishment, would die. However

a survey of ten populations, all but two from the seventeenth through nineteenth centuries, George Masnick showed that birth intervals were usually six to eleven months longer when a preceding child had survived; but he pointed out that not all of this lengthening can be attributed to post-partum amenorrhea extended by breast-feeding.[33]

Given the difficulty in getting any independent evidence about lactation, one is tempted to explain variations in fertility by different nursing practices, and then prove that there were these nursing practices by the variations in fertility.[34] There is a little independent evidence, albeit fragmentary, about whether (and how) the English Quakers nursed their babies. It comes from the journals and letters of four mothers (and one father) from the latter half of the eighteenth and first part of the nineteenth centuries.[35] Four mothers attempted to nurse their children; the fifth sent hers to the countryside to be nursed. Two mothers encountered difficulty producing enough milk for at least one of their children, which may explain why these sources mention nursing at all.

A non-random sample of five out of some tens of thousands of Quaker mothers alive at the time, while typical of work with literary sources, poses obvious statistical problems. We can add, however, that there would have been strong ideological support for maternal nursing. It was a standard recommendation of Puritan handbooks on family life,[36] and the commonest objections to it (that it would ruin women's figures or interrupt sexual relations) would have sounded worldly to the Quakers.

Nevertheless, it is necessary to try the indirect approach to this question, by studying the effect of previous deaths of infants on the interval before the next birth. This is done in Table 4.11. Except in the cities, there is a tendency for a slight hastening in the next pregnancy if the immediately previously born baby died as an infant, but the

Henry and Gautier were able to show that in Crulai in the great majority of cases the death of the earlier infant antedated the presumed date of the new conception.
[33] George S. Masnick, "The demographic impact of breast feeding: a critical review," *Human Biology* 51 (1979), 109–25.
[34] A trap fallen – or rather plunged – into by Dorothy McLaren, "Fertility, infant mortality, and breast feeding in the 17th century," *Medical History* 22 (1978), 378–96. U.-B. Lithell, "Breastfeeding habits and their relation to infant mortality and child fertility," *Journal of Family History* 6 (1981), 182–94 is not free of the same problem.
[35] We were unable to improve on the comprehensive search for these sources made by Linda A. Pollock in *Forgotten Children: Parent-Child Relations from 1500 to 1900* (Cambridge, 1983). Since the Quakers were such avid keepers of journals, they furnish a disproportionate share of the evidence she cites. Her discussion of the extent of breast-feeding is on pp. 212–22.
[36] Fildes, *Breasts, Bottles and Babies*, 98–99.

Table 4.11   *Effect of death of previous child on birth interval before conception of next child*

	n	Mean	s.d.
Southern England			
When previous child has died	607	20.5	6.3
When previous child survives	5189	22.2	6.5
Northern Britain			
When previous child has died	367	21.4	NA
When previous child survives	5499	22.2	NA
Urban			
When previous child has died	819	20.7	6.3
When previous child survives	3972	20.7	6.7
Ireland			
When previous child has died	652	20.7	6.2
When previous child survives	5632	22.0	6.5

difference is much less than the six to eleven months reported by
Masnick. Furthermore, the fertility of the urban Quakers rose most
remarkably in the period when their babies were enjoying much better
chances of survival (Table 5.2).

As we have seen, the length and intensity of nursing matter a great
deal. Data on age at weaning are even more sparse than on the
prevalence of breast-feeding; but it appears that there was a significant
tendency in the eighteenth century to wean children earlier. Medical
authorities, whose tracts were increasingly addressed to lay readers,
were recommending earlier weaning, partly because more acceptable
artificial foods were becoming available.[37] Estimates of actual mean
ages at weaning in the eighteenth century range from seven and a half
to ten and a half months; the four Quaker children we know about
were weaned at an average age of thirteen months.[38]

If it was the custom of Quakers to nurse children for any substantial

---

[37] *Ibid.*, 370.

[38] The lower estimate (disproportionately based on eight children of royal family!) is
from Fildes, *Breasts, Bottles and Babies*, 355; the higher one was made by Pollock,
Forgotten Children, 220. Pollock actually gives a mean of 9.5 months, but she has
included one child (a Quaker) who was taken from the breast aged one week because
its mother had no milk. We do not consider this a genuine case of weaning,
particularly since in all likelihood the child was then sent to a wet-nurse, so we have
recalculated the mean omitting this figure.

period of time – seventeen months, let us say[39] – Table 4.11 should have told a different story. There should have been more nursing (and thus a longer period of amenorrhea) when a larger percentage of children were surviving infancy; but this would produce fewer, not more, babies. So either lactation did not do much to prevent renewed ovulation or (more likely) babies were not nursed very long by their mothers in any case.

Finally, let us consider the possible effects of differing frequencies of intercourse. Total abstinence is of course the perfect contraceptive. As we have seen, complete abstinence from intercourse for substantial periods of time is most likely to be the contraceptive measure which seventeenth-century Friends took. In the seventeenth century also, Quaker couples were sometimes parted by the imprisonment of one or even both; and the extensive traveling which many Friends undertook may have had an inhibiting effect on their chances of having children. Though couples who never have sexual relations will engender no children, it is not clear how infrequent intercourse must become to have a substantial effect on fertility. "Moderate" rather than "low" frequencies enhance the chances of conception; but intercourse daily, as opposed to every other day, apparently adds little to the chances of conception, and may even impair them.[40] Not surprisingly, there is no quantitative evidence about the frequency of sexual relations among the Quakers, and even what we know about the separations of Quaker couples is hard to evaluate quantitatively. We think, though, that abstinence from intercourse played some role in limiting fertility, although not often with that intention.

What we have found about the reproductive behavior of the Quakers seems to confound the conventional wisdom of demographers and dramatize the uniqueness of their way of life; but we believe there is a way of making sense of it. If, as we have argued, the Southern English Quakers were employing family limitation in the late seventeenth century, they appear to be the only people – except possibly the famous Colytonians – to have been doing so. This would mean that for them the conventional chronology of the adoption of family limitation

---

[39] This is the mean for the twenty-four children in the sixteenth and seventeenth centuries whose ages at weaning are presented by Fildes, 355. We have again removed one child "weaned" at one week from the calculation.

[40] R. G. Potter and S. R. Millman, "Fecundability and the frequency of marital intercourse: a critique of nine models," *Population Studies* 39 (1985), 461–70; C. F. Westoff, R. G. Potter, and P. C. Sagi, *The Third Child* (Princeton, 1963), which finds only a weak association (cited in Peter A. Lachenbruch, "Frequency and timing of intercourse: its relation to the probability of conception," *Population Studies* 21 [1967], 23).

was in reverse order; prudential checks to marriage are supposed to operate *until* the nineteenth century, and then contraception was introduced, first in urban areas and among the middle classes, then spreading to the countryside, so that couples married early and still had a family no larger than they could comfortably support.

We find the reproductive behavior of the Quaker better explained by the concept of "adjustment" rather than "innovation" in fertility control. As Gösta Carlsson has written:

Birth control, and especially contraception, need not be regarded as new or recent in human society. There may have been a "steady state" in which birth control was practised by part of a population, or it may have been practised with higher fertility targets. The decline in fertility is then regarded as an adjustment to a new set of forces, defining a new equilibrium level of modern or "controlled" fertility.[41]

Further support of this contention can be found in data from the Genevan bourgeoisie and British peerage. Fertility of the Genevan bourgeoisie was measured in terms of birth intervals; that of the British nobility mainly in family size (completed families were not treated separately). Family limitation in Geneva began in the latter part of the seventeenth century; it was introduced not just to avoid having very large families, but to remain at or below the average family size.[42] Their fertility was consequently consistently lower than that of the British, and substantially lower than that of the Irish, Quakers. Henry, however, finds no evidence of a "spacing" as against a "stopping" strategy. The interval between marriage and first birth (which might be disturbed to an undeterminable degree by pre-nuptial pregnancies) varied remarkably, from a very long 22.6 months in the last half of the seventeenth century to only 15.4 in the eighteenth and 18.1 in the nineteenth. (The numbers here are small, which may account for these wide swings.) There is, as Henry notes, no apparent evolution towards a longer interval before the first birth; the mean for all cohorts (going back before 1600) is 18.4 months.[43] The Genevans accomplished their family limitation by longer intervals before later births, and especially by very long intervals (more than four years) before the last one.[44] In Southern England, where we think the

[41] Gösta Carlsson, "The decline of fertility: innovation or adjustment process," *Population Studies* 20 (1966), 150. Carlsson does not produce any historical evidence before the census era, but tries to make the case by showing that fertility control was just as advanced in rural areas as in the metropolises, and that some Swedish regions had markedly lower fertility than others in 1860, which must have been the result of a long historical development (156–60).

[42] Louis Henry, *Anciennes familles genevoises, étude démographique, XVIᵉ–XXᵉ siècles* (Paris, 1956), 83, 107.

[43] *Ibid.*, 93.   [44] *Ibid.*, 94–95.

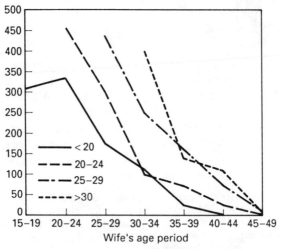

Genevan bourgeoisie, eighteenth century

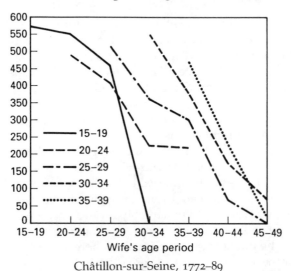

Châtillon-sur-Seine, 1772–89

Fig. 4.3 Age-specific fertility, groups practicing family limitation.
Sources: Henry, *Anciennes familles genevoises*; Antoinette Chamoux and Cécile Dauphin, "La Contraception avant la Révolution française: l'exemple de Châtillon-sur-Seine," *Annales: Economies, Sociétés, Civilisations* 24ᵉ année (1969), 672.

evidence for a spacing strategy is strongest, the interval before the first birth was around twenty months. Even 18.4 months seems to us rather long (among the Irish Quakers it was never more than 16) and we believe that the Genevan bourgeoisie may also have employed both spacing and stopping strategies.

A comparison with the families of the peerage is made in Table 4.12.

Table 4.12   *Children ever born, British and Irish Quaker and British peerage families*

	British peerage		Southern English Quakers		Urban Quakers		Irish Quakers	
	Mean	s.d.	Mean	s.d.	Mean	s.d.	Mean	s.d.
1650–74	4.54	NA						
1675–99	4.46	NA						
1650–99			4.0	3.0	3.5	3.3	5.4	3.4
1700–24	3.83	NA						
1725–49	4.51	NA						
1700–49			4.0	3.1	3.6	3.5	6.1	3.8
1750–74	4.91	NA						
1775–99	4.98	NA						
1750–99			4.3	3.5	4.3	3.6	6.1	4.1
1800–24	4.64	NA						
1825–49	4.06	NA						
1800–49			3.7	3.4	4.4	3.5	5.6	4.3

Note: Figures for the British peerage are from Hollingsworth, *Demography*, Table 19, p. 30 (combined for families of secondary males and secondary females, and adjusted for all forms of underenumeration). Quaker figures are for all families formed, at all marriage ranks, but excluding those where the date of marriage, date of the end of the marriage, or date of the wife's birth are unknown. No adjustment for possible underenumeration has been made in the Quaker figures.

If Hollingsworth's allowances for underenumeration are approximately correct, it appears that the children of peers had consistently larger families than the English Quakers, but quite a bit smaller than those of the Irish. This does not, however, mean that their marital fertility was higher than that of the Southern English and urban Quakers; virtually all the difference can be explained by the lower ages at first marriage of the wives and sisters of the peers. A more intriguing point is that unlike the rest of the population, but like the Quakers, the peers' children not only experienced a sharp increase in fertility in the second half of the eighteenth century, but also did so despite a higher age at first marriage.[45]

[45] T. H. Hollingsworth, *The Demography of the British Peerage* (Supplement to *Population Studies* 18 [1965]), 26, 31. Table 4.12 is not a pure comparison of fertility. Besides the obvious effect of different ages at marriage, all families, rather than completed ones only, are included, so mortality influences the figures, in that some marriages were prematurely terminated by the death of one of the spouses.

Since marital fertility was capable of such an increase, the question must also arise whether the nobility were at some time practicing family limitation. One surprising aspect of their family life is the high number of infertile unions; during the period from 1675 to 1850 it was usually around 20 percent,[46] about three times the level that the Irish ever experienced and seldom approached by the British Quakers. It is hard to believe that purely physiological factors could produce so many childless unions. Probably some of the nobility were controlling marital fertility, *à la* the Count and Countess Almaviva, by simple refusal to cohabit. Hollingsworth believes it "likely that some form of family limitation, however crude, was used and was effective as early as 1650";[47] yet he admits there is no positive evidence of it and does not attempt to infer it from the fertility statistics. He dates the possible onset of family limitation very close to the time Henry suggests for the Genevan bourgeoisie, Wrigley argues for the inhabitants of Colyton, and we have claimed for the Southern English Quakers. If his surmise is correct it strengthens the case that family limitation was practiced by at least some subgroups in the population in the seventeenth and eighteenth centuries.

The long interval between marriage and first births among the Southern English Quakers, otherwise inexplicable, would fit a "spacing" strategy in which all intergenesic intervals were somewhat lengthened. (We have no direct evidence about nursing practices before 1750, but it is reasonable to suppose that mothers by and large nursed their own children, and for a considerable period of time, thus contributing to the leisurely pace of child-bearing.)

As we explained in chapter 3, it was primarily cultural factors, the effect of the religious discipline and the growing clannishness of the Quakers, that resulted in the elevated ages at first marriage after 1750. Marrying later, Friends (at least before 1800) had less anxiety about the total numbers of children they might have, and fertility rebounded to a high "natural" level. If, as we surmise, mothers were weaning their children earlier, and giving them supplementary food at an early age as well, periods of amenorrhea would be shorter, contributing to the shorter birth intervals.

One problem with this explanation is the fact that fertility rose so much after 1750 while infant mortality was falling. Table 4.11 showed that the death of the immediately previous child made comparatively little difference to the timing of the next conception, suggesting that nursing was not protracted nor intensive; but nevertheless in some

[46] *Ibid.*, Table 36, p. 46.   [47] *Ibid.*, 51.

populations there has been a strong relationship between high infant mortality and higher fertility, as though there were some mechanism, as yet unaccounted for, which could trigger a faster replacement even when there was no relationship with lactation or family limitation.[48] This may be simply another peculiarity of the Quakers, but it amplifies the phenomenon of rapid population growth after 1750.

In these, and other, respects, either our findings are wrong or else the conventional wisdom does not universally apply. We have pointed to the uncertainties which are commonly experienced in trying to measure the true fertility of past populations, and we do not claim to be exempt from them. Our temporal and geographical cohorts may be so small that random fluctuations weigh heavily. There may have been underregistration of children who did not live long. Some families may have moved in and out of our areas, or in and out of close association with Friends, and had children where or when they could not be registered and thus figure in our sample. We may have discarded from our analysis families whose records appeared to be incomplete when in fact they simply had no children. By estimating, in a few cases, mothers' ages, we may have increased or decreased the age-specific fertility ratios.

Having admitted all these possibilities, we can draw two logical conclusions. First, if there were errors in the records, or in our handling of them, they will be on the side of underenumeration of children. Thus the high fertility figures which we show must be more reliable than the low ones. Second, if there were any wrong attributions of children to families or cohorts, these cannot have had a systematic bias, but must have canceled one another out.

Since we are convinced that our records were kept as carefully as any others which historical demographers have exploited – not excluding the British peerage or the Genevan bourgeoisie – we believe other scholars are just as likely, or perhaps even more likely, to have got wrong results, especially if they have applied some general correction factor to compensate for what they believe to be universal underregistration. We have shown in detail why the Quakers, and their records, were *sui generis*; and so we cannot reject our findings simply on grounds that they stand out as significantly different from those about other populations.

Since we stand by the substantial accuracy of our findings, we have the further duty of interpreting them. We dismiss the possibility that

[48] Knodel and van de Walle, "Breast feeding," 129–30; John Knodel, "Child mortality and reproductive behavior in German village populations in the past: a micro-level analysis of the replacement effect," *Population Studies* 36 (1982), 177–200.

some inherited biological factor was at work leading to serious variations in fecundability, since almost all our families came from the same general genetic pool. The most that could have happened would have been that owing to intermarriage (not to kin as close as first cousins) some characteristics were perpetuated or others became more important as time went on (which could have shown up in an unusual frequency of sterility or twinning); but we found no evidence for such a supposition.

If genetic influences cannot explain the rise and subsequent fall in fertility, and the different extent to which this occurred in our various subpopulations, there appear to be only two other possibilities: either the changes, and their local incidence, reflect physiological conditions which were part of the local environments at different times, or there were behavior patterns (that is, response of individuals or groups to changing economic influences and social perceptions) which led different groups at different times to produce families of varying sizes.

Physiological differences may have been at work, in that our most striking contrast, between the Southern English and the Irish, could have been in some degree owing to a high incidence of gastrointestinal illnesses in Southern England, which had a deleterious effect on the chances of carrying pregnancies to term. We have also shown that there was a somewhat higher incidence of definitive sterility among the Southern English families, which again may reflect physiological effects of the environment. But there is also some evidence of family limitation, especially in Southern England before 1750 and again in the genealogies after 1825, achieved as much through spacing from the first birth onward as by stopping once the target-size family was achieved.

Some of the puzzles we raised on p. 143 are as yet unsolved. The timing of the onset of family limitation in England and in the American colonies remains somewhat mysterious; but at least we think we can establish that family limitation (probably effected in the seventeenth century through abstinence from intercourse) was part of the repertoire of behavior patterns which the American Quaker settlers brought over with them. (It may be significant, in this connection, that when London Yearly Meeting appointed a committee to give advice on marriage in 1933, the committee's report did not condemn contraceptives, at a time when almost all other religious bodies were still doing so.)

The apparent anomalies in our findings are not surprising, since even after twenty years of concentrated work, demographic history is still too new for a comprehensive and convincing theory of fertility to emerge. The troubles we found in adapting a model fertility schedule (discussed in the Appendix to this chapter) are symptomatic of a more general difficulty; even the demographic theory that we have, based as it is on the kinds of data which can be produced by modern states and the distinctive biological and sociological regimes of modern societies, often fits only perplexingly (or Procrusteanly) the data from a pre-industrial population – especially one with the distinctive character-istics of the Society of Friends.

But our lack of direct evidence about such matters as nursing or child care, and the plethora of unverifiable hypotheses which seem to address the particular demography of the British and Irish Quakers, should not obscure the brute facts. At least in this segment of the population, fertility rose substantially after 1750, and since infant mortality was falling, the result had a strong tendency to increase the population (though the total number of Quakers was diminished by emigrations and disownments). Quakers in all parts of Britain and Ireland seem to have shared in this increasing fertility, though the rise was naturally not so pronounced among the populations which already had high fertility, especially the Irish. The period of the greatest rise was the twenty-five years on either side of 1800 (which makes the conventional cohorts of 1750–99 and 1800–49 in this case rather misleading). In the cities, where more and more Quakers were coming to live, fertility continued to climb strongly even after 1800. Only after 1850, in the genealogies, do we see unmistakable signs of general and conscious fertility control, although the more prominent families represented in the genealogies had probably begun employ-ing it at least a generation earlier.

We have already had occasion to refer to the relationship between fertility and mortality, since neither can be fully understood without knowledge of the other. Now it is time to turn our attention to the other side of the eternal equation between life and death.

Appendix

The most recently developed, and statistically elegant, test for family limitation depends on a "natural fertility" schedule developed by Ansley Coale and T. James Trussell.[1] Coale and Trussell averaged age-specific marital fertility rates for ten modern populations presented by Louis Henry as examples of natural fertility.[2] They then constructed an index of the degree of fertility control, m, which depends purely on the steepness of decline in age-specific fertility in the later years.[3]

[1] Ansley Coale and T. James Trussell, "Model fertility schedules in the age structure of childbearing in human populations," *Population Index* 40 (1974), 185–258. In an erratum note they presented revised figures in *ibid*. 41 (1975), 572.

[2] Coale and Trussell did not bother to disclose which ten populations they used for their model fertility schedule, but they came from the following thirteen presented by Henry in "Natural fertility," 81–91: (American) Hutterites married between 1921 and 1930; French Canadian women married from 1700 to 1730; Hutterites married before 1930; wives of Genevan bourgeois men born between 1600 and 1649; Europeans of Tunis (except notables) married from 1840 to 1859; marriages and baptisms in Sotteville-les-Rouen, Normandy, from 1760 to 1790; Crulai, Normandy, marriages from 1674 to 1742; Norwegian marriages from 1874 to 1876; marriages in Iranian villages, 1940 to 1950; wives of Genevan bourgeois men born before 1600; Taiwanese women from the rural region of Yunlin born about 1900; Hindu villages of Bengal in India, marriages of 1945 and 1946; and the villages of Fouta-Djalon in Guinea, marriages from 1954 to 1955. Since the article was published in 1961, when the couples married in the 1940s and 1950s could not have completed their fertility, we presume it was the Iranian, Bengali, and Guinean populations which were omitted.

[3] The basic formula is:

$$m = \log[r(a)/M \cdot n(a)]/v(a)$$

Here $n(a)$ is the standard fertility schedule derived from Henry's ten populations; $r(a)$ is the fertility schedule to be tested; M is a scale factor equal to the ratio of $r(a)$ to $n(a)$ at age 20–24; and $v(a)$ is also an empirically derived function representing a typical age pattern of voluntary fertility control. The values of $n(a)$ and $v(a)$ as presented by Coale and Trussell in the revised version of their figures are:

	20–24	25–29	30–34	35–39	40–44	45–49
$n(a)$	0.460	0.431	0.395	0.322	0.167	0.024
$v(a)$	0.000	−0.279	−0.677	−1.042	−1.414	−1.671

The differences that might be made by varying ages at marriage and duration of marriages are not considered, and the fertility level at age 20–24 is taken to be the maximum fertility achieved by that population.[4] When the decline from that maximum is less sharp than in the average populations, the value of m is negative; where there is no fertility control, it will be close to zero, while 1.0 represents the level of family limitation found in a typical modern population.

We have computed the value of m for all cohorts of our total population and also for the one where family limitation is most likely to have been practiced, the Southern English group. The results are inconclusive, but cast considerable doubt on the utility of this method when applied to our population (and probably to all pre-industrial populations). In one cohort, that for all British Quakers between 1800 and 1824, there is a practically perfect fit with the model of populations not practicing family limitation (that is, all m values were close to zero), but the results from most of the others suggest that there was a different age structure of child-bearing in pre-industrial populations. It will be recalled from Table 4.1 that in three of the seven quarter centuries, age-specific fertility was greater in the 25–29 age-group than in the 20–24 one; this is also true of two of the four cohorts in Southern England. (In fact, it was also consistently true of the Hutterites, those models of natural and high fertility.)[5] This naturally leads to large negative values for m in several of the cohorts for this age period, which in fact did not have a single positive value anywhere. Other negative m values were not uncommon, and when we took the means of the five m values for the age period from 25–29 to 45–49, there was a high standard deviation, suggesting considerable divergence both ways from the model population.

In general, m values did move towards the positive after age 29, and were usually moderately positive for women in their thirties and forties. Overall, however, the means of m values were usually negative. The only cohorts consistently positive at all ages above 30 were 1725–74 for all British Quakers and 1750–99 for the Southern English. It will be recalled that there was a strong upswing in general fertility after 1750.

---

[4] The age-group 15–19 is ruled out because some of the populations had a substantial number of pre-nuptial pregnancies in that age-group, and also because of teenage subfecundity.

[5] J. W. Eaton and A. J. Mayer, *Man's Capacity to Reproduce: The Demography of a Unique Population* (Glencoe, IL, 1954), 24. They attribute this effect to combining the women into five-year age groups.

In summary: most Quakers had more children in their late twenties
and fewer in their thirties and forties than the model fertility schedule
would predict. Their fertility curve is thus different; and this may have
been because of family limitation (though it need not have been so).

The value of the model fertility schedule in revealing the existence of
family limitation has been debated by E. A. Wrigley and Richard B.
Morrow in connection with a discussion of family limitation in
Colyton.[6] Colyton's population at the time when, according to
Wrigley, family limitation was being practiced also had a higher
fertility in the 25–29 age-group than in the 20–24 one, and the strong
negative m value for that age-group overwhelmed the positive values
in the next three age-groups to yield a negative m overall. So Morrow,
adhering strictly to the model fertility schedule, claimed there was no
family limitation, in spite of the positive m values from age 30 to 44.
Wrigley, however, contended that the higher fertility in age-group
25–29 is an anomaly which arises from the ages at marriage characteristic of Colyton women. Comparatively few married before age 25, and
many of these married at age 24, thus contributing one woman-year
lived to that group before having their first child in the next age-group.
He points out that if the anomaly is removed by standardizing peak
fertility at the level for age-group 25–29, the evidence for family
limitation after age 30 looks much stronger.[7] If the same operation
were performed on the figures for the British Quakers, the case for
family limitation among them would be similarly strengthened.

"Anomalies" such as Colyton are by no means isolated cases. In fact
they may seem anomalous only if we think modern populations must
be normal. Age at marriage is a crucial variable, as Wrigley pointed out
with respect to Colyton. Since the interval between marriage and the
first birth was almost always the shortest in a pre-industrial population, if many women married between the ages of 25 and 29, fertility
would necessarily be particularly high in that age period.

It is also possible that subfecundity in pre-industrial populations
may have lasted on well into the twenties, so that the late twenties
really did see peak fertility. The question hinges on when menstruation began. In England and Scotland in the mid nineteenth century,
menarche seems to have come, on the average, at age 15 or 16. If
menarche came that late, Rose Frisch has argued, fitness for procreation would be reached at age 22 and the ages best suited for

---

[6] Richard B. Morrow, "Family limitation in pre-industrial England: a reappraisal,"
Economic History Review 2nd ser. 31 (1978), 419–28 and E. A. Wrigley, "Marital fertility
in seventeenth-century Colyton: a note," *ibid.*, 429–36.
[7] Wrigley, "Marital fertility," 430–34.

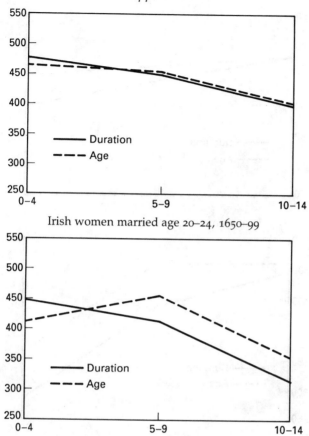

Irish women married age 20–24, 1650–99

Irish women married age 25–29, 1650–99
Fig. 4.A1 Comparison of age- and duration-specific fertility.

procreation would be 25 to 29.[8] Age at menarche is certainly lower
now than it was then; but it is not safe to conclude that the figures
for the mid nineteenth century must be, in turn, lower than those for
the seventeenth century. One of the earliest and most thorough
students of this subject, Gaston Bachmann, believed that the age of
menarche was at its height in the nineteenth century – it may have
been as high as 17, on average, just after 1800 – but had been only 14 in
the Middle Ages. After 1500, he believed, the average age at menarche
slowly rose.[9] The evidence is so sparse, and depends so greatly on the

[8] Rose E. Frisch, "Population, food intake, and fertility," *Science* 199 (1978), 23. We wish
to thank Professor Frisch for having given us the correct citation for this article.
[9] Gaston Bachmann, "Die beschleunigte Entwicklung der Jugend," *Acta Anatomica* 4
(1947–48), 421–80. A good summary of research on the ancient and medieval periods is

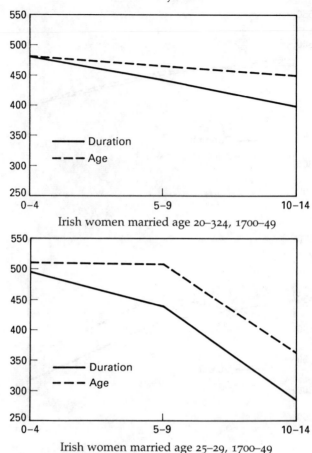

Irish women married age 20–324, 1700–49

Irish women married age 25–29, 1700–49

opinions of physicians, that the question will probably never be satisfactorily resolved.

offered by C. J. Diers in "Historical trends in the age at menarche and menopause," *Psychological Reports* 34 (June 1974), 931–37. She notes, however, that there is very little evidence for the period 1500–1800. She and D. W. Amundsen wrote on the age of menarche in classical antiquity (*Human Biology* 41 [1969], 125–32) and in the Middle Ages (*ibid.* 45 [1973], 363–69); they believe the average was 13.5 in the classical period. J. B. Post in "Age at menarche and menopause: some medieval authorities," *Population Studies* 25 (1971), 83–87 collects the opinions of medieval writers, who generally thought menarche occurred in the thirteenth or fourteenth year. These estimates rest on medical and legal writings. The best body of quantifiable data bearing on the question seems to be the census of Belgrade in 1733–34; making the assumption that menarche must have occurred before marriage (which was early and nearly universal, in Hajnal's "eastern European" pattern) Peter Laslett has concluded that menarche must have usually occurred before age fifteen and perhaps even earlier. Out of thirty-one women he studied from a community listing at Chilvers Coton, Warwickshire, in 1684, ten conceived before age 20 ("Age at menarche in Europe since the eighteenth century," *Journal of Interdisciplinary History* 2 [1971–72], 221–36).

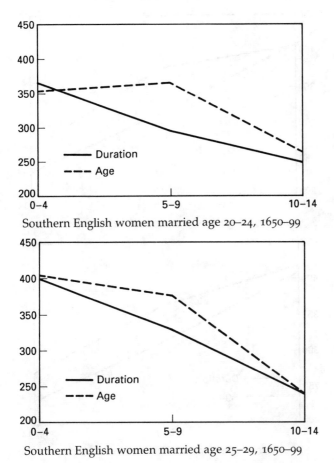

Southern English women married age 20–24, 1650–99

Southern English women married age 25–29, 1650–99

It is also possible, of course, that women's child-bearing ability was more impaired by previous pregnancies than it would be today, so that they bore fewer children in their late 30s and 40s because they were less fecund, not because they were trying to have no further children.

There is a way to see whether higher fertility at age 25–29 is real or a statistical artifact arising from the way the groups were constructed. This is to look at both age-specific and duration-specific fertility. If there was a real peak in fertility after age 25, women married between ages 20 and 24 might be expected to show some such peak in the fifth to ninth years of their marriages; and women who married after age 25 should have had more children in the first five years of their marriages than those who married earlier. Figure 4A.1 unfortunately gives inconclusive results. When the age-specific figures are graphed

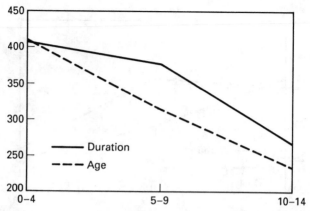

Southern English women married age 20–24, 1700–49

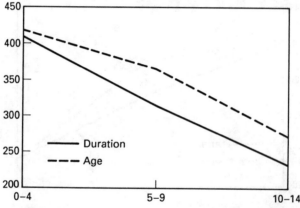

Southern English women married aged 25–29, 1700–49

against the duration-specific ones for Southern England and Ireland, there is a steady decline in fertility as the marriage continues, not the rise in the age 25–29 age period which is familiar from the age-specific fertility figures alone. On the other hand, when we compare the fertility during the first five years of their marriages of women married between age 20 and 24 with that of those married aged 25 to 29, the latter have equal or slightly higher fertility. This may be owing to a bunching of marriages just before the age-bound change; but it may also be evidence that there is something to the argument that fecundity might be higher at this age, or at the very least that it did not decline as fast as in a modern population.

In any case the use of the model fertility schedule does not seem able to prove that there was family limitation, though it is suggestive. It ignores the important difference made by varying ages at marriage and duration of marriage; and it is unlikely that norms of "natural fertility" of modern populations are valid for all past eras. As Hilary Page has demonstrated, these are serious shortcomings.[10]

[10] Hilary J. Page, "Patterns underlying fertility schedules: a decomposition by both age and marriage duration," *Population Studies* 31 (1977), 85–106. See also the critique of the Coale-Trussell technique in John Knodel, "Family limitation and the fertility transition: Evidence from the age-patterns of fertility in Europe and Asia," *Population Studies* 31 (1977), 219–49.

5

The quality and quantity of life

The measurements of births and marriages which we have presented assume their full significance only when we know what toll death was taking. The same level of fertility will obviously have very different consequences if only half the children survive to adulthood than if three-quarters of them do so. Furthermore, it is often easier to detect the impact of conditions like poor nutrition in higher mortality than in lower fertility. This has made mortality rates, especially those of infants and children, the best indicator of standards of living in general: quality and quantity of life come close together.

As with fertility and nuptiality, deaths can either be considered aggregatively, in terms of the numbers occurring in any given period, or by age-specific rates. Since the latter measurements, especially life expectancy, are more discriminating, these are the ones on which we shall concentrate; but some useful information can come from looking at what appear to be "crisis" years in British and Irish Quaker mortality.

A "crisis" of mortality can be variously defined, but in our usage it refers to a season when mortality in a given quarter of a year was more than one and a half times greater than the nine-year moving average for that quarter. We must caution, however, against misconstruing our series of total deaths. Only persons who the registers show had already formed families, and the members of those families, will appear in our mortality figures. The difference this makes can be seen most dramatically in the figures we have for deaths in London in 1665. Although the Quaker burial registers show that dozens of Quakers died in the great plague epidemic, only two were recorded on our forms. In the seventeenth century the age structure of the Quakers was probably quite different from that of the general population, which would make a total death figure misleading, and from about

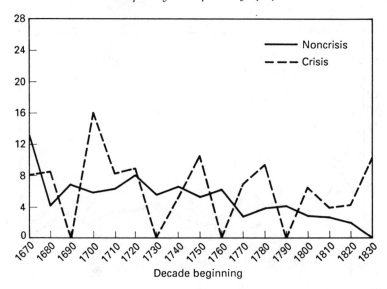

Urban

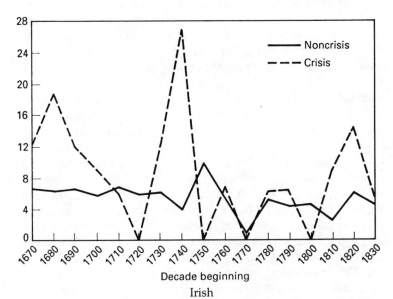

Irish

Fig. 5.1 Percentage of "clustered" deaths, "crisis" and "non-crisis" years, urban, Irish, and Southern English Quakers.

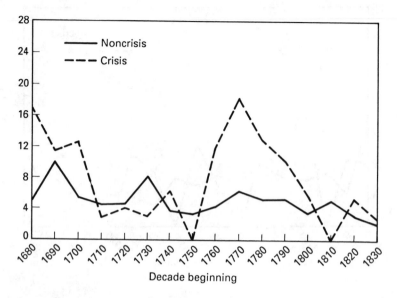

Decade beginning

1760 on disownments and resignations were also frequent enough to disturb death totals. Since our aggregative series are subject to these perturbations, the index of crisis mortality which we use has to do with deaths which occur in the same family during a period of heavy mortality (on the supposition that famine or epidemic would be more likely to strike people living together).

Deaths within the same family in a quarter, which we call "clustered" deaths, are shown as a percentage of total mortality by decade in Figure 5.1. Such deaths occur with some frequency in "non-crisis" years as well (death in childbed accompanied by the death of the infant is a typical instance) but the curve for clustered deaths in crisis years is much more volatile, and usually exceeds that for non-crisis years. London generally shows a lower percentage of clustered deaths, whether in crisis or not; but the over-all mortality there was generally higher. In the metropolis many infectious diseases were endemic, taking a high but steady toll; the rest of the country was liable to epidemics which would suddenly push up their generally lower death rates.[1] The worst single crisis quarter appears to have been among the Irish Quakers in April to June of 1741, a year which saw a general harvest failure in Europe, a failure of the potato crop, and a smallpox

---

[1] John Landers, "Mortality and metropolis: the case of London 1675–1825," *Population Studies* 41 (1987), 59–76.

epidemic in Ireland.[2] The 1670s, especially 1673, seem to have been particularly unhealthy in Southern England, though there is a surprising upsurge again in the 1770s and 1780s. Although London Quakers never again endured mortality as high as the 1665 outbreak, the 1670s were also unhealthy for them; July to September 1705 was also a crisis period. The general tendency of clustered deaths was to decline sharply from peaks in the period before 1720, and then much more gradually for the rest of our period, suggesting that deaths from infectious disease became progressively less important.

When we turn to age-specific rates of mortality, the easiest index to calculate is infant mortality – that is, the proportion of babies born alive but dying before their first birthday to all live births. Even when birth and burial registers are somewhat incomplete there are techniques which suggest what the true level of infant mortality might have been. As children grow older, however, it becomes progressively more difficult to establish their rates of survival, because they are likely to pass out of observation, especially in England, where it was the custom to send many young people in their early to mid-teens to other households for service or apprenticeship.[3] In English family reconstitution studies done from parish registers, data are available about the survival rates of children up to the age of 15, and the tables showing the life expectancy of adults are done exclusively from the married population, beginning when the newly wed couple come into observation. Although more of the Quaker youth remained in observation, thanks to the regional character of the registration system and the habit of sending them out to other Quaker households for service, it still proved impossible to establish a true figure for life expectancy at birth. It will therefore be convenient to discuss the more reliable figures, those for infant and child mortality, first, and then those for adults, which rely to some extent on interpolation and conjecture.

As it happens, some of our most dramatic findings about the demography of the British and Irish Quakers relate to the degree of infant and child mortality. As usual, we will start with the most general presentation, that which comprehends all of the British Quakers by quarter-century cohorts. Figure 5.2 sets forth the relevant data for the Quakers as a whole. There is a very marked spike for both

[2] K. H. Connell, *The Population of Ireland, 1750–1845* (London, 1950), 144–46, 209; John D. Post, *Food Shortage, Climatic Variability, and Epidemic Disease in Preindustrial Europe: The Mortality Peak in the Early 1740s* (Ithaca, 1985), 96–97.
[3] On this see Richard Wall, "Age at leaving home," *Journal of Family History* 3 (1978), 181–202 and Christabel M. Young, "Factors associated with the timing and duration of the leaving-home stage of the family life cycle," *Population Studies* 29 (1975), 61–73.

Friends in life and death

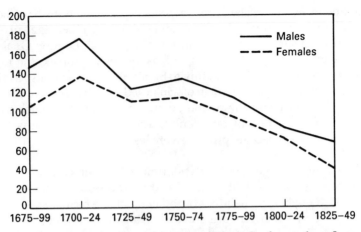

Fig. 5.2 Infant mortality, all British and Irish Quakers, 1675–1849.

males and females in the first quarter of the eighteenth century, when infant mortality for boys rose to around 175. (The fact that clustered deaths were not so prominent then suggests that conditions were generally more unhealthy, but without such sharp individual crises.) The prospects for both genders improved substantially in the next quarter century, but there was a slight worsening between 1750 and 1774. After 1774 the descent to modern values continued uninterrupted.

As would be expected, regional variations are particularly marked. These are shown in Table 5.1. (Because of the diversity within regions, our figures by twenty-five-year cohorts have to be taken with particular caution. In particular, we do not know whether our high-mortality "urban" families are represented in the same proportions in our sample as they were in the whole Quaker population.) By Quaker, or any other, standards, the urban infant mortality rate is quite high, especially the staggering figure for London alone, while that for Northern England and Scotland is on the low side. One of the most striking findings is that the very high infant mortality in London declined markedly after 1750. An alternate estimate of London Quaker infant mortality gives somewhat higher figures: 341 for a cohort born 1725–49, 231 for the 1775–99 cohort, and 194 for the cohort born between 1800 and 1824.[4]

---

[4] John Landers, "Mortality, weather and prices in London 1675–1825: a study of short-term fluctuations," *Journal of Historical Geography* 12 (1986), 347–64. We do not know how to account for the difference between Landers' infant mortality figures and ours. It is not clear from this article how Landers reached his estimates (some inflation

When it comes to making a comparison with English society generally, we are in a somewhat better position than with fertility, though there are considerable anomalies in the findings thus far reported. Rates in individual parishes sometimes show sudden and dramatic declines (usually a sign that a new and more careless incumbent is keeping the parish register); but there are also wide variations among parishes, even when, as in the Felden of Warwickshire, the parishes were close together.[5] A further difficulty is that the interval between birth and baptism became steadily longer in the eighteenth century; by 1750 the interval was sufficiently long to make a substantial difference in the calculation of infant mortality rates, because the ages of children would be miscalculated if their date of birth was taken to be a day or so before their baptism (as had been the custom in the sixteenth century). Also, the deaths of unbaptized children might not be recorded at all, because such children were denied funeral rites.[6] For this reason E. A. Wrigley and R. S. Schofield have introduced a correction factor in their calculations of infant mortality, which fortunately is not necessary with the Quaker materials.[7] Bearing these difficulties in mind, we can still say that almost all studies show a decline in infant mortality in the course of the

---

factor may have been introduced). The article does not state which two monthly meeting records were used, but from Landers' other work we presume they were Peel and Southwark, among the unhealthiest parts of the city.

[5] The most comprehensive study, based on a large number of parishes in Shropshire, is by R. E. Jones, "Infant mortality in rural North Shropshire," *Population Studies* 30 (1976), 305–17 and "Further evidence on the decline in infant mortality in pre-industrial England: North Shropshire 1561–1810," *ibid.*, 34 (1980), 239–50. Besides the articles by Wrigley and Schofield and Smith cited in Table 5.2, some local studies have been published by David Levine in *Family Formation in an Age of Nascent Capitalism* (New York, 1977). See also Glynis Reynolds, "Infant mortality and sex ratios at baptism as shown by reconstruction of Willingham [Cambs.]" *Local Population Studies* no. 22 (1979), 31–37 and F. West, "Infant mortality in the East Fen parishes of Leake and Wrangle," *Local Population Studies* no. 13 (1974), 43–44. In compiling his series, Michael Flinn chose only nine of the seventy parishes in Shropshire studied by R. E. Jones. Presumably these are the ones with the "best" registers (i.e., the ones that show the highest infant mortality figures). He has not used a few which showed extremely low infant mortality, such as St. Michael Cornhill. Otherwise, however, the figures seem to be taken straight. See *The European Demographic System, 1500–1820* (Baltimore, 1981), 94, 132–33. The variations in Shropshire are among the many things to which Michael Martin drew our attention.
[6] Robert Rankin, *A Familiar Treatise on Life Assurances and Annuities* (London, 1830), 17.
[7] E. A. Wrigley and R. S. Schofield, "English population history from family reconstitution: summary results 1600–1799," *Population Studies* 37 (1983), 175–77. See further E. A. Wrigley, "Births and baptisms: the use of Anglican baptism registers as a source of information about the numbers of births in England before the beginning of civil registration," *Population Studies* 31 (1977), 281–312 and B. Midi Berry and R. S. Schofield, "Age at baptism in pre-industrial England," *Population Studies* 25 (1971), 453–63.

eighteenth century, but they differ on the absolute level. The highest general level is that proposed by Michael Flinn, who, on the basis of fifty-three parish registers prior to 1750, argues that the mean level of infant mortality was 187. The figure for 1740–90 was 161 and that for 1780–1820 only 122, based on only eight and thirty-one parish registers, respectively. The ESRC Cambridge group has published two studies, which give the figures set forth in Tables 5.1a,b and 5.2. Not surprisingly, the two are in broad agreement, although Wrigley's, not based on full family reconstitutions, dates the peak of infant mortality earlier than does Smith. The increasing interval from birth to baptism in the eighteenth century makes this hard to establish; but the pooled data for thirteen parishes presented by Wrigley and Schofield, when subjected to correction factors for the growing birth–baptism gap and for the rules of observation about maternal mortality, show rates between 162.3 and 169.7 throughout the period from 1600 to 1799, except for a peak of 195.3 in the first half of the eighteenth century. (The first entirely reliable figures come from the life table of 1841, which shows a male infant mortality of 159 and a female one of 133.)[8]

In Ireland, there are no comparable figures for the general population prior to the census of 1841, when the infant mortality rate was between 220 and 225.[9] In rural England, Scotland, and Ireland, Quaker infant mortality does not seem to have fallen very much in the latter eighteenth century, and the level in the first half of that century was usually higher than in the last half of the seventeenth. Quaker infant mortality (even in the cities) appears lower than that in the general population in settlements of comparable size, even if we take the figures of the ESRC Cambridge Group, and was only about two-thirds what Flinn's selection of parishes suggests. It would thus appear that the health of Quaker infants living outside the large cities was already roughly at a level which the rest of the population did not

---

[8] *Fifth Annual Report of the Registrar-General* (2nd edn, London, 1843), 354.

[9] Joel Mokyr and Cormac Ó Gráda, ''New developments in Irish population history, 1700–1850,'' *Economic History Review* 2nd ser. 37 (1984), 484. Regional variations were very marked; the poverty-stricken westernmost province of Connaught (where there were few Quakers) had in the years from 1838 to 1840 an average infant mortality of 235 in the rural areas and 355 in its towns, while the comparable figures for Ulster were 179 and 291 (Joel Mokyr, *Why Ireland Starved: A Quantitative and Analytical History of the Irish Economy, 1800–1850* [London, 1983], 37). Notwithstanding these data, Peter Razzell claims that at all ages under 35, Irish mortality was less severe than English (''Population growth and economic change in eighteenth and early nineteenth-century England and Ireland,'' in *Land, Labour and Population in the Industrial Revolution: Essays Presented to J. D. Chambers*, ed. E. L. Jones and G. E. Mingay [London, 1967], 268). The rate for 1841 might have been abnormally high owing to the first distress in the great Irish famine.

Table 5.1a. *Quaker infant and child mortality rates by sex and region*

	Ireland				Southern England				Northern Britain			
	M		F		M		F		M		F	
	n	Rate	*n*	Rate	*n*	Rate	*n*	Rate	*n*	Rate	*n*	Rate
1650–99												
Under 1	1,244	121	1,156	95	1,004	133	962	101	420	100	395	53
1–4		105		106		116		96		66		73
5–9		18		45		49		35		28		19
10–14		26		23		19		25		44		36
0–14		248		245		285		235		219		170
1700–49												
Under 1	1,336	132	1,266	102	1,308	135	1,268	114	630	100	562	77
1–4		171		148		106		89		98		80
5–9		54		49		28		25		23		24
10–14		35		21		13		21		14		8
0–14		343		288		258		230		218		178
1750–99												
Under 1	970	121	903	95	1,285	125	1,242	117	957	92	848	72
1–4		143		130		76		80		61		72
5–9		34		44		33		30		30		14
10–14		29		11		20		20		23		35
0–14		293		256		234		228		192		181
1800–49												
Under 1	390	59	360	39	527	93	545	83	1,230	54	1,079	45
1–4		48		71		51		48		47		36
5–9		36		23		35		35		5		24
10–14		39		8		0		26		24		17
0–14		170		135		169		179		124		117
1850–99												
Under 1									586	41	615	31
1–4										26		26
5–9										9		10
10–14										17		4
0–14										90		69

Table 5.1a. (*cont.*)

| | London | | | | Bristol Norwich | | | |
| | M | | F | | M | | F | |
	n	Rate	*n*	Rate	*n*	Rate	*n*	Rate
1650–99								
Under 1	184	353	146	329	373	196	318	138
1–4		250		260		189		205
5–9		65		0		69		61
10–14		29		0		67		10
0–14		559		503		434		363
1700–49								
Under 1	285	277	234	248	483	224	507	164
1–4		245		227		276		247
5–9		57		36		69		33
10–14		108		31		39		12
0–14		541		457		497		430
1750–99								
Under 1	142	155	158	127	547	163	515	128
1–4		110		150		187		111
5–9		100		43		40		52
10–14		0		0		31		23
0–14		323		290		367		282
1800–49								
Under 1	37	162	35	57	280	86	225	111
1–4		83		74		71		79
5–9		67		0		33		84
10–14		143		111		18		26
0–14		386		224		194		270

Note: n means the number of live births (the denominator of the fraction of which the numerator is the number dying). "Northern Britain" includes families reconstituted from the family histories. The 1850–99 cohort is composed entirely of families from the family histories.

Table 5.1b. *Infant and child mortality, from British and Irish Quaker and English parish registers*

Period	Southern England *n*	Rate	Northern Britain *n*	Rate	Ireland *n*	Rate	Urban *n*	Rate	13 English parishes Rate	inflated
Infants										
1650–99	1966	117	815	77	2400	116	1021	225	166.7	169.7
1700–49	2576	125	1192	89	2602	117	1509	217	169.2	195.3
1750–99	2527	121	1805	83	1873	108	1362	145	133.4	165.5
1800–49	1072	88	2309	50	750	49	577	99	NA	NA
Children										
1–4										
1650–99	1330	106	590	69	1672	105	614	212		
1700–49	1824	98	922	89	1806	159	941	253		
1750–99	1911	78	1404	66	1329	137	973	146		
1800–49	810	49	1842	42	560	59	428	75		
5–9										
1650–99	890	42	421	24	1017	32	368	57		
1700–49	1270	26	746	44	1157	51	556	49		
1750–99	1430	32	1058	23	846	49	655	49		
1800–49	597	35	1440	14	372	30	303	53		
10–14										
1650–99	636	22	325	40	624	25	257	31		
1700–49	932	17	524	9	821	28	420	38		
1750–99	1093	20	807	29	598	20	488	24		
1800–49	450	13	1174	21	247	24	205	29		

Source: E. A. Wrigley and R. S. Schofield, "English population history from family reconstitution: summary results 1600–1799," *Population Studies* 37 (1983), 179. Their figures are inflated to compensate for the effects of underregistration and mistaken age calculations and for maternal mortality as it affects staying in observation.

attain until a century later; but that having attained that level, infant mortality showed no further improvement during the eighteenth century. (The pattern for the Quakers in the large cities is of course much different; there infant mortality dropped remarkably after 1750). To see whether this appearance is deceptive we need to investigate the credibility of the Quaker figures and to discuss the causes of infant mortality, besides taking into account the figures for Northern England and Scotland and the cities, which seem to follow a different pattern.

Table 5.2 Infant and child mortality from English parish registers
(Alcester, Aldenham, Banbury, Colyton, Gainsborough, Gedling, Hartland, Terling)[a]

	MALE				FEMALE			
	1550–99	1600–49	1650–99	1700–49	1550–99	1600–49	1650–99	1700–49
0–1 Mean	138	136	147	170	123	117	133	151
1–4 Mean	72	92	95	99	68	87	105	94
5–9 Mean	32	42	41	41	28	40	44	43

Infant mortality[b]

	1580s	1630s	1680s	1730s	1780s
Mean	138	135	174	137	99

Barton-under-Needwood; Bromfield; Bruton; Dymock; Eastham; Farnham (Yorks.); St. Martin, Coney Street, York; St. Michael, Cornhill, London; Middleton; Ottery St. Mary; Tatenhill; St. Vedast; London; Wedmore; Wem; Widecombe-in-the-Moor[b]

Infant and child mortality, various parish reconstitutions[c]

	Pre-1750		1740–90		1780–1820	
	n	Rate	n	Rate	n	Rate
Infants	101	187	8	161	31	122
Children 1–4	6	164			1	94
Children 5–9	6	66			1	33

Sources: (a) R. M. Smith, "Population and its geography in England, 1500–1730," in An Historical Geography of England and Wales, ed. R. Dodgshon and R. Butlin (New York, 1978), Table 8.3.
(b) E. A. Wrigley, "Births and baptisms as sources," Population Studies 31 (1977), 281.

We have two ways to approach the causes of infant mortality. The first is to establish as nearly as possible the exact age at death. This is often not available to us, because many registers entered the deaths of very young infants in the burial register rather than recording their births as well; the register then noted that they died in their first year. (In such cases, as explained in chapter 1, we have entered an inferred date of birth,[10] so that the fertility figures will take into account this birth even though it was not entered in the birth registers). Despite being unable to discover the exact ages at death of all infants, we do have information for a good many, which is presented in Table 5.3. Within the first year of a child's life, demographers distinguish between "endogenous" and "exogenous" causes of death. Some of those occurring within the first month are called "endogenous" in the belief that only the genetic constitution of the baby or traumas associated with birth would cause such an early death. The remaining deaths in the first month and those in the subsequent eleven are attributed to environmental causes (chiefly infectious disease) and so are termed "exogenous."

The interpretation of these figures depends on what we expect the distribution of infant deaths to be. One (quite rough) estimate for early modern populations is that half of the infant deaths generally occurred within the first month.[11] The Quaker figures are clearly well below this level; the percentage of infant deaths occurring within the first month among English and Scottish Quakers was just under 30 prior to 1750 and about 25 in the first half of the nineteenth century. But there is reason to believe the percentage of infant deaths within the first month was often less than 50; nor is this a biologically dictated constant. It seems to have declined steadily during the eighteenth century; in 1841 only one-third of the deaths which befell infants in the whole English population struck those aged one month or less.[12] Furthermore, the combination of a relatively low over-all mortality rate and a comparatively low percentage dying within the first month is not unique to the Quakers; in the parish of Hillmorton, Warwickshire, where infant mortality was lower than in the other Warwickshire parishes studied by Michael Martin, the percentage of infant mortality before the end of the first month was well under half. This is a parish where – unusually – the interval between births and baptisms

---

[10] We use this term in preference to "dummy birth," employed by Wrigley, "Births and baptisms," 285–86. Since ages at death were so often specified in days in the Quaker registers, an exact date of birth can frequently be inferred, even though there was no corresponding entry in the birth registers.

[11] Wrigley, "Births and baptisms," 283.

[12] *Fifth Annual Report of the Registrar-General*, 142.

is known to be very low, which lends substantial credibility to these figures. Even the fact that the death rate for infants under a month old fell in the first half of the eighteenth century when mortality in the remaining months was substantially higher is not unique to Quakers; E. A. Wrigley reports similar findings in some Anglican parishes.[13]

Furthermore, it may be that almost all deaths in the first month are influenced by environmental factors, thus undermining the whole distinction. In particular, some nursing practices may prove immediately fatal to infants. Valerie Fildes has pointed out that prior to 1747 most advice to nursing mothers called for them to delay – for a few days, or even a few weeks – putting the baby to the breast. Instead the hapless infant was to be given a "purge," or nauseous mixture of oil or butter and honey, sugar, and syrup, every two to four hours. Besides the dubious merits of this purging, this regimen would deprive the infant of the mother's first milk, or colostrum, which is rich in antibodies helping to protect against intestinal and respiratory infections. (The colostrum was regularly expressed and then thrown away as "unpurified".)[14]

Fildes goes on to argue that better medical advice, advocating immediate nursing, was the main reason for the decline in endogenous infant mortality during the eighteenth century. Using yet another set of ESRC Cambridge Group figures (not otherwise in print) she puts the endogenous rate at 88 in the 1680s, 74 in the 1730s, 51 in the 1780s, and only 23 in 1840. At the same time over-all infant mortality declined from 204 to 181, 165, and 150, or about 10 percent each fifty years. By contrast, the endogenous rate declined 16, 31, and 55 percent in the three periods. Fildes apparently makes the mistake of calling all deaths that occurred within the first twenty-eight days of life "endogenous," thus exaggerating the rate; but the general level of endogenous deaths does bear some relationship to the total death rate within the first four weeks.

The literate and scientifically inclined Society of Friends ought to have been one group that might nurse by the book. We have a rare glimpse of one such mother; when Hannah Rathbone was weaning her son (in the 1790s) she anticipated that he would be upset by the process; and so, she reports: "I gave him 6 drops of laudanum and do. antiminial wine, but had a very bad night."[15] (Giving opiates to babies

---

[13] The decline of mortality within the first month during the eighteenth century can be seen in the sixteen parishes studied by Wrigley, "Births and baptisms," 286.

[14] Valerie Fildes, "Neonatal feeding practices and infant mortality during the 18th century," *Journal of Biosocial Science* 12 (1980), 313–24.

[15] *Reynolds–Rathbone Diaries and Letters 1753–1839*, ed. Emily Greg (London, 1905), 53, quoted in Linda A. Pollock, *Forgotten Children: Parent-Child Relations from 1500 to 1900* (Cambridge, 1983), 221.

is not recommended by Dr. Spock, but Hannah Rathbone was following current medical advice, and was careful to give the precise
dosages.) If we judge the efficacy of colostrum by the decline in the
mortality rate within the first month, however, our figures give only
modest support to Fildes' hypothesis. The biggest declines in mortality in the first month show up in the early eighteenth century, when it
decreased by about a third in the cities and in the Southern counties. In
the next half-century, after the publication of better advice on nursing,
there was a further, more gentle decline (18 percent) in the cities and
28 percent in Northern Britain, but an actual rise in the Southern
counties and in Ireland. Not until the first half of the nineteenth
century do rates for the first month of life show a uniform and steep
reduction. The protection given by colostrum may have shielded
infants for longer than a month, however, so infant mortality rates
throughout the first year may be relevant to Fildes' argument.

The decline in the rate of infant mortality in the first month for the
first half of the eighteenth century may, however, be deceptive. It may
be just the result of underregistration. We know from independent
evidence that this was the period of greatest slackness in registration;
and we know that very early deaths, especially those occurring in the
first few days, are the least likely to be recorded. Since our figures for
all aspects of infant mortality are lower than those presented by Flinn
or the ESRC Cambridge Group for the whole population, perhaps we
should have added an inflation factor to offset possible negligence in
registering burials of infants. Had we inflated the figures for 1700–49,
first-month deaths would have been enlarged enough to show a
decline everywhere in the latter eighteenth century, which could then
serve as evidence that infants were getting colostrum because their
parents had attended to the medical advice books of the mid
eighteenth century.

We decided not to inflate our figures, because we believe there is no
presumption that they should approximate national averages. Such a
subgroup of the population – and on the whole a privileged one – could
well have lower infant mortality than the rest of the population. In this
they would be like some of the individual parishes comprised in Table
5.2. The rate for Dymock, Gloucestershire was 47 in the 1730s and for
Widecombe-in-the-Moor, Devon, only 46 in the 1780s. Even in
London, St. Michael, Cornhill, had a rate of only 53 in the 1580s.
Furthermore, as we have already noted, the Quaker registers are free
from one cause of underregistration which afflicts the parish registers,
namely that infants who died very young, before they could be baptized, might not be entered in either the baptismal or burial registers.

But though the Quaker registers do not suffer from any difficulties

Table 5.3 *Ages at death of Quaker infants who died in their first year*

		≤24 hours	1–6 days	7–29 days	30–59 days	60–89 days	90–179 days	180 days– one year	% Dying <1 month
Southern England									
1650–99	*n* at risk	1,974	1,955	1,921	1,859	1,828	1,797	1,740	
	Rate	6	10	30	16	14	24	31	43
1700–49	*n* at risk	2,597	2,589	2,565	2,500	2,468	2,429	2,324	
	Rate	2	5	23	12	13	32	44	25
1750–99	*n* at risk	2,555	2,540	2,504	2,449	2,394	2,365	2,285	
	Rate	4	9	21	21	10	27	39	28
1800–49	*n* at risk	1,073	1,065	1,055	1,042	1,032	1,019	994	
	Rate	6	7	11	10	11	21	30	26
Northern Britain									
1650–99	*n* at risk	765	758	751	739	730	723	711	
	Rate	7	5	15	11	4	12	25	35
1700–49	*n* at risk	1,106	1,103	1,094	1,069	1,056	1,044	1,018	
	Rate	1	2	21	12	10	20	33	25
1750–99	*n* at risk	1,551	1,549	1,533	1,513	1,500	1,480	1,433	
	Rate	1	7	11	7	11	24	38	21
1800–49	*n* at risk	1,810	1,802	1,795	1,774	1,770	1,755	1,723	
	Rate	2	3	9	1	5	13	23	22

Table 5.3. (cont.)

	≤24 hours	1–6 days	7–29 days	30–59 days	60–89 days	90–179 days	180 days–one year	% Dying <1 month
Ireland								
n at risk	2,383	2,371	2,344	2,293	2,252	2,228	2,180	
1650–99								
Rate	3	8	21	17	9	16	38	30
n at risk	2,612	2,601	2,580	2,528	2,499	2,465	2,379	
1700–49								
Rate	3	5	19	11	10	25	51	23
n at risk	1,882	1,875	1,855	1,821	1,794	1,774	1,719	
1750–99								
Rate	3	9	17	14	9	20	42	27
n at risk	751	749	747	740	735	732	723	
1800–49								
Rate	1	1	8	7	1	7	25	22
Urban								
n at risk	1,054	1,045	1,018	970	937	916	861	
1650–99								
Rate	9	16	47	31	19	50	87	31
n at risk	1,584	1,569	1,546	1,528	1,442	1,392	1,306	
1700–49								
Rate	6	11	31	31	28	47	102	21
n at risk	1,399	1,387	1,368	1,333	1,307	1,278	1,231	
1750–99								
Rate	6	10	24	18	18	34	54	26
n at risk	587	582	578	564	558	552	540	
1800–49								
Rate	9	5	22	11	9	14	41	36

about possible gaps between birth and baptism, it would be facile to assert that because they did not have to be baptized in order to be registered, no Quaker child was ever born whose birth was not entered in the birth registers. At best an average of two weeks would elapse before reports of a child's birth could be given to the registrar appointed by the monthly meeting, and that interval was surely sometimes even longer. So we experimented with a correction factor based on the supposition that there were unreported deaths almost all of which came in the first month. If we assume that the total infant mortality rate was double the rate for the last eleven months, so as to attain a notional figure where half the deaths would have been in the first month, the figure for Southern English Quakers before 1750 would be higher than that for thirteen parishes before 1700 and only slightly below that for 1700–50 (Table 5.1), while the rate for Northern England and Scotland would come up to 127. Since all our direct evidence of underregistration suggests that it was at its worst in the first half of the eighteenth century, there almost certainly was a shortfall in the registration of very early infant deaths during this period, and probably some underregistering of them at other times as well. This undoubtedly is pertinent to the evaluation of Fildes' claims; but in our view does not require introducing a correction factor based on the idea that half of all infant deaths occurred within the first month of life. As we have seen, this cannot be relied on as a biological constant, and first-month deaths were usually under half in the eighteenth century. If we had introduced such a correction factor for Southern England, the inflated total of deaths within the first month would have been over twice the number actually registered, and we find it hard to believe that there was underregistration on such a heroic scale. It therefore seems safe to conclude that despite some unknown degree of underregistration, the apparent advantage in health enjoyed by Quaker children as against those in the population as a whole was real and was not an artifact arising from greater underregistration of early infant deaths.

The reasons for the greater health of Quaker infants are probably related to their position in the social structure. In a recent study of Cartmel, Cumbria, Roger Finlay has shown a direct connection between wealth and low infant mortality; the infant mortality rate of families with goods worth over £60 in probate inventories was only 81 percent of that in families with goods worth less than £60. The advantage of the wealthier families was even greater later in childhood, as the rates of the three later periods were, respectively, 70, 65, and 59 percent as high.[16] In the Felden of Warwickshire, too, there are clear signs that children had higher chances of survival if their families were well off. The parish register of Priors Marston recorded the occupations of all males between 1698 and 1750. In the period from 1730 to 1779, children of farmers suffered an infant mortality rate of 112, whereas that of children of cottagers and laborers was 140. In the

---

[16] Roger Finlay, "Differential child mortality in pre-industrial England: the example of Cartmel, Cumbria, 1600–1750," *Annales de démographie historique* (1981), 76.

Table 5.4. *Child mortality rates (0–14), Quakers and British peerage*

	Peerage		Southern England		Northern Britain		London		Bristol & Norwich	
	M	F	M	F	M	F	M	F	M	F
1650–74	379	357								
1675–99	333	322								
1650–99			285	235	219	170	559	503	434	363
1700–24	325	314								
1725–49	323	342								
1700–49			258	230	218	178	541	457	497	430
1750–74	236	225								
1775–99	199	198								
1750–99			234	228	192	181	323	290	367	282
1800–24	174	179								
1825–49	144	134								
1800–49			169	179	124	117	386	224	194	270
1850–74	124	127								
1875–99	74	88								
1850–99					90	69				

Source: Hollingsworth, *Demography*, Table 46, p. 60; our Table 5.1.

nearby parish of Napton-on-Hill, the figures were 117 as against 132 in the period from 1730 to 1769, and from 1770 to 1819 the children of farmers had the very low rate of 45, while that for children of cottagers and laborers was 121.[17]

Finally, the Genevan upper bourgeoisie and the British nobility provide a test of our suggestion that levels of mortality should be lower in higher social ranks. In Geneva, Henry notes that improved sanitation began to improve the health of adults born from 1650 to 1699 and that of children in the following half-century. The result was a dramatic increase in life expectancy at birth, from 32 to 42 years – figures which are somewhat higher than those for the Norwich and Bristol Quakers, not to mention those in London. Geneva evidently escaped the high mortality of early eighteenth-century Britain. Mortality was steadily, although slightly, lower in the *haute bourgeoisie* than in the Genevan population as a whole.[18]

[17] Unpublished material made available to us by Michael Martin. In "A Warwickshire market town in adversity: Stratford-upon-Avon in the sixteenth and seventeenth centuries," *Midland History* 7 (1982), 40 he points out that in the poorer sections of Old Stratford mortality was at least 25 percent higher.

[18] Louis Henry, *Anciennes familles genevoises, étude démographique, XVI⁻ᵉ–XXᵉ siècles* (Paris, 1956), 155–58.

Hollingsworth presents no data on infant mortality, but it is possible to compare (in Table 5.4) the mortality in childhood experienced by the British peerage with that sustained by the Quakers. Since comparatively few of the children of the peerage lived in cities, and the mortality of Quaker children there was so extraordinarily high, the most reasonable comparison is with Southern England and Northern Britain. The worst mortality experience of the peers' children struck the cohort born between 1650 and 1675; after that there was a steady, if slow, decline until 1750. Thus from 1650 to 1750 more children of peers died than of Quakers; it is possible that their childhood mortality was as bad or worse than that of the general population. But their mortality declined sharply after 1750, dipping for the next century below that of the Southern English Quakers. (In this substantial fall they resembled the London Quakers.) We have no data about the causes of death of the children of noble families, and thus no idea why child mortality declined so much after 1750.

Even with the same level of childhood mortality, one would expect the Quakers – the men, at least – to have a lower risk of death as adults. After 1700 they had very little chance of being killed, whereas inflicting, and occasionally sustaining, violent death was the noblemen's *métier*. There is of course considerable guesswork in estimating life expectancies of adults; but our estimates are that before 1750 Quakers of both genders had a substantially higher life expectancy than the nobility. Their lower childhood mortality must have been largely responsible for this, but the reduced chance of violent death was not insignificant for the men. After 1750 the life chances of the nobility considerably improved, but the Quakers – except for those in the cities – still held a slight advantage.

One of the central problems presented by Quaker infant mortality is why it declined at a time when birth rates were rising, since higher birth rates usually provoke higher infant mortality. It has even been claimed, by T. C. McKeown and R. G. Brown, that in large families the later children were so likely to die that the entire effect of higher fertility would be negated.[19] Of course they would all have to die for

[19] Thomas McKeown and R. G. Brown, "Medical evidence related to English population changes in the eighteenth century," *Population Studies* 9 (1955), 119–41. The logic of their argument does not survive the critique in Roger Schofield, "Population growth in the century after 1750: the role of mortality decline," in *Pre-Industrial Population Change: The Mortality Decline and Short-term Population Movements*, ed. T. Bengtsson, G. Fridlizius, R. Ohlsson (Stockholm, 1984), 21–22. Besides these logical problems, there is not even any good evidence, once other factors in regression models have been controlled, that birth orders of four or higher are more hazardous. See J. N. Hobcraft, J. W. McDonald, and S. O. Rutstein, "Demographic determi-

this to happen, which is unlikely; but it is worth investigating whether a rise in family size was accompanied by higher infant mortality rates. We have some evidence bearing on this issue, which is given in Table 5.5. This provides only an indirect test of the thesis of McKeown and Brown, because the age of mothers is not controlled for and we are only considering previous births, regardless of whether these children were still surviving at the birth of subsequent children. With these caveats, Table 5.5 suggests that McKeown and Brown have somewhat exaggerated the differential mortality of the later children, at least in Quaker families. When seven children had already been born, subsequent children did have a considerably higher risk of dying in infancy, but the risk for middle children was not much above the average, and that for the first four was as a rule only slightly below average. Differential mortality thus runs in the same direction predicted by McKeown and Brown, but the effect is quite weak and certainly could not cancel out increases in the number of children born into the family. Even more important, the secular decline in infant mortality for all children was much more significant than the higher mortality suffered by late-born children; recall that infant mortality did not rise after 1750, and even declined considerably in the cities, at the same time that the fertility surge was creating more large families. Here we should mention again that there is a mechanism linking higher fertility with lower rather than higher infant mortality; as we pointed out in chapter 4, the same unsanitary conditions that might cause high infant mortality could lead to a higher number of miscarriages. Improvement in these conditions could thus be reflected both in a higher birth rate (through fewer fetal deaths) and lower infant mortality.

Another way to approach this question is to examine the danger to a child's life when its mother conceives shortly after its birth. Table 5.6 shows that if this occurs within six – or especially within three – months, the child is dramatically more likely to die, and die quickly; whereas a child who lives two years before its mother conceives again almost always has a better chance of surviving the first two years of its life. But the greatest risk is confined to those less than six months old when their mothers conceive again; for those who have lived a year, the risk is usually only a little greater – and sometimes even less – than for those who have survived for two years.

Even in Ireland, comparatively few mothers conceived as quickly as three months after their last birth; such births were only 4 to 5 percent

nants of infant and early child mortality: a comparative analysis," *Population Studies* 39 (1985), 368.

Table 5.5. *Infant mortality rates, by rank order of birth*

		Southern England				Northern England				Ireland				Urban			
		1–4	5–7	≥8	All	1–4	5–7	≥8	All	1–4	5–7	≥8	All	1–4	5–7	≥8	All
1650–99	*n* at risk	1401	331	86	1816	478	146	64	688	1044	431	197	1672	962	261	98	1321
	Rate	108	129	127	112	75	89	94	80	102	113	142	109	223	195	234	218
1700–49	*n* at risk	1430	381	101	1912	688	226	77	991	1265	461	232	1958	1216	337	156	1709
	Rate	118	133	257	128	86	115	142	97	119	119	133	121	209	237	320	224
1750–99	*n* at risk	1092	374	187	1653	849	365	158	1372	813	338	238	1389	885	318	149	1352
	Rate	110	149	197	128	85	96	101	90	111	112	126	113	162	147	140	156
1800–49	*n* at risk	467	136	49	652	1073	392	184	1649	330	131	69	530	373	133	56	562
	Rate	92	29	122	81	59	64	87	63	52	22	86	49	102	90	178	106

Table 5.6 *Infant and child mortality rates if next child conceived within two years and all other cases*

Urban If child at next conception is aged:	Within 3 mos.		Between 3 & 6 mos.		Risk of dying Between 6 & 12 mos.		Within 1 year	Between 1 & 2 yrs.	
		n		*n*		*n*			*n*
1650–99									
0–89 days	58	220	45	44	40	150	366	34	147
90–179 days	117	215	92	98	83	133	386	69	72
180–364 days	227	159	191	79	175	97	301	138	138
1–2 years	292	65	273	38	268	78	171	240	121
All above	694	134	601	52	566	97	259	481	121
All others	187	37	180	33	174	75	139	161	137
1700–49									
0–89 days	92	152	76	26	71	99	256	59	102
90–179 days	218	151	185	70	170	159	336	131	115
180–364 days	320	125	280	68	261	123	285	212	127
1–2 years	425	66	397	28	386	91	175	341	147
All above	1,055	109	938	48	888	114	248	743	132
All others	231	65	216	46	206	53	155	151	79
1750–99									
0–89 days	56	179	45	67	41	146	269	34	118
90–179 days	131	107	117	51	111	81	221	98	82
180–364 days	351	97	317	38	305	56	180	272	88
1–2 years	490	22	479	29	465	47	106	428	68
All above	1,028	67	958	37	922	59	150	832	78
All others	89	45	164	30	81	12	85	154	52
1800–49									
0–89 days	8	375	5	0	4	0	375	4	0
90–179 days	74	108	66	61	62	32	189	57	18
180–364 days	171	35	165	6	164	73	111	143	35
1–2 years	192	36	185	5	184	27	67	169	36
All above	445	54	421	14	414	70	133	373	32
All others	77	26	74	14	73	14	53	74	54

Table 5.6 (*cont.*)

Southern England

If child at next conception is aged:	Risk of dying								
	Within 3 mos.		Between 3 & 6 mos.		Between 6 & 12 mos.		Within 1 year	Between 1 & 2 yrs.	
	n		*n*		*n*			*n*	
1650–99									
0–89 days	70	257	52	0	50	0	257	49	61
90–179 days	133	218	104	77	95	63	324	79	76
180–364 days	335	90	305	46	291	55	180	246	33
1–2 years	664	33	642	9	636	25	66	597	49
All above	1,202	82	1,703	25	1,072	35	136	971	47
All others	440	32	426	5	424	19	55	417	34
1700–1749									
0–89 days	102	78	93	43	85	24	139	81	12
90–179 days	224	138	193	114	169	75	294	138	58
180–364 days	480	73	445	52	422	52	167	360	42
1–2 years	846	20	829	14	817	39	71	760	43
All above	1,652	55	1,560	39	1,493	48	135	1,339	43
All others	508	41	487	14	480	21	74	470	51
1750–1799									
0–89 days	85	212	67	75	59	102	345	51	39
90–179 days	264	129	230	52	217	55	220	191	42
180–364 days	591	64	553	33	535	49	139	484	37
1–2 years	817	32	791	15	779	39	84	736	31
All above	1,757	59	1,641	29	1,590	47	129	1,462	35
All others	406	52	384	18	377	16	84	370	24
1800–1849									
0–89 days	17	118	15	0	15	67	177	14	71
90–179 days	100	130	87	57	82	24	199	79	0
180–364 days	292	45	279	32	270	52	124	236	13
1–2 years	351	14	346	3	345	20	37	331	33
All above	760	43	727	21	712	34	95	660	23
All others	172	29	167	18	164	12	58	162	43

Table 5.6 (*cont.*)

Ireland	Risk of dying								
If child at next conception is aged:	Within 3 mos.		Between 3 & 6 mos.		Between 6 & 12 mos.		Within 1 year	Between 1 & 2 yrs.	
	n		*n*		*n*			*n*	
1650–99									
0–89 days	83	157	69	14	64	78	234	58	86
90–179 days	200	125	175	17	172	70	200	149	67
180–364 days	404	114	361	42	345	43	188	305	75
1–2 years	1,012	33	979	8	971	35	74	905	49
All above	1,699	67	1,584	17	1,552	42	121	1,417	58
All others	535	28	520	12	514	21	60	513	33
1700–1749									
0–89 days	113	150	96	42	82	73	245	75	80
90–179 days	290	128	253	55	237	68	232	195	144
180–364 days	556	63	521	44	498	80	176	417	110
1–2 years	935	19	917	14	904	44	75	839	82
All above	1,894	56	1,787	30	1,721	59	138	1,526	98
All others	464	9	460	11	455	24	43	444	59
1750–1799									
0–89 days	68	191	54	56	49	61	283	45	44
90–179 days	287	84	262	19	255	43	140	231	74
180–364 days	534	54	505	32	489	65	144	419	74
1–2 years	634	22	620	8	615	29	58	575	64
All above	1,523	53	1,441	20	1,408	45	114	1,270	69
All others	194	46	185	11	183	27	82	178	34
1800–1849									
0–89 days	29	69	27	37	26	115	207	23	87
90–179 days	63	63	59	0	59	0	63	56	18
180–364 days	222	18	218	5	217	37	59	193	26
1–2 years	284	7	282	7	280	11	25	264	34
All above	598	20	586	7	582	24	50	536	32
All others	97	0	97	0	97	21	21	95	32

of the total in Ireland and never exceeded 7 percent (the urban percentage prior to 1750). Even conceptions within six months are relatively uncommon, ranging between one-eighth to one-fifth of the total. When fertility began its dramatic rise after 1750, very short birth-to-next-conception intervals actually declined, but there was a large increase in the proportions of such intervals between three months and a year. Had differential infant mortality rates remained unchanged, this development would have increased over-all infant mortality; but the secular decline in infant mortality visible in other tables, especially in urban families, shows up again here and counterbalances the effect of the shorter intervals.

The most important thing to explain is clearly this secular decline. The age- or rank-distribution of infant deaths do not get us very far towards an explanation. The only other evidence about the cause of the secular decline in infant mortality can be found in the London figures. Although London's infant mortality was among the highest in the country, and certainly was the highest experienced in our sample of the British and Irish Quakers, it may exhibit, in exaggerated form, tendencies found elsewhere in the country. Happily we do have for London some evidence about causes of death, because the searchers whose reports were compiled to make up the bills of mortality were supposed to state the cause of death for those they reported. Although Quaker burials were not included in the bills of mortality, until about 1795 the Quaker registers of burials from time to time included information about causes of death. Before 1700, this was done for most adult deaths and for many infant and child deaths as well. The practice became much less common in the first half of the eighteenth century – once again this is the slack period of registration – but was resumed from 1750 to 1770, and then petered out before the end of the century. It is not clear whether the information about causes of death was supplied by doctors, chemists, or apothecaries, by the family, or by people like the searchers whose job was to view the corpse.

Besides the frequent omissions of the reported causes of death, these data pose considerable difficulties in interpretation. Some diseases were fairly easy to diagnose, such as plague and smallpox – even though these were sometimes confused with typhus and measles, respectively.[20] Most frequently, however, the searchers simply reported the most prominent symptoms displayed by the dead person

---

[20] Andrew B. Appleby, "Nutrition and disease: the case of London, 1550–1750," *Journal of Interdisciplinary History* 6 (1975), 7.

– fever,[21] convulsions, or general debilitation, which was described as "decline" or "consumption." (Tuberculosis was apparently most often called "tissick," i.e. phthisic.) Some causes of death were given simply as "suddenly," which probably refers most often to strokes or heart attacks, although its occasional application to infants reminds us that a frequent cause of infant death today is still called "sudden infant death syndrome." Finally some "causes" of death were reported which should not have proven mortal at all; occasional adults had the misfortune of being "blasted and planet-struck."[22]

From the late seventeenth century onwards the London bills of mortality became an object of interest to "political arithmetic," and there were discussions about what reliance could be placed on reported causes of death, especially since the searchers were usually elderly women. "The low capacity of the person usually chosen for this office," wrote Thomas Birch in 1759,

has been made an objection to the truth and justice of the bills. But with regard to natural deaths, there seems no other capacity necessary in these searchers, than that of relating what they hear. For the wisest person in the parish would be able to find out very few distempers from a bare inspection of the dead body, and could only bring back such an account, as the family and friends of the deceased would be pleased to give.[23]

To John Graunt, in 1676, in many cases the precise cause of death did not matter, while in many "such as *Drowning, Scalding, Bleeding, Vomiting, making away themselves, Lunatick, Sores, Smallpox &c* their own senses are sufficient, and the generality of the World are able pretty well to distinguish the *Gout, Stone, Dropsie, Falling sickness, Palsie, Agues, Pleurisie, Rickets, from one another*."[24]

Unfortunately among the causes which did not readily yield to the senses of the searchers were two which were very commonly reported, "convulsions" and "consumption." The former seems to have come to designate, though not exclusively, diseases of infancy. As Thomas Short noted in 1750, the bills of mortality had ceased to record any entries of "Chrysoms and Infants" (those dying within the

---

[21] The fevers that could prove mortal were cholera, diphtheria, dysentery, influenza, measles, scarlet fever, smallpox, typhoid, and typhus. The latter three were particularly dangerous during our period. See J. A. Johnston, "The impact of the epidemics of 1727–1730 in South West Worcestershire," *Medical History* 15 (1971), 283.

[22] This appears to be the astrological explanation of apoplexy. Thomas R. Forbes, *Chronicle from Aldgate* (New Haven, 1971), 99–117 has done his best to elucidate this and other unusual terms (such as "mother" and "wolf") as causes of death.

[23] [Thomas Birch], *A Collection of the Yearly Bills of Mortality, from 1657 to 1758 inclusive* (London, 1759), 7.

[24] John Graunt, *Natural and Political Observations . . . upon the Bills of Mortality* (5th edn, London, 1676), 21.

Table 5.7 *Reported causes of death, London population covered by bills of mortality, 1670–1795*
(to nearest 1,000)

	1670–1709		1710–49		1740–95	
	No.	%	No.	%	No.	%
Diseases relating to childhood						
Abortive and stillborn	25	3.0	25	2.4	29	3.0
Convulsions	159	19.1	290	28.1	247	25.4
Teething	49	5.9	57	5.5	30	3.1
Chrisoms and infants	10	1.1	1[a]	0.1	—	—
Rickets	15	1.7	4	0.4	0.2[b]	
Thrush and Canker	4	0.4	6	0.6	6	0.6
Overlaid, starved at nurse	3	0.4	3	0.3	0.4[b]	
Coughs, whooping cough	—	—	1[c]	0.1	13	1.3
Miscellaneous	1	0.1	8	0.8	11	1.1
	265	31.8	394	38.2	323	33.3
Fevers (unspecified)	116	13.9	156	15.1	133	13.7
Smallpox	51	6.1	83	8.0	93	9.6
Measles	3	0.4	7[d]	0.6	11	1.1
Typhus ("spotted fever")	6	0.8	—	—	—	—
	177	21.2	245	23.7	237	24.4
"Consumption"	136	16.3	149	14.4	210	21.6
Swelling of the lungs ("Rising of the lights")	5	0.6	2	0.2	—	—
Asthma, phthisic	—	—	21	2.1	18	1.8
Cold, quinsy	2	0.2	2	0.2	1	0.1
Pleurisy	1	0.1	2	0.2	1	0.1
	143	17.2	176	17.1	230	23.6
"Suddenly"	4	0.4	8	0.8	10	1.1
Dropsy and tympany	16	2.0	40	3.8	42	4.3
	21	2.5	48	4.6	52	5.3
Gastrointestinal Surfeit, gripes, flux, colic, stopping of the stomach	110	13.3	30	2.9	4	0.4
Others	117	14.0	140	13.6	126	12.9
Total	833		1,033		971	

Notes: [a]Chrisom children (those aged under 1 month) not reported after 1725; infants not reported after 1722.
[b]Not reported after 1790.
[c]Not reported before 1740.
[d]Measles was tabulated together with smallpox from 1690 to 1700 (here the combined figure is entered under smallpox).
Source: J. Marshall, *Mortality of the Metropolis* (London, 1832), following p. 82.

first month of life) and "Hence the present Article of *Convulsions* (besides the real Increase of the Disease) is monstrously swelled beyond its just Bounds, by thrusting into it, all that die within the Month of Diseases not obvious and certain." He characterized "consumption" as "a most extensive Article, comprehending not only most Distempers of the Breast, but all *Atrophies, Emaciations, slow lingering Disorders,* and probably Haemorrhages, as that Article is now dropped in the bills."[25] The Quaker John Fothergill, who thought that only smallpox reports could be trusted, commented: "If the body is emaciated, which may happen from an acute fever, it is enough for [the searchers] to place it to the account of consumption, though the death of the party was perhaps owing to a disease specifically different."[26]

There is, then, a thick screen of vague nomenclature separating us from real knowledge of what caused the deaths of London Quaker infants;[27] but in an area where there is almost no other direct evidence at all, the reported causes of death have to be used, albeit with due circumspection.

The over-all picture of London mortality which is suggested by J. Marshall's 1832 tabulation of the bills of mortality is given in Table 5.7. Stated causes of death are grouped roughly by the bodily system affected (respiratory, circulatory, gastrointestinal), with fevers and Marshall's category of "diseases relating to children" tabulated separately. (When we come to age-specific data, we will discover that the category of "diseases relating to childhood" is a questionable one.)

Drawing inferences about London mortality as a whole is made even more tricky by the limited coverage of the bills and the possible decline in the efficiency of the system in the later eighteenth century. By the time the bills of mortality ceased to be compiled, from one-third to one-half the parishes in London, including St Marylebone, St Pancras, and those in Kensington and Chelsea, were not

---

[25] Thomas Short, *New Observations, Natural, Moral, Civil, Political, and Medical, on City, Town, and Country Bills of Mortality* (London, 1750), 206, 211. Short did not stint on his "moral" observations; he attributes the real increase in convulsions to "Parents too general and fatal Acquaintance with spiritous Liquors" (210).

[26] Quoted in Charles Creighton, *A History of Epidemics in Britain* (Cambridge, 1894), II, 530.

[27] The comments of M. D. Grmek on this subject are very much to the point; see "Préliminaires d'une étude historique des maladies," *Annales: Economies, Sociétés, Civilisations* 24ᵉ année (1969), 1482–83. The best study of the difficulty of translating eighteenth-century medical terminology is by Jean-Pierre Peter, "Une enquête de la Société Royale de Médecine: malades et maladies à la fin du XVIIIᵉ siècle," *Annales: Economies, Sociétés, Civilisations* 22ᵉ année (1967), 711–51, translated by Elborg Forster as "Disease and the sick at the end of the eighteenth century," in *Biology of Man in History,* ed. Robert Forster and Orest Ranum (Baltimore, 1982), 81–124.

Table 5.8. *Stated causes of death, by age at death, all London Quakers*

Males	1670–99		1700–24		1725–49		1750–74		1775–94	
Cause	No.	%	No.	%	No.	%	No.	%	No.	%
<1 Month										
Convulsions	138	33.6	19	5.1	27	12.1	29	32.6	10	11.6
Gastrointestinal	79	19.1	4	1.1	0		3	3.3	0	
Pulmonary (including "consumption")	10	2.4	5	1.3	4	1.8	4	4.4	1	1.2
Smallpox	2	0.5	0		0		0		0	
Fevers	3	0.7	0		1	0.4	0		0	
Other stated	4	1.0	5	1.3	4	1.8	1	1.1	0	
Unstated	175	42.6	341	91.2	188	83.9	52	58.4	75	87.2
Total	411		374		224		89		86	
1 Month–1 Year										
Convulsions	198	25.5	12	1.8	59	14.0	80	32.4	37	19.0
Gastrointestinal	135	17.4	5	0.8	2	0.5	1	0.4	0	
Pulmonary (including "consumption")	29	3.7	9	1.4	12	2.9	23	9.3	14	7.2
Smallpox	40	5.2	24	3.7	16	3.8	14	5.7	16	8.2
Fevers	35	4.5	13	2.0	4	1.0	9	3.6	2	1.0
Other stated	84	10.8	30	4.6	24	5.7	17	6.9	4	2.1
Unstated	254	32.8	557	85.7	303	72.1	103	41.7	122	62.6
Total	775		650		420		247		195	
1–4 Years										
Convulsions	69	9.1	8	1.8	35	9.8	41	19.5	16	9.4
Gastrointestinal	73	9.6	2	0.5	1	0.3	3	1.4	0	
Pulmonary (including "consumption")	71	9.4	10	2.3	19	5.3	29	13.8	28	16.5
Smallpox	95	12.5	56	12.6	77	21.6	60	28.6	37	21.8
Fevers	105	13.9	29	6.5	28	7.8	19	9.0	13	7.6
Other stated	167	22.1	46	10.4	44	12.3	20	9.5	2	1.2
Unstated	177	23.4	293	66.0	153	42.9	38	18.1	74	43.5
Total	757		444		357		210		170	
5–9 Years										
Convulsions	10	5.9	3	2.4	4	4.3	7	10.8	1	2.5
Gastrointestinal	19	11.2	0		1	1.1	0		0	
Pulmonary (including "consumption")	38	22.5	11	8.7	14	14.9	10	15.4	9	22.5
Smallpox	30	17.6	27	21.4	27	28.7	27	41.5	4	10.0
Fevers	37	21.9	18	14.3	15	16.0	11	16.9	3	7.5
Other stated	18	10.7	3	2.4	7	7.4	5	7.7	0	
Unstated	17	10.1	64	50.8	26	27.7	5	7.7	23	57.5
Total	169		126		94		65		40	
10–14 Years										
Convulsions	6	7.2	2	3.2	2	3.7	2	8.0	1	5.0
Gastrointestinal	8	9.6	1	1.6	0		0		0	
Pulmonary (including "consumption")	23	27.7	10	15.9	16	29.6	9	36.0	10	50.0
Smallpox	15	18.1	9	14.3	5	9.3	3	12.0	2	10.0
Fevers	9	10.8	6	9.5	6	11.1	5	20.0	4	20.0
Other stated	13	15.7	8	12.7	10	18.5	4	16.0	0	
Unstated	9	10.8	27	42.9	15	27.8	2	8.0	3	15.0
Total	83		63		54		25		20	

Table 5.8 (*cont.*)

Females	1670–99		1700–24		1725–49		1750–74		1775–94	
Cause	No.	%	No.	%	No.	%	No.	%	No.	%
<1 Month										
Convulsions	113	32.8	10	3.4	20	22.0	15	21.1	6	11.5
Gastrointestinal	45	13.0	1	0.3	2	1.1	1	1.4	0	
Pulmonary (including "consumption")	5	1.4	3	1.0	5	2.8	4	5.6	0	
Smallpox	1	0.3	0		1	0.6	2	2.8	0	
Fevers	3	0.9	0		0		0		0	
Other stated	5	1.4	1	0.3	1	0.6	0		1	1.9
Unstated	173	50.1	278	94.9	152	84.0	49	69.0	45	86.5
Total	345		293		181		71		52	
1 Month–1 Year										
Convulsions	142	23.2	25	5.1	40	12.0	51	28.8	24	15.1
Gastrointestinal	88	14.4	1	0.2	1	0.3	2	1.1	1	0.6
Pulmonary (including "consumption")	13	2.1	2	0.4	8	2.4	18	10.2	11	6.9
Smallpox	19	3.1	15	3.1	12	3.6	12	6.8	9	5.7
Fevers	29	4.7	9	1.8	7	2.1	8	4.5	6	3.8
Other stated	74	12.1	20	4.1	11	3.3	1	0.6	8	5.0
Unstated	246	40.3	416	85.2	255	76.3	85	48.0	100	62.8
Total	611		488		334		177		159	
1–4 Years										
Convulsions	72	9.7	6	1.3	28	8.6	31	15.2	8	4.9
Gastrointestinal	67	9.0	2	0.4	0		0		0	
Pulmonary (including "consumption")	46	6.2	7	1.5	17	5.2	31	15.2	18	17.1
Smallpox	66	8.9	53	11.4	55	16.9	42	20.6	24	14.6
Fevers	88	11.8	30	6.5	37	11.3	24	11.8	17	10.4
Other stated	170	22.8	46	9.9	34	10.4	18	8.8	6	3.7
Unstated	236	31.7	320	69.0	155	47.5	58	28.4	81	49.4
Total	745		464		326		204		164	
5–9 Years										
Convulsions	11	7.7	1	0.8	4	4.6	7	11.7	4	8.0
Gastrointestinal	13	9.2	0		0		0		0	
Pulmonary (including "consumption")	24	16.9	15	11.5	11	12.6	15	25.0	7	14.0
Smallpox	19	13.4	31	23.8	21	24.1	20	33.3	9	18.0
Fevers	38	26.8	14	10.8	11	12.6	10	16.7	5	10.0
Other stated	8	5.6	4	3.1	1	1.1	1	1.7	1	2.0
Unstated	29	20.4	65	50.0	39	44.8	7	11.7	24	48.0
Total	142		130		87		60		50	
10–14 Years										
Convulsions	2	2.8	0		2	5.7	5	14.3	0	
Gastrointestinal	4	5.6	0		0		0		0	
Pulmonary (including "consumption")	21	29.6	11	16.4	8	22.9	16	45.7	3	21.4
Smallpox	11	15.5	13	19.4	4	11.4	4	11.4	2	14.3
Fevers	16	22.5	5	7.5	8	22.9	8	22.9	3	21.4
Other stated	7	9.9	6	9.0	3	8.6	2	5.7	1	7.1
Unstated	10	14.1	32	47.8	10	28.6	0		5	35.7
Total	71		67		35		35		14	

included.[28] The population of London, even within the restricted area covered by the bills of mortality, was apparently increasing then, yet the number of reported deaths was smaller. Conceivably the death rate fell substantially, perhaps because many more young people were moving into the city; but underregistration is another possible explanation for this. Even more seriously, although from 1728 the bills of mortality tabulations gave the age at death, they do not associate the reported causes of death with the ages of the deceased. This means we cannot estimate mortality rates from the different reported causes of death at various ages. With the London Quakers, however, we can to some degree specify both age at death and reported cause of death, and thus come a little closer to an explanation of their patterns of infant and child mortality.

The first step is to tabulate reported causes of death by age, as is done in Table 5.8. The main difference between this table and the one preceding is of course the large number of cases in the Quaker records where no cause of death was mentioned in the burial note. It is noteworthy that the younger the child, the less likely it was that the cause of death would be stated, as though infancy itself was a sufficient explanation for dying. (In the bills of mortality prior to 1720, infancy was in fact regularly given as a cause of death.) As noted, the registration is least comprehensive in the first part of the eighteenth century, and our best information starts in 1750, when more of the entries have a stated cause of death and pseudo-causes such as teething are less often mentioned. Having such a large number of unknown causes, especially for the youngest children, is of course a major difficulty, if perhaps not an insuperable one; we shall return to a technique which may mitigate its effects.

Turning for the time being only to those cases where a cause of death was stated, we can see at a glance some refinements of the data for the whole of London. Gastrointestinal disease, for example, seems to have been a major killer of infants and children before 1700. Smallpox also claimed a heavy toll, even among infants; Sarah Ebrall was said to have died of it on the nineteenth of the seventh month (September) 1683, aged only two weeks. "Consumption" could also be fatal to infants under a month old, so contemporaries clearly did not confine use of the word to the wasting diseases of adulthood.[29] On the

---

[28] Creighton, *Epidemics*, II, 567.

[29] Frederick Smith, a Friend who was born in 1757, describes an accident which befell his young daughter as follows: "[T]he nursemaid carelessly suffered her to fall off the bed, which occasioned the formationof an abcess inwardly, and a consequent gradual decay; so that she became reduced, to all appearance, to the last stage of a consumption" (*Autobiographical Narrations of the Convincement and Other Religious*

other hand "convulsions" or "fits" did strike adults as well; in fact Table 5.14 shows quite a few adults who were said to have perished from one of these two causes.

Having toured the pitfalls of trying to use the bills of mortality without any notion of ages at death, we shall now convert Table 5.8 into an estimate of death rates from various causes by multiplying the death rates we have established for our sample of London Quakers by the distribution of deaths of all London Quaker infants and children. In doing this (in Table 5.9) we assume that the distribution of deaths where no cause of death was stated was the same as where it was stated, deferring for the moment a discussion of the plausibility of this assumption.

From rough-and-ready statistics such as these, inferences should be cautious; but one, at least, seems very tempting: that the main cause of the reduction in infant mortality in the first part of the eighteenth century was the remarkable decline in gastrointestinal diseases. If we assume the "unknowns" were distributed in the same way as the known causes, total mortality from all other causes taken together in the first part of the eighteenth century was almost exactly the same as it had been fifty years earlier; but that from gastrointestinal disease was only one-tenth as great.

A similar decline in reported causes of death from gastrointestinal disease has been noted for the very large London parish of St. Giles without Cripplegate. "Griping of the guts" declined from 8.5 percent of reported causes in the period from 1654–93 to only 0.1 percent in 1729–43, while in the same time span incidence of fatal "stoppage of the stomach" went from 2.6 to 0.1 percent and "surfeit" from 2 percent to none. By a half-century later (1774–93) designation of gastrointestinal illness as a cause of death in the bills of mortality had altogether ceased.[30]

The medical writer William Black, writing at the end of the eighteenth century, was the first to notice this. His explanation, repeated by most subsequent writers, was "that many infant diseases and deaths, which were formerly crowded into colick and gripes, are in modern times transferred to the vortex of convulsions." "I am aware," he continued, "that, in reply, it may be suggested that drains, sewers, drier lodgings, less damp, alteration in diet, and the more

Experiences of Samuel Crisp, Elizabeth Webb, Evan Bevan, Margaret Lucas, and Frederick Smith [London, 1848], 188.) Not having any way to correlate ages at death with the statements of cause of death in the bill of mortality, Appleby takes "consumption" to designate exactly this sort of long-lasting degenerative disease.

30 Thomas R. Forbes, "Births and deaths in a London parish: the record from the registers, 1654–1693 and 1729–1743," *Bulletin of the History of Medicine* 55 (1981), 390.

Friends in life and death

Table 5.9 *Estimated mortality rates from various causes, London Quaker infants and children*

Cause	1670–99		1700–49		1750–95	
	M	F	M	F	M	F
Died aged under 1 year						
Convulsions	157	156	116	121	91	68
Gastrointestinal	100	81	11	6	2	3
Pulmonary (including "consumption")	18	11	30	23	25	23
Smallpox	20	12	40	36	18	16
Fevers	18	20	18	20	6	10
Other stated	41	48	63	42	13	7
Died aged 1 to 4 years						
Convulsions	30	37	30	25	23	27
Gastrointestinal	31	34	2	1	1	0
Pulmonary (including "consumption")	31	23	20	17	23	34
Smallpox	41	34	92	78	40	45
Fevers	45	45	39	48	13	28
Other stated	72	87	62	58	9	16
Died aged 5 to 9 years						
Convulsions	4	0	3	2	10	6
Gastrointestinal	8	0	0	0	0	0
Pulmonary (including "consumption")	16	0	11	8	25	12
Smallpox	13	0	24	17	40	16
Fevers	16	0	14	8	18	8
Other stated	8	0	4	2	6	1
Died aged 10 to 14 years						
Convulsions	2	0	6	1	0	0
Gastrointestinal	3	0	1	0	0	0
Pulmonary (including "consumption")	9	0	37	10	0	0
Smallpox	6	0	20	9	0	0
Fevers	4	0	17	7	0	0
Other stated	5	0	27	5	0	0

Note: Estimated rates were obtained by multiplying age-specific mortality rates for our sample of London Quaker families (those with surnames beginning with "B") by the percentage distribution among stated causes of death of all London Quakers (given in Table 5.8). Causes of death were much less frequently stated for girls, accounting for the frequent zeroes in their columns.

plentiful use of vegetable and fermented liquors, have decreased dysenteric complaints in this city"; but he concluded that nevertheless much infantile diarrhea was being ascribed to convulsions.[31]

This looks somewhat plausible if we assume that every case attributed to convulsions was really a gastrointestinal disease and then add the figures for intestinal diseases and "convulsions" in Table 5.8; taken together they amount to 32.4 percent of all reported deaths occurring at all ages in 1670–1709 and 31 percent in 1710–49, falling to 25.8 percent in 1740–95. Furthermore it seems absurd to claim that gastrointestinal diseases could have fallen so rapidly, in an age not especially noted for sanitary improvements, to such a minute fraction as the searchers' reports would indicate. We nevertheless believe there was a real and substantial decline in fatal infantile diarrhea, and appeal to Tables 5.7 and 5.8 for support. Bedevilled as they are by the monstrously large total of unknowns, they nevertheless give no evidence that an undiminished mortality from diarrhea was now being rechristened convulsions. Even if we multiplied the percentages attributed to convulsions and gastrointestinal disorders ten-fold (since there were proportionally ten times as many stated causes of death in the figures before 1700) there would still be a 20 percent decline from the 1670–99 figures in 1700–24 for infants under a month old, and proportional declines at higher ages.

Probably the real decline in the incidence of fatal gastrointestinal diseases was not so great as the disappearance of this category from the bills of mortality would have one believe, but it does show up in the general population as well. Since the incidence of fatal gastrointestinal disorders also declined among children aged 1 to 4, a more general improvement in hygiene among infants and children would seem to be a part, at least, of the explanation. Here seems to be another case where the Quaker population was a leading sector, anticipating changes which occurred more slowly in the population as a whole.

In infants, in particular, gastrointestinal illnesses in the past were generally the result of contaminated water and food supplies. Babies who were breast-fed during their entire first year would have run much less risk of contracting such infections, so the dramatic decrease in their incidence could be taken as a sign that more Quaker women were breast-feeding in the eighteenth century than in the seventeenth, and beginning immediately so that the infants received their prophy-

---

31 William Black, *An Arithmetical and Medical Analysis of the Diseases and Mortality of the Human Species* (London, 1789), reprinted with an introduction by D. V. Glass (n.p., 1973), 160. Forbes, who compiled the statistics from St Giles Cripplegate, appears to believe that there was no real decline in mortality from gastrointestinal diseases, but rather that the searchers simply began calling them "fevers."

lactic colostrum. The continued low incidence of such disorders could then count as evidence that breast-feeding remained the custom into the nineteenth century. But as we have seen in chapter 4, breast-feeding by Quaker mothers is more likely to have been less intensive and prolonged in the eighteenth than in the seventeenth century. On the other hand, the benefits of colostrum were available if babies were put to the breast immediately; and we also have evidence that supplementary feeding had improved by the middle of the eighteenth century. In some more affluent parts of London, too, more sanitary supplies of water and milk were becoming available. These seem the most likely reasons for the decline in infantile diarrhea.

The further decline in infant mortality in the last half of the eighteenth century has no obvious explanation. Virtually every stated cause of death (including such pseudo-causes as teething) declined. The most important change was the increasing incidence of "convulsions," since these were said to be the principal cause of the deaths of infants, especially those under a month old. We obviously need to know more about the reasons why so many infants perished from such disorders. Convulsions were doubtless in many cases the result of high fevers; but there also must have been some which could be classed as "endogenous," especially among very young infants. They can be caused by teething; rickets (arising from Vitamin D deficiency); spasmophilia, owing to lack of calcium in the diet; birth injury; smallpox; Vitamin B_6 deficiency; or possibly even lead poisoning (nipple shields in the eighteenth century were often made of lead). The real causes of death associated with teething could have been diarrhea, infantile scurvy, convulsions, or mercuric poisoning.[32] The steepest decline, however, was in mortality from smallpox, especially in the last quarter of the century.

When we turn from infant to child mortality, the importance of smallpox becomes even more pronounced. In the eighteenth century it was the greatest single killer of children between the ages of 1 and

[32] J. Rendle-Short, "The causes of infantile convulsions prior to 1900," *Journal of Pediatrics* 47 (1955), 733–39 and "The history of teething in infancy," *Proceedings of the Royal Society of Medicine* 48 (1955), 132–38. "Convulsions" and diarrhea, taken together, accounted for a quarter of all infant deaths in London as late as 1845 and 30 percent of infant deaths in England and Wales in 1870 (D. V. Glass, *Numbering the People: The Eighteenth-Century Population Controversy and the Development of Census and Vital Statistics in Britain* [Farnborough, Hants., 1973], 189). Although William Cadogan's *Essay upon Nursing and the Management of Children* (London, 1748), which was the first book to advocate immediate nursing, also was the first to deny that teething was necessarily morbid, it was still given as a considerable cause of death of infants as late as the bills of mortality of 1897 (Samuel X. Radbill, "Teething in fact and fancy," *Bulletin of the History of Medicine* 39 [1965], 339–45).

10. It has been claimed that children under 2 were the principal victims of smallpox,[33] but we find it still a major cause of death in children over 10. In fact, it was the cause of at least 10 percent of all deaths which occurred even among people aged 15 to 34 in London. Since smallpox was endemic in the metropolis, there was (before the popularity of inoculation) a high probability that every child born there would catch it sooner or later (there appears to be a natural immunity in only about 5 percent of the population).[34] The case mortality has been estimated at 15 percent,[35] so that it is not surprising that it figures prominently in the mortality rates. Many of its older victims among the London Quakers had been born and brought up in the country (probably in towns where smallpox was not endemic) and they died of the disease when exposed to it in London.

Since prevention or mitigation of smallpox by inoculation is one of the major innovations of eighteenth-century medicine, it is necessary to examine its possible impact on the decline of infant and child mortality in the second half of the eighteenth century. Was it a consequence of widespread adoption of inoculation by the Quakers? We do know that Friends were free of religious prejudice against inoculation, which was found in the Church of England and also in some Dissenting churches, such as the Independents. Inoculation, besides being disapproved of by some religious leaders, could be expensive; but the Quakers were less affected by either hindrance than most groups, so inoculation might have been adopted earlier by them. A Quaker girl living in Hertfordshire, Mary Batt, was successfully

[33] Flinn, *European Demographic System*, 98. Peter Razzell thinks that 87 percent of all mortality from smallpox struck those aged under 10 years; but that in London, because it was endemic there, "practically all cases of smallpox occurred amongst children under the age of seven" (*The Conquest of Smallpox* [Firle, Sussex, 1977], vi, 70). The latter statement, at least, is incompatible with our findings about the Quakers.

[34] Razzell, *Conquest*, vi.

[35] Michael Flinn, "The stabilization of mortality in pre-industrial Western Europe," *Journal of European Economic History* 3 (1974), 317. Razzell states that the case mortality among infants was 40 percent ("Population growth," in *Land, Labour and Population*, 273). This estimate seems too high. On the same page Razzell suggests that but for inoculation, from one-fifth to one-fourth of infant and child deaths in the period from 1838 to 1844 would have been from smallpox (we derive this figure from his claim that in the whole country during those years infant and child mortality would have been one-third to one-fourth higher than it was except for the conquest of smallpox). It is hard to see how the case mortality could be as high as 40 percent, and natural immunity only 5 percent, if smallpox constituted only a quarter or a third of the total infant and child mortality. The two smallpox censuses which Razzell cites (*Conquest*, 116–17) show case mortalities of only 12 and 16 percent. James Jurin, in a paper to the Royal Society in 1723, concluded that the risk of dying from smallpox was about 2 in 17, and the case mortality in recent epidemics had been 1 out of 5 or 6 (quoted in Donald R. Hopkins, *Princes and Peasants: Smallpox in History* [Chicago, 1983], 50).

inoculated as early as 1721, and one of the most famous inoculators was the Quaker Thomas Dimsdale.[36] Inoculation seems to have been generally slower to catch on in the metropolis; in 1781 it was said as yet to have "made very little progress in London."[37] Rural Friends may have been just as slow to take up the practice, though; it does not seem to have made much of an impact on over-all mortality outside the cities. It will be recalled that rural infant mortality actually rose in the third quarter of the eighteenth century, and declined only a bit in the fourth quarter. It is possible that adoption of inoculation prevented an even steeper rise in infant mortality, but the evidence does not seem to support the enthusiastic claims about inoculation made by Peter Razzell. As for London itself, the Quakers seem just as retrograde as everyone else in taking up inoculation. As Table 5.9 shows, there was no substantial decline in deaths from smallpox until after 1775; as a percentage of all infant and child deaths, smallpox actually increased in the twenty-five years after 1750, and in the next quarter-century the decline in mortality from smallpox in infants and children was less pronounced than that from convulsions and other fevers, against which, except for improved sanitary measures, no effective therapy had been devised.

Of course, even with smallpox we must remember the fallibility of eighteenth-century diagnoses. In fact, even in the twentieth century clinical diagnoses are often erroneous and death certificates often misstate causes of death; a study of almost 10,000 autopsies in England and Wales showed a disagreement between the clinical diagnosis and the autopsy over the cause of death in almost 30 percent of the cases.[38] Apparently there was in eighteenth-century Britain a kind of fulminating smallpox which could kill before the characteristic pustules had time to develop; in young children it might thus be put down to "convulsions" or "bloody flux."[39] Its incidence, however, seems to have been quite low.[40] But if there were really more smallpox cases than the Quaker registers show, this is further evidence for our conclusion that inoculation was not yet widespread among London Quakers. Insofar as mortality from smallpox declined, this may be explained in part by mutations towards less virulent strains of the micro-organism, just as the appearance of more virulent strains in the

[36] Razzell, *Conquest*, 26–27, 51.   [37] Quoted in *ibid.*, 70.

[38] M. A. Heasman, "Accuracy of death certification," *Proceedings of the Royal Society of Medicine* 55 (1962), 733–36.

[39] Razzell, *Conquest*, 104–6; Hopkins, *Princes*, 5. Eversley has pointed out that in eighteenth-century Germany there were four different strains of smallpox, each with its own pattern of virulence and age-specific incidence (*Population Growth and the Brain Drain*, ed. Bechhofer, Discussion, 229).

[40] At least this is the opinion of William Brass (*Population Growth and the Brain Drain*, 231).

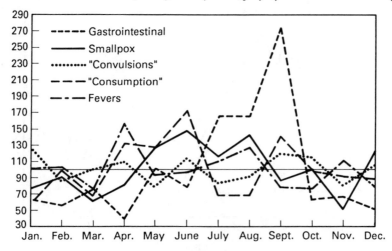

Fig. 5.3 Seasonality of deaths from stated causes, London Quaker children, 1675–1795.

seventeenth century appears to account for the sudden surge in mortality from smallpox then.[41]

These arguments do depend on the assumption, heretofore unexamined, that the distribution of causes of death among those for whom no cause was stated was the same as among those where there was such a statement. Even where only 10 percent were known, this would be an entirely adequate sample if causes were reported randomly. That, unfortunately, is most unlikely. Spectacular or unusual causes of death, such as accidents, might be reported in almost every case, and much-feared or easily diagnosable diseases such as plague or smallpox might stand a better chance of being reported than

[41] Leslie Clarkson, *Death, Disease and Famine in Pre-Industrial England* (London, 1975), 56; Ann G. Carmichael and Arthur M. Silverstein, "Smallpox in Europe before the seventeenth century: virulent killer or benign disease?" *Journal of the History of Medicine and Allied Sciences* 42 (1987), 147–68. Alfred Perrenoud has recently laid enormous stress on mutations of pathogens (and perhaps also sunspots) in the decline of mortality in France, England, and Sweden at the end of the eighteenth century; see "Le Biologique et l'humain dans le déclin séculaire de la mortalité," *Annales: Economies, Sociétés, Civilisations* 40e année (1985), 113–35. On the other hand, some scholars deny that any decrease in the virulence of smallpox played a part in its decline in the eighteenth century; see B. Luckin, "The decline of smallpox and the demographic revolution of the eighteenth century," *Social History* no. 6 (1977), 793–97. Some strain of smallpox, at least, was taking a deadly toll in India even in the early twentieth century. Nobody has produced a series of case mortality figures, which would be at least a first step in deciding this question (though comparisons of the general health of the populations at risk would obviously be necessary to interpret such figures even if they existed).

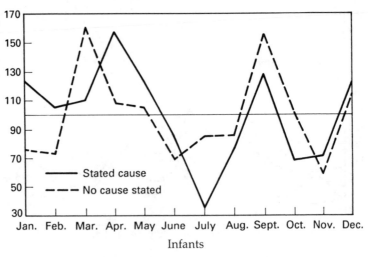

Infants

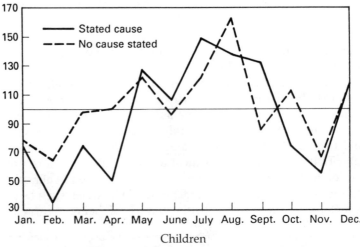

Children

Fig. 5.4 Seasonality of infant deaths from stated and unstated causes, London Quaker infants, 1 month to 1 year, 1670–1709, and children, 1 to 4 years, 1710–1749.

"consumption" or teething, not to mention disgraceful causes of death such as suicide or venereal disease.

We have thought of only one way of finding out anything about deaths from unstated causes, and that is to study their seasonal distribution as compared to the seasonality of deaths from the major reported causes. This cannot be done for all groups, since subdividing into twelve cells can produce numbers so small that random variations would play an undesirably large part; but where it can be done, we can at least compare one property of the sample with the whole population. This becomes particularly useful because some of the stated causes of death display marked seasonal variations, as is shown in Figure 5.3. This is especially true of gastrointestinal diseases, which rose to a spectacular peak in September and generally were most prevalent in the late summer. (This peak was still clearly noticeable in 1841, when the seasonal distribution of most illnesses in London seems to have been the same as in our records.)[42] Our task would be easier if other diseases had sharply different patterns, but in fact they display a broadly similar seasonal incidence, almost all taking the heaviest toll in the six months from April to September. More people died from small-pox in June, July, and August, for example, than in the rest of the year. This was even true of "consumption," suggesting that when this term was used for a children's disease, it was sometimes not a respiratory one, since whooping cough and inflammations of the mouth and throat like quinsy and thrush were slightly more likely to prove fatal in the winter months and were less common in the late summer.[43]

If the seasonal distribution of deaths from unstated causes had been quite different than that from stated ones, then inferences about the pattern of all-over mortality could not safely be drawn from the latter. In fact, however, they fit together reasonably well (especially when the likelihood of high random variation from small numbers is borne in mind). Figure 5.4 shows two representative seasonal distributions. In general, the comparisons which can be made for those aged 1 month to 5 years at death, most revealing for the highly seasonal gastrointestinal diseases, suggest that its incidence in the whole Quaker population was probably less in the late seventeenth century and somewhat more in the early eighteenth than our figures drawn only from the stated causes of death would suggest. On the other hand, "fevers" have quite a different seasonal pattern from gastrointestinal diseases, which casts doubt on Forbes' claim that the incidence of such diseases continued, but they were simply reported as "fever." Though the rate of decline in gastrointestinal disease may not have been quite so dramatic as Table 5.9 indicates, we find no reason to believe that the distribution of fatal diseases as stated in the Quaker records was wildly different from that among all London Quaker children.

42 *Fifth Annual Report of the Registrar-General*, 272–83.
43 *Observations on the Bill of Mortality, in Chester, for the Year 1772. By Doctor* [John] Haygarth notes the promiscuous use of the word "consumption" in England, and says that "to prevent every error of this kind, with all possible accuracy, strict injunctions were given, that no disorder, unless attended with a cough, should be called consumption" (reprinted in *Mortality in Pre-Industrial Times: The Contemporary Verdict* ed. John Cassedy [London, 1973], 73). Regrettably Dr Haygarth was not giving such instructions to the searchers for the London bills of mortality.

We are left, therefore, with a picture of a reduction in gastrointestinal disease in the first half of the eighteenth century and a general decline in mortality from infections of all kinds among younger children in the last half. Inoculation for smallpox may have played some part in this, especially after 1775, but at best it was not a great one, and the explanation of the general reduction in mortality must remain in doubt.

So it remains somewhat mysterious why London infant mortality declined so much after 1750, especially since this decline seems earlier and sharper than that for the rest of the population; but since more children still died in London than in the countryside, why did Quakers not leave London for a healthier environment – which after all was close at hand in the green fields of western Middlesex and Hertfordshire?[44] They cannot have been totally resigned to God's will in thus decimating their beloved offspring. However, it could well be that especially the London Quakers who were affluent had important business affairs to attend to. They needed to live within walking, or at least within riding, distance of their countinghouses, and they may therefore have fairly coolly calculated the gains from their commercial activities against the greater risks to their health and that of their children. This explanation would also be consonant with their later behavior: when infant mortality was finally brought down to much lower levels, they began to restrict fertility.

Coolly calculating Quakers? Why not? We are so bemused by the normal Quaker biography, or hagiography, that we overlook the fact that these multi-millionaires (in modern terms) had to make their fortunes by hard-headed business methods before they could devote some or all their time to philanthropy. The household names of Fry and Gurney, William Allen and Peter Bedford, John Bellers and John Howard are those of families for whom the accumulation of great wealth was a prerequisite to their freedom of action. We do not say that they acted dishonestly, or even callously, by the standards of their time; but, invariably, they bought cheap and sold dear (whether we are talking about commodities or labor). Then why should we balk at the thought that they may have kept their families in London even if this meant higher mortality?

Of course we historians are really the ones who can coolly calculate.

---

[44] We have in mind exactly the sort of calculation – retrospective, of course – in Jeffrey G. Williamson, "Was the industrial revolution worth it? Disamenities and death in 19th-century British towns," *Explorations in Economic History* 19 (1982), 221–45. There the infant mortality rate is taken as a proxy for all the other "disamenities" of nineteenth-century towns and compared with differentials in the real wages of workers to see how much extra in real wages would be required to make them move to somewhere with higher infant mortality. Significantly, no increase in real wages was required to induce workers to move to London, where real wages were lower in spite of slightly higher infant mortality (224–25).

The Quakers of eighteenth-century London not only had to weigh the passion for gain against solicitude for their children's health; they also made comparisons of infant mortality with that they remembered from their own childhood and with that they saw about them. High as it was, London Quaker infant mortality was usually below that estimated for the rest of the London population.[45] And they had no idea of the low level of infant mortality which we now accept as normal.

Thus far we have spoken only of mortality rates; but these can be put into a different and perhaps more comprehensible perspective if we hazard a guess as to what life expectancy at birth would have been, given infant and childhood mortality at the levels we have found. Such an estimate depends on recourse to model life tables, with all the risks, already discussed in chapter 4, that application of such models to historical populations entails. Neither the choice of life tables nor the fitting of data to the tables selected is subject to any precise decision rules. We have decided to use the Ledermann life tables, which were based on 154 mortality tables, though none were earlier than 1816–40 (for Sweden).[46] There is no perfect fit of our data to any model life table; in fact, in both the Ledermann and the UN ones, there are none which match child mortality as severe as that experienced by the Quakers in London before 1700. The closest fit between Quaker infant- and child-mortality figures and the life expectancies in the various life tables is set forth in Table 5.10. The small numbers at risk in Northern England and Scotland and the genealogies prohibit us from attaching too much certainty to these numbers, but they can be compared to contemporary estimates for Southern England as represented in the life table for Lichfield in 1694 prepared by Gregory King and the late eighteenth-century life table for Carlisle, which has been called the first life table based on English data to give a realistic view of mortality.[47] Quaker longevity (life expectancy at birth) in Bristol and Norwich was a bit above that of Lichfield, which was a considerably smaller town. King thought that there life expectancy at birth would have been 32 years. The comparable figure for Carlisle a century later was 38.7. This may represent a real improvement, comparable to what the Quakers seem to have experienced; but it may also simply show the advantage that a smaller settlement usually had. Using an unspecified statistical technique (probably

45 John Landers, "Some problems in the historical demography of London 1675–1825," Cambridge University PhD Thesis, 1984, 73 estimates infant mortality (from the London bills of mortality) as 306 in 1680–99 and 359, 375, 331, and 262 in the four quarters of the eighteenth century, falling to 218 in 1800–19.

46 Sully Ledermann, *Nouvelles tables-types de mortalité* [INED Travaux et Documents no. 53] (Paris, 1969).

47 Joshua Milne, *A Treatise on the Valuation of Annuities and Assurances on Lives and Survivorships* (London, 1815), II, 564–65; praised by Glass, *Numbering the People*, 16.

Table 5.10. *Estimated life expectancy at birth, British and Irish Quakers*

Period	Ireland		Southern England		Northern Britain		Bristol & Norwich		London	
	M	F	M	F	M	F	M	F	M	F
1650–99	47.0	50.0	46.4	50.4	52.3	57.6	36.6	38.9	26.0	26.4
1700–49	41.3	45.8	45.8	49.8	49.4	54.2	30.1	34.8	29.1	31.4
1750–99	44.1	47.9	49.0	50.3	53.5	55.6	38.2	46.8	44.0	43.5
1800–49	58.3	59.4	54.4	57.0	59.1	63.1	53.1	51.1	45.3	57.0
1850–99					63.2	66.6				

Note: Figures are for Quaker infant and child mortality (0–4 survival rates) fitted to the life tables in Sully Ledermann, *Nouvelles table-types de mortalité*, INED Travaux et Documents, no. 53 (Paris, 1969), Réseau 101, pp. 102–19. When our values differed from those in the model life tables, we interpolated.

taking the median of reported ages at death) Michael R. Watts has calculated the life expectancy (presumably at birth) of the Quakers in London Quarterly Meeting during the first decade of the eighteenth century at 32.06 years.[48] This is very close to our figure of 31.4 for the first half of the eighteenth century. (London was of course more unhealthy than Bristol or Norwich.)

Our figures are also close to the figures derived from parish family reconstitution studies, where life expectancy at birth was reckoned to be 39.5 years between 1650 and 1750 and 45 in the latter half of the eighteenth century.[49] For England as a whole in 1841, life expectancy at birth was 40.2 years for males and 42.2 for females.[50]

In the consideration of adult mortality, we are in a position to construct our own life expectancy tables. One (Table 5.11) is done for that part of the married population where the exact age at death is known. Though this is in one sense the most accurate procedure, since it uses only data of complete reliability, it also represents a relatively small part of the population. Also, mortality is likely to be exaggerated if only those whose exact ages at death are considered, since such a procedure would overrepresent those who died before they could move away and thus possibly pass out of observation. For these reasons our computations also include life tables prepared on "optimistic" and "pessimistic" estimates of the longevity of persons

[48] Michael R. Watts, *The Dissenters* vol. 1 (Oxford, 1978), 506. Watts believes we can be "certain" of the death rate among Friends in this meeting during this decade; since the life expectancy figure was 32.06, the death rate must have been 31.2.
[49] E. A. Wrigley and R. S. Schofield, *The Population History of England 1541–1871: A Reconstruction* (Cambridge, Mass., 1981), 252.
[50] *Fifth Annual Report of the Registrar-General*, 25.

Table 5.11 Life expectancies, exact ages at death known only

Cohort	Urban M	Urban F	Southern England M	Southern England F	Ireland M	Ireland F	Northern Britain M	Northern Britain F	Genealogy M	Genealogy F
Age group 25–29										
1650–99	29.8	25.7	28.9	24.5	34.1	27.4	NA	29.1	35.7	34.7
1700–49	28.1	26.7	32.9	30.1	33.9	29.9	35.3	35.4	40.8	35.7
1750–99	33.0	30.6	37.0	33.9	32.7	31.2	34.4	28.4	39.5	36.4
1800–49	27.1	32.1	35.4	33.4	NA	29.1	NA	NA	43.5	35.9
All cohorts	29.8	27.6	32.9	29.3	33.8	29.6	33.3	31.1	40.7	35.9
Age group 30–34										
1650–99	27.7	26.0	27.2	24.4	29.9	26.4	26.2	26.3	31.9	34.4
1700–49	25.3	25.1	29.6	29.3	30.8	28.3	31.5	31.8	35.8	33.3
1750–99	29.7	30.0	33.9	31.2	29.6	29.0	32.1	26.8	36.0	34.5
1800–49	30.2	29.3	33.9	34.4	29.0	28.8	NA	31.7	39.2	34.1
All cohorts	27.4	26.8	30.2	28.7	30.2	28.1	29.9	28.8	36.5	34.0
Age group 35–39										
1650–99	25.5	26.0	24.8	22.5	26.6	25.2	24.7	24.6	28.7	30.5
1700–49	22.9	23.9	26.3	27.6	28.0	25.9	29.4	29.6	32.0	32.1
1750–99	27.2	28.4	30.2	28.1	26.8	25.7	28.9	24.9	32.6	31.7
1800–49	27.6	26.9	30.0	31.5	25.9	26.2	29.1	31.9	34.5	31.5
All cohorts	25.4	25.4	27.2	26.6	27.2	25.7	27.8	27.1	32.8	31.6
Age group 40–44										
1650–99	22.8	24.4	23.0	21.8	23.8	24.4	21.7	22.3	26.0	26.5
1700–49	20.4	21.4	24.0	24.8	25.6	24.0	26.3	26.3	29.1	28.6
1750–99	24.1	26.3	27.0	26.0	23.1	24.1	25.6	23.0	28.4	28.9
1800–49	24.4	24.1	27.5	28.9	23.1	26.3	27.9	29.2	30.3	28.9
All cohorts	22.7	23.1	24.9	24.7	24.3	24.3	24.9	24.6	29.2	28.7
Age group 45–49										
1650–99	19.2	19.6	20.0	19.5	21.1	22.4	19.1	18.5	21.8	24.3
1700–49	18.5	18.8	21.2	22.2	22.4	21.3	23.6	23.1	25.1	24.9
1750–99	20.6	24.4	24.0	23.1	20.8	21.7	23.6	21.8	24.7	25.4
1800–49	20.9	22.3	22.8	26.8	20.1	22.4	24.0	25.2	26.6	26.0
All cohorts	19.5	20.6	21.8	22.2	21.5	21.7	22.3	21.7	25.4	25.7
Age group 50–54										
1650–99	16.1	17.5	17.3	16.8	17.9	18.8	18.2	16.8	18.0	20.1
1700–49	15.8	16.1	18.4	19.3	18.6	19.3	19.7	19.7	22.1	21.1
1750–99	17.4	21.3	20.1	20.2	19.2	19.8	19.2	19.3	20.5	22.5
1800–49	17.3	18.3	21.4	23.5	17.6	18.3	21.9	21.9	22.7	22.1
All cohorts	16.4	17.9	18.9	19.4	18.5	19.3	19.4	19.1	21.8	22.3

Table 5.12 Estimated life expectancy at birth, British and Irish Quakers (average of "optimistic" and "pessimistic" assumptions)

Cohort	Urban M	Urban F	Southern England M	Southern England F	Ireland M	Ireland F	Northern Britain M	Northern Britain F	Genealogy M	Genealogy F
Age group 25–29										
1650–99	31.0	29.4	32.2	29.2	33.5	32.7	35.8	33.7	36.1	36.7
1700–49	29.6	28.8	34.1	31.9	35.8	36.3	35.0	32.8	40.8	36.9
1750–99	33.6	32.2	36.7	35.0	35.3	31.3	34.4	33.4	38.6	37.0
1800–49	30.5	35.2	36.0	35.1	NA	33.3	35.9	32.6	41.4	36.6
Age group 35–39										
1650–99	25.6	26.2	26.3	25.7	26.1	26.8	27.5	28.4	28.8	30.7
1700–49	24.6	25.0	26.9	28.2	29.0	29.7	28.0	27.5	32.0	31.9
1750–99	27.0	28.7	29.6	28.7	29.0	26.6	27.4	27.1	31.1	31.1
1800–49	27.4	28.5	29.0	31.0	29.2	31.0	27.2	27.9	32.6	31.0
Age group 45–49										
1650–99	19.5	20.9	20.9	21.3	19.9	20.6	21.2	22.9	21.8	24.1
1700–49	19.5	19.8	21.2	22.6	22.6	23.1	21.8	22.1	25.1	24.6
1750–99	20.8	23.9	23.2	23.1	22.8	22.3	20.9	22.2	23.8	24.7
1800–49	20.6	22.6	21.9	25.2	22.7	24.1	20.5	22.6	25.1	25.0

Cohort	Urban M	Urban F	Southern England M	Southern England F	Ireland M	Ireland F	Northern Britain M	Northern Britain F	Genealogy M	Genealogy F
Age group 30–34										
1650–99	28.4	28.5	29.4	28.0	28.6	29.4	31.3	31.2	32.3	34.8
1700–49	26.7	26.7	30.4	30.2	31.7	32.6	31.4	30.2	35.8	33.9
1750–99	30.0	30.8	33.4	32.0	32.5	29.1	30.8	30.6	34.8	34.4
1800–49	30.7	31.8	33.1	34.3	32.8	33.2	31.0	31.0	37.0	34.2
Age group 40–44										
1650–99	22.7	23.9	23.9	23.9	22.8	24.2	24.3	25.9	26.0	26.8
1700–49	22.0	22.4	24.0	25.3	25.5	26.3	25.0	25.0	29.1	28.2
1750–99	24.0	26.3	26.3	26.2	25.4	24.2	23.6	24.9	27.2	28.1
1800–49	24.0	25.3	25.9	27.9	26.4	27.7	23.8	26.3	28.6	28.0
Age group 50–54										
1650–99	16.7	18.3	17.9	18.3	18.1	18.2	18.0	19.6	18.1	20.2
1700–49	16.9	16.9	18.4	19.6	19.0	19.8	18.4	19.6	22.1	21.0
1750–99	17.6	20.7	19.5	20.1	19.1	19.5	18.7	19.8	20.1	21.7
1800–49	17.2	18.9	19.7	22.0	20.1	20.9	17.8	18.9	21.5	21.4

for whom no date of death was recorded.[51] We present in Table 5.12 life tables based on an average of the "optimistic" and "pessimistic" estimates.

These tables show that the general tendency of adult mortality, like that of infant and child mortality, was downward, although the improvements were irregular and were not highly correlated with commensurate improvements among infants and children. In Ireland, for example, life expectancies for adults in almost all age groups were higher than in England in the seventeenth century; but after a slight improvement in the next fifty years they declined in the last half of the eighteenth century. This decline appears to have continued into the first half of the nineteenth century, but the statistics which show life expectancy then at its lowest level are misleading, because of a "truncation effect." (No effort was made to find out exactly when people in Ireland who married before 1837 but died after that date died; so the result was that only people who died relatively early had a chance of figuring in the sample.)

In England, on the other hand, life expectancies for men rose throughout the eighteenth century and held steady or declined slightly in the first half of the nineteenth. (Almost all registers after 1837 were searched in the Southern English group, so the truncation effect would be very small.) In the cities the tendency at all age groups was for life expectancies for adult males to fall in the first half of the eighteenth century. Since this was the period which also saw a rise in child mortality but a decline in infant mortality, the unhealthy conditions of the cities at that time seem to have affected almost everyone over the age of one. After 1750 the men in the cities enjoyed better survival prospects than earlier, though still inferior to those in the rest of England. Their life expectancy seems to have changed very little in the first half of the nineteenth century.[52]

---

[51] "Optimistic" and "pessimistic" estimates are made as follows: "For each person two dates are identified: one at which they were last known to be alive, and one by which they are known to have been dead, though in most cases the latter date cannot be assigned, and so it is taken to be 100. Since death must have occurred between these two dates, an age at death is assigned according to the relative probabilities of dying given by an "optimistic" and "pessimistic" mortality schedule. In fact these were taken from Princeton model life tables, region west, levels 1 and 20, corresponding to expectations of life of 20.00 for females and 18.03 for males, and 67.50 for females and 63.64 for males respectively" (R. S. Schofield, personal communication, 2 February 1984).

[52] The single – and inexplicable – exception is urban men aged 25 to 29, whose life expectancy was about three years higher in the latter eighteenth than in the early nineteenth century. Since births in Bristol and Norwich were followed into the registers after 1837, this cannot have been entirely owing to a truncation effect, although this affected the life expectancy figures for London.

Women in the eighteenth and early nineteenth centuries shared the general tendency to live longer, and in fact the improvement in their longevity was more marked than that of the men, particularly at the younger ages. The most spectacular example comes from Southern England; and since this was our largest subgroup, and the one least affected by truncation effects, it presents us with a problem which requires explanation. In the three youngest age groups, the longevity of men improved by 2.7 to 3.7 years (Table 5.12), but that for women went up 5.3 to 6.3 years by the first half of the nineteenth century. By that time, except in the youngest age group, adult women were for the first time enjoying a higher life expectancy than men, the typical pattern in a modern population.

It will be recalled from Figure 5.1 that throughout childhood female children enjoyed better health than males; their chances of surviving to age 15 were always and everywhere greater. Why should this advantage not have persisted into adulthood? The considerable improvement in women's life expectancies, especially in the younger years, strongly suggests that a lessening of the hazards of childbirth was to some degree responsible, even though it should be pointed out that there was also a strong improvement in the longevity of Southern English women in the older age groups as well. At ages 50 to 54, women in the early nineteenth century could expect to live almost four years longer than their counterparts in the late seventeenth century, while the improvement for men was less than two years. Clearly these women were past the hazards of childbirth, and it may be argued that the increase in their longevity at this age was as noteworthy as the longer one at earlier ages.

We do have a way of getting some information about the hazards of childbirth, which is to tabulate the number of instances where the mother died within three months of the live birth of a child. This is done in Table 5.13. These figures are subject to both an upward and a downward bias. They do not take into account maternal mortality associated with a stillbirth. Stillbirths were about five times as likely to lead to maternal death as a live birth; but fewer than 3 percent of confinements led to a stillbirth. On the other hand, some maternal deaths which occurred within three months of the birth of the child were not the result of childbirth.[53]

---

[53] The most careful work on maternal mortality, treating all the possible biases in family reconstitutions from parish registers and drawing on the much superior Swedish records from the mid eighteenth century, is in Roger Schofield, "Did the mothers really die? Three centuries of maternal mortality in 'The World We Have Lost'," in *The World We Have Gained: Histories of Population and Social Structure*, ed. Lloyd Bonfield, Richard M. Smith, and Keith Wrightson (Oxford, 1986), 231–60.

Table 5.13 *Maternal mortality rates*

Cohort	Southern England n at risk	rate	Northern Britain n at risk	rate	Ireland n at risk	rate	Urban n at risk	rate	London n at risk	rate
1650–99	2388	19	911	10	2767	10	1264	17	388	23
1700–49	2985	10	1305	10	3002	12	1791	12	576	13
1750–99	2729	9	2274	8	2187	5	1524	9	340	11
1800–49	1164	13	1422	6	836	19	648	7	82	12

Our figures nevertheless are fairly close to estimates for the national toll of maternal mortality. Roger Schofield estimates this mortality rate at just under 16 for the end of the seventeenth century, just over 10 for the first half of the eighteenth and just under 8 for the second half, falling to between 5 and 6 per 1,000 in the first half of the nineteenth century.[54] The Quakers in Southern England and the urban centers share in the high maternal mortality at the end of the seventeenth century, after which it declined sharply and then after 1750 levelled off somewhat. The maternal mortality rate at its worst was something like 17 or 19 per 1,000 birth events, which is close to the rate estimated by Thomas Short in 1750; he thought there would be about 1 childbed death for every 61 christenings, which would mean a rate of 16 per 1,000.[55] In St. Giles without Cripplegate parish, London, the maternal mortality rate has been estimated at 19.3; in St. Botolph without Aldgate it was 23.5 from 1583 to 1599 and 15.9 in the bills of mortality in London from 1666 to 1758.[56] Since this was the risk at each confinement, the risk of dying in childbed over a lifetime has to be ascertained by multiplying the risk for each confinement by the number of times that each woman would give birth. Thus, if a woman had five confinements, the chances that one would end fatally would be about one in twelve.

Although childbirth was not a hazard to men, maternal mortality is not necessarily enough to account for the differences in life expectancy

[54] Schofield, "Maternal mortality," 250.   [55] Short, *New Observations*, 219.
[56] Forbes, "Births and deaths," 381; B. M. Willmott Dobbie, "An attempt to estimate the true rate of maternal mortality, sixteenth to eighteenth centuries," *Medical History* 26 (1982), 79–90. Dobbie thinks that even with corrections, E. A. Wrigley's – and doubtless also our – figures from family reconstitutions are "much too low." In his view the true rate of maternal mortality was more like 25. Schofield's calculations show this estimate is much too high.

Table 5.14 *Stated causes of death, London adult Quakers*

Cause	1670–99		1700–24		1725–49		1750–74		1775–94	
	No.	%	No.	%	No.	%	No.	%	No.	%
Males										
15–34										
Fevers	213	33.7	156	30.6	163	36.3	75	29.2	33	23.7
Pulmonary (including "consumption")	162	25.6	110	21.6	133	29.6	87	34.0	55	39.6
Smallpox	70	11.1	52	10.2	45	10.0	33	12.9	2	1.4
Gastrointestinal	68	10.8	7	1.4	1	0.2	2	0.8	1	0.7
Convulsions	11	0.2	28	5.5	30	6.7	19	7.4	8	5.8
Circulatory	17	2.7	12	2.4	13	2.9	8	3.1	3	2.2
(Dropsy)	(11)		(8)		(11)		(5)		(3)	
Other stated	35	5.5	41	8.1	31	6.9	14	5.5	14	10.1
Unstated	56	8.9	103	20.2	33	7.3	18	7.0	23	16.6
Total	632		509		449		256		139	
35–54										
Fevers	199	38.2	114	25.3	131	26.6	70	21.4	29	15.2
Pulmonary (including "consumption")	185	35.5	159	35.3	183	37.2	141	43.1	82	42.9
Smallpox	9	1.7	9	2.0	5	1.0	7	2.1	4	2.1
Gastrointestinal	29	5.6	14	3.1	4	0.8	6	1.8	1	0.5
Convulsions	4	0.8	29	6.4	51	10.4	28	8.6	8	4.2
Circulatory	46	8.8	49	10.9	46	9.3	37	11.3	20	10.5
(Dropsy)	(38)		(36)		(30)		(26)		(16)	
Other stated	28	5.4	35	7.8	47	9.6	29	8.9	28	14.7
Unstated	21	4.0	42	9.3	25	5.1	9	2.8	19	9.9
Total	521		451		492		327		191	
Females										
15–34										
Fevers	179	29.1	99	22.0	105	26.6	51	24.5	17	12.2
Pulmonary (including "consumption")	136	22.1	82	18.2	110	27.9	73	35.1	57	41.0
Smallpox	70	11.4	53	11.8	29	7.4	22	10.6	5	3.6
Gastrointestinal	58	9.4	9	2.0	6	1.5	0		1	0.7
Convulsions	13	2.1	27	6.0	58	14.7	14	6.7	6	4.3
Circulatory	27	4.4	23	5.1	17	4.3	9	4.3	4	2.8
(Dropsy)	(24)		(19)		(9)		(9)		(4)	
Other stated	82	13.3	45	10.0	35	8.9	26	12.5	16	11.5
Unstated	45	7.3	112	24.9	34	8.6	13	6.3	33	23.7
Total	615		450		394		208		139	
35–54										
Fevers	168	27.5	116	23.3	129	21.7	57	18.1	15	7.5
Pulmonary (including "consumption")	165	27.0	118	23.7	192	32.3	120	38.1	76	38.2
Smallpox	8	1.3	8	1.6	4	0.7	3	1.0	1	0.5
Gastrointestinal	54	8.8	17	3.4	6	1.0	2	0.6	1	0.5
Convulsions	10	1.6	37	7.4	80	13.5	32	10.1	12	6.0
Circulatory	87	14.2	63	12.7	83	24.0	41	13.0	30	15.1
(Dropsy)	(76)		(57)		(64)		(39)		(24)	
Other stated	82	13.4	46	9.2	64	10.8	38	12.1	17	8.5
Unstated	38	6.2	93	18.7	36	6.1	22	7.0	47	23.6
Total	612		498		594		315		199	

between young men and women before 1750, much less after 1750, when there was little further improvement. Alfred Perrenoud, surveying family reconstitution results in Geneva, where the figures for maternal mortality were comparable to those obtaining among the Quakers, points out that even if all the women who died in childbed had been spared and lived to the age of 50, life expectancy of women (at birth) would have risen by less than a year.[57] Furthermore, improvements in maternal mortality are of course irrelevant to those women past their childbearing years, whose life expectancy was also improving.

If we look beyond maternal mortality for an explanation, the same sort of information about causes of death which was available for infants and children among the London Quakers can also be compiled for adults – subject, of course, to the same difficulties of interpretation. Table 5.14 gives the relevant data. The picture is not unlike that which the bills of mortality give for the whole population (Table 5.7). Wasting diseases – if that is what we take both "consumption" and "decline" or "decay of nature" to be – slowly became more important as life expectancy in general improved; fevers, on the other hand, took a lesser toll. There is not much significant difference in the mortality from different diseases of men and women, leaving accidents and childbed deaths as the only strongly gender-specific causes of death. Since about three-quarters of the accident victims were men, part of the differential impact of deaths in childbed was cancelled out.

The reasons why men's life expectancy remained for so long above that of women thus remain elusive; but it may be the problem lies more in our expectations than in the data. That women live longer than men in modern populations need not mean that this is a law of nature, and that any deviation from this pattern requires an explanation. Richard Wall points out that the typical nineteenth-century pattern, in which mortality of the two genders was almost the same, may have been more nearly "natural," and that excess male mortality in the twentieth century may be the result of cultural factors (such as that more men smoke cigarettes).[58]

It is these, we believe, that most dramatically show the effects of the Quaker way of life upon the length of their lives. Greater longevity for men than women has been noted in other pre-industrial populations,

---

[57] Alfred Perrenoud, "Surmortalité féminine et condition de la femme (XVIIᵉ–XIXᵉ siècles): une vérification empirique," *Annales de démographie historique* (1981), 102. Several other articles in this issue of this journal are devoted to maternal mortality and examples of excess female mortality.

[58] Richard Wall, "Inferring differential neglect of females from mortality data," *Annales de démographie historique* (1981), 133.

but it would appear that men "of the world" did not come as close as Quaker men did to keeping up with the improvements in female life expectancy.[59] Of course Quaker men benefited directly from the establishment of religious toleration in the 1690s. Even though no English Quakers were executed for their religious beliefs, records of sufferings would warrant the estimate that perhaps 1 percent of the men either died in prison or had their health substantially impaired by imprisonment. After 1689 the Quakers ran very little risk of coming to a violent end; so far as we know, none were victims of homicides during this period (suicides, if there were any, were hushed up).[60] This, however, would not account for very much of the difference between Quaker mortality and that of the general population, since everywhere in England violent deaths were too infrequent to make much of an impact on life expectancies.[61] The Quakers, and especially the men, probably also benefited – though to an indeterminable degree – from religious values directed to minimizing stress and risk-taking behavior, and enjoining moderation of the appetites. This was particularly true since the Quaker discipline stood prepared to enforce this behavior. Drunkards were disowned; businessmen who seemed to be trading beyond their capacities were visited by the overseers, exhorted not to be greedy and overreach themselves, and advised how to set their affairs in order. If they persisted in reckless trading, they also were likely to be disowned. Friends thus enjoyed the advantages of a comfortable subsistence without suffering some of the anxieties and intemperance that often accompany wealth.

The Quakers included among their numbers, from the early eighteenth century onwards, a much higher proportion of doctors, chemists, manufacturers of food and drugs, scientists, and experimental engineers than could be found in the population at large. They knew cause and effect because many were essentially trained observers; and people brought up to silence and a contemplative way of life should see more than those used to relentless activity, a busy social life, and conformity to accepted beliefs and behavior. They were concerned with education, of infants as well as older children, at a time when for the rest of the middle-class population the teaching of children was full of barbarous practices.

---

[59] E. A. Wrigley, "Mortality in pre-industrial England: the example of Colyton, Devon, over three centuries," *Daedalus* 97 (Spring, 1968), 574; Wall, 131.

[60] William Allen notes the suicide of S. Whitbread on the sixth of July, 1815; but this is not recorded in the register of burials. See *Life of William Allen, with Selections from His Correspondence* (London, 1846), I, 233.

[61] On this see P. E. H. Hair, "Deaths from violence in Britain: a tentative secular survey," *Population Studies* 25 (1971), 5–24.

Table 5.15 *Life expectancies in Bristol, c. 1825: the poor, Quakers, and the whole city*

At age:	Quakers	Poor	All Bristol	At age:	Quakers	Poor	All Bristol
Birth	40.40	20.36	28.78	12	45.16	36.65	38.45
1	45.90	25.90	34.42	13	44.41	36.26	37.85
2	47.66	29.26	37.44	14	43.65	35.87	37.15
3	48.73	32.98	39.45	15	42.90	35.34	36.45
4	48.69	35.80	40.74	20	39.51	32.32	33.17
5	48.42	37.25	41.27	25	36.78	29.93	30.57
6	48.15	37.99	41.37	30	33.34	27.25	28.01
7	47.90	38.12	41.13	35	29.99	24.61	25.53
8	47.65	38.05	40.84	40	26.98	22.14	23.12
9	47.41	37.77	40.38	45	23.29	19.51	20.63
10	46.67	37.46	39.79	50	20.97	16.90	18.12
11	45.92	37.05	39.19	55	17.13	14.48	15.50

Note: Calculations for the poor, based on 4,061 individuals, were also included in the figures for all of Bristol.
Source: Robert Rankin, *A Familiar Treatise on Life Assurances and Annuities* (London, 1830), 76–80.

We can hardly accept volumes of evidence about Quaker pre-eminence in medicine, science, and industrial innovation, and a mass of literature about their belief in a certain lifestyle (or "testimonies") with its attendant valuation of the human individual, and at the same time suppose that these abundantly documented practices and ideas are not in any way reflected in their experience of sickness and death. Their mortality should have been below that of the population in general, and also below that of Britain's usually dissolute and occasionally vicious aristocracy. In fact contemporary actuaries believed there was no doubt that the middle classes would enjoy longer life than the upper class.[62]

Indeed it does appear that when systematic comparisons first become possible, in the 1830s, the Quakers enjoyed better health than the general population. For the period 1861–65, for example, their death rate was 20.3 compared to 22.6 in the general population; by 1896–1900 it was 14.3 as against 17.6.[63] These advantages were already known to the people who insured lives in the early nineteenth

[62] Milne, I, li.
[63] John Thurnam, *Observations and Essays on the Statistics of Insanity* (London, 1845), Appendix II, Table 14.

century. Robert Rankin, one of the actuaries of that time, compiled life tables for the city of Bristol as a whole, for the poor of that city (derived from the records of cemeteries offering cheap burials), and for the Bristol Quakers. The results can be found in Table 5.15. Rankin exhibited unbounded enthusiasm about the merits of the Quaker lifestyle:

This Table contains a lesson of inestimable value, for it teaches us how to extend human existence and augment its happiness. The moral habits for which the members of the Society of Friends are proverbially eminent, tend as certainly to the prolongation and enjoyment of life, as their opposites tend to abridge and embitter it.[64]

The Quakers exemplify Péguy's aphorism that we die of our whole lives. Being heavenly minded served also to lengthen their days on earth.

[64] Rankin, *Life Assurances*, 81.

Conclusion

In some ways the sources available to the student of British and Irish Quaker demography are the best that historical demographers have used. We are able to track the mobile part of the population; births, not baptisms, are recorded; there was a centralized system to oversee the activities of individual registrars; and we have a good deal of literary evidence from the Quakers themselves. These rich sources make it possible to offer with some confidence a summary view of the demography of the British and Irish Quakers; but we shall also give something like a concluding unscientific postscript – unscientific in the sense that of necessity the ratio of speculative inferences to straight conclusions from hard statistical evidence may be somewhat higher than in the preceding chapters.

For analytical purposes, nuptiality, fertility, and mortality were treated in separate chapters. Where necessary we sketched the relationships among the three, but without assessing their joint impact on population change. We do not have the sort of aggregative figures that could allow the computation of a net reproductive rate, and we know that emigration, disownment, and conversions had a very great effect on the total numbers of Quakers. We can, however, offer a crude technique for estimating what the effect of purely demographic changes would have been *if* the population had been closed and if the families for which we know the number of children ever born are representative of the whole. We have made this computation by multiplying the average number of live births per family formed by the percentage of such children who lived to the age of 15 (since we have no information about mortality between the ages of 15 and 25). The contribution of fertility is represented by number of live births per family, which is a function of the age at marriage and marital fertility rates. (We have not factored in percentages ever

Table C.1 *Numbers of children per family surviving to age 15*

Period	Ireland		Southern England		Northern* Britain		Urban	
	Mean	n	Mean	n	Mean	n	Mean	n
1650–99	5.4	67	4.0	109	5.3	30	3.5	116
1700–49	6.1	131	4.0	331	5.2	113	3.6	285
1750–99	6.1	62	4.3	444	5.4	185	4.3	227
1800–49	5.6	27	3.7	182	5.1	274	4.4	75
1850–99	NA	NA	NA	NA	4.1	129	NA	NA

Note: *"Northern" includes also families reconstituted from the family histories. The 1850–99 cohort is composed entirely of families from the family histories.

marrying). The impact of mortality is shown in the percentage of unions prematurely terminated by the death of one of the spouses and in the failure of children to survive until the age of 15.

The result of these calculations – with all these reservations – is shown in Table C.1. The pattern for all English regions is quite clear: family size remained almost the same for the first 100 years, then rose (most sharply in the cities and least so in the northern area) during the last half of the eighteenth century. Then (except in the cities) family size fell back again in the first half of the nineteenth century, while in the cities it rose slightly (and perhaps not significantly).

The situation in Ireland is very striking. Overall family size always exceeded that in England, and usually by a substantial amount. In fact, the Irish Quakers were one of the most fertile populations known to historical demography. The eighteenth century saw the largest families, but the figure for the first half of the nineteenth century was nevertheless larger than that for the last half of the seventeenth.

This table would make it appear that even after the transition to lower fertility had begun, the Quakers were still having surviving children at a pace way above net replacement. However, it exaggerates, for at least three reasons, the growth potential of their population (if emigration, disownment, and conversion are left out of account). Some children would have died between the ages of 15 and the average age at first marriage (which in the early nineteenth century, it will be recalled, was from 26 to 30 for English women and 30 and over for English men). In the nineteenth century proportionately fewer families were formed, since more and more Quaker women were not marrying at all. Finally, the rising ages at first marriage not only diminished the number of children born, but also slowed the growth of population by lengthening the period between generations.

Thus the demographic pattern of British Quakers falls into three stages. For the first hundred years, despite a relatively low age at first marriage, fertility was fairly low, and heavy infant mortality, especially in the cities, meant that a closed population probably would have barely reproduced itself. In the second stage, lasting from 1750 to around 1825, marital fertility shot up, although its full effect was mitigated by a rise in the age at first marriage and (probably) by an increase in definitive celibacy. For the British Quakers as a whole, the rise in age at first marriage for women was about three years between the late seventeenth and mid-nineteenth centuries. If other things had remained equal, this should have reduced the average family size by at least one child. There were however two counteracting tendencies which more than offset the delay in marrying. The first, and weaker, one was the increased expectation of life and consequently greater duration of marriages. Although the tendency for marriages to last longer was quite marked, its effects on fertility were relatively modest, because the extra years came at the end of the child-bearing period, when women would have been bearing relatively few children.

Considerably more significant is the fact that although women were marrying later, they were then having their children at shorter intervals. The Irish Quakers, of course, led the way, but throughout England and Scotland as well fertility in the half-century from 1775 to 1825 was extraordinarily high, and in the cities the surge continued until the mid-nineteenth century. For one privileged section of the English bourgeoisie, then, fertility could climb dramatically in spite of later ages of marriage. In this they resemble twentieth-century Irish women, late marriers who nevertheless manage to have fairly large families. We await with some eagerness reports which will tell us whether this was a peculiarity of Friends or was found in other sectors of the population in the late eighteenth and early nineteenth centuries.

However this turns out, our findings that there was room for age-specific marital fertility to rise sharply at the end of the eighteenth century corroborates the contention of Wrigley and Schofield that pre-industrial England was a relatively low fertility society, and that rises in fertility played a major role in the increase of English population during the late eighteenth century. Before 1750, and perhaps again after around 1825, most married Quaker women, for whatever reason, were not bearing as many children as ordinary French Catholics, not to mention the Irish Quakers or the Québecois. But the very fact that it is not changes in age at marriage but in age-specific fertility

Friends in life and death

makes explaining this pattern much more difficult, since there is much more evidence about marriage arrangements than there can be about reproductive behavior. We think that family limitation was involved before 1750, along with possible physiological problems in carrying pregnancies to full term.

The rise in fertility in the late eighteenth century was complemented by declines in infant and child mortality from its peak in the first quarter of the eighteenth century. In the regional breakdowns, the familiar unhealthiness of pre-industrial cities appears in the figures for Bristol and Norwich, but even more so for London, where the Quakers in the late seventeenth and early eighteenth century were trying to bring up their children in conditions of infant and child mortality comparable to those obtaining in Calcutta today. It is small wonder that the cities of England could not reproduce their own populations, and had to depend on a steady influx of people from the countryside.

From these much higher starting levels, however, there was a remarkable reduction in infant mortality in the cities in the later eighteenth century, accompanied by a fall in child mortality that was almost as impressive. Infant mortality in London fell within a mere fifty years to little more than half the levels of the early eighteenth century. There was also a sharp decline in Bristol and Norwich, though of nothing like such proportions; there infant mortality declined by about one-quarter and child mortality by a slightly greater amount. In the first half of the nineteenth century, the benefits of a healthier childhood were enjoyed especially in Southern England, Ireland, and Bristol and Norwich. Even London, though it seems to have shown no further improvements, was now healthier for Quaker children than was the rest of England for the general population, while mortality in Bristol and Norwich was even lower. No doubt having ten times the average income had a good deal to do with this, but steady habits, temperate eating and drinking, and the serene approach to life which Quaker piety inculcated must have also been important.

Most historical demographers now reject the simple theses of the social historians of two generations ago (like Talbot Griffith and M. C. Buer), who thought that population growth owed much to general improvement in hygiene; yet they also seem to reject the specific alleged causes of reduced mortality from known diseases, as in the works of McKeown and Brown or Razzell. In fact the major effort of Wrigley and Schofield in reinstating fertility increases, rather than mortality decreases, as the major cause of eighteenth-century population growth is evidence of this rejection of the conventional wisdom of two generations ago. But even if these arguments are valid for the population at large, there is no reason to ignore the sharp decline in Quaker urban infant mortality, and the slower decline elsewhere. The Quakers lived longer, and this helps explain the relatively early restrictions on their fertility which the Quakers accepted.

The final phase started around 1825, only fifteen years before our work with the registers ended, and so is reflected mainly in the genealogies. Here the evidence is that family limitation, which had probably always been employed by a few Quaker families – and more than a few in the late seventeenth century – became sufficiently general to have an appreciable effect in depressing fertility. At the same time mortality continued to fall.

The Irish pattern was somewhat like that in Britain. Fertility was so high, even in the seventeenth century, that further increases were inevitably less dramatic, but there was nevertheless a slight rise in the first half of the eighteenth century and the familiar peak in the second half, followed by a decline to roughly the same levels as before 1750 in the first half of the nineteenth century.

In this third period, beginning around 1825, the absolute size of families was still larger than it had been prior to 1750. Furthermore, at some periods before 1750, we argue, family limitation had been practiced, at least on a small scale. In what sense, then, had a "demographic transition" begun?

It is, of course, more a matter of tendency than of absolute size of families or level of population growth. Though still high, fertility began a fall, never reversed, in the second generation of the nineteenth century, while mortality continued the decline that had commenced around 1750. A further aspect of the demographic transition was the degree of volitional and rational control of demographic processes. In these the Quakers had a long apprenticeship. Their style of marriage emphasized that proposed matches must face the scrutiny of the business meeting; unsuitable or impulsive ones were either quashed or led to disownment. Through a combination of religious and sociological motives this emphasis on prudent marriage gradually raised the age at which marriage was entered; but at the same time there is no reason to confuse unions among Friends with the unsentimental contracts entered into by some pre-modern European peasants. Contemporary observers noted the unusual sociability of Quaker spouses with one another, and the fact that the ages of marriage of men and women drew closer together suggests an early practice of affectionate, if not romantic, marriage, which is itself characteristic of the transition to modern family life.

Although the evidence of this is scanty, there is reason to believe that in these affectionate marriages there were efforts to bear only the number of children who could best be loved and provided for. Techniques of family limitation, especially by abstinence, probably appear in the repertoire of Quaker behavior as early as the late seventeenth century; they are certainly found among American Quakers in the eighteenth century, and with increasing frequency in Britain in the nineteenth.

Our results, we believe, add some modifying detail to the developing picture of demographic changes in eighteenth- and nineteenth-century Britain and Ireland; but they also modify the traditional picture of the Society of Friends. This is particularly true of the restriction on fertility. The degree to which the Quakers were, from the very beginning, to some degree aiming at conscious control of their fertility shows that the Puritan/activist strand in the Quaker heritage, seeking to dominate nature, could predominate over the contemplative and mystical strand, at least as far as the practical decisions of life were concerned.

We are not arguing that these decisions were taken in a spirit of Malthusian rationalism. The advantage of that version of the "new home economics" put forward by Valerie Oppenheimer (discussed at the start of chapter 3) is that it takes into account the total environment in which decisions about family size might be taken, including the likelihood of changing perceptions during the duration of the marriage (so that age at marriage cannot be an adequate regulator of eventual family size, and lengthening of intergenesic intervals or early cessation of reproduction may have to be brought into play). Her theory also shows more adequately the importance of peer or reference group influences; and it directs attention to the role women play in decisions of this kind (which, given the prominent role which women took in the Society of Friends, was probably far from negligible).

Religion, of course, was a most important part of the total environment of the Quakers, and anything that might be called a "fertility strategy" would have to be congruent with their religious values. In the seventeenth century, abstinence from sexual intercourse would be consonant with a general (and for some, pre-millennial) asceticism; yet it would have the effect also of limiting family size. In the period of highest fertility, in the late eighteenth century, the restriction of marriage partners to other Quakers safeguarded the purity and religious unity of the Quaker family; yet it also helped to concentrate capital, solidify commercial relationships, and mitigate the effects on family size of high fertility. Only in the early nineteenth century, perhaps, were spiritual considerations first beginning to be moistened by the icy waters of egotistical calculation; for by then many Quakers (especially the ones represented in our family histories) had substantial businesses to protect, professional educations or apprenticeships to pay for, and above all standards of living and a comfortable lifestyle to preserve. And so, we believe, they anticipated the English upper bourgeoisie in adopting the rational familial allocation of material and emotional resources that we know in the small families of today.

People have always sought to avoid death, but some religious traditions have inculcated a passive acceptance of the fate which God inflicted upon Adam and Eve as a consequence of their primal sin. Not so Quakerism. Although the practice of inoculation seems not to have been widespread among them in the eighteenth century, it was important that they raised no religious objection to it, just as (in the twentieth century) they propounded no religious objection to contraception. It is not too fanciful to speculate that all the repressed intelligence and imagination that could not take the form of rhetoric, fiction writing, music, and the visual arts issued in the great Quaker tradition of medicine and science. Quietist as they often were in their spiritual lives, they believed not only in the precepts of a healthy life but also that diseases were obstacles to be conquered, not chastisements to be accepted.

The Quakers were in some ways like endogamous sects native to or transplanted to America, such as the Hutterites, the Amish, and the Mormons – especially in their relatively high fertility. However, during most or all of their history the members of these American sects lived a secluded agricultural or pastoral life, quite unlike the commercial and industrial pursuits of most of the British Quakers. Within the British Isles, the Quakers can be compared – as we have already done here and there – with the peerage; in pre-industrial Europe, the best available comparison is with the upper bourgeoisie of Geneva.

These comparisons derive much of their interest from the fact that the Quakers were a group which came into being in the mid seventeenth century and only gradually assumed a largely endogamous and socially homogeneous character, while the peerage and the Genevan upper bourgeois families had been upper class for centuries (Louis Henry studied the descendants of nineteen families admitted to the

Bourgeoisie of Geneva before the Reformation). It took a century for a truly distinctive Quaker pattern of fertility and nuptiality to emerge. Its hallmark was the extremely high age at first marriage. In all these elite social groups, a substantial number of women never married, and for the wives and sisters of peers, like the Quakers, the number of late marriages increased as more and more women remained celibate. Quaker men, like the men in peerage families, also delayed marrying at a time when the age at marriage of men in the whole population was declining. This delay seems to be a genuine cultural innovation, not a case of hanging on to a tradition which no longer held for peasant or proletarian England; and we have identified it, speculatively, with the increase in companionable marriages as both spouses were fully adult and closer together in age.

The evidence suggests that all three groups practiced family limitation in the period from 1650 to 1700. This seems to be undeniable for the Genevans; for the peerage families and the Quakers our conclusion must be more tentative. The Genevan bourgeoisie mostly employed a "stopping" strategy, trying to keep their families at or below average size after the target had been reached, but there are indications that some also spaced their births widely even from the beginning of marriage. The Quakers used the spacing strategy more commonly, although there are some signs of premature termination of their reproductive careers. Like that of the Quakers, the marital fertility of the peerage families rose considerably after 1750 as their ages at marriage also rose, showing that this apparently odd combination may have been general in the upper strata of English society.

The three groups are most similar in their death rates. All would appear to be comparatively low, and to begin to decline before any such improvements were enjoyed by the population in general. Ruskin said, "There is no wealth but life"; but all too often in early modern Europe, there was less life without wealth.

Much was distinctive about the Quakers, but a full understanding of their demography demands that we raise again the question of how representative they were of the larger populations they tried to convert. Contrary to expectations, it was not the mortality of the British Quakers but their nuptiality and fertility during the first 100 years that seems closest to that of the people around them.[1] While they were most strongly upholding their cultural deviation from the societal norm, by paying scant attention to the ecclesiastically prohi-

[1] See Allan Sharlin, "Methods for estimating population total, age distribution and vital rates in family reconstitution studies," *Population Studies* 32 (1978), 512.

bited seasons for marriage, they were marrying at just about the same age as their Anglican contemporaries. The major deviation began only after 1750, when the Quakers began marrying later and later while the rest of English society was doing the opposite. The scattered evidence that we have about the Protestant population of Ireland suggests that like the Irish Quakers they also married earlier than their English counterparts – perhaps even earlier than the Irish Quakers.

The age-specific fertility of the British Quakers outside the cities during the first century was only 2 to 5 percent higher than that of the English population as a whole (if we make the rather large assumption that the thirteen parishes appearing in Table 4.2 are representative of that population). But, as with the age at first marriage, the situation was very different after 1750; the age-specific fertility of the non-urban Quakers was almost 19 percent higher than that of the families in the thirteen parishes, and that of the urban Quakers was 22 percent higher.

Comparable data about the age-specific fertility of other Irish Protestants or of the Catholic peasantry are almost entirely lacking before the 1841 census. At that time, though, marital fertility of the total population was 21 percent higher than that of the whole English population, and the best (though still poorly) informed guess is that high marital fertility was an important aspect of Irish population growth in the century before 1840. Furthermore, it was highest in largely Protestant Ulster.[2] As we have seen, the marital fertility of the Irish Quakers was always higher than that of the British. Prior to 1800 it had been from 24 to 29 percent higher, and in the first half of the nineteenth century, although it was falling, it was still 11 percent higher. Thus, although it is impossible to compare the fertility of the Irish Quakers with that of the rest of the Irish population, or even that of other Irish Protestants, it seems probable that in this respect they resembled their fellow Irish more than British Friends.

Because so many English parish registers are defective after about 1810, it is impossible to determine whether the families represented in the parish registers experienced the slight decline in fertility after 1825 which we believe signals the onset of the demographic transition for the British and Irish Quakers. The evidence from Irish parish registers is even scantier, but given the high levels of marital fertility shown in the 1841 census, it seems likely that of the Irish Quakers began to decline well before that of the Irish population as a whole.

Although the fertility and nuptiality of the early British Quakers

---

[2] Joel Mokyr and Cormac Ó Gráda, "New developments in Irish population history, 1700–1850," *Economic History Review* 2nd ser. 37 (1984), 480–81.

seem to have been close to that of the population as a whole, this was much less true of their mortality. In Southern England, we believe infant mortality was only two-thirds to three-quarters of that in the mixture of (mostly Southern) parishes reconstituted by collaborators with the ESRC Cambridge Group. Even the extraordinarily high London infant mortality before 1750 was only about 70 percent of that estimated from the London bills of mortality.[3]

Infant mortality among the Irish Quakers was always slightly lower than among the Southern English. It took an amazing plunge in the 1800–50 cohort, to less than half the level of the previous half-century. These figures, based on a small number of cases, look implausible; but even if it was only a little lower than in the last half of the eighteenth century, Irish Quaker infant mortality was about half that reported for the rest of Ireland. Any refined comparisons are made difficult not only by the lack of census data prior to the 1830s but also by our not having made any regional break-down or distinguished Dublin and Cork from the countryside, since regional variations and the usual correlation of settlement size and infant mortality are important.[4]

Child and adult mortality is more difficult to measure. The evidence we have suggests that the Quakers also had an advantage, although a less marked one, over the general population. This advantage seems to have increased after 1750, leading in the early nineteenth century to such encomia as that pronounced by Robert Rankin.

This demographic behavior is of course complexly related to religious values as well as to social milieu. Our final task will be an attempt to assess their relative weight. The early Quakers proudly bore the label of "a peculiar people" – peculiar not in the sense of "weird" but in the sense of "distinctive," "set apart." Their garb and their refusal of merely conventional courtesies proclaimed this even to people who cared nothing about the inerrancy of the biblical text, whether hymns should be a part of worship, or whether outward elements should be used in the sacraments. But their *demographic* peculiarities, so far as fertility and nuptiality are concerned, were not at all marked in the century when the movement experienced its first great in-gathering and then accommodated itself to its status as one group among the Protestant Dissenters. While Friends were going to jail for not paying tithes or wearing their hats in court they were marrying at about the

---

[3] Based on the estimates made by John Landers, "Some problems in the historical demography of London 1675–1825," Cambridge University PhD Thesis, 1984, 73.

[4] Joel Mokyr, *Why Ireland Starved: A Quantitative and Analytical History of the Irish Economy, 1800–1850* (London, 1983), 37.

same age, and having about as many children as "the people of the world." On the other hand, their advantage in infant, child, and adult mortality was marked from the very beginning, probably because there were so few aristocrats or paupers among them.

In the second century of Quakerism, the evidence is that many of these religious scruples or "testimonies" were laid aside by increasing numbers of Friends. Their traveling ministers filled the air, and many pages, with laments about the worldliness which had all but extinguished the inner light. When the Quaker affirmation came to be accepted in legal contexts, it ceased to be a challenge to the insincerity and hypocrisy of society as a whole and became simply one more custom becoming increasingly quaint. (This may be one reason why use of the plain language ceased to be universal.) The "gay Quakers" wore wigs and lace, and took tea. But while the outward distinctions which set off Friends appeared to contemporary observers to be diminishing, their fertility and nuptiality for the first time became quite distinctive.

The response of the most serious-minded Quakers to this perception of growing worldliness was the intense effort to enforce the prohibition of mixed marriages. In mid-century, if the experience of Southwark Monthly Meeting is at all typical – and it seems to have been one of the more rigorous monthly meetings – Friends were taking a fairly relaxed attitude towards those of their number who married outside the meeting. In the great revival of the discipline that was accomplished in the 1760s Friends made lists of those who had made irregular marriages in the previous ten or twenty years, visited them with an eye to bringing them to repentance, and disowned those who were obdurate. Afterwards the full rigors of consideration for a month or so by the women's and men's monthly meetings, certificates of "clearness" (from other engagements), and declarations of the consent of parents were enforced.

These efforts were of course often unsuccessful, if success is defined (as the Quakers themselves eventually came to define it) as maintaining the largest possible membership. In the eighteenth century Friends valued purity more than size of membership. But insofar as they succeeded in maintaining a society free from non-Quaker spouses (at the cost of disowning many of their own children), it was only in part owing to fidelity to Quaker principles. The mixture of religious motives and socio-economic ones helped uphold the testimony against mixed marriages; and we resist declaring that either determined the other.

These socio-economic motives reflect the differences in the social composition of the Society of Friends between the late eighteenth and the late seventeenth centuries. In the late seventeenth century the range of occupations in the Society of Friends in England, although narrow in that laborers and the poverty-stricken on the one end and the gentry and aristocracy on the other were almost entirely absent, was nevertheless closer to the distribution of occupations within the general population than it became in the late eighteenth century. As the Industrial Revolution was beginning, the concentration of Quakers within banking, chemical-related manufacturing, the wholesale grain trade, and professions like accountancy put a high premium on waiting to save up money for dowries and concentrating capital through intermarriage between closely related families. Such marriages were easier to arrange within the Society of Friends than outside it; but even those marriages outside meeting, though probably contracted at a slightly earlier age than those approved by Friends, were usually confined to the same social milieux.

The rise in fertility in the whole English population in the eighteenth century appears to have been entirely the result of two changes in nuptiality: a larger number of people were able to marry, and those marrying were able to do so earlier. The increase in proportions marrying, which was chiefly important before 1750, seems to have been a consequence of rises in real wages, which allowed more workers to accumulate enough savings to make the capital outlay necessary to form a new family. Rises in real wages would seem the obvious candidates to explain declines in the age at first marriage as well; but there is an awkward fact in the way – real wages were *not* rising at the end of the eighteenth century, when ages at first marriage were falling. There are various attempts to account for this: as that falling ages at first marriage were in fact a response to rising real wages, only to those that rose forty (or, alternatively, fifteen to twenty) years previously. Or, it has been claimed, more and more of the population was becoming proletarianized by the early stages of industrialization, and it was reasonable prospects of continued employment rather than the level of real wages *per se* which allowed the new proletarians to marry. Sometimes the emphasis has been placed on cultural institutions or traditions which were being disrupted by industrialization, as though some people in the late eighteenth century broke out of a traditional pattern of late marriage, while the majority stayed within it. (Institutions like the boarding-in of farm laborers obviously fit such a pattern; insofar as they were no longer treated as dependent members of their employers' families, such workers had less incentive to remain unmarried.)[5]

It is not our task – fortunately – to adjudicate among these conflicting explanations. We need only point out that none of them can apply to more than a handful of Quakers, almost none of whom were proletarians, servants in husbandry, or receivers of wages. They were thus immune from the developments that allowed (or precipitated) a good many English men and women into the ranks of earlier marriers. So it may be that the inertial force of the earlier tradition of late marriages – conceived, of course, as the religious duty not to enter matrimony without the requisite sobriety and maturity – as well as positive advantages of capital accumulation and concentration played a role in their later and later marriages.

Our distinctive problem is to account for two significant breaks in the trends in age-specific fertility: higher between 1750 and 1825, lower before and afterwards. These changes in recorded behavior cannot be related to changes in recorded doctrine, though they may be connected with interpretations of such doctrine, or even underlying beliefs. We have dismissed as highly unlikely the notion that increasing natural fecundity had anything to do with it. Thus the only remaining possible explanations for the rise in fertility are that a larger proportion of all conceptions resulted in live births and/or no – or very few – couples restricted their progeny during this period.

The theory that spontaneous abortions were less frequent is discussed in chapter 4, where we gave it only limited importance. It is possible that improvements in general health, reflected in lower mortality, also influenced the rate of conceptions; but there is so little evidence for this explanation that we are forced to examine alternative, behavioral theories.

At this point we need to leave for a moment the inferences from the statistics to which we have adhered until now. It seems an inescapable conclusion that part of the explanation for higher fertility after 1750 was that before then fertility had been limited by more than physiological factors. Some degree of conscious restraint was apparently exercised – perhaps due in part to a spiritual value attached to chastity, rather than solely to economic prudence. What happened between 1750 and 1799, then, could be explained in part by a lower value attached to chastity, and in part by secular concerns.

[5] This discussion is based on David Weir, "Better never than late: celibacy and age at marriage in English cohort fertility," *Journal of Family History* 9 (1984), 2–20, and J. A. Goldstone, "The demographic revolution in England: a re-examination," *Population Studies* 40 (1986), 5–33.

In chapter 4 we did not speculate much about why it might have been possible that in the last part of the eighteenth century Quakers allowed themselves – temporarily, as it turned out – the luxury of larger families. Though real wages were not rising, most Quakers made their livings from profits, fees, and salaries – all of which probably were rising. Above all, at a time of more rapidly expanding population, employment opportunities were also increasing, particularly in the sectors of the economy in which the Quakers were strongly represented: trade (especially overseas trade), finance and banking, extractive industries, engineering, and food and drink (including beer).

We can therefore connect demographic behavior with economic developments at least in this way: opportunities for the next generation, in the eyes of the parents of the last part of the eighteenth century, were increasing; and this would make it possible to contemplate a quiverful of employable sons and marriageable daughters. But by 1825 economic prospects did not seem so rosy, and even later marriages were now complemented by increasing family limitation.

Comparison of Quaker mortality with that of the general population presents a more anomalous picture. Just as the rates of fertility and ages at marriage were beginning to diverge sharply from those of the general population, mortality rates (outside the cities) began to converge, since there was less further improvement after 1750 than was exhibited by the rest of the English population. This suggests that even though the income gap was, as far as we know, not closing, improvements of other kinds, perhaps in public sanitation, were becoming more widely accessible.

The most important causes of general and infant mortality described in chapter 5 were, to a greater or lesser extent, common to all parts of the population. Thus the much higher infant and child mortality of urban Quakers as compared to those in the countryside reflects the situation in the country as a whole. The causes were much the same: high-density living, poor water supply, polluted air, contaminated food, and the speed with which infections traveled through the close networks of human contacts, especially those involving personal services, which made people in cities much more vulnerable to infectious diseases, whether air or water-borne. We have discussed whether the Quakers found a way to minimize the impact of smallpox, the worst killer among infectious diseases, and concluded that they remained very vulnerable indeed; and it does not appear that the Quakers were more immune from gastrointestinal infections which were the concomitants of food shortages and bad seasons generally.

Deaths directly due to food shortages are not evident among the middle-class Quakers, but they probably would not have shown up among the middle-class British and Irish populations in general, if we had class-specific statistics. Among the Irish Quakers, 1846 does not show up as a mortality peak. There are some causes of mortality which did not affect Quakers: violent deaths from duels or warfare. Similarly, Quakers were presumably less subject to death from excessive consumption of alcohol or venereal disease. These, however, are minor causes of death: to a very large extent Quakers had the same fears of sickness as the general population, and this was because they were, at least potentially, equally exposed to these dangers. If their mortality was from the beginning less than that of the general population, we can only conclude that their mode of life afforded them some degree of protection against catching, or succumbing to, the prevailing sicknesses. For if they did contract some of these diseases, their more hygienic practices, and quite possibly greater knowledge of nutrition and therapeutic medicine than was available to the rest of the population, may have saved the lives of some patients. If we look at their situation this way, the contrast explained in chapter 5 between the older "medical" explanations of decreased mortality and the newer "environmental" – and in part anti-medical – explanations becomes less important. It would appear that the benefits which the Quakers were already enjoying spread slowly to the larger population, allowing it to approach, though not catch up with, the Quaker mortality levels.

The Quakers, then, were a people set apart, and yet they lived in the midst of a population experiencing important changes in economic organization and social structure. Not only were they not comparable to the Hutterites or Amish; the English and Ulster Quakers were in the forefront of the Industrial Revolution, from the beginning of the eighteenth century with the Darbys of Coalbrookdale onward. They were pioneers of technological change, with a share of inventions a matter of record as well as of legend. The same applies to the origins of English banking, to science, and to medicine. They were, assuredly, "of this world" at least by 1750, and we cannot treat their behavior as though the Quakers were in the vanguard of rapid industrial and commercial changes, but not participating in the concomitant social and cultural changes affecting the rest of the population.[6] They should

[6] In this respect the Quakers were in a similar position to that of the Central European Jews, who like the Quakers had a leading position in banking and finance, and later in

rather have exhibited more strongly, and at an earlier period, the demographic behavior which became common in the English managerial and professional classes in the nineteenth century.

The final question then is this: can we use the findings of this research to illuminate the demographic developments of the rest of the British and Irish population? On this point we remain agnostic, awaiting comparable family reconstitution analysis of much larger sections of the Anglican population. (Such material apparently will never be found for the Roman Catholic population of Ireland, as their parish registers have not survived.) Such work is in progress, but if data for specific social classes, or occupational and income groupings, are not presented, it may not even then yield a basis for comparison. We cannot prejudge this issue.

As far as aggregative analysis is concerned, we have seen that the Quaker experience does exhibit the same trends in mortality as seen in the general population – but with such marked differentials in absolute values (especially in infant mortality) that the Quaker statistics are relevant mainly in demonstrating a "lag" effect. Because of their class, income, lifestyle, and practical knowledge, the Quakers experienced reductions in mortality which did not show up in the population in general until two or three generations later.

As regards fertility, we know only that that of the Quakers rose at about the same time as that of the general population. But once again the regime is so different in respect of certain fundamental measures (especially marital fertility) that the greatest caution would be required before embarking on a complete set of inferences based on the similarities which do exist.

The same caution must apply to the later periods of fertility decline. We can again hypothesize about lags. It does rather look, on our evidence, that the decline in fertility set in earlier among the Quakers than in the population as a whole – but quite possibly not earlier than among the English middle classes. Statistical elucidation of the problem will have to await class-specific figures from further Anglican family reconstitutions. If literary evidence is sought, Malthus and his predecessors and followers provide the clearest evidence of middle-class prudential (rather than moral) restraint.

As a concluding hypothesis for our own work, and as a starting point for others, we can only say that the Quakers may have been in the vanguard here as elsewhere. Perhaps because they were predominantly members of the middle class, they exhibit collectively patterns

industry and the professions, and in the process underwent demographic changes parallel to, but in many cases preceding, those found in the population at large.

which became general in the English population only in the last quarter of the nineteenth century, and in Ireland, after the disaster of the Great Famine, far later than that. But even if this is true, the methods by which English Quakers limited their family size would not necessarily be the same as those in general use in the wider population at a later date. History has not sufficiently advanced into the bedrooms of middle-class English men and women to tell us by what devices they first attempted to control their fertility.

We can thus conclude with certainty only about the demography of the British and Irish Quakers themselves. Even the American Quakers behaved quite differently in some respects, and even greater variations can be seen when the comparison is extended to the peerage, the Genevan bourgeoisie, or the British and Irish population as a whole. But we believe we have demonstrated that the techniques of modern demographic analysis can reveal historical changes calculated from material which has not been previously used in Britain (except for the peerage). This may set a kind of benchmark for further studies; our own unresolved questions must form the starting point for other researchers' analysis.

Furthermore, we have shown that the spiritual, social, and economic history of the Society of Friends in England, Scotland, and Ireland is mirrored in the demographic history of Quaker families. This does not mean that the image is a perfect reflection; that would be absurd. However, the claim that historical demography cannot be studied in isolation has always been a theoretical desideratum. In Quaker history, the interconnectedness has visible reality. The Society of Friends, as it existed in 1850, was the outcome both of general socio-economic forces and of specific cultural influences. The age and household structure of friends was formed by a demographic regime which in some respects must have been unique, and in others reflects much more general changes in the experiences of life and death.

Bibliography

(Place of publication is London unless otherwise stated.)

Adams, Thomas, compiler, *Bessbrook: A Record of Industry in a Northern Ireland Village Community and of a Social Experiment, 1845–1945* (Bessbrook, 1945).

Allen, William, *Life of William Allen, with Selections from his Correspondence* (3 vols.: 1846).

Almquist, Eric L., "Pre-famine Ireland and the theory of European proto-industrialization," *Journal of Economic History* 39 (1979), 699–718.

Amundsen, D. W., and Diers, C. J., "The age of menarche in Classical Greece and Rome," *Human Biology* 41 (1969), 125–32.

"The age of menarche in medieval Europe," *Human Biology* 45 (1973), 363–69.

Anderson, A., "The social origins of the early Quakers," *Quaker History* 68 (1979), 33–40.

Annual Monitor . . . or Obituary of Members of the Society of Friends in Great Britain and Ireland (established in 1813; titles and publishers vary).

Appleby, Andrew B., "Nutrition and disease: the case of London, 1550–1750," *Journal of Interdisciplinary History* 6 (1975), 1–22.

Armstrong, Alan, *Stability and Change in an English County Town* [York, 1801–51] (1974).

Ashton, T. S., *The Industrial Revolution 1760–1830* (1948).

An Economic History of England: The 18th Century (1955).

Bachmann, Gaston, "Die beschleunigte Entwicklung der Jugend," *Acta Anatomica* 4 (1947–48), 421–80.

Backhouse, Hannah C., *Extracts from the Journals and Letters of Hannah Backhouse* (1858).

Backhouse, Katharine, *A Memoir of Mary Capper* (London and York, 1847).

Banks, J. A., *Prosperity and Parenthood: A Study of Family Planning among the Victorian Middle Classes* (1954).

Barclay, John, ed., *Some Account of the Life of Joseph Pike: Also, a Journal of the Life and Gospel Labours of Joseph Oxley* (1837).

Barclay, Robert, *Inner Life of the Religious Societies of the Commonwealth* (1876).

Bardet, J.-P., K.-A. Lynch, G.-P. Mineau, M. Hainsworth, and M. Skolnick, "La Mortalité maternelle autrefois: une étude comparée (de la France de l'ouest à l'Utah)," *Annales de démographie historique* (1981), 31–48.

Barnard, T. C., *Cromwellian Ireland: English Government in Ireland* (Oxford, 1955).

Bechhofer, F., ed., *Population and the Brain Drain* (Edinburgh, 1969).

Beck, William and Ball, T. Frederick, *The London Friends' Meetings: Showing the Rise of The Society of Friends in London: Its Progress, and the Development of Its Discipline* (1869).

Behar, L., "Des tables de mortalité aux XVIIe et XVIIIe siècles: histoire-signification," *Annales de démographie historique* (1976), 173–200.

Benson, R. S., *et al.*, *Descendants of Isaac and Rachel Wilson, Photographic Pedigree* (privately printed, Middlesbrough, 1949), 4 vols.

Berry, B. Midi and Schofield, R. S., "Age at baptism in pre-industrial England," *Population Studies* 25 (1971), 453–63.

Bevan, Joseph Gurney, *Extracts from the Letters and Other Writings of the Late Joseph Gurney Bevan* (1821).

Biraben, Jean Noël, "Quelques aspects de la mortalité en milieu urbaine," *Population* 30e année (1975), 509–22.

Birch, Thomas, *A Collection of the Yearly Bills of Mortality, from 1657 to 1758 inclusive* (1759).

Black, William, *An Arithmetical and Medical Analysis of the Diseases and Mortality of the Human Species* (1789) reprinted with an introduction by D. V. Glass (Farnborough, Hants, 1973).

Bongaarts, John, "Why high birth rates are so low," *Population and Development Review* 1 (1975), 289–96.

"Does malnutrition affect fecundity? A summary of evidence," *Science* 208 (1980), 564–69.

[Bougrenet] de la Tocnaye, *Promenade d'un Français dans l'Irlande* (Dublin, 1797).

Bower, David, and Knight, John, *Plain Country Friends: the Quakers of Wooldale, High Flatts and Midhope* (Wooldale, 1987).

Boyle, Phelim P., and Ó Gráda, Cormac, "Fertility trends, excess mortality, and the Great Irish Famine," *Demography* 23 (1986), 543–62.

Braithwaite, William C., *The Beginnings of Quakerism*, 2nd edn revised by Henry J. Cadbury (Cambridge, 1955).

Buer, M. C., *Health, Wealth and Population in the Early Days of the Industrial Revolution* (1926).

Burnet, George B., *The Story of Quakerism in Scotland 1650–1850* (1952).

Butterfield, Rebecca, Diary (manuscript in Friends House Library, London).

Bytheway, William R., "The variation with age of age differences in marriage," *Journal of Marriage and the Family* 43 (1981), 923–27.

Cadogan, William, *Essay upon Nursing and the Management of Children* (1748).

Caldwell, John C., *Theory of Fertility Decline* (1982).

Calvo, Thomas, "Familles mexicaines au XVIIe siècle: une tentative de reconstitution," *Annales de démographie historique* (1984), 149–74.

Carlsson, Gösta, "The decline of fertility: innovation or adjustment process," *Population Studies* 20 (1966), 149–74.

Carmichael, Ann G., and Silverstein, Arthur M., "Smallpox in Europe before the seventeenth century: virulent killer or benign disease?" *Journal of the History of Medicine and Allied Sciences* 42 (1987), 147–68.

Carney, F. J., "Aspects of pre-famine Irish household size: composition and differentials," in *Comparative Aspects of Scottish and Irish Economic and Social*

History 1600–1900, ed. L. M. Cullen and T. C. Smout (Edinburgh, n.d. [1977], 32–46.

Carr-Saunders, A. M., *The Population Problem* (Oxford, 1922).

Carter, Charles F., "Unsettled friends," *Journal of the Friends Historical Society* 50 (1967), 143–53.

Cassedy, John, *Mortality in Pre-Industrial Times* (1973).

Chapman, G. R., *An Historical Sketch of Grange Meeting* (Grange, Co. Tyrone, 1960).

——— compiler, *The History of Ballyhagan and Richhill Meetings, 1654–1793–1979* (Richhill, 1979).

Clarkson, Leslie, *Death, Disease and Famine in Pre-Industrial England* (Dublin, 1975).

——— "Irish population revisited, 1687–1821," in *Irish Population, Economy, and Society*, ed. Goldstrom and Clarkson (Oxford, 1981), 13–35.

——— "Marriage and fertility in nineteenth-century Ireland," in *Marriage and Society: Studies in the Social History of Marriage*, ed. R. B. Outhwaite (New York, 1982), 237–55.

——— "Population change and urbanisation, 1820–1940," in *An Economic History of Ulster 1820–1940* ed. Liam Kennedy and Philip Ollerenshaw (Manchester, 1985), 137–57.

Clarkson, Thomas, *A Portraiture of Quakerism* (3 vols.: 1806).

Cleland, John, and Wilson, Christopher, "Demand theories of the fertility transition: an iconoclastic view," *Population Studies* 41 (1987), 5–30.

Coale, Ansley, and Trussell, T. James, "Model fertility schedules in the age structure of childbearing in human populations" *Population Index* 40 (1974), 185–258 (and *ibid.*, 41 [1975], 572).

Cohen, Joel E., "Childhood mortality, family size, and birth order in pre-industrial Europe," *Demography* 12 (1975), 35–66.

Cole, Alan, "The social origins of the early Friends," *Journal of the Friends Historical Society* 48 (1957), 99–118.

Connell, K. H., *The Population of Ireland, 1750–1845* (Oxford, 1950).

——— "Some unsettled problems in English and Irish population history, 1750–1845," *Irish Historical Studies* 7 (1951), reprinted in *Population in Industrialization*, ed. Michael Drake (1969), 30–39.

Cousens, S. H., "The restriction of population growth in pre-famine Ireland," *Proceedings of the Royal Irish Academy* vol. 64, Section C (1965), 85–99.

Crafts, N. F. R., and Ireland, N. J., "The role of simulation techniques in the theory and observation of family formation," *Population Studies* 29 (1975), 75–95.

——— "Family limitation and the English demographic revolution: a simulation approach," *Journal of Economic History* 36 (1976), 598–623.

Crawford, W. H., "The origins of the linen industry in North Armagh and the Lagan Valley," *Ulster Folklife* 17 (1971).

——— "Drapers and bleachers in the early Ulster linen industry," in *Négoce et industrie en France et en Irlande aux XVIIIe et XIXe siècles*, ed. L. M. Cullen and P. Butel (Paris, 1980).

Creighton, Charles, *A History of Epidemics in Britain*: vol. 2, *From the Extinction of the Plague to the Present Time* (Cambridge, 1894).

Cressy, David, *Coming Over: Migration and Communication between England and New England in the Seventeenth Century* (Cambridge, 1987).

"The seasonality of marriage in Old and New England," *Journal of Interdisciplinary History* 16 (1985), 1–21.

Crisp, Samuel, *et al.*, *Autobiographical Narrations of the Convincement and Other Religious Experiences of Samuel Crisp, Elizabeth Webb, Evan Bevan, Margaret Lucas, and Frederick Smith* (1848).

Cullen, L. M., *An Economic History of Ireland since 1660* (1972).

"Population trends in seventeenth-century Ireland," *Economic and Social Review* [Dublin] 6 (1975), 149–65.

"Population growth and diet, 1600–1850," in *Irish Population, Economy and Society*, ed. Goldstrom and Clarkson (Oxford, 1981), 89–112.

Dailey, Barbara Ritter, "The husbands of Margaret Fell: an essay on religious metaphor and social change," *Seventeenth Century* 2 (1987), 55–71.

Davis, Kingsley, and Blake, Judith, "Social structure and fertility," *Economic Development and Cultural Change* 4 (1956), 211–35.

Demos, John, "Notes on life in Plymouth colony," *William and Mary Quarterly* 3rd ser. 22 (1965), 246–86.

"Families in colonial Bristol, Rhode Island: an exercise in historical demography," *William and Mary Quarterly* 3rd ser. 25 (1968), 40–57.

Deparcieux, Antoine, *Essai sur les probabilités de la durée de la vie humaine* (Paris, 1746).

Diers, C. H., "Historical trends in the age at menarche and menopause," *Psychological Reports* 34 (June 1974), 931–37.

Dixon, Ruth B., "Late marriage and non-marriage as demographic responses: are they similar?" *Population Studies* 32 (1978), 449–66.

Dobbie, B. M. Willmott, "An attempt to estimate the true rate of maternal mortality, sixteenth to eighteenth centuries," *Medical History* 26 (1982), 79–90.

Drake, Michael, "Marriage and population growth in Ireland, 1750–1845," *Economic History Review* 2nd ser. 16 (1963–64), 301–13.

ed., *Population in Industrialization* (1969).

Duchen, M. R., and McNeilly, A. S., "Hyperprolactinaemia and long-term lactational amenorrhoea," *Clinical Endocrinology* 12 (1980), 621–27.

Dudley, Elizabeth, *The Life of Mary Dudley* (1825).

Memoirs of Elizabeth Dudley (1861).

Dupâquier, Jacques, "Réflexion sur la mortalité du passé: mesure de la mortalité des adultes d'après les fiches de famille," *Annales de démographie historique* (1978), 31–48.

Dupâquier, Jacques, and Lachiver, M., "Sur les débuts de la contraception en France ou les deux malthusianismes," *Annales: Economies, Sociétés, Civilisations* 24e année (1969), 1391–406.

"Du contresens à l'illusion technique," *Annales: Economies, Sociétés, Civilisations* 36e année (1981), 489–92.

Eaton, Joseph W., and Mayer, Albert J., "The social biology of very high fertility among the Hutterites," *Human Biology* 25 (1953), 206–64.

Man's Capacity to Reproduce: The Demography of a Unique Population (Glencoe, Ill., 1954).

Eccles, Audrey, "Obstetrics in the 17th and 18th centuries and its implications for maternal and infant mortality," *Society for the Social History of Medicine Bulletin* 20 (June 1977), 8–11.

Edin, K. A., "Studier i svensk fruktsamhetsstatistik," *Ekonomisk Tidskrift* 17 (1915), 251–304.

Emden, Paul H., *Quakers in Commerce: A Record of Business Achievement* (1940).

Erickson, Julia A., *et al.*, "Fertility patterns and trends among the Old Order Amish," *Population Studies* 33 (1979), 255–76.

Eustace, P. B., and Goodbody, O. C., eds., *Abstracts of Wills*, in Irish Historical Manuscripts Commission, *Church Records* (Dublin, 1957).

Eversley, David, "A survey of population in an area of Worcestershire from 1660 to 1850 on the basis of parish registers," *Population Studies* 10 (1957) reprinted (in slightly amended form) in *Population in History*, ed. Glass and Eversley (1965), 394–419.

Social theories of Fertility and the Malthusian Debate (Oxford, 1959).

"Exploitation of Anglican parish registers by aggregative analysis," in *An Introduction to English Historical Demography*, ed. Wrigley, 44–95.

"The validity of family and group statistics as indicators of secular population trends," in *Population Growth and the Brain Drain*, ed. F. Bechhofer (Edinburgh, 1969), 179–95.

"The demography of the Irish Quakers, 1650–1850," in *Irish Population, Economy, and Society*, ed. Goldstrom and Clarkson (Oxford, 1981), 57–88.

Fifth Annual Report of the Registrar General (2nd edn, 1843).

Fildes, Valerie A., "Neonatal feeding practices and infant mortality during the 18th century," *Journal of Biosocial Science* 12 (1980) 313–24.

Breasts, Bottles and Babies: A History of Infant Feeding [to 1800] (Edinburgh, 1986).

Finlay, R. A. P., "The accuracy of the London parish registers, 1580–1653," *Population Studies* 32 (1978), 95–112.

"Gateways to death? London child mortality experience, 1570–1653," *Annales de démographie historique* (1978), 105–34.

"Population and fertility in London, 1580–1650," *Journal of Family History* 4 (1979), 26–38.

"Differential child mortality in pre-industrial England: the example of Cartmel, Cumbria, 1600–1750," *Annales de démographie historique* (1981), 67–79.

Fitzpatrick, David, *Irish Emigration 1801–1921* (Dublin, 1984).

Flinn, Michael W., "The stabilization of mortality in pre-industrial Western Europe," *Journal of European Economic History* 3 (1974), 285–318.

The European Demographic System, 1500–1870 (Baltimore, 1981).

Forbes, Thomas R., *Chronicle from Aldgate* (New Haven, 1971).

"By what disease or casualty: the changing face of death in London," *Journal of the History of Medicine and Allied Sciences* 31 (1976), 395–420.

"Births and deaths in a London parish: the record from the registers, 1654–1693 and 1729–1743," *Bulletin of the History of Medicine* 55 (1981), 371–91.

Ford, John, *Memoir of Thomas Pumphrey* (London and York, 1864).

Ford, Kathleen, and Kim, Young, "Distributions of postpartum amenorrhea: some new evidence," *Demography* 24 (1987), 413–30.

Fourth Annual Report of the Registrar General (1842).

Fox, George, *Friends Fellowship Must Be in the Spirit* (1668).

Freedman, R., *et al.*, "Fertility trends in Taiwan, tradition and change," *Population Studies* 16 (1963), 219–36.

Friedlander, Dov, and Ben-Moshe, Eliahu, "Occupations, sex ratios, and nuptiality in nineteenth century English communities: a model of relationships," *Demography* 23 (1986), 1–13.

Friedlander, Dov, Shellekens, Jona, Ben-Moshe, Eliahu, and Keysar, Ariela, "Socio-economic characteristics and life expectancies in nineteenth-century England: a district analysis," *Population Studies* 39 (1985), 137–51.

Frisch, Rose E., "Demographic implications of the biological determinants of female fecundity," *Social Biology* 22 (1975), 17–22.

"Population, food intake, and fertility," *Science* 199 (1978), 22–30.

"Nutrition, fatness and fertility: the effect of food intake on reproductive ability," in *Nutrition and Human Reproduction*, ed. H. W. Mosley (New York, 1978), 91–122.

and Revelle, Roger, "Height and weight at menarche and a hypothesis of menarche," *Archives of Disease in Childhood* 46 (1971), 695–701.

Fuller, Abraham and Holme, Thomas, *A Compendious View of Some Extraordinary Sufferings of the People Call'd Quakers in the Kingdom of Ireland* (2 vols.: Dublin, 1731).

Gallman, James Matthew, "Relative ages of colonial marriages," *Journal of Interdisciplinary History* 14 (1984), 609–17.

Galloway, P. R., "Annual variations in deaths by age, deaths by cause, prices, and weather in London 1670 to 1830," *Population Studies* 39 (1985), 487–505.

Gaskin, Katherine, "Age at first marriage in Europe before 1850," *Journal of Family History* 3 (1978), 23–36.

George, M. Dorothy, *London Life in the XVIII Century* (1925).

Gill, C., *The Rise of the Irish Linen Industry* (Oxford, 1925).

Glass, D. V., *Numbering the People: The Eighteenth-Century Population Controversy and the Development of Census and Vital Statistics in Britain* (Farnborough, Hants., 1973).

and Eversley, David, eds., *Population in History* (1965).

Glick, Paul, C., Heer, David M., and Beresford, John C., "Family formation and family composition: trends and prospects," in *Sourcebook in Marriage and the Family*, ed. Marvin B. Sussman (2nd edn: New York, 1963), 30–40.

Goldstone, J. A., "The demographic revolution in England: a re-examination," *Population Studies* 40 (1986), 5–33.

Goldstrom, J. M., and Clarkson, L. A., eds., *Irish Population, Economy, and Society: Essays in Honour of the Late K. H. Connell* (Oxford, 1981).

Goodbody, Olive C., *Guide to Irish Quaker Records 1654–1680*, with contributions on Northern Irish records by B. C. Hutton (Dublin, 1967).

Graunt, John, *Natural and Political Observations ... upon the Bills of Mortality* (5th edn, 1676).

Green, E. R. R., *The Lagan Valley, 1800–1850* (1949).

The Industrial Archaeology of County Down (Belfast, 1963).

Greg, Emily, ed., *Reynolds–Rathbone Diaries and Letters 1753–1839* (1905).

Greven, Philip, *Four Generations: Population, Land, and Family in Colonial Andover, Massachusetts* (Ithaca, 1970).

Griffith, Talbot G., *Population Problems of the Age of Malthus* (Cambridge, 1926).

Grmek, M. D., "Préliminaires d'une étude historique des maladies," *Annales: Economies, Sociétés, Civilisations* 24ᵉ année (1969), 1473–83.

Gross, B. A., and Eastman, C. J., "Prolactin secretion during prolonged lactational amenorrhoea," *Australian & New Zealand Journal of Obstetrics and Gynaecology* 19 (1979), 95–99.

Grubb, Geoffrey B. W., *The Grubbs of Tipperary: Studies in Heredity and Character* (Cork, 1972).

Grubb, Isabel, "Social condition in Ireland in the seventeenth and eighteenth centuries as illustrated by early Quaker records," (London University M.A. thesis, 1916).

Quakers in Ireland, 1654–1900 (1927).

"Guide to Meeting Records," (MS. in Friends' House Library, London).

Habakkuk, H. J., "English population in the eighteenth century," *Economic History Review* 2nd ser. 6 (1953), 117–33.

Population Growth and Economic Development since 1750 (Leicester, 1971).

Habicht, J.-P., Davanzo, Julie, Butz, W. P., and Myers, Linda, "The contraceptive role of breastfeeding," *Population Studies* 39 (1985), 213–32.

Hair, P. E. H., "Deaths from violence in Britain: a tentative secular survey," *Population Studies* 25 (1971), 5–24.

Hajnal, John, "European marriage patterns in perspective," in *Population in History*, ed. Glass and Eversley (1965), 101–43.

"Two kinds of preindustrial household formation system," *Population and Development Review* 8 (1982).

Hall, David S., *Richard Robinson of Countersett 1628–1693 and the Quakers of Wensleydale* (York, 1989).

Harrisson, Barnard, *A Memoir of Barnard Harrisson* (1830).

Hatt, Paul K., Farr, Nellie Louise, and Weinstein, Eugene, "Types of population balance," *American Sociological Review* 20 (1955), 14–21.

Haygarth, Doctor [John], *Observations on the Bill of Mortality, in Chester, for the Year 1772* (reprinted in *Mortality in Pre-Industrial Times: The Contemporary Verdict* ed. John Cassedy [London, 1973], 73).

Heasman, M. A., "Accuracy of death certification," *Proceedings of the Royal Society of Medicine* 55 (1962), 733–36.

Henripin, Jacques, "La Fécondité des ménages canadiens au début du XVIIIᵉ siècle," *Population* 9ᵉ année (1954), 61–84.

La Population canadienne au début du XVIIᵉ siècle: nuptialité, fécondité, mortalité infantile (Paris, 1954).

Henry, Louis, "La Fécondité des mariages au Japon," *Population* 8ᵉ année (1953), 711–30.

Anciennes familles genevoises, études démographique, XVIᵉ–XXᵉ siècles (Paris, 1956).

"Some data on natural fertility," *Eugenics Quarterly* 8 (1961), 81–91.

"Perturbations de la nuptialité résultant de la guerre 1914–1918," *Population* 21ᵉ année (1966), 273–332.

"Schémas de nuptialité: déséquilibre des sexes et âge au mariage," *Population* 24ᵉ année (1969), 1067–122.

"Nuptiality," *Theoretical Population Biology* 3 (1972), 136–52.

"Schéma d'évolution des mariages après de grandes variations des naissances," *Population* 30ᵉ année (1975), 759–80.

"Mobilité et féconditè d'après les fiches de famille," *Annales de démographie historique* (1976), 279–302.

and Blanchet, Didier, "La Population de l'Angleterre de 1541 à 1871," *Population* 38ᵉ année (1983), 781–825.

and Gautier, Emile, *La Population de Crulai, paroisse normande* (Paris, 1959).

and Hollingsworth, T. H., "Généalogies et démographie historique," *Annales de démographie historique* (1976), 73–75 and 167–70.

and Houdaille, Jacques, "Célibat et âge au mariage aux XVIIIᵉ et XIXᵉ siècles en France," *Population* 33ᵉ année (1978), 43–84.

Higgs, Robert and Stettler, H. Louis, "Colonial New England demography: a sampling approach," *William and Mary Quarterly* 3rd ser. 27 (1970), 282–94.

Hobcraft, J. N., McDonald, J. W., and Rutstein, S. O., "Child-spacing effects on infant and early child mortality," *Population Index* 49 (1983), 585–618.

"Demographic determinants of infant and early child mortality: a comparative analysis," *Population Studies* 39 (1985), 363–85.

Hobson, M. A. B., *Memoirs of Six Generations* (Belfast, 1947).

Hodgkins, M. A., ed., *Friends in Ireland* (Dublin, 1910).

Hollingsworth, T. H., *The Demography of the British Peerage* (Supplement to *Population Studies* 18 [1965]).

"Mortality in the British peerage families since 1600," *Population* 32 (numéro spécial, Sept. 1977), 323–49.

Hopkins, Donald R., *Princes and Peasants: Smallpox in History* (Chicago, 1983).

Houdaille, Jacques, "Démographie de la Nouvelle Angleterre aux XVIIᵉ et XVIIIᵉ siècles," *Population* 26ᵉ année (1971), 963–66.

and Tugault, Yves, "Une bourgeoisie peu malthusienne dans un pays neuf: généalogies américaines du XIXᵉ siècle," *Population* 42ᵉ année (1987), 305–20.

Howie, P. W., McNeilly, A. S., Houston, M. J., Cook, A., and Boyle, H., "Effect of supplementary food on suckling patterns and ovarian activity during lactation," *British Medical Journal* 283 (1981), 757–59.

Huffman, Sandra L., Chowdhury, A. K. M. Alauddin, Chakraborty, J., and Mosley, W. Henry, "Nutrition and post-partum amenorrhoea in rural Bangladesh," *Population Studies* 32 (1978), 251–73.

Huffman, Sandra L., Chowdhury, A. K. M. Alauddin, and Sykes, Zenas M., "Lactation and fertility in rural Bangladesh," *Population Studies* 34 (1980), 337–47.

Hunt, Norman C., *Two Early Political Associations: The Quakers and the Dissenting Deputies in the Age of Sir Robert Walpole* (Oxford, 1961).

Hurwich, Judith, "The social origins of the early Quakers," *Past and Present* no. 48 (1970), 155–64.

"Dissent and Catholicism in English society: a study of Warwickshire, 1660–1720," *Journal of British Studies* 16 (1976), 24–58.

Imhof, Arthur E., "La Surmortalité des femmes mariées en âge de procréation: un indice de la condition féminine au XIXᵉ siècle," *Annales de démographie historique* (1981), 81–87.

"From the old mortality pattern to the new: implications of a radical change from the sixteenth to the twentieth century," *Bulletin of the History of Medicine* 59 (1985), 1–29.

Isichei, Elizabeth, *Victorian Quakers* (Oxford, 1970).

James, W. H., "The causes of the decline in fecundability with age," *Social Biology* 26 (1979), 330–34.

Jette, René and Charbonneau, Hubert, "Généalogies déscendantes et analyse démographique," *Annales de démographie historique* (1984), 45–54.

Johnston, J. A., "The impact of the epidemics of 1727–1730 in South West Worcestershire," *Medical History* 15 (1971), 278–92.

Jones, R. E., "Population and agrarian change in an eighteenth-century Shropshire parish," *Local Population Studies* no. 1 (1968), 6–29.

"Infant mortality in rural North Shropshire," *Population Studies* 30 (1976), 305–17.

"Further evidence on the decline in infant mortality in pre-industrial England: North Shropshire 1561–1810," *Population Studies* 34 (1980), 239–50.

Jones, Rufus, *Studies in Mystical Religion* (1909).

Spiritual Reformers in the Sixteenth and Seventeenth Centuries (1914).

The Later Periods of Quakerism (2 vols.: 1921).

Kantrow, Louise, "Philadelphia gentry: fertility and family limitation among an American aristocracy," *Population Studies* 34 (1980), 21–30.

Kendall, John, *Memoirs of the Life and Religious Experience of John Kendall* (1815).

Kennedy, Liam and Ollorenshaw, Philip, eds., *An Economic History of Ulster 1820–1940* (Manchester, 1985).

Kett, J. F., "Provincial medical practice in England, 1730–1815," *Journal of the History of Medicine and Allied Sciences* 19 (1964), 17–29.

Knodel, John, "Family limitation and fertility transition: evidence from the age-patterns of fertility in Europe and Asia," *Population Studies* 31 (1977), 219–49.

"Breast feeding and population growth," *Science* 198 (1977), 111–15.

"Natural fertility in pre-industrial Germany," *Population Studies* 32 (1978), 481–510.

"Espacement des naissances et planification familiale; une critique de la méthode Dupâquier-Lachiver," *Annales: Economies, Sociétés, Civilisations* 36e année (1981), 473–88.

"Child mortality and reproductive behaviour in German village populations of the past: a micro-level analysis of the replacement effect," *Population Studies* 36 (1982), 177–200.

"Starting, stopping, and spacing during the early stages of fertility transition: the experience of German village populations in the 18th and 19th centuries," *Demography* 24 (1987), 143–62.

and van de Walle, Etienne, "Breast feeding, fertility and infant mortality: an analysis of some early German data," *Population Studies* 21 (1967), 109–31.

Krause, John T., "Some neglected factors in the English Industrial Revolution," *Journal of Economic History* 19 (1959), 531.

"Some aspects of population change, 1690–1790," in *Land, Labour and Population in the Industrial Revolution: Essays Presented to J. D. Chambers*, ed. E. L. Jones and G. E. Mingay (1967), 187–205.

Küchemann, C. F., Boyce, A. J., and Harrison, G. A., "A demographic and genetic study of a group of Oxfordshire villages," *Human Biology* 39 (1967), 252–76.

Kuczynski, R. R., "British demographers' opinions on fertility, 1660 to 1760," in *Political Arithmetic*, ed. L. A. Hogben (New York, 1938), 283–327.

Kunitz, Stephen J., "Speculations on the European mortality decline," *Economic History Review* 2nd ser. 36 (1983), 349–64.

"Mortality since Malthus," in *The State of Population Theory*, ed. David Coleman and Roger Schofield (Oxford, 1986), 279–302.

Kussmaul, Ann, "Time and space, hoofs and grain: the seasonality of marriage in England," *Journal of Interdisciplinary History* 15 (1985), 755–79.

Lachenbruch, Peter A., "Frequency and timing of intercourse: its relation to the probability of conception," *Population Studies* 21 (1967), 23–31.

Ladurie, Emanuel LeRoy, "L'Aménorrhée de famine (XVIIe–XXe siècles)," *Annales: Economies, Sociétés, Civilisations* 24e année (1969); translated by Elborg Forster and Patricia M. Ranum in *Biology of Man in History*, ed. Robert Forster and Orest Ranum (Baltimore, 1975).

Landers, John, "Some problems in the historical demography of London, 1675–1825" (Cambridge University PhD Thesis, 1984).

"Mortality, weather and prices in London 1675–1825: a study of short-term fluctuations," *Journal of Historical Geography* 12 (1986), 347–64.

"Mortality and metropolis: the case of London 1675–1825," *Population Studies* 41 (1987), 59–76.

Laslett, Peter, "Age at menarche in Europe since the eighteenth century," *Journal of Interdisciplinary History* 2 (1971–72), 221–36.

The World We Have Lost (2nd edn, New York, 1973).

Family Life and Illicit Love in Earlier Generations: Essays in Historical Sociology (Cambridge, 1977).

Leadbeater, Mary, *Memoirs and Letters of Richard and Elizabeth Shackleton, Late of Ballitore, Ireland* (1822).

Biographical Notices of Members of the Society of Friends Who Were Resident in Ireland (1823).

Annals of Ballitore, ed. John McKenna (Athy, 1986).

Ledermann, Sully, *Nouvelles tables-types de mortalité* (INED Travaux et Documents no. 53, Paris, 1969).

Lee, Joseph, "Marriage and population in pre-famine Ireland," *Economic History Review* 2nd ser. 21 (1968), 283–95.

Leites, Edmund, *The Puritan Conscience and Modern Sexuality* (New Haven, 1986).

Leridon, Henri, *Natalité, saisons et conjoncture économique* (Paris, 1973).

"Sur l'estimation de la sterilité," *Population* 32e année (1977), 231–48.

Lesthaeghe, R. J., and Page, H. J., "The post-partum non-susceptible period: development and application of model schedules," *Population Studies* 34 (1980), 143–69.

Levine, D., "The demographic implications of rural industrialization: a family reconstitution study of Shepshed, Leicestershire, 1600–1851," *Social History* 2 (1976), 177–96.

"The reliability of parochial registration and the representativeness of family reconstitution," *Population Studies* 30 (1976), 107–22.

Family Formation in an Age of Nascent Capitalism (New York, 1977).

"Proto-industrialization and demographic upheaval," in *Essays on the Family and Historical Change*, ed. Leslie Page Moch and Gary D. Stark (College Station, 1983), 9–34.

"Production, reproduction, and the proletarian family in England, 1500–1851," in *Proletarianization and Family History*, ed. David Levine (Orlando, 1984), 87–127.

Lévy, Claude, and Henry, Louis, "Ducs et pairs sous l'Ancien Régime: caractéristiques démographiques d'une caste," *Population* 15ᵉ année (1960), 807–30.

Lindert, Peter, "Child costs and economic development," in *Population and Economic Change in Developing Countries*, ed. Richard Easterlin (Chicago, 1980), 5–69.

"English occupations, 1670–1811," *Journal of Economic History* 40 (1980), 685–712.

"English living standards, population growth, and Wrigley–Schofield," *Explorations in Economic History* 20 (1983), 131–55.

and Williamson, Jeffrey G., "Reinterpreting Britain's social tables, 1688–1913," *Explorations in Economic History* 20 (1983), 94–109.

Lithell, Ulla-Britt, "Breastfeeding habits and their relation to infant mortality and marital fertility," *Journal of Family History* 6 (1981), 182–94.

Lloyd, Arnold, *Quaker Social History 1669–1738* (1950).

Lockridge, Kenneth, "The population of Dedham, Mass., 1636–1736," *Economic History Review* 2nd ser. 19 (1966), 318–44.

London Yearly Meeting, *Directions for a More General Uniformity in Keeping Records* (1774).

The Method to be Observed in Recording Marriages, Births, and Burials (1774).

Loschky, David J., and Krier, Donald F., "Income and family size in three eighteenth-century Lancashire parishes: a reconstitution study," *Journal of Economic History* 29 (1969), 429–48.

Loudon, Irvine, "The nature of provincial medical practice in eighteenth-century England," *Medical History* 29 (1985), 1–32.

"Deaths in childbed from the eighteenth century to 1935," *Medical History* 30 (1986), 1–41.

Luckin, B., "The decline of smallpox and the demographic revolution of the eighteenth century," *Social History* no. 6 (1977), 793–97.

MacAfee, W. and Morgan, V., "Irish population in the pre-famine period: evidence from County Antrim," *Economic History Review* 2nd ser. 37 (1984), 182–96.

"Population in Ulster, 1660–1760," in *Plantation to Partition: Essays in Ulster History in Honour of J. L. McCracken* (Belfast, 1981), 46–63.

Macfarlane, Alan, *The Family Life of Ralph Josselin* (Cambridge, 1970).

Mackenroth, Gerhard, *Bevölkerungslehre: Theorie, Soziologie und Statistik der Bevölkerung* (Berlin, 1953).

Malthus, Thomas Robert, *An Essay on the Principle of Population, As It Affects the Future Improvement of Society* (1798).

Marriott, John, *A Short Account of John Marriott* (Doncaster, 1803).

Marshall, J., *Mortality of the Metropolis* (1832).

Marshall, T. H., "The population problem during the Industrial Revolution: a note on the present state of the controversy," *Economic History* 1 (1929), reprinted in *Population in History*, ed. D. V. Glass and D. E. C. Eversley, 247–68.

Martin, J. M., "Marriage and economic stress in the Felden of Warwickshire during the eighteenth century," *Population Studies* 31 (1977), 519–35.

"A Warwickshire market town in adversity: Stratford-upon-Avon in the sixteenth and seventeenth centuries," *Midland History* 7 (1982), 26–41.

Martineau, Harriet, *Illustrations of Political Economy* (9 vols., 1832–34).

Masnick, George S., "The demographic impact of breast-feeding: a critical review," *Human Biology* 51 (1979), 109–25.
Matras, Judah, "Social strategies of family formation: data for British female cohorts born 1831–1906," *Population Studies* 19 (1965), 167–81.
Maw, Lucy, *A Memoir of Louisa Maw* (York, 1828).
McKeown, Thomas and Brown, R. G., "Medical evidence related to English population changes in the eighteenth century," *Population Studies* 9 (1955), 119–41, reprinted in *Population in Industrialization*, ed. Drake, 40–72.
and Gibson, J. R., "A note on menstruation and conception during lactation," *Journal of Obstetrics and Gynaecology of the British Empire* 61 (1954), 824–26.
The Modern Rise of Population (1976).
McLaren, Angus, *Birth Control in Nineteenth-Century England* (New York, 1978).
Reproductive Rituals: The Perception of Fertility in England from the Sixteenth Century to the Nineteenth Century (1984).
McLaren, Dorothy, "Fertility, infant mortality, and breast feeding in the 17th century," *Medical History* 22 (1978), 378–96.
"Nature's contraceptive: wet-nursing and prolonged lactation: the case of Chesham, Bucks., 1578–1601," *Medical History* 23 (1979), 425–41.
Menken, Jane, Trussell, James, and Watkins, Susan, "The nutrition fertility link: an evaluation of the evidence," *Journal of Interdisciplinary History* 11 (1981), 425–41.
Mercer, A. J., "Smallpox and epidemiological-demographic change in Europe: the role of vaccination," *Population Studies* 39 (1985), 287–307.
Milligan, E. H., *Britannica on Quakerism* (1965).
Milne, Joshua, *A Treatise on the Valuation of Annuities and Assurances on Lives and Survivorships* (1815), vol. 2.
Mokyr, Joel, "Malthusian models and Irish history," *Journal of Economic History* 40 (1980), 159–66.
Why Ireland Starved: A Quantitative and Analytical History of the Irish Economy, 1800–1850 (1983).
and Ó Gráda, Cormac, "New developments in Irish population history, 1700–1850," *Economic History Review* 2nd ser. 37 (1984), 473–88.
"Poor and getting poorer? Living standards in Ireland before the famine," *Economic History Review* 2nd ser. 41 (1988), 209–35.
Morgan, Valerie, "The Church of Ireland registers of St. Patrick's, Coleraine, as a source for the study of a local pre-famine population," *Ulster Folklife* 19 (1973), 56–67.
and MacAfee, W., "Irish population in pre-famine period: evidence from County Antrim," *Economic History Review* 2nd ser. 37 (1984), 182–96.
Morrell, C. C., "Tudor marriages and infantile mortality," *Journal of State Medicine* 74 (1935), 173–81.
Morrow, Richard B. "Family limitation in pre-industrial England: A reappraisal," *Economic History Review* 2nd ser. 31 (1978), 419–28.
Mortimer, Jean, and Mortimer, Russell, eds., *Leeds Friends' Minute Book, 1692 to 1712* (Yorkshire Archaeological Society Record Series, vol. CXXXIX for 1977 and 1978) (Leeds, 1980).
Mueller, Eva, "The economic value of children in peasant agriculture," in

Population and Development, ed. Ronald G. Ridker (Baltimore, 1976), 98–153.

Muhsam, H. V., "The marriage squeeze," *Demography* 11 (1974), 291–99.

Murray, Lindley, *Memoirs of the Life and Writings of Lindley Murray, with a Preface, and a Continuation of the Memoirs by Elizabeth Frank* (York, 1826).

Myers, A. C., *Immigration of the Irish Quakers into Pennsylvania, 1682–1750, with Their Early History in Ireland* (Swarthmore, Pa., 1902).

Neale, Samuel, ed., *Some Account of the Life and Religious Exercises of Mary Neale, formerly Mary Peisley* (Dublin, 1795).

Newenham, Thomas, *A Statistical and Historical Inquiry into the Progress and Magnitude of the Population of Ireland* (1805).

Nuttall, Geoffrey, *The Holy Spirit in Puritan Faith and Experience* (Oxford, 1946).

Ó Gráda, Cormac, "The Population of Ireland 1700–1900: a survey," *Annales de démographie historique* (1979), 281–99.

Ohlin, G., "Mortality, marriage, and growth in pre-industrial populations," *Population Studies* 14 (1961), 190–97.

Oppenheimer, Valerie Kincade, *Work and the Family: A Study in Social Demography* (New York, 1982).

Osterud, Nancy and Fulton, J., "Family limitation and age at marriage: fertility decline in Sturbridge, Massachusetts, 1730–1850," *Population Studies* 30 (1976), 481–94.

Outhwaite, R. B., "Age at marriage in England from the late seventeenth to the nineteenth century," *Transactions of the Royal Historical Society* 5th ser. 23 (1973), 62–70.

Page, Hilary J., "Patterns underlying fertility schedules: a decomposition by both age and marriage duration," *Population Studies* 31 (1977), 85–106.

Palloni, Alberto and Tienda, Marta, "The effects of breastfeeding and pace of childbearing on mortality at early ages," *Demography* 23 (1986), 31–52.

Pearce, Carol G., "Expanding families: some aspects of fertility in a mid Victorian community," *Local Population Studies* no. 10 (1973), 22–35.

Perrenoud, Alfred, "Malthusianisme et protestantisme: 'un modèle démographique weberien,'" *Annales: Economies, Sociétés, Civilisations* 29ᵉ année (1974), 975–88.

"Surmortalité féminine et condition de la femme (XVIIᵉ–XIXᵉ siècles): une vérification empirique," *Annales de démographie historique* (1981), 89–104.

"Le Biologique et l'humain dans le déclin séculaire de la mortalité," *Annales: Economies, Sociétés, Civilisations* 40ᵉ année (1985), 113–35.

and Zumkeller, D., "Caractères originaux de la démographie genevoise du XVIᵉ siècle: structure ou conjuncture?" *Annales de démographie historique* (1980), 125–41.

Peter, Jean-Pierre, "Une enquête de la Société Royale de Médicine: malades et maladies à la fin du XVIIIᵉ siècle," *Annales: Economies, Sociétés, Civilisations* 22ᵉ année (1967), 711–51; translated by Elborg Forster in *Biology of Man in History,* ed. Robert Forster and Orest Ranum (Baltimore, 1982), 81–124.

Petty, William, "Political anatomy of Ireland," in *The Economic Writings of Sir William Petty,* ed. Charles Henry Hull (Cambridge, England, 1899), vol. 1.

Phillips, Catherine, *Memoirs of the Life of Catherine Phillips* (1797).

Pollock, Linda A., *Forgotten Children: Parent–Child Relations from 1500 to 1900* (Cambridge, 1983).

Porter, Roy, "Lay medical knowledge in the eighteenth century: the evidence of the *Gentleman's Magazine*," *Medical History* 29 (1985), 138–68.

Post, J. B. "Ages at menarche and menopause: some medieval authorities," *Population Studies* 25 (1971), 83–87.

Post, John D., "Famine, mortality, and epidemic disease in the process of modernization," *Economic History Review* 2nd. ser. 29 (1976), 14–37.

Food Shortage, Climatic Variability, and Epidemic Disease in Preindustrial Europe: The Mortality Peak in the Early 1740s (Ithaca, 1985).

Potter, J., "The growth of population in America, 1700–1860," in *Population in History*, ed. Glass and Eversley (1965), 631–88.

Potter, Robert G., "Birth intervals: structure and change," *Population Studies* 17 (1963), 155–66.

and Parker, M. P., "Predicting the time required to conceive," *Population Studies* 18 (1964), 99–116.

and Kobrin, F. C., "Distributions of amenorrhea and anovulation," *Population Studies* 35 (1981), 85–94.

and Millman, S. R., "Fecundability and the frequency of marital intercourse: a critique of nine models," *Population Studies* 39 (1985), 461–70.

Pratt, David H., *English Quakers and the First Industrial Revolution: A Study of the Quaker Community in Four Industrial Counties – Lancashire, York, Warwick, and Gloucester, 1750–1830* (New York, 1985).

Pressat, Roland, *L'Analyse démographique* (Paris, 1961).

Radbill, S. X., "Teething in fact and fancy," *Bulletin of the History of Medicine* 39 (1965), 339–45.

Raistrick, Arthur, *Quakers in Science and Industry, being an Account of the Quaker Contributions to Science and Industry during the 17th and 18th Centuries* (1950).

Rankin, Robert, *A Familiar Treatise on Life Assurances and Annuities* (1830).

Ransom, Mercy, *Some Remarks by Way of Diary* (1816).

Razzell, P. E., "Population change in eighteenth-century England: a reinterpretation," *Economic History Review* 2nd ser. 18 (1965), reprinted in *Population in Industrialization*, ed. Drake, 128–56.

"Population growth and economic change in eighteenth and early nineteenth-century England and Ireland," in *Land, Labour and Population in the Industrial Revolution: Essays Presented to J. D. Chambers*, ed. E. L. Jones and G. E. Mingay (1967), 260–81.

The Conquest of Smallpox (Firle, Sussex, 1977).

Reay, Barry, "The social origins of Early Quakerism," *Journal of Interdisciplinary History* 11 (1980–81), 55–72.

The Quakers and the English Revolution (New York, 1985).

Redford, A., *Labour Migration in England, 1800–1850* (Manchester, 1926).

Rendle-Short, J., "The causes of infantile convulsions prior to 1900," *Journal of Pediatrics* 47 (1955), 733–39.

"The history of teething in infancy," *Proceedings of the Royal Society of Medicine* 48 (1955), 132–38.

Reynolds, Glynis, "Infant mortality and sex ratios at baptism as shown by reconstruction of Willingham [Cambs.]," *Local Population Studies* no. 22 (1979), 31–37.

Richardson, J. M., *Six Generations of Friends in Ireland* (1893).

Richardson, J. N., *The Quakri at Lurgan and Grange* (n.p., 1899).

Rowntree, J. S., *Quakerism, Past and Present* (London, 1859).

"The Friends' registers of births, deaths, and marriages, 1650–1900," *The Friend* new ser. 43 (1903), 53.

"Some lessons of the Friends' registration figures," *The Friend* new ser. 43 (1903), 72.

Rutty, John, *A History of the Rise and Progress of the People Called Quakers in Ireland, from the Year 1653 to 1700*, 4th edn (1811).

Sabagh, Georges, "The fertility of French–Canadian women during the seventeenth century," *American Journal of Sociology* 47 (1942), 680–89.

Salber, E. J., Feinlaub, M., and MacMahon, B., "The duration of post-partum amenorrhea," *American Journal of Epidemiology* 82 (1965), 347–58.

Saville, J., *Rural Depopulation in England and Wales, 1851–1951* (1957).

Schofield, Roger, "Perinatal mortality in Hawkshead, Lancashire, 1581–1710," *Local Population Studies* no. 4 (1970), 11–16.

"Historical demography: some possibilities and some limitations," *Transactions of the Royal Historical Society* 5th ser. 21 (1971), 119–32.

"The relationship between demographic structure and environment in pre-industrial Western Europe," in *Sozialgeschichte der Familie in der Neuzeit Europas*, ed. Werner Conze (Stuttgart, 1976), 147–60.

"Representativeness and family reconstitution," *Annales de démographie historique* (1972), 121–25.

"Population growth in the century after 1750: the role of mortality decline," in *Pre-Industrial Population Change: The Mortality Decline and Short-term Population Movements*, ed. T. Bengtsson, G. Fridlizius, and R. Ohlsson (Stockholm, 1984), 21–22.

"English marriage patterns revisited," *Journal of Family History* 10 (1985), 2–20.

"Did the mothers really die? Three centuries of maternal mortality in 'The World We Have Lost'," in *The World We Have Gained: Histories of Population and Social Structure*, ed. Lloyd Bonfield, Richard M. Smith, and Keith Wrightson (Oxford, 1986), 231–60.

Scrimshaw, N. S., Taylor, C. E., and Gordon, J. E., *Interactions of Nutrition and Infection* (Geneva, 1968).

Sharlin, Allan, "Methods for estimating population total, age distribution and vital rates in family reconstitution studies," *Population Studies* 32 (1978), 511–21.

Short, Thomas, *New Observations, Natural, Moral, Civil, Political, and Medical, on City, Town, and Country Bills of Mortality* (1750).

Skipp, V., *Crisis and Development: An Ecological Case-Study of the Forest of Arden, 1570–1674* (Cambridge, 1978).

Skolnick, Mark, *et al.*, "Mormon demographic history: nuptiality and fertility of once-married couples," *Population Studies* 32 (1978), 5–19.

Smith, C. Fell, *James Nicholson Richardson of Bessbrook* (1925).

Smith, Daniel Scott, "The demographic history of Colonial New England," *Journal of Economic History* 32 (1972), 165–83.

"A homeostatic demographic regime," in *Population Patterns in the Past*, ed. Ronald Demos Lee (New York, 1977), 19–51.

Smith, Frederick, *Autobiographical Narrations of the Convincement and Other Religious Experience of Samuel Crisp, Elizabeth Webb, Evan Bevan, Margaret Lucas, and Frederick Smith* (1848).

Smith, Richard M., "Population and its geography in England, 1500–1730," in

An Historical Geography of England and Wales, ed. R. Dodgshon and R. Butlin (New York, 1978).

"Transfer incomes, risk and security: the roles of the family and the collectivity in recent theories of fertility change," in *The State of Population Theory: Forward from Malthus*, ed. David Coleman and Roger Schofield (Oxford, 1986), 188–211.

Smith, T. E., "The Cocos-Keeling Islands: a demographic laboratory," *Population Studies* 14 (1960), 94–130.

Souden, David, "Migrants and the population structure of later seventeenth-century provincial cities and market towns," in *The Transformation of English Provincial Towns 1600–1800*, ed. Peter Clark (1984), 133–68.

"Movers and stayers in family reconstitution populations," *Local Population Studies* no. 33 (Autumn 1984), 11–28.

Southwark Monthly Meeting, Minutes 1667–1837 (manuscript in Friends House Library, London).

Spufford, Margaret, *Contrasting Communities* (Cambridge, 1974).

Stansfield, Samuel, *Memoirs of Ruth Follows* (Liverpool, 1829).

Steel, Donald John, *Sources for Nonconformist Genealogy and Family History* (1973).

Stycos, J. M., *Family and Fertility in Puerto Rico* (New York, 1955).

Swift, David, *Joseph John Gurney: Banker, Reformer, Quaker* (Middletown, CT, 1962).

Temkin-Greener, Helena, and Swedlund, A. C., "Fertility transition in the Connecticut Valley: 1740–1850," *Population Studies* 32 (1978), 27–41.

Thestrup, P., "Methodological problems in Danish family reconstitution," *Scandinavian Economic History Review* 20 (1972), 1–26.

Thomas, Mair E. M., and Tillett, Hilary E., "Diarrhoea in general practice: a sixteen-year report of investigations in a microbiology laboratory, with epidemiological assessment," *Journal of Hygiene* 74 (1975), 183–94.

Thurnam, John, *Observations and Essays on the Statistics of Insanity* (1845).

Tietze, Christopher, "Probability of conception resulting from a single unprotected coitus," *Fertility and Sterility* 11 (1960), 485–88.

Tilly, Charles, ed., *Historical Studies of Changing Fertility* (Princteon, 1978).

Tranter, N. L., *Population since the Industrial Revolution: The Case of England and Wales* (New York, 1973).

Population and Society 1750–1940: Contrasts in Population Growth (1985).

Trumbach, Randolph, *The Rise of the Egalitarian Family: Aristocratic Kinship and Domestic Relations in Eighteenth-Century England* (New York, 1978).

Trussell, J. and Wilson, C., "Sterility in a population with natural fertility," *Population Studies* 39 (1985), 269–86.

Tual, Jacques, "Les Quakers en Angleterre: naissance et origines d'un mouvement, 1649–1700: illuminisme et révolution" (3 vols.: Doctorat d'Etat es Lettres, Université de Paris III, 1986).

"Sexual equality and conjugal harmony: the way to celestial bliss. A view of early Quaker matrimony," *Journal of the Friends' Historical Society* 55 (1988), 161–74.

Vann, Richard T., *The Social Development of English Quakerism 1655–1755* (Cambridge, Mass., 1969).

"Nurture and conversion in early Quakerism," *Journal of Marriage and the Family* 31 (1969), 639–43.

"Quakerism and the social structure in the interregnum," *Past and Present* no. 43 (1969), 71–91.

"Friends' sufferings – collected and recollected," *Quaker History* 61 (1972), 24–35.

Wakefield, Edward, *An Account of Ireland, Statistical and Political* (2 vols.: 1812).

Wall, Richard, "Age at leaving home," *Journal of Family History* 3 (1978), 181–202.

"Inferring differential neglect of females from mortality data," *Annales de démographie historique* (1981), 119–40.

Waring, Mary, *A Diary of the Religious Experience of Mary Waring* (1809).

Watts, Michael R., *The Dissenters* vol. 1 (Oxford, 1978).

Weir, David R., "Better never than late: celibacy and age at marriage in English cohort fertility," *Journal of Family History* 9 (1984), 340–54.

Wells, Robert V., "Family size and fertility control in eighteenth-century America: a study of Quaker families," *Population Studies* 25 (1971), 73–82.

"Quaker marriage patterns in a colonial perspective," *William and Mary Quarterly* 3rd ser. 29 (1972), 415–42.

West, F., "Infant mortality in the East Fen parishes of Leake and Wrangle," *Local Population Studies* no. 13 (1974), 43–44.

Westoff, C. F., Potter, R. G., and Sagi, P. C., *The Third Child* (Princeton, 1963).

Whitelaw, James, *An Essay on the Population of Dublin, being the Result of an Actual Survey Taken in 1798* (Dublin, 1805).

Williamson, Jeffrey G., "Was the Industrial Revolution worth it? Disamenities and death in 19th-century British towns," *Explorations in Economic History* 19 (1982), 221–45.

Wilson, C., "Natural fertility in pre-industrial England 1600–1799," *Population Studies* 38 (1984), 225–40.

Worrall, Arthur J., "The impact of the discipline: Ireland, New England, and New York," *Quaker History* 68 (1979), 83–91.

Wrigley, E. A., "Family limitation in pre-industrial England," *Economic History Review* 2nd ser. 19 (1966), 82–109.

"Mortality in pre-industrial England: the example of Colyton, Devon, over three centuries," *Daedalus* 97 (Spring, 1968).

Population and History (1969).

"Births and baptisms: the use of Anglican baptism registers as a source of information about the numbers of births in England before the beginning of civil registration," *Population Studies* 31 (1977), 281–312.

"Marital fertility in seventeenth-century Colyton: a note," *Economic History Review* 2nd ser. 31 (1978), 429–36.

"Fertility strategy for the individual and the group," in *Historical Studies in Changing Fertility*, ed. Charles Tilly (Princeton, 1978), 135–54.

"Marriage, fertility and population growth in eighteenth-century England," in *Marriage and Society: Studies in the Social History of Marriage*, ed. R. B. Outhwaite (New York, 1982), 137–85.

"The growth of population in eighteenth-century England: a conundrum resolved," *Past and Present* 98 (1983), 121–50.

ed., *An Introduction to English Historical Demography* (1966).

and Schofield, R. S., *The Population History of England, 1541–1841: A Reconstruction* (Cambridge, Mass., 1981).

"English population history from family reconstitution: summary results 1600–1799," *Population Studies* 37 (1983), 157–84.

Yasumoto, Minoru, "Industrialisation and demographic change in a Yorkshire parish," *Local Population Studies* no. 27 (1981), 10–25.

Young, Arthur, *A Tour of Ireland* (1780), II.

Arthur Young's Tour in Ireland, ed. A. W. Hutton (2 vols.: 1846).

Young, Christabel M., "Factors associated with the timing and duration of the leaving-home stage of the family life cycle," *Population Studies* 29 (1975), 61–73.

Yow, M. D., Melnick, J. L., Blattner, R. J., Stephenson, W. B., Robinson, N. M., and Burkhardt, M. A., "The association of viruses and bacteria with infantile diarrhoea," *American Journal of Epidemiology* 92 (1970), 33–39.

Index

Nassau Senior, 120
Nayler, James, 66
net reproductive rates, 239
New Jersey, 64, 142
New York, 142
Newgarden, Leinster, 47
Newry, Ulster, 36
Nicholson family, 53
Norfolk, 21, 68, 74
Norfolk Quarterly Meeting, 32–33
Northamptonshire, 36
Northumberland, 59
Norwich, 8, 32, 36, 41, 43, 74, 228, 242
Norwich Monthly Meeting, 32
Nottinghamshire, 114
nudity, homiletic, 65
nuptiality, age at marriage, 1, 4, 6–7, 63, 80–81, 86–104, 111–28, 136, 142, 173–74, 180, 184, 239–41, 243–44, 246–47; cultural influences on, 107, 122–24, 127–28, 243–44; economic influences on, 74, 81, 94, 111–15, 118–22; effects on fertility, 80–81; emigration and age at marriage, 97, 104, 124; illegitimacy, 88; and inheritance, 82, 115–16, 122–23; and life cycle, 122; and longevity of parents, 115–16; and migration, 2, 123; proportions never marrying, 2, 25, 80–81, 88, 107–9, 111, 127, 144, 240, 246, 250; turning points in, 6; *see also* marriage, prenuptial pregnancies, remarriage, weddings
nutrition, influence on fertility, 165–66; on mortality, 1, 186, 220

obstetrics, *see* midwifery
Oppenheimer, Valerie, 82–83, 244
ovulation, 6, 147, 164, 167
Oxford University, 66
Oxley, Joseph, 120

Page, Hilary, 185
parish registers, English, 3, 7, 12, 15; Irish, 93
peerage, 78, 245, 255; age at first marriage (British), 104–7, 127–28;

(French and other European), 106; child mortality of, 203–4; fertility of, 172–73; as leading sector, 46; mortality of, 8, 204, 237; proportions never marrying, 108–9, 128, 246; record-keeping, 175
Peete family, 50
Péguy, Charles, 238
Pennington family, 49
Pennsylvania, 50, 64, 142
Penrose family, 50
Perrenoud, Alfred, 235
Petty, Sir William, 95
Phillips, Catherine, 120
Phillips, William, 120
Pim family, 51, 60
plague, decline in frequency of, 2; diagnosis of, 210, 223; and mortality crises, 186
poverty, Poor Laws, 1, 94; Quaker poor relief, 16, 47
prenuptial pregnancies, 162, 171
Presbyterians, Irish, 36, 52, 58–59, English, 65
Priors Marston, Warwickshire, 202
probate inventories, 56, 60, 202
proto-industrialization, *see* cottage industry
Public Record Office, English, 12, 29; Irish, 93
Puerto Rico, 78
Puritanism, 65, 84, 168, 244

Quakers, adult mortality, 212–15, 248; autobiographies (journals), 9, 52, 54, 75, 118, 120, 168; biographies, 54, 75, 118, 226; burials, 16–18; child mortality, 196, 203–4, 214–17, 231, 248; convincements, 19, 66–67, 239; and demographic transition, 9, 77, 133, 170–71, 177, 243, 245, 247, 254; discontinued meetings, 68; disownments, 12, 19, 55, 58, 63, 123–24, 177, 188, 239; emigration of, 22, 239; family histories, 9; infant mortality, 8, 142–43, 177, 189–90, 192–95, 197–212, 214–27, 241–43, 248; marriage discipline,

Quakers (*cont.*)
  10, 15, 18–21, 67, 83–84, 122–24,
  243, 245, 249–50; monthly
  meetings, 14–15; occupational
  distribution, 8–9, 34, 47–51, 53–63,
  68–74, 111–14, 250; poor relief, 16,
  47; preservation of records, 19;
  Public Friends, 54; quarterly
  meetings, 14; registration system,
  8, 12–19, 201, 239; resignations,
  14, 19, 188; testimonies, 10, 14, 68,
  236–37, 248–49
Quebec, 96
Québecois, 134–35, 137, 167, 241

Rankin, Robert, 237–38, 248
Rathbone, Hannah, 200
Razzell, Peter, 5, 222, 242
real wages, 2, 6, 71, 81, 250–51
Registrar General, 12
remarriage, 109, 111, 126
respiratory diseases, seasonality,
  225; *see also* "consumption"
Rhode Island, 49
Richardson family, 52, 53, 61–62
Robinson family, 76–77
Rodgers, James, 20
Roman Catholics, Irish, 36, 52, 60,
  63–64, 95, 97, 254; French, 134–35,
  241

sanitation, 1–2, 7, 203, 217–20, 222,
  252–53
Saville, J., 78
Schofield, Roger, xi, xiii, 30, 136,
  191, 233, 241–42
Scoryer, Richard, 17
Scotland, 46, 59
servants, 63, 64, 71, 94, 189; in
  husbandry, 7, 81, 84, 250–51
Severn River, 36
sex ratios, at burial, 107–8; in
  genealogies, 42; and marriage, 2,
  107–8, 124–25
sexual intercourse, frequency, 147,
  150, 162, 165, 170, 174, 244, 251;
  coitus interruptus, 162
Shillitoe, Thomas, 39
Short, Thomas, 211, 233
Sinton family, 53, 61–62

smallpox, diagnosis, 210, 223;
  incidence, 8, 189, 212–16, 218,
  220–21, 234, 252; inoculation
  against, 1, 5, 7, 221–22, 226, 245;
  vaccination against, 221;
  seasonality of, 225; varieties, 222
Smith, Adam, 6–7
Smith, Daniel Scott, 133
Smith, Richard, 192
Smith, T. E., 78
South Hams, Devonshire, 78
Southwark Monthly Meeting, 17–18,
  20–21, 38, 249
Spock, Benjamin, 200
standard of living, 82
sterility, 21, 42, 144–46, 174–76; *see
  also* fecundity
stillbirths, 129, 163, 232
Strangman family, 49, 51
Stranraer, Scotland, 60
Stuchbury, John, 17
Stycos, J. M., 78
subsistence crises, *see* famines
suicide, 224, 236
Surrey, 120
Sussex & Surrey Quarterly Meeting,
  32, 38
Sweden, 80

Taiwan, 78
Tewkesbury, Gloucestershire, 50
Tipperary, Munster, 51
tithes, 47, 52, 66
Tranter, N. L., 4
Trieste, 88
truncation effects, 87, 115, 231
Trussell, T. James, 155, 178
typhus, 210, 212
Tyrone (county), Ulster, 61

Ulster, 36, 49, 56, 62, 63, 75
UN life tables, 227
underregistration, 15, 18, 21–22, 25,
  27–28, 143, 175, 201–2, 216
Unitarians, 52
urbanization, and demographic
  transition, 4; in Ireland, 57

Vann, Richard T., xi, 32
Virginia, 49

Cambridge Studies in Population, Economy and Society in Past Time

Titles available in paperback are marked with an asterisk